Religious Conversion

ISSUES IN CONTEMPORARY RELIGION

Series editors: Christopher Lamb and M. Darrol Bryant

The volumes in this series are interdisciplinary and present their subjects from global and cross-religious perspectives, examining issues that cut across traditions and emerge in distinctive ways in different religions and cultural settings. Based on sound scholarship, the books are intended for undergraduate courses and for professionals involved in inter-faith dialogue.

Also available in the series:

Dan Cohn-Sherbok, *Understanding the Holocaust: An Introduction*

Religious Conversion

Contemporary Practices and Controversies

Edited by
Christopher Lamb and M. Darrol Bryant

CASSELL
London and New York

Cassell
Wellington House, 125 Strand, London WC2R 0BB
370 Lexington Avenue, New York, NY 10017-6550

First published 1999

British Library Cataloguing in Publication Data
A catalogue record for this book is available from the British Library.
ISBN 0 304 33842 7 Hardback
    0 304 33843 5 Paperback

Library of Congress Cataloging-in-Publication Data
Religious conversion : contemporary practices and controversies /
  edited by Christopher Lamb and M. Darrol Bryant.
     p. cm. — (Issues in contemporary religion)
  Includes biographical references and index.
  ISBN 0-304-33842-7. — ISBN 0-304-33843-5 (pbk.)
  1. Conversion. I. Lamb, Christopher, 1937- . II. Bryant, M.
Darrol. III. Series.
BL639.R45 1999
291.4'2–dc21   99–10551
                                                        CIP

Typeset by BookEns Ltd, Royston, Herts.
Printed and bound in Great Britain by Biddles Ltd,
Guildford and King's Lynn

Contents

CONTENTS

The Contributors

Dr M. Darrol Bryant, Professor of Religion and Culture, Renison College, University of Waterloo, Ontario.

Dr Lorne L. Dawson, Department of Sociology, University of Waterloo, Ontario.

Dr Homi B. Dhalla, Researcher in BJPC Institute, Bombay.

Dr Yasin Dutton, Lecturer in Arabic and Islamic Studies, University of Edinburgh.

Father Tim Edgar, Assistant Director of Studies, Missionary Institute, London.

Rev Dr Martin Eggleton, Ecumenical Chaplain, Middlesex University, London.

Charles E. Farhadian, PhD student, Boston University, Massachusetts.

Dr Frank K. Flinn, Adjunct Professor of Religious Studies, Washington University, St Louis, Missouri.

Dr Sophie Gilliat-Ray, Lecturer in Religious and Theological Studies, University of Wales, Cardiff.

Dr Tamal Krishna Goswami, Governing Body of ISKON, Dallas, Texas.

Dr Graham Harvey, Lecturer in Religious Studies, King Alfred's College, Winchester.

Dr Irving Hexham, Professor of Religious Studies, University of Calgary, Alberta.

Doris R. Jakobsh, PhD student, University of British Columbia, Vancouver, British Columbia.

Christopher Lamb, Head of the Centre for Inter-Faith Dialogue, Middlesex University, London.

Rabbi Rodney Mariner, Convenor of the Court of the Reform Synagogues of Great Britain, London.

Dr Jordan Paper, Professor of Religious Studies, York University, Ontario.

Dr Karla Poewe, Professor of Anthropology, University of Calgary, Calgary, Alberta.

Dr Lewis R. Rambo, Professor of Psychology and Religion, San Francisco Theological Seminary, California.

Dr K. L. Seshagiri Rao, Professor Emeritus, University of Virginia, Columbia, South Carolina.

Darshan Singh Rudel, a French Sikh living in India.

Rev Dame Macrina Sitzia OSB, Benedictine nun, Stanbrook Abbey, Callow End, Worcester.

Dr Donald Taylor, formerly Head of Religious Studies, Middlesex University, London.

A note on diacritics

The editors have omitted diacritics in transliterated foreign language terms on the principle that scholars do not need them and they only make reading more difficult for others.

Introduction: Conversion: contours of controversy and commitment in a plural world

M. Darrol Bryant and Christopher Lamb

The questions

What is conversion? Is it a mighty work of God? Or is it a human choice? Is it a dramatic emotional event in a person's life that fades as suddenly as it occurs? Or is it a gradual and growing conviction in one's mind that life's meaning and purpose lie in a particular direction? Or is conversion a sham, a psychological trick to dupe you of your money, possessions, or your autonomy? Is conversion always a dramatic encounter with spiritual reality or can it be the pressure of a community to ensure conformity with the group? Is conversion simply another word for changing one's institutional religious affiliation? Is conversion a Christian phenomenon or is it also found within other religious traditions? Is there conversion to Hinduism? Islam? Buddhism? Confucianism? Why do Zoroastrians oppose conversion? Is conversion the basis for the Christian life, as some Christians contend? Can one distinguish an authentic conversion from an inauthentic one? Does conversion have a meaning outside the context of explicit religious traditions? Can one speak about personal transformations, whatever their context or content, as conversions? These are but some of the questions that surround 'conversion' at the end of the twentieth century. To address some of these issues we have invited a group of scholars from several religious traditions and from different academic disciplines to contribute to this volume.

1

In a classic study at the beginning of the twentieth century William James, the American philosopher and psychologist, described conversion in the following terms:

> to be converted, to be regenerated, to receive grace, to experience religion, to gain an assurance, are so many phrases which denote the process, gradual or sudden, by which a self hitherto divided, and consciously wrong, inferior, and unhappy becomes unified and consciously right, superior, and happy in consequence of its firmer hold upon religious realities.[1]

Such persons are, to use James's other phrase for converted souls, the 'twice-born'. While James's study remains important, we can now see that it was limited in at least two important respects. It limited the phenomenon of conversion to Christianity and it interpreted conversion wholly in psychological terms. Although the psychological approach to conversion has remained central to the study of conversion through most of the twentieth century, more recent studies of the phenomenon have regarded it in more sociological terms. These changes are reflected in the theoretical contribution of Lewis Rambo and Charles Farhadian where they outline the stages of the conversion process. As we see in Rambo and Farhadian, as well as in the contribution of Frank Flinn, conversion involves not only an inner event but it often involves a move from one religious community to another.

This volume explores conversion as a contemporary religious issue. This means three things: (1) it explores the theoretical meaning of conversion; (2) it examines the significance of conversion within diverse religious traditions; and (3) it points to the tensions between traditions over the issue of conversion.

Conversion is usually thought of as an issue within Christianity, where the acceptance of Jesus as the only way to salvation is primary: 'No one comes to the Father but by me' (John 14:6), but it has a wider significance. It has also been important for the so-called 'universal' religions. The 'universal' religions have a historical founder who gives his message to a small group of followers who in turn pass on to their followers a mission to spread the message to all humanity. Into this category fall the teachings of the Buddha, Jesus and Mohammed. Zoroastrianism, Jainism and Sikhism likewise had founders with a universal message − Zoroaster / Zarathustra, Mahavira and Guru Nanak. But there is a noticeable absence of a strong mission or proselytizing tendency in these traditions. Indeed, in the case of Indian Zoroastrians (Parsees), there has been a tendency to move towards an ethnic religion, that is, one open only to members of a given ethnic community.

The so-called ethnic religions like Hinduism and Judaism, though matrices of two universal religions, seem less concerned with conversion except in so far as it is a negative force they have to confront (e.g. Jews for Jesus, Christian missionaries in the Hindu kingdom of Nepal). Historically they have both sought converts in certain circumstances though today it is not always considered appropriate to convert into Judaism and it is not made easy. One enters Hinduism through birth into one of the castes, though people in the contemporary period have entered with varying levels of formality by means of the modern guru-led movements such as Hare Krishna, Ramakrishna mission, and Ramana Maharshi or, as in the case of Christopher Isherwood, through Vedanta. Orthodox Hindus may not always know quite what to make of this, as is made clear in the chapter by Tamal Krishna Goswami, a North American convert to Hinduism through the Hare Krishna movement. At the extreme of non-conversion stands Zoroastrianism in India (Parsees) which does not have a mechanism for the reception of converts. Indeed, most Indian Zoroastrians or Parsees believe that conversion is simply not possible. This position of Zoroastrianism is interesting because by all accounts it should be a universal religion, but often acts as an ethnic one. Has it been ethnicized due to historical circumstances? Homi Dhalla's chapter in this volume gives an account of the debate currently going on in the Zoroastrian or Parsee community in India.

Conversion among the primal traditions or non-universal religions was virtually unknown. Thus this collection pays little attention to these traditions. What are they? The primary religions of the First Nation Peoples of North, Central and South America and Australia, African traditional religion, and Siberian Shamanism, are usually defined as such. These ancient traditions precede the invention of writing. They do not have written scriptures like the Bible, the Qur'an or the Dhammapada. They passed narrative traditions down through oral transmission within the matrix of a living community. Hinduism started like this with the Vedas that were *sruti*, 'heard' by the ancient *rsis*, 'seers', but in the course of ages these were eventually set in writing. Similarly, the traditions of the primary religions may contain creation accounts but they do not

3

have an identifiable historical founder. Where these traditions have survived into the modern era, there are cases of conversion. Within the last three decades, for example, there has been a remarkable growth of the Yoruba tradition of Nigeria among black populations in Brazil, the United Kingdom, and the United States. And we have seen non-native people inducted into the tribes of the First Nation Peoples of the Americas.

Hinduism, Judaism, Confucianism, Taoism, Shintoism, and Bon-po – the indigenous religion of Tibet prior to Buddhism (though modern Bon-po has been influenced by Buddhism and has restructured itself along Buddhist lines) – are not so clear-cut. In any event, in those religions whose world-view includes reincarnation across myriads of lives there is less sense of urgency to achieve salvation in a single lifetime. Some traditions are often called ethnic religions because they seem so closely woven into, if not identified with, an ethnic identity. Indeed, it is sometimes difficult to identify the boundary between the two and thus it is difficult, if not impossible for that boundary to be crossed by those not born into a particular ethnic community. Judaism possibly has the strongest sense of its peoplehood, but in the first centuries when it developed out of Israelite religion it was a proselytizing religion. In the period of the Second Temple it actively sought to make converts to monotheism. And, as we see from Rabbi Rodney Mariner's chapter, modern Judaism accepts converts with an attitude ranging from reluctance to eagerness, though not yet through proselytization. John Bowker pointed out that 'if there is a conversion priority in Judaism, it lies in the sense which some Jews (e.g. Lubavitch, Hasidim) have that all Jews should convert to Judaism (to the observance of Torah in orthodox form)'.[2] In the Chinese traditions, as Jordan Paper shows in his chapter, conversion was virtually unknown.

Emergent global pluralism

Throughout history, the great religious traditions lived in relative isolation from one another, especially in the West. The whole of the Western world has been overwhelmingly Christian for centuries. The exception was the Jewish community and indigenous peoples in the Americas who were often subject to enforced 'conversions'. The Muslim world was the great crescent stretching from North Africa to

Indonesia. The manifold streams of Hindu religious life dominated the Indian subcontinent, with a sizeable Muslim minority beginning in the Middle Ages. Buddhism emerged in India but moved north and east into China, Tibet, Korea and Japan and south and east into Sri Lanka and Southeast Asia. It virtually disappeared in India, though some streams of Hinduism regard the Buddha as an *avatar* of Visnu. In China, the Confucian, Taoist, and later the Buddhist traditions came to permeate Chinese culture and to interface with the earlier folk traditions. In North Africa, Muslims came to dominate all across northern Africa, but below the Sahara there were the traditional African religions. The missionary movements of Christianity beginning in the eighteenth century spread across sub-Saharan Africa as, to a lesser extent, did Muslim missionary efforts. The whole of Latin America became Roman Catholic as the traditional religions were either destroyed following the Conquest or absorbed into Catholicism. Today there is an evangelical and pentecostal movement sweeping across Latin America where 'conversion' is central. But in this instance, conversion is an intra-Christian event, as millions move from a nominal Roman Catholic allegiance to evangelical or pentecostal churches.

For centuries European and North American Christians assumed that 'conversion' was a dramatic change that led one into the Christian community. The dark side of conversion in the Christian era was the 'enforced conversion' of Jews especially in medieval Europe, and the legally sanctioned efforts to convert Catholics to Protestants in Ireland and to convert Protestants to Catholics in other European contexts. What this had to do with conversion as theologically understood within the Christian world is difficult, if not impossible to see. It was clearly a wholly external change forced upon persons against their will. Moreover, it simply never occurred to most Christians that one could legitimately belong to another religion or that conversion could ever involve becoming a member of a religion other than Christianity. But in the twentieth century this religious chauvinism has been broken. In a predominantly Christian Europe and North America, people are converting to non-Christian religious traditions like Tibetan or Zen Buddhism or to new religious movements.

In California, a young woman in her twenties with shoulder-length blond hair turns her blue eyes brimming with devotion towards her Guru and bows before a Tibetan Rimpoche and utters her determination to 'take refuge in the Buddha, the Dharma, and the Sangha'. While at the same moment in the UK a man in his thirties enters the baptismal waters of a *mikveh* to become a Jew in order to marry the woman with whom he has fallen in love. In far-off India a young Frenchman is being initiated into the Sikh tradition through the *amrit* ceremony, as we see in the story of Dharshan Singh. And in Norway a young woman has just announced her sense of homecoming in a pagan ritual. Sometimes, perhaps rarely, the conversion experience can come to deepen one's empathy to people one has moved away from. In Westminster Cathedral, London, a young married man is ordained as a Roman Catholic priest and recognizes that the joy he feels is surprisingly the same as that experienced by those women he left behind in the Church of England as they are priested. But in general those in the Christian traditions have been forced, in recent decades, to see the phenomenon of conversion in relation to traditions other than Christianity.

These are the events that have generated considerable controversy in the twentieth century. Some wonder if these are true conversions and if they are valid religious choices. Others simply observe that as modern societies become more plural religiously, it is inevitable that one will see more and more of these conversions to other religious traditions. Besides, the focus on 'conversion' to non-Christian religious traditions obscures what is the larger tendency in predominantly Christian societies. In Canada, for example, there are yearly many more 'converts' to Christianity from non-Christian religions than there are 'converts' from Christianity to non-Christian religions. The reason for this is quite simple, namely, marriage. In Canada, when a non-Christian marries a Christian, it is much more likely for the non-Christian spouse to join the Christian community than vice versa. But is this 'conversion?' What do we mean by conversion?

A common meaning of conversion?

Conversion, as we have already suggested and as becomes clearer in the chapters that follow, is understood differently in different religious and social contexts. What Christians call conversion or *metanoia*, Muslims would probably call 'submission' and Buddhists would speak of 'Going for Refuge'. In some countries (Egypt and some other Muslim countries, and until recently, Nepal) 'conversion' is forbidden by law, while in other societies we encounter 'rice-bowl' conversions. What is genuine conversion? Can conversion be a group experience or decision? Whole villages 'converted' to neo-Buddhism in Maharashtra, India, in the 1950s. Or, is conversion an intensely dramatic and personal event? This came to be the classic image of conversion in Christianity. These diverse meanings and understandings of conversion pose difficulties for the theorists of conversion.

The chapters in this volume by Lewis Rambo and Charles Farhadian of the United States, Donald Taylor of the United Kingdom, and Frank Flinn of the United States all seek to offer a more comprehensive understanding of the phenomenon of conversion. For Rambo and Farhadian, conversion is the name for all forms of 'religious change'. In their model of conversion, it is a complex process involving seven stages. Those stages are context, crisis, quest, encounter, interaction, committing, and consequences. Seen in such a process perspective, conversion is not just a moment in a person's life, but involves a complex set of factors that are at once social, psychological and spiritual. Donald Taylor explores the meaning of conversion in relation to its usages in the context of the relationships between religions. Here he finds that conversion is an evaluative term used positively by those in the religion to which one converts and negatively by that religion which one abandons. Frank Flinn draws mainly upon the Christian traditions in exploring the meaning of conversion, especially in relation to the evangelical and pentecostal movements in Christianity.

When we look at the phenomenon of conversion across the range of religious traditions, we can see that the substance of conversion varies. And so do the formal conditions for the acceptance of a convert. Those conditions can be extremely stringent, less so, or completely non-existent. Anyone converting to Judaism has to satisfy the Beth Din as to the integrity of his or her motivation, adequacy of knowledge about Jewish law, custom and practice, and has to fulfil certain ritual requirements. There are also 'gatekeepers' in Roman Catholicism. Only a priest can formally admit a convert into the church after a period of instruction in the tenets of the faith that then leads to baptism. For in the sacramental traditions of Christianity, the formal way into the church is through the sacrament of baptism. And in the sacramental traditions, baptism is performed by a priest though it can in fact be performed by anyone, baptized Christian or not, who uses the right formula, and has the intention to do what the church requires. However, canon law in the Catholic tradition forbids this except in the case of imminent death, and the situation would have to be regularized should death not occur. Islam requires the act of submission to Allah to be made in the presence of witnesses, but clearly more than a recitation of the *shahada* – There is no God but God and Mohammed is His Messenger – is envisaged. A convert is also expected to say yes to the full tradition of Qur'anic teaching, *hadiths* and *shari'a*, as Yasin Dutton makes clear in his chapter on conversion in Islam. Would the convert also have to locate himself or herself in the Shi'ite, Sunni or Sufi stream of Islam as converts do in identifying Christianity with one or another denomination? In Mahayana Buddhism, one usually 'takes Refuge' in relation to one's Sensai, Master, Lama, or Teacher. Here the mechanism for admission to a community of faith might be less formal than in some other traditions.

Ideological issues

In Christianity and Islam the ideology of mission has without doubt been perceived with a greater sense of urgency than in Buddhism. The reasons for this difference may have to do with the more 'provisional' nature of Buddhist teaching conveyed in the story of the raft. In that story, religion is likened to a raft with which one crosses a stream, but when the stream is crossed one does not continue to carry the raft. It is left behind. So, the purpose of religious practice and discipline is to lead one from suffering to enlightenment and once that goal is achieved then one leaves the religion behind. Nonetheless, there is a strong missionary mentality within Buddhism – after all, the Bodhisattva vow is to remain in this world until all sentient beings achieve enlightenment. But the ideology of mission has been most prevalent in traditions like Christianity which, through most of its history, has tended to regard all other religions as 'false'. And thus, all others must be converted to the Christian way – if they are to be saved.

Serial conversion

In the modern world there is an unprecedented opportunity for persons to move freely from one religion to another. Some have moved out of their own tradition for a time, only to 'rediscover' the tradition they left behind. This has happened with a number of those Anglicans who converted to Rome over the issue of women priests. About 16 per cent have returned, though none of those who have have been (re-)ordained. Some people's pilgrimage takes them on through one tradition after another but never finally arriving at any settled place. Such questing or 'religion hopping' is rarely approved of, but perhaps in an unstructured way the move between religions is expressing a deeper need for movement and change in the spiritual life. Hinduism offers a structured pattern of commitment according to four stages of life in the idea of *varnasramadharma*. The devotee moves from being a student of the Vedas, through the householder to the hermit stage. Then, for a few, there follows the last stage of complete renunciation as a wandering *sannyasin*. In this fourth stage a kind of conversion takes places as the renunciant abandons household, ownership and caste. He dies to the world symbolically by burning an effigy of himself and taking the saffron robe, spends his time in meditation, even eschewing temple-worship, completely dependent on the alms he may receive from others. These are dramatic changes within a given religious tradition, one that builds into its own self-understanding an awareness of different spiritual outlooks at different stages of life.

We are also finding more and more people asking if it is possible to belong to more than one religion. The 'supermarket' or 'pick and mix' approach to religion found in the modern West is often criticized as a feature of the rootlessness of modern culture. But people in East Asia have for centuries seen themselves as part of more than one tradition. In Japan, for example, people have Shinto weddings and Buddhist funerals without thinking it strange. The boundaries between traditions are more porous in Eastern traditions than in the West. We may lament the loss of a monolithic certainty that belonging to a tradition once gave, but some people have challenged the desirability or even the possibility of belonging to just one religion for life. Don Cupitt, a British Anglican theologian, is just such a voice. He finds that Buddhist insights illumine his Christianity so completely that he defines himself as a Buddhist

Christian. Phil Jackson, coach of basketball's Chicago Bulls including Michael Jordan, describes himself as a 'Zen Christian'. Some people feel most comfortable at the threshold of a tradition, defining themselves, for example, as Catholic Hindus or as having a Christian heart but a Buddhist head; they feel not completely in, not completely out, like a 'flying buttress supporting the Church from without', as Winston Churchill was supposed to have said. Diana Eck, that powerful voice for religious inclusiveness, has said

> I know that this image of the river of life [flowing from the throne of God] is not our image alone. I cannot read the final chapters of Saint John's imaginative vision without seeing the Ganges in my mind's eye. For Hindus it is the River of Heaven flowing from the foot of Vishnu, falling on the head of Shiva, touching the earth on top of the highest mountain, Mount Meru, and then generously splitting into four channels to flow in four directions, watering the whole earth with streams of blessing.[3]

Contours of controversy

Of one thing we can be sure: conversion is a controversial issue in today's world. Christian officials in the United Kingdom bemoan the 'conversion' of nominal Christians to Paganism. Jewish leaders in the United States worry that conversions to Christianity and new religious movements are destroying the Jewish community. Hindu leaders of some extreme factions in India decry the 'conversions of Hindus to Islam' four to six centuries ago and urge Indian Muslims to reclaim their historic Hindu faith. Conversion is legally disallowed by the state constitutions of several Muslim nations. In Latin America, Roman Catholic leaders are dismayed by the numbers of Roman Catholics who have now become Pentecostals as the pentecostal movement sweeps across Latin America. Russian Orthodox officials in the former Soviet Union are perplexed by the appearance of many North American-based evangelical Christian groups in post-Communist Russia because of their aggressive calls for 'conversion to Christ'. Some Christian missionaries seek the conversion of those who 'live in darkness' or adhere to 'false religions'. Some North African Muslims call on the 'infidels' to submit to Allah as the only true God. Indian gurus and Tibetan lamas in the West invite nominal Christians to follow their paths to liberation and enlightenment. Parents of young adults in their twenties get very upset and suspect illicit means when their 'children' forsake their family religion and join new religious movements. Conversion is the troubling issue underlying these discordant voices. And it is at the very heart of the new religious pluralism that is sweeping the planet.

Conversion and priesthood

Hinduism has come to be thought of as a single religion by Western students of religion and many Hindus have come to accept this view. However, it is the most plural of religions, with something to offer every kind of religious seeker, and with many different forms of God for the devotee to choose from. These different forms of the Absolute may be male or female or both or neither. The forms of Hindu life range from popular cults to non-theistic, non-dualistic Vedanta. Village Hinduism has its own kinds of priests, but in the classical orthodox tradition the fourfold caste-system of *varnas* – *brahmin, ksatriya, vaisya, sudra* – is intrinsic. And priests come only from the brahmin *varna* in Brahmanical Hinduism. What about persons not born into the tradition, can they be priests?

In Christianity there are diverse ideas of priesthood. Catholics speak of the (usually) celibate male priest, Protestants speak of men and women called to the ministry and the Orthodox have married priests and celibate monks. In Hinduism and Judaism it is quite different: the priesthood is an inherited status passed through membership of the priestly family. In both religions it entails the highest degree of ritual purity which must be safeguarded if the priestly function is not to be impugned.

In Hinduism this has become an issue because of the growing acceptance among Hindus of the diaspora of the ministry of the International Society for Krishna Consciousness (ISKCON). Many caste-Hindus in Britain flock to Bhaktivedanta Manor for the great festivals and follow the temple worship led by non-Indian swamis who were not born brahmins but have become assimilated according to the teachings of Caitanya. Caste purity is not a matter of birth but right-mindedness. This is similar to the Buddhist redefinition of *arya*, 'noble', to mean the spiritually advanced person who conducts himself rightly.

Conversion: the sliding scale

Though the term 'conversion' is often associated with dramatic and emotional religious experiences in relation to Christianity, the notion predates Christianity and has its parallels in other religious traditions as the chapters below make clear. Conversion was known in ancient Judaism, but it was not so much a dramatic experience as a process unfolding over time of learning the Torah under the direction of a rabbi and undergoing some ritual events. Thus it is important to realize the various meanings of conversion both across the religious traditions and even within a given religious tradition. The chapters in the section on conversion in the world's religions document some of these differences both across and within the religious traditions.

Here it is worth noting something of the sliding scale that surrounds conversion – from the dramatic personal and inward experience of being turned around, to a very external institutional and formal process of induction into a religious community. While the founder of Methodism, John Wesley, wrote of his 'heart being strangely warmed' in response to a sermon by a Moravian preacher in seventeenth-century London on justification by faith alone, a Buddhist monk in Sri Lanka might quietly enter a temple monastery and spend years learning Pali and studying the Sutras and learning ritual practices on his way to enlightenment. In one case, conversion was dramatic and personal, in the other more formal and institutional. And one could also find this range within a given tradition: conversion to Roman Catholicism is very different from conversion to Pentecostalism or even charismatic Catholicism.

It is also important to recognize the sociological and institutional dimensions of conversion. Conversion is not just a personal spiritual awakening, it is also an entry into a particular religious community. As we have already seen, there is the 'gatekeeper' dimension to conversion, the religious official or office or institution that recognizes and acknowledges one's experience and/or intention and validates it in relation to a religious community or institution. If one, for example, were converted to the Jewish Way it would not be sufficient to say that Yahweh called me to be a Jew or that I was persuaded of the truth of the Torah. One would also have to meet certain requirements to be admitted to the Jewish tradition.

Conversion, deprogramming and new religious movements

One of the most controversial aspects of conversion in the contemporary world concerns the new religious movements and the 'cults'. The phrase 'new religious movements' covered a wide range of religious groups. At one end were groups that were not really new, but only new to North America and Europe. The Hare Krishna movement is one example of a religious movement that was five hundred years old in India, but burst on to the North American scene in the 1960s when Swami Prabhupada came to the US and founded the International Society for Krishna Consciousness. At the other end of the scale were truly new religious groups like Scientology that emerged in the 1950s from the work of L. Ron Hubbard, a science fiction writer who created the Scientology religion. There were also small Christian groups like the infamous Jonestown group that met its tragic end in Guyana and the fundamentalist community in Waco. There were also syncretistic and gnostic groups that combined elements from more than one religious traditions into their own distinct constellation. There were literally hundreds of groups. Many of these groups had a very short life, others have now been around for decades.

When in the 1960s, the twenty-something-year old-sons and daughters of the middle class began joining these groups there was a huge outcry. Parents were often outraged to see their 'children' chanting Hare Krishna at the airport or following a Korean Messiah like Sun Myung Moon rather than pursuing their studies or professions. Some opponents to these new religious movements alleged that people did not voluntarily join these movements but were illicitly seduced into them, they had been 'brainwashed'. Adherents of these newer communities offered another account, speaking of how they had been converted and found the true Lord Krishna in this group or discovered their Real Self in another. But opponents insisted that these were *not* only the words of the seduced, they were not really religious movements at all but cynical schemes to rip off the unsuspecting. In North America, the opposition to these new religious movements turned to 'deprogramming'. The idea was literally to abduct or kidnap the person who had joined a 'cult' or 'new religious movement' to hold them against their will and subject him or her to a process of 'deprogramming' to get them to renounce their – to the deprogrammer – pseudo-faith and false religion. The services of the deprogrammer cost between a few thousand and tens of thousands of dollars. And the promise was to 'free the children' – to use the title of a book by Ted Patrick, the most notorious of the American deprogrammers. During the 1970s, hundreds of members of new religious movements in North America were subject to 'deprogramming'. Some left their religious groups – having been 'deprogrammed' they then turned on their former group and commitment – but more returned to their groups after escaping the deprogrammers. Ted Patrick was sentenced to prison for kidnapping and abduction in the 1980s. The deprogrammers not only worked on 'young people' from the so-called 'new religious movements', they also 'deprogrammed' Catholics, Protestants, vegetarians, and persons who had declared themselves 'gay'. Unfortunately, this controversy continues down to the present. It is symptomatic of how controversial and troubling conversion to a different religious community can be. New religious movements (NRMs) have an unsubstantiated reputation for 'brainwashing', when most observers find familiar modes of religious persuasion. What is the difference between a person who wants to give his life to following a New Age cult which demands separation from the world and someone who feels he is being called to join a strictly contemplative religious order with all the rules of monastic enclosure? How is conversion experienced in an NRM or how is a sense of calling to the monastic life or the 'Baptism in the Spirit' of charismatics or the 'Toronto Blessing' of some evangelicals to be compared?

Commitment, continuity and conversion

In order to put the contemporary controversy into perspective, it is important to recall that most human beings simply follow the religious tradition into which they are born. And when there is change in religious commitment among Christians, it is usually a change from one denomination or sect to another within the larger tradition. For example, Old Order Mennonites become town Mennonites or join an evangelical denomination, Baptists become Episcopalians, Lutherans become Roman Catholics, Roman Catholics become Pentecostals. Perhaps the more prevalent characteristic of the modern era is the numbers of human beings who abandon religion altogether. But the vast majority of human beings remain of the religious tradition into which they were born and in which they were raised. The percentage that even explore another tradition amount to less than 10 per cent of the population.

Conversion and secularity: conversion as a non-religious phenomenon

Conversion is normally seen in a religious context. It is part of joining one or another religious community. It becomes linked to identity and membership in a community. But the language of conversion also appears in non-religious contexts. It has become a way of speaking of personal transformation and growth. For example, some women have spoken of their movement into feminism as a conversion, as a homecoming or a realization of a truth about who or what they are. Other men and women who have 'come out' in relation to their gay or lesbian nature have also spoken about that in terms of 'conversion'. Registrar's offices in North American universities speak of 'conversion rates' in relation to applicants to the university – how many of those initially contacted by the university actually proceed through the stages of applying, accepting, and actually coming to the university? And in the human potential movement, you often encounter the use of the language of conversion to speak about life-transforming experiences.

Coming out as a gay man or lesbian woman frequently leads to a complete transformation of life. Many gay and lesbian people experience something like a conversion when they take control of their own lives and 'come out'. They feel that now they can be who they truly are. If they are religious people, they see this as accepting themselves as God made them and discover that their authentic spirituality is to be gay. Fr Bernard Lynch, a priest who worked with people with AIDS in New York described how he felt when the question 'Father, are you homosexual?' was unexpectedly and unfairly sprung on him by Gay Burne in the TV *Late, Late Show*.[4] Later he was to say:

> My heart fell to the floor. Everything in me wanted to say 'no, I am not, but I *am* gay'. Because I don't like the word homosexual, it's a medicinal word, it's a clinical word. It's too genital. It is not 'wholesome'. But I stopped at the 'no'. That to me was the biggest sin I've ever committed. To deny my createdness in God.

15

Yet he had every justification. The question was designed to undermine everything he had been saying, not to say his reality as a human being. Nevertheless, the experience made him reconsider and decide to come out in his book *Priest on Trial* and later in a TV programme about his life and work because 'I would rather be hated for what I am than loved for what I am not.'[5]

What has this in common with religious conversion? The feeling of joy and release from the burden of self-hatred and internalized homophobia, accompanied by a renewed sense of strength and vigour and self-worth which was never experienced before has made coming out for many people akin to a religious conversion. In the case of coming out the new status is permanent: it can hardly be gainsaid. Coming out, as against being outed, is said to be truly life-transforming.

Gay people themselves have been the target of deprogramming probably longer than any other group. Many psychiatrists have tried to alter sexual orientation by using techniques even more abusive than those used by the religious deprogrammers. Their rationale was couched in the language of sickness, though this is now completely discredited among reputable bodies such as the American Psychiatic Association and the British Medical Association. Many people, among them Christians, find the procedures morally reprehensible because they deliberately set out to increase the guilt feelings, alienation and self-hatred of the subject. Since it has been reported to work in no more than 27 per cent of patients 'under optimum conditions', despite their high motivation and wish to be 'cured', it fails for the other 73 per cent, leaving them unconverted but 'burdened with false guilt and shame concerning their incurable condition'.[6]

Nevertheless, some evangelical groups, unable to accept that God might love his gay children unconditionally, try to promote the idea that homosexuality is a chosen, not a given, from which the subject can be released. They use deprogramming techniques and even exorcism to cast out the 'spirit of homosexuality'.

A critique of conversion

Conversion has also had its critics. Some have seen Christian evangelical conversion experiences as bogus and fleeting emotional experiences that have little lasting impact on people. The critic looks, for example, at the Billy Graham 'Crusade for Christ' events as manipulated events, orchestrated by his effective preaching and the music, that lead the one who comes forward at the 'altar call' to a very temporary state of remorse about his or her life and a temporary commitment to Jesus as their personal Saviour. But the next day, the moment has passed and the 'convert' quickly returns to his pre-conversion life. In this view, conversion is not a deep turning of the human being to God, but a superficial manipulation of people's emotions.

Similarly, within the context of many new religious movements, the critics have alleged that people are drawn into these movements through illicit methods rather than through any genuine conversion or conviction. More sober scholarly investigation of these allegations, like that of Lorne Dawson in this volume, have not verified the allegations, though they have revealed an amazing array of reasons for people joining religious groups – and they are not all noble or profound. And here too one finds that many alleged conversion experiences prove to be very shallow and temporary.

Conversion in Christianity

We have grouped together here four chapters exploring various facets of conversion in relation to the Christian traditions. We felt it important to give this much attention to Christianity because it is the tradition in which 'conversion' has loomed largest, it is the world's largest religious tradition, and it is the tradition in which conversion has generated the most controversy. Yet we must hasten to add that we have not been able to deal with the issue of conversion in relation to Christianity in a comprehensive way. Some aspects of this question have not been touched upon where others have only been alluded to. For example, we could well have had a essay exploring the phenomenon of intra-Christian conversion, specifically, the pentecostal movement that is sweeping across Latin America and is drawing most of its 'converts' from nominal Catholics. We could also have given more attention to the independent Christian churches of Africa where conversion is sometimes related to tradition African religious practices.

In a general way, it is perhaps worth noting that while conversion is found in all streams of Christianity, there is a marked difference in the understanding of conversion between the more sacramental and evangelical streams of Christianity. In the sacramental traditions (Roman Catholic, Orthodox, Anglican, Lutheran) the conversion process is through participation in the sacraments of baptism (a dying and rising with Christ), eucharist, confirmation. In the evangelical traditions it is a personal experience of giving your life to Jesus or being baptized in the Spirit, or the experience of being born again.

In Christianity conversion has been the 'big issue' in so far as it was perceived for centuries, and still is in some quarters, that outside the Church there is no salvation. Based on the image derived from Noah's Ark, by which God gave Noah the opportunity to save the uniquely righteous family from the universal flood, the Church saw itself as the One Ark of Salvation.

Later, Protestant Christians judged a person as saved or not by his commitment to Jesus as saviour. This is to put it at its simplest. The picture is more complex and complicated when conversion is perceived as a calling or an 'election' – especially if, as Calvin taught, not all are of the elect.

It has been an issue within Christianity where some people have moved across traditions. The primary group were the Reformers, Luther, Calvin and others who set up what some might see as an alternative tradition when they broke communion with the Pope. But from their side this was perceived as a reconstruction of Testamental Christianity which had been lost.

But the Church tried to retrieve the lost territory when it launched the Counter-Reformation which in many ways defined Catholic–Protestant relations to the present day. The old antagonism has been largely mollified except in Northern Ireland. Until Vatican II the Catholic Church sought converts from other Christian groups quite aggressively and in England after the repeal of anti-Catholic laws, was triumphant about the conversion of high-profile people like Cardinal Newman and Father Faber, claiming them as part of the reclamation of England as Mary's Dowry. Now, though conversions across Christian traditions still go on, the Catholic Church seems more conciliatory and perceives it more as a generous accommodation of people on a spiritual journey. This happened in the case of those Anglicans who went Romewards when women were ordained as priests in the Church of England.

There are voices, too, which question the morality of the very concept of mission itself. Missiology has undergone criticism and revision. There are those that think it should be stopped altogether. They may allow religions to express themselves to others but would limit the activity to dialoguing in order to learn something. Darrol Bryant discusses the problem in his chapter on Christianity.

Contemporary conversion

We end with a collection of cases about contemporary conversion: people who have a personal story to tell, Graham Harvey who has come out Pagan; Father Tim Edgar who has found his home in one of the most traditional forms of Christianity but who also brings something new to that tradition in his status as a married priest; Darshan Singh Rudel and Tamal Krishna Goswami who have 'gone East'. Other chapters in this final section observe the growth of non-Christian religions in the West.

Notes

1. William James, *The Varieties of Religious Experience: A Study in Human Nature. The Gifford Lectures on Natural Religion, given at Edinburgh 1901–1902*, (London and New York: Longman, Green & Co, 1902). This edition 1920, Lecture 9 'Conversion', p. 189.
2. John Bowker (ed.), *The Oxford Dictionary of Religions* (Oxford and New York: Oxford University Press, 1997), p. 236.
3. Diana L. Eck, *Encountering God: A Spiritual Journey from Bozeman to Banaras* (Boston: Beacon Press, 1993), p. 231.
4. *The Late, Late Show*, April 1987 networked on Irish Television and Channel 4, UK.
5. Father Bernard Lynch, *A Priest on Trial* (London: Bloomsbury, 1993); 'A Priest on Trial' and 'AIDS - A Priest's Testimony' Irish TV and Channel 4, written and directed by Conor McAnally.
6. John J. McNeill, *The Church and the Homosexual* (4th edn, Boston: Beacon Press, 1993), p. 122.

Part I
Conversion: theoretical perspectives

1. Converting: stages of religious change[1]

Lewis R. Rambo and Charles E. Farhadian

Introduction

Religious change characterizes an enduring quality of the human predicament. Whether it entails converting from one religious tradition to another, changing from one group to another within a tradition, or the intensifying of religious beliefs and practices, instances of conversion can be found in many cultures, historical periods, economic conditions and social categories. Although 'conversion', as a theological word, is used most often within the Christian tradition, it has come to refer to the general notion of religious change. Because definitions of conversion abound, the phenomenon of conversion continues to be an elusive concept.

This chapter proposes that 'converting' is the most appropriate term to signify that religious change is an ongoing complex process involving many different dimensions, and provides a heuristic stage model which can serve as a framework in which the nature of the converting processes can be seen more adequately.[2]

Given our assumption that converting is a process, a stage model is useful in portraying phases of a process that takes place over time. We realize that speaking of 'stages' involves the use of metaphorical language. Human life is rarely so simple and orderly. We believe that a stage model is valuable as a map of the features of change over time. We propose seven stages in this model. *Context* is the overall environment in which change takes place. Contextual factors either facilitate or constrain change. The *crisis* stage is generally a rupture in the taken-for-granted world that triggers the *quest* stage in which persons actively seek new ways of confronting their predicament. *Encounter* is the contact between questing persons and the advocate of a new alternative. *Interaction* is an intensification of the process in which the advocates and potential converts 'negotiate' changes in thoughts, feelings and actions. *Commitment* is a phase in which persons decide to devote their life to a new spiritual orientation. *Consequences* involve cumulative effects of various experiences, actions and beliefs that either facilitate or hinder converting.

A major theme of this chapter will be that converting is a process of religious change that takes place in a dynamic force field of people, events, ideologies, institutions, expectations and experiences. It is assumed that converting is always an ongoing process, rather than a single event. Converting cannot be extricated from the fabric of relationships, processes and ideologies which provide the matrix of religious change. Dimensions of the converting process are multiple, interactive and cumulative.

To understand converting in all its richness, variety and complexity, the domains of anthropology, sociology, psychology and religious studies must be taken into account. Three preliminary comments should be made concerning this stage model. First, this stage model must not be seen either as unilinear or as universal. Second, this model is intended to be heuristic. The usefulness of the model lies in its ability to systematically organize the complex phenomena of religious change as well as some of the technical issues emerging in conversion scholarship. Third, stages are not to be seen as always occurring in the same order. Reality is far more complex, and converting is frequently characterized by a spiralling effect – a going back and forth between the stages – and thus not a unidirectional movement.

Stage 1: context: dynamic force fields

The context is the ecology in which converting takes place. It could be argued that the context is not strictly speaking a stage but rather the total environment of religious change. The context influences each stage, and each stage can have a reciprocal impact upon the context. A pervasive dialectic transpires among and between stages and the context.

The context consists of three interconnected spheres: macro-context, microcontext and mesocontext. The macrocontext includes such large-scale domains as political systems, religious organizations, multinational corporations, relevant ecological considerations and economic systems. The microcontext focuses upon the more personal world of the individual, such as family and friends, vocation, and other aspects of a person's life which have a direct impact on the person's thoughts, feelings and actions. Finally, the mesocontext includes those aspects of the context which mediate between the macrocontexts and microcontexts, such as local government, regional politics and economics, and local religious institutions.

The diversity of contexts is immense. For instance, even within a nuclear family that shares many of the same features of the macrocontext, each member may be involved in different local political or religious movements, hold conflicting views on personal or public issues, or be engaged in separate vocations. Contextual infrastructures provide a range of mobility, flexibility, resources and opportunities as well as different powers of access, support, control and repression. Given the countless variety of contexts that shape a person's and / or group's life, the scholar of conversion should be careful to be systematic in detailing the contours of the context so that patterns, themes and issues can be made explicit.

Understanding the dynamic force field of the converting person and / or group is a crucial first step in the study of religious change. For instance, fourth-century Rome, the context in which Emperor Constantine was converted to Christianity, is profoundly different from that of modern Oceania, where there has been an explosion of conversions to Mormonism, Seventh-Day Adventistism, and the Jehovah's Witnesses since the Second World War.

Stage 2: crisis: catalyst for change

Crises are disordering and disrupting experiences that call into question a person's or group's taken-for-granted world. Crises are triggered by the interaction of external and internal forces. External influences may include, for example, colonial contact for the sake of exploration and trade and/or the imposition of military force which involves coercion, manipulation or threat. On a personal level a crisis may be triggered by people (an evangelist, family member) or events (an illness, mystical experience).[3] Much of the human science literature has emphasized social disintegration, political oppression, or something very dramatic as instigating crises. Also important to keep in mind is that some cultures, societies, persons and religions are able to withstand a severe crisis and adapt to it in a productive manner. Others are more fragile, and may be rendered vulnerable and malleable to outside influence. Crucial features of the crisis stage to be considered are the intensity (degree of severity), duration (length of time), scope (degree of pervasiveness), and source (internal / external) of the crisis.

The films *Black Robe* (1991) and *The Mission* (1986) retell the stories of Roman Catholic missions to the 'New World' and the ensuing conflict between Church authority and indigenous peoples. Contact with Europeans introduced diseases, against which the people had no immunity. The impact of disease and death combined with overwhelming power devastated the local people, thus undermining native religious beliefs and practices. Colonial legacy often entailed the imposition of the colonizers' religion on local peoples. For instance, the Spanish colonialization of the Philippines in the sixteenth century included both the introduction of Spanish political and economic dominance as well as Roman Catholicism. Moreover, when Japan extended its sovereignty over parts of East Asia and Southeast Asia (1942–45) it also attempted to enforce participation in Shinto religious practices. An externally stimulated crisis therefore can be a powerful motivator for religious change.

Internal catalysts for conversion may include mystical or near-death experiences, illness, existential questions about the purpose of life, desire for transcendence, altered states of consciousness, pathology, or apostasy. There are countless examples of internal incentives for conversion. Within Christianity, the conversion of Saul of Tarsus serves as a paradigmatic example of a conversion that was stimulated by an extraordinary mystical experience. While on a mission to persecute followers of Jesus in the city of Damascus in Syria, he had an experience that transformed his life. The writer of the Gospel of Luke says that Saul was confronted by the resurrected Jesus. Whatever the precise nature of the experience, it is clear that Saul's life was profoundly altered, for he became the leading proclaimer of Christianity. Although the nature of Saul's crisis can be described as of relatively short duration, it was extraordinarily intense.

On college campuses religious groups often find their most successful outreach periods to be early fall, when new and returning students experience increased social dislocation and therefore seek ways to meet their need to belong and for social intimacy. Crises of transition may give rise to greater openness to accept religious options which were either rejected previously or simply ignored.

Stage 3: quest: searching for salvation

The quest stage encompasses different ways in which people respond to crises and / or the way in which people orient themselves to life, especially the religious life. Three important factors are involved in the quest stage: response style, structural availability, and motivational patterns. Response style describes whether a person responds actively or passively to conversion. Did the conversion occur because he or she simply followed the desire of the group to convert or was the conversion something he or she actively sought?

A significant factor in understanding the quest stage is the assessment of motivational structures. What motivated the individual to convert? Typically, human motivations are complex, involving emotional, intellectual and religious features. For instance, a person yearning for relationships may find a proselytizer's friendship a wonderful balm; this friendship could then be the beginning of the conversion process. On a larger scale, in many countries, because of the presence of a powerful religious majority, persons seeking public office or positions of economic power may be prevented from doing so if they do not share the religion of the majority. This can serve as a strong impetus for conversion – to obtain social rank. Sharing the religion of the powers-that-be may enhance political or personal aspirations. Likewise, having a different religious perspective may preclude one's political, educational or social opportunities.

The assumption at the quest stage is that people seek to maximize meaning and purpose in life. Under abnormal or crisis situations this active searching becomes more compelling; people look for resources for growth and development in order to 'fill the void' and / or enrich life. The quest stage may intensify during times of crisis. In the United States the notable conversions of Malcolm X to Islam and Nixon advisor Charles Colson to Christianity each occurred while they were serving time in prison. Personal crises in the lives of Malcolm X and Charles Colson precipitated their trajectory of religious transformations.

Other motivations that may stimulate an individual or group to seek religious change include the desire to experience pleasure and avoid pain, enhance self-esteem, establish and maintain relationships, obtain power, or experience transcendence. The quest stage often entails a combination of these motives. Evidence of complex motives is demonstrated in the life stories of members of such diverse religious groups as Jim Jones's People's Temple in San Francisco, Mormonism, Krishna Consciousness, Baha'i World Faith, Islam, Protestantism, Roman Catholicism, and Buddhism.

Stage 4: encounter: engaging new options

The encounter stage describes the contact between the potential convert and the advocate / proselytizer.[4] It should be noted that this initial contact can precipitate the converting process, triggering a crisis, and fostering a quest for new solutions. Three major components of the encounter are the advocates, the potential converts, and the setting of the encounter. First, concerning the religious advocate, one should ask what is his or her theory of conversion? Is conversion central to their mission? What do they understand conversion to be? What is their personal experience of conversion? Does the advocate's strategy for conversion focus on particular individuals within a society, for instance people on the margins of society, or does the advocate circulate widely within a community and seek to persuade large numbers of people, especially community leaders, with the intention of converting the entire community? Religious advocacy may include particular strategies such as encountering the potential convert publicly or privately, personally or impersonally.

Missionary strategies of the Jehovah's Witnesses and Mormons can be described as private and personal. Jehovah's Witnesses often canvass neighbourhoods in pairs or small groups and distribute literature to potential converts. Similarly, Mormon missionary strategy includes walking or cycling throughout neighbourhoods (typically in pairs) and building friendships with local people. Examples of public encounter on a large scale are the revivalist crusades of the Billy Graham Evangelistic Association and the rallies of the Ayatollah Khomeini. Both Graham and Khomeini are charismatic religious personalities that have had profound effect on individual lives. Held frequently in large sports arena, the Billy Graham crusades deliver a Christian message that climaxes with a call for conversion at the conclusion of the service. Khomeini led the Islamic revolution in Iran, and became the spiritual and political leader of the nation until his death in the 1980s. His encounter style, like Graham's, focused on large gatherings, indeed a nation, and through personal charisma converted an entire country to a scriptural Islam.

The second feature to consider in order to understand the encounter stage is the potential convert and what he or she perceives as the benefits of conversion. The type and degree of benefits will vary according to individual need and are usually mixed. Conversion may provide a system of meaning, emotional gratification, techniques for living, leadership, and power. For instance, a powerful benefit is that the religious option may provide a sense of belonging and a compelling sense of meaning.

Finally, the setting of the encounter provides the background for conversion. Religious group members may seek private encounters in a public setting. For instance, members of newer religious movements in the West, such as Krishna Consciousness, Baha'i World Faith, Jews for Jesus, or fundamentalist Christians sometimes gather at public locations (e.g. university campuses, airports and train stations), engage passing individuals in conversations, and distribute literature. The use of huge public gatherings, by such charismatic persons as Billy Graham and Martin Luther King Jr, has the potential to create a sense of transcendence; the individual feels part of something much greater than himself or herself. On the other hand, private one-on-one encounters, typified by Mormon or Jehovah Witness mission strategy (i.e. going door-to-door) may provide the personal intimacy that enables the conversion process.

Stage 5: interaction: creating new identities

If an individual continues with the religious group after the encounter, the interaction intensifies. Here the converting person or group learns more about the teachings, lifestyle and expectations of the group, and is required to begin making a decision for commitment. It is important to note that not all religious groups encourage conversion. Some groups actively seek new members while others remain passive. Orthodox Jews, for instance, do not encourage converts, and the potential convert must be very direct and assertive in seeking a rabbi willing to provide instruction in Judaism. Other groups, such as pentecostal Christians, Southern Baptists, the Krishna Consciousness movement, or the Unification Church actively seek converts.

Four features of interacting immerse the converting person or group into the new religious option: *ritual, relationships, rhetoric,* and *roles*. First, the development of personal relationships serve as networks of transformation. These affiliations, which are crucial to the learning process, may follow the lines of family, friends or teachers. Generally, the closer the relationship between the advocate and potential convert, the greater likelihood for religious change.[5]

Second, deep-level learning of the religious tradition is facilitated by participation in ritual practices. Rituals enable converting persons to experience religion beyond the merely intellectual level. Through community activities such as singing, recitation of scriptures, and prayer, ritual action consolidates persons and groups and instils a deeper sense of belonging. Within the religious community rituals are events that embody and enact interactions between the deity and the faith community. Among Christian, Muslim, and Buddhist groups, for instance, prayer serves as a central ritual that fosters a sense of intimacy with the deity and members of the religious tradition. Other notable rituals among Christians include baptism, shared communion, and contribution of an offering to the work of the church or para-church organization. Examples of Muslim rituals include the pilgrimage to Mecca, giving alms to the poor, and observance of the fast during the month of Ramadan.

Third, the converting person or group begins to employ the specific rhetoric of the religious group, thereby incorporating into their lifeways the language of transformation inherent to the particular group.[6] The religious terminology serves as a new interpretative system that has the potential to dramatically transform the worldview of the converting person. For instance, Christians utilize terms such as 'sinner', 'heaven' and 'hell'; Buddhists '*samsara*', '*dhamma*' and '*Nirvana*'; and Muslims '*shirk*', '*sharia*' and '*jihad*'.

Finally, converting persons learn the expected roles and conduct required before the deity/God and others.[7] Group members explicitly or implicitly communicate to the converting person or group the expected changes that should take place were they to convert. These changes will encompass different levels of the personality: self, behaviour, values and attitudes. Some groups expect total rejection of the former self and the creation of a new self. For instance, morally restrictive Christian groups prohibit smoking, alcohol, dancing, and, among some of the most conservative, even men's facial hair. However, most Muslim groups also forbid drinking alcohol and interactions which they deem inappropriate socially, yet among more conservative members men are encouraged to grow facial hair. While the requirements for religious membership are diverse, the important issue at this point in the converting process is that the interaction stage provides the guidelines for new behaviour and values.

Stage 6: commitment: consolidating new spiritual orientations

At this stage a decision is required and, in many cases, some sort of public demonstration of the status change is expected. The potential convert has been confronted with a choice between the way of life and the way of death. Converts experience a sense of surrender, a 'giving in' to the religious option, that often gives rise to feelings of relief and liberation. A common method for publicly displaying commitment is the personal testimony, a narrative of the convert's life before and after conversion. The testimony serves to reconstruct biographical information, integrating the convert's and religious community's story. The individual's commitment will be more conspicuous when the group requires public testimony from the new convert.

Evangelical Christian testimonies, for instance, are marked frequently by a deep sense of sin, crisis, and surrender to Christ, whereas testimonies of Jehovah's Witnesses typically tell of a progressive enlightenment and discovery of cognitive truth. Research indicates that what people profess before a group consolidates belief. Conversion narratives can also be published to reach a wider audience, thereby solidifying their commitment in the public arena.[8] The stories of Charles Colson, Malcolm X, Eldridge Cleaver, and countless ex-gang members, athletes, politicians and musicians have been published in the popular press in the form of magazine and newspaper articles, books and testimonial tracts.

Another crucial set of expectations are the rituals in which the convert must participate. Rituals help consolidate a convert's beliefs and involvement in a group. They may involve, for instance, renaming the convert (e.g. acquiring a Muslim or Christian name), wearing particular clothes, or participating in transformative rites such as a Muslim pilgrimage to Mecca on Christian baptism.

In groups that demand total submission to the religious authority, converts may be required to leave their residences in order to live communally with other group members in order to intensify commitment to the group and its ideals, and in some cases even giving up their lives in martyrdom.

Stage 7: consequences: assessing the effects of converting

In order to assess the converting process in a sophisticated manner, the nature and extent of conversion depend in part on how many aspects of the convert's life are affected and how comprehensive these changes are.[9] Many scholars believe that authentic conversion is an ongoing process of transformation. The initial change, while crucial, is a first step in a long trajectory of transformation. For converting to be authentic (as judged by particular religious traditions), converts must change aspects of their life according to the prescriptions and proscriptions of specific religious communities. These dimensions include affective, intellectual, ethical, religious, and social / political domains. In addition to the criteria within a religious system, scholars should be cognisant of their own values and the criteria from their particular scholarly discipline. For example, psychologists may employ criteria derived from individualistic and 'rational' standards of 'normal functioning' to judge whether a conversion is 'healthy' or 'pathological'.

The impact of individual and group religious change can foment profound changes within social and political arenas. For instance, under the influence of the Ayatollah Khomeini, as noted above, many Iranians turned to a radical form of Islam, which quickly led to an Islamic revolution that deposed the Shah and his family and established Khomeini as Iran's spiritual and political leader. Conversions of large numbers of individuals (i.e. mass conversion) may deeply impact the social, economic and political lifeways of a nation. For instance, on 14 October 1956 an estimated five hundred thousand people gathered in the western Indian state of Maharashtra. The Mahars renounced their Hindu faith and embraced Buddhism, transforming them from being Untouchables to being Buddhists. In Indonesia, following the failed *coup d'état* of 30 September 1965 and the subsequent violence directed at members of the Indonesian Communist Party, hundreds of thousands of Javanese converted to Christianity. Both of these dramatic large-scale instances of conversion had a profound effect on converts' self-understanding as well as their social position in their respective societies.

Conclusion

The process of converting evinces enormous diversity in the contemporary world. This model provides a cartography of the converting process. Each stage will impact the converting person or group with different degrees of intensity. One life may be marked by a lifelong, relatively serene quest that lacks a dramatic turning-point, whereas another's spiritual journey is an intense pursuit.

The stages of converting are uneven, at times imbued with explosive vitality and at other times with relative quiescence. They are marked by advances and declines. Their trajectories are unpredictable and reversals are common. Nevertheless, as persons experience movement between and among stages, their way of life, values and perceptions are intimately involved in the dynamic process of converting.

Notes

1. The authors wish to thank Dr Araceli Suzara, of Spring Arbor College, Spring Arbor, MI, for her assistance in the writing of this chapter.
2. For a comprehensive discussion of the converting process and an extensive bibliography, see Lewis R. Rambo, *Understanding Religious Conversion* (New Haven, CT: Yale University Press, 1993).
3. For a splendid psychological interpretation of crisis, see Curtis D. Smith, 'Religion and Crisis in Jungian Analysis', *Counseling and Values* 34 (1990), pp. 177–85.
4. Three recent books provide excellent case studies of the complexities of the processes of encountering: Robert W. Hefner (ed.), *Conversion to Christianity: Historical and Anthropological Perspectives on a Great*

Transformation (Berkeley, CA: University of California Press, 1993); Steven Kaplan (ed.), *Indigenous Responses to Christianity* (New York: New York University Press, 1995); and Peter van der Veer (ed.), *Conversion to Modernities: The Globalization of Christianity* (New York: Routledge, 1996).

5. Because of space limitations, this chapter cannot consider the so-called brainwashing theory of conversion. For an overview of the issues, see Larry D. Shinn, 'Who Gets to Define Religion? The Conversion / Brainwashing Controversy', *Religious Studies Review* 19 (1993), pp. 195–207.

6. For a detailed and provocative study of the role of language in the converting process, see Peter G. Stromberg, *Language and Self-Transformation: A Study of the Christian Conversion Narrative* (New York: Cambridge University Press, 1993).

7. The discussion of role theory and conversion also points to a vast literature on self theory. It is imperative that psychology and the other human sciences become more aware of cross-cultural issues. I believe that conversion studies can be greatly improved by adopting the perspectives of scholars like Alan Roland. See his groundbreaking book *In Search of Self in India and Japan: Toward a Cross-Cultural Psychology* (Princeton, NJ: Princeton University Press, 1988).

8. A recent and very important development in conversion studies is the examination of the distinctive experience of women in the converting process. See Virginia Lieson Brereton, *From Sin to Salvation: Stories of Women's Conversions, 1800 to the Present* (Bloomington, IN: Indiana University Press, 1991).

9. An important topic that could not be discussed in this brief chapter are the consequences of the converting process for the missionary. Research indicates that the advocate or missionary is influenced by the interplay with converting persons. On a historical and theological level, see James C. Russell, *The Germanization of Early Medieval Christianity: A Sociohistorical Approach to Religious Transformation* (New York: Oxford University Press, 1994).

2. Conversion: inward, outward and awkward

Donald Taylor

What is meant by conversion, and what light does it throw upon inter-religious relationships in the world today?

First of all, meanings are notoriously difficult to arrive at, and the meaning of 'conversion' is no exception. Like the word 'religion', we think we know what it means, but when we come to define it we have difficulty. And the same applies to 'conversion'. It simply means so many things that we have difficulty in pinning it down.

It was Wittgenstein who suggested that the meaning of a word was to be found in its use.[1] Thus if we use a word correctly then we have understood its meaning. So even if we cannot define a word, we can at least convey its meaning by showing how it is used. So using Wittgenstein's approach I will try to explore how the word is used (or *not* used) in general conversation. And I will divide my exploration into three parts: inward 'conversion', outward 'conversion', and 'conversion' that may never be called 'conversion', or 'awkward conversion'.

Inward 'conversion'

Consider the following sentences:[2]

'He is a convert to Christianity (or Islam, or Judaism).' The speaker can be a non-Christian (or non-Muslim or non-Jew), or even an atheist, referring to a third party who has adopted the religion of his choice. We all think we know what is meant here.

'He is a convert to Catholicism.' If the speaker is a Catholic, he may be referring to anyone who has embraced the Catholic Christian tradition (i.e. from the Church of England) or from a non-Christian tradition (i.e. from a New Guinea tribal religion) or from Judaism, for instance. On the other hand the speaker might use such an expression if he were referring objectively to someone who had become a Catholic.

There seems to be an element of evaluation in the words 'convert' or 'conversion', for they seem to imply moving away from an inferior to a superior tradition (in the eyes of the convert and of those in the receiving tradition but not in the eyes of the giving tradition). Thus Catholics regard their tradition to be superior (because they believe they possess all truth necessary for salvation) to all other traditions, whether Christian or non-Christian (e.g. Judaism, Islam, etc.). So Catholics can talk about 'converts' from the Church of England (Anglicans) as well as 'converts' from Islam, or Judaism, or from a tribal religion, since each is the recipient of the truth which none of them held before his or her 'conversion'.

But this is not peculiar to Catholicism. It is found in Islam and in Judaism as well as in most other world religions. Islam regards itself as superior to Judaism and Christianity; Judaism regards itself as superior to Islam and Christianity. Thus Muslims will speak of 'converts' to Islam, Jews of 'converts' to Judaism (though more often than not the word 'proselyte', of Greek origin, would be used).

The reason for this is not hard to find, for each major religion classifies other religions in relation to itself, and it always puts itself first and foremost at the top of the classification. It regards itself as superior to other religions which automatically rank below it.

Thus Pentecostals in Latin America make 'converts' from Latin American Catholics, because they regard themselves as superior to Catholics, and Anglicans refer to 'converts' from tribal peoples for the same reason.

Outward 'conversion'

Now consider the expression 'He has gone over to Rome'. The speaker will almost certainly be an Anglican, and the expression 'going over to Rome' refers to an Anglican who has left the Anglican fold to become a Catholic. 'Going over to Rome' is another way of expressing ultramontanism, or 'going over the mountains to Rome' or 'coming under the jurisdiction of the Pope of Rome'. An Anglican who remains one would not accept that a person becoming a Catholic is thereby embracing a superior Christian tradition. For him, Anglicanism is just as good as, if not superior to, Roman Catholicism. Thus by refusing to use the word 'conversion' here, he is acknowledging the evaluative element built into it, and omits to use it in the case of Catholicism.

Thus from the giving tradition's point of view a person who leaves the fold to take up with another tradition is not entering a superior tradition, and so the word 'conversion' is hardly ever used. Various words may be used, depending on the degree of animosity the transfer of allegiance has aroused.

Apostasy is possibly the strongest word for such a move. In Islam apostasy is regarded as punishable by death, so strong are the feelings aroused by it. And sometimes mass apostasy arouses strong feelings that persist over the centuries, as witnessed by the bloody encounter between Serbian Orthodox Christians and the Bosnian Muslims. The latter were Slavs who had followed the Manichaean teachings of the Bogomils and were persecuted by the Orthodox clergy from the twelfth century onwards before converting *en masse* to Islam when the Ottomans overran their country. This they did to escape their Christian persecutors. But the Serbs never forgot this; nor does it seem that they have forgiven them for it either.

But in less charged language the expression 'has become' could be used. 'He has become a Catholic' is a fairly neutral way of saying that a person has converted to Catholicism. And the expression can be used in a neutral sense for almost any other change of religious allegiance. 'He has become a Muslim' or 'He has become a Greek Orthodox Christian' is acceptable and neutral. But we have to be careful, as the expression cannot be used in all circumstances. At least there are reservations about its use in ethnic religions or religions restricted to small groups. So there are reservations about saying 'He has become a Jew' or 'He has become a Hindu' because for either of these there is the feeling that to be a Jew or to be a Hindu one must be born a Jew or a Hindu. But more of that later.

Another neutral expression, where the speaker is not necessarily from the giving tradition, is 'has joined'. Thus one can say 'he has joined the Salvation Army', or 'he has joined the Moonies (or the Hare Krishna or the Sathya Sai Baba or the New Age movement)'. The expression is on a par with the secular notion of joining a club. In the same way one can say 'he has become a Moonie (etc.)'. The underlying meaning is that these religious movements are similar to secular movements which one can join and leave at will (though the reality may be quite different).

There are other instances where no evaluation is implied, and where again the word 'conversion' is not used. These are when someone moves from one Christian denomination to another, or from one accepted form of Islam (Sunni, say) to another (Shi'ite). Thus a Presbyterian who begins to attend the Baptist Church would not be said to be a 'convert' to the Baptist Church. One would say 'He is going to the Baptist Church now', and this would be accepted as a neutral statement indicating the individual's preference for the time being. There would be no surprise if after some time the individual would be seen 'going to the Presbyterian Church again'. In fact the existence of denominations, especially in the United States, has enabled Protestantism to flourish in a pluralist society, where all religions are tolerated and therefore regarded as equal. There is no question of superior or inferior status here, even though some rigorists might regard their own tradition as better than others. But this 'denomination switching' is quite common, especially in the United States.

As indicated above, something equivalent to denomination switching may happen in Islam, especially in Sunni and Shi'ite Islam. But one has to be careful here, as the situation is not exactly parallel. A Shi'ite in London may worship at a Sunni Mosque (such as the Regent's Park Mosque in London), and would be accepted by his fellow worshippers, but this does not mean that he would be accepted as a Sunni Muslim. He remains a Shi'ite. Nor would his fellow Shi'ites regard him as an apostate for worshipping with Sunni Muslims. His identity as a Muslim supersedes his identity as a Sunni or as a Shi'ite at this level only.

There is no idea of 'conversion' in either of the two examples above. Another instance where no idea of conversion is intended is 'falling away' from one's religious tradition, or 'lapsing ' from it. Thus one can meet 'lapsed' Catholics or 'lapsed' Anglicans, who have 'fallen away' from Catholicism or Anglicanism without taking up another tradition, or 'becoming' anything else. Such a person is not regarded as being 'converted', nor even of being an 'apostate'. He is simply 'lapsed'.

What about lapsed members who wish to return to the fold? Are they 'converts'? Indeed they are, and their experience whether in solitude or at a revival meeting is referred to as a conversion experience. Some Protestant denominations put great emphasis upon conversion experience, and those people who have such an experience are also known as 'Born Again Christians'. Here again the idea is a move from the inferior to the superior, and is often expressed in phrases such as 'see the light'.

'Conversion' and ritual

What seems to come from the above exploration so far is the fact that a boundary wall appears to exist between one world religion and another. 'Conversion' implies a one-way movement – inwards. But a convert cannot move in of his or her own accord. The move is regarded as official and is marked by the performance of rituals by the appropriate functionary.

Every major religion has its rituals for incoming members. In Christianity the ritual is baptism, and embedded within the ritual is the idea that the one to be baptized is moving from a world of sin, the flesh and the Devil (definitely inferior) to the world of the Kingdom of God (definitely superior). In fact the change of status is so stark that the former is regarded as darkness and death and the latter as light and life. And usually the move from one status to the other can only be effected by the superior on the inferior, and not by the incoming member willing it onto himself or herself. In Islam the convert has to recite the *Shahada*³ and if he was a Christian, he has to renounce belief in the Trinity. By reciting the *Shahada* the convert accepts the Unity of God, the Apostleship (*Rasul*) of Muhammad, and by implication, the divine origin of the Qur'an. By renouncing belief in the Trinity, the convert is distancing himself from his Christian origins, the implication being that he has now achieved the superior status of believing in the Unity of God, rather than in three gods (which belief in the Trinity is erroneously thought to imply).

In Judaism the proselyte must seek conversion without any ulterior motive. Seeking to be a proselyte because of marriage is not acceptable to Orthodox Judaism, and a person must want to be a proselyte for its own sake. Again this is accompanied by the performance of a series of rituals.

Awkward 'conversion'

In spite of the use of rituals to mark the importance of 'conversions' from one religion to another, the boundary walls between them are not always as impenetrable as they may at first seem. For instance one can traverse the boundary wall by means of marriage. Thus a Catholic man can marry a non-Catholic on condition that the children issuing from the marriage are brought up as Catholics. A Muslim man may marry a Christian or Jewish woman without her having to convert to Islam. A Jewish man may marry a Christian woman though their children would never be considered to be Jewish. And a Christian man may marry a Jewish woman. But a Muslim woman may not marry either a Christian or a Jew. She must marry a Muslim alone, and may never marry outside Islam. Thus marriage provides a route through the impenetrable boundary walls between religions, making them more porous than it at first seemed.

Intra-religious boundaries and 'awkward conversions'

When we come to consider the movement between the internal divisions within a religious tradition, then the boundaries are even more porous. We have already noted the example of denomination switching in Christianity, which takes place without mention of 'conversion' and is not marked by ritual.

The boundaries between the internal divisions of Islam are fairly porous, as has been indicated above. The main internal divisions of Islam are between the Sunni and the Shi'ite – especially the Imamite version of Shi'ite Islam. Though there are differences between some Sunni and Shi'ite doctrines (mainly the notion of the Imam and the priority of Ali and his descendants as leaders of the Muslim community), a Shi'ite Muslim will worship with a Sunni Muslim in the same mosque. So the boundary wall here is fairly porous, as happens between one Protestant denomination and another. But Shi'ite Islam has fragmented into smaller groups apart from Imamite Islam which is its official form in Iran from before the Iranian Revolution. And these smaller groups, such as the Druzes, tend to be more exclusive, not permitting the free movement of people between one group and another. Yet they do not prohibit conversions from other traditions, especially through marriage.

Orthodox Judaism, on the other hand, regards itself as superior to Reform, Conservative and Reconstructionist Judaism, and so cannot accept anyone from these traditions without due ritual. But the movement between Reform, Conservative and Reconstructionist Judaism is permitted without too much fuss, and the boundaries are considered to be fairly porous.

I shall return later to inter-religious 'conversion' according to the practitioners of liberation theology in Catholicism, and of political Islam among Islamists.

Inter-religious boundaries and 'awkward conversions'

Even boundaries between one religion and another are not always impenetrable. For instance, Islam might be thought to be particularly rigorous about boundaries between itself and other religions. But in the past Islam has shown itself to be fairly tolerant towards both Christianity and Judaism, members of which were regarded as *Dhimmi* (or People of the Book), having some affinity with the teaching of Islam. In some instances the boundaries between Islam and non-Islamic traditions have been fairly porous, especially where people have been introduced to Islam by their Sufi (mystical) tradition. The latter has played an important part in converting members of animist and polytheist traditions to Islam, especially in Africa, India, Indonesia and elsewhere. Because the Sufis were able to communicate with the mystics of other traditions they were able to appeal to the divine–human experience of religious men and women and so draw them into their sphere of influence and ultimately into Islam. But both Sunni and Shi'ite Islam have always been wary of the Sufis and converts made by them have been regarded by mainstream Islam with suspicion.[4]

Where the Sufi tradition in Islam has probably had the greatest response is possibly in India, especially in the fourteenth and fifteenth centuries. It was here that the Sufis were able to communicate with the Hindu Sant tradition of mysticism, and arising out of that encounter came such saintly men as Kabir in Benares in the fifteenth century and later, Nanak, the founder of the Sikh tradition in the sixteenth century in the Punjab. These were two of many saintly men who sought to reconcile the Muslim and Hindu traditions.[5]

'Awkward conversions' and Hinduism

The intra- and inter-religious boundaries of Hinduism are particularly interesting. Hinduism is a complicated nexus of religions in which major deities, such as Vishnu, Shiva, Ganesha, Rama, Krishna, and the female deity Durga are worshipped on an India-wide scale (the worship of whom together with a few others is sometimes referred to as the Great Tradition of Hinduism) while lesser known (but equally important) deities are worshipped at the regional and village level (sometimes known as the Lesser Tradition).[6] At the same time sectarian, devotional (*bhakti*) worship is offered to individual deities regarded as the one and only supreme deity – the best known being Vishnu, Shiva, and Krishna.[7] But there are others such as Murukan, and Ayyapan in Tamil Nadu and Kerala. Another important form of sectarian Hinduism is the Sathya Sai Baba movement, originating in Andra Pradesh near Bangalore but now to be found in many countries outside India. The worship is centred upon the founder calling himself Sathya Sai Baba who claims to be the incarnation of Shiva-Shakti, regarded as the supreme deity above all others.[8]

The transfer of allegiance from one form of Hinduism to another is fairly informal, a Hindu being able to participate in the festivals and pilgrimages of any of these traditions – either the Great or the Lesser. For instance, there is no formal ritual to mark the transfer of allegiance from one form of Hinduism to the Sathya Sai Baba movement. Merely acknowledging the miraculous powers of the founder and discoursing with other devotees in a manner that acknowledges these powers is sufficient to be accepted into the fold. The parallel with denomination switching in Protestantism is to be noted.

Boundary walls do exist, however, in the socio-religious sphere of castes. Transfer from one caste to another is regarded as impossible, though a certain amount does take place without the knowledge or consent of the majority. One of the major principles behind the caste system is purity, and the lowest caste is regarded as the least pure. The application of this principle produces an ontological hierarchy from which no one can escape.[9] The individual Hindu is born with a degree of purity which has been passed on by his parents who themselves possess the degree of purity relative to their caste. Thus although anyone can join in a religious festival, not everyone can participate in the worship in the same way. Only the high caste Brahman priest can enter the sanctuary of the temple. He can go where even some of his lower ranking priests cannot enter. As for the ordinary Hindu, only the accepted castes can enter the precinct and at one time the lowest (outcastes) could not do so, or even pass by a temple within a certain distance. Their lack of purity was regarded as polluting even at a distance.

With this strict internal division within Hinduism due to caste differentials, the boundary walls between them were (and still are) almost impenetrable. But this applies mainly to Brahman-led temple and domestic worship. Such rigid boundaries are not to be found so firmly applied in sectarian Hinduism where devotion, rather than ontology is the predominant principle, and where a sect is seeking to show itself to have universal appeal.

Although 'conversion' is not a burning issue within Hinduism, it does become an issue when Hindus come into contact with other religions. Hindus, especially the low caste Hindus, have converted to Christianity in order to shake off the stigma of their low status in the eyes of other Hindus. But these have usually come about by means of mass conversions of low caste members of a community in a small sub-region. Similarly low caste members have been converted to Islam and Buddhism.

But when it comes to being converted to Hinduism the matter is not quite not so straightforward. The traditional (conservative) Hindu, such as the member of the Rashtrya Swayamsek Sangh, or the Arya Samaj, would not accept that a non-Hindu can convert to Hinduism. According to their way of thinking, a person must be born a Hindu; he cannot become one. The reasoning behind this is quite logical. If a person is born with a certain degree of purity relative to his caste, and there can be no movement between one caste and another, then the person born outside Hinduism is so polluted that nothing can be done about it. It is true that Hinduism has its rites of passage, similar to those found in other religions. These are the *samskara* and are carried out at various stages of an individual's life, providing the degree of purification that is required for that particular stage.[10] But no *samskara* ritual can provide sufficient purification to elevate a person into a higher, purer caste. Thus there is no ritual that can change the ontology of the polluted non-Hindu into one that is acceptable to the caste Hindu.

But for all that, unofficially non-Hindus have been accepted into the Hindu system, especially as sadhus and gurus. These have opted out of the caste system, in the same way as the *sannyasin* (who has become a wandering ascetic) is regarded as no longer belonging to the caste system.[11] In fact the *sannyasin* renounces his caste ties by going through a ceremony in which an effigy of himself is burned, symbolizing his death and the disposal of his physical body on the funeral pyre, and the severance of his caste and social ties. Although the sadhu and guru are not regarded as *sannyasin*, there is a long tradition in India which recognizes their validity because of their behaviour. In fact, the tradition in India is that a guru never declares himself to be a guru. Rather, he is recognized by people to be a guru, and if anyone is in need of a guru, a guru will appear and be recognized as such by the one in need. Thus if someone behaves as a sadhu or a guru, then he is accepted as such by the majority of ordinary Hindus. Even Europeans in the past have been accepted as sadhus and gurus, because they have behaved as such. This is the 'awkward conversion', not by ritual, but by behaviour.

The importance of behaviour in Hinduism

Such a view expressed above may appear to contradict the ontological nature of caste purity as a measure of ranking castes within the hierarchy of castes. But even the ontology of such a hierarchy is not altogether straightforward. For though caste rank may indicate the degree of purity, the individual can theoretically move from caste to caste through the cycle of reincarnation driven by the effects of *karma* (action). By performing 'good' actions (i.e. those appropriate to the caste) a person may accumulate 'good' *karma* that would survive the physical body's destruction and enable him to be born into a higher, purer caste at the next cycle of reincarnation. *Karma* or the nature of behaviour thus determines the ranking of caste purity within the whole system.

Appropriate behaviour plays an important part in inter-religious action, especially in India and those countries where there are large populations from the Indian subcontinent. In Sri Lanka, for instance, the Hindu pilgrimage centre at Kataragama is looked after by Buddhists.[12] When the major Hindu festival takes place, it is attended by Hindus, Buddhists and Muslims. A few years ago one of the most important participants in a mortificatory ritual was a

Muslim. He was swung from hooks that had been pierced through the flesh of his back, and while swinging to and fro he read the scriptures and was worshipped as a holy man by the attendant Hindus. In Mauritius, Catholics and Hindus participate in the annual pilgrimage to the tomb of the local saint (St Père Laval); Catholics participate in the Hindu festival of *Kavati* (which involves a mortificatory pilgrimage to the temple of the Hindu deity Murukan, as well as firewalking), while Sunni Muslims used to participate in the Shi'ite mortificatory ritual associated with the martyrdom of Hussein. Even Hindus, ever willing to participate in such rituals, were known to have joined in. At the unofficial level, behaviour plays a significant part in inter-religious interaction.

A similar tendency is taking place among Hindus who have left India and are settling in countries outside India. For instance, Hindus in Britain would accept the presence of outcaste Hindus at their temple rituals as long as they behaved as good caste Hindus.[13] Here behaviour is almost equivalent to purity. A similar process is happening in the Hare Krishna movement. Those Americans and Britons who have made their way up in the movement sufficiently to perform rituals that otherwise would be performed by Brahman priests are increasingly being accepted in their priestly functions by the majority of Hindus who attend these ceremonies. The acceptance is based on the fact that they are behaving like Brahman priests and therefore must be acknowledged to be equivalent to them.[14] Once again behaviour is regarded as being equivalent to purity, and 'conversion' is sidestepped. At the popular, unofficial level the boundary walls between one religious tradition and another are so porous as to hardly exist at all.

Even in Hinduism there are Hindus who do not accept either the validity of the Hare Krishna movement, or of their rituals. For in traditional Hinduism it is not the right performance of a ritual that makes it valid, but the presence of the right person – that is to say the Brahman priest, who alone can chant the Vedic mantras. Other persons can do what they like, but if they do not have the purity of the Brahman priest, no amount of chanting and of ritual manipulation will validate the ritual. Indeed, the Hare Krishna movement in Britain is aware of the peripheral nature of its Hindu membership, and attempts to attract many more Hindus to its fold.

The importance of behaviour in Protestantism

In Protestantism, the importance of behaviour is well illustrated by the civil rights movement in the 1960s when the black churches in the United States under the leadership of Dr Martin Luther King began their peaceful protests against the infringement of Afro-American civil rights that existed at the time. The issue highlighted the different approaches of the traditionalist, conservative Protestants and the liberal Protestants. Traditionalists of the white Protestant churches believed that what was necessary for the enforcement of black civil rights was a firmer commitment to the values of American society such as justice, equality and freedom which they thought were the values of Christianity as well, so that the greater the commitment to religion, the greater would be the Christian's commitment to a fair, just and equitable society. Thus they gave support to the black churches' civil rights movement by verbally endorsing what they were doing, and calling for greater Christian commitment to their religion. The logic was that behaviour would stem from commitment to religious values. But this is not always the case, since most people act out of self-interest, and often find religious justification for their behaviour. The liberal Protestants on the other hand argued that belief and verbal justification were not enough, and religious commitment had to be put into effect by the appropriate behaviour. Thus a small minority of liberal Protestants went on the freedom rides with Afro-American activists in Alabama and joined in their marches, and participated in their confrontation with the state authorities. In doing so they welcomed anyone else who would join them, including liberal Jews and Catholics, who wished to do the same.

This highlights the importance of behaviour as a means of participating in the religious convictions of others. Nor does it end with the civil rights movement of the 1960s. American Protestantism has 'reconstructed' itself making use of Special Purpose Groups, according to the thesis of Robert Wuthnow,[15] and many of these Groups operate interdenominationally, drawing members from across the religions as well. The more influential Special Purpose Groups become, the more the emphasis is placed upon behaviour, without any concern for conversion.

The importance of behaviour in Catholicism and Islam

We should not be surprised at this shift towards behaviour especially in intra-religious interaction. In Catholicism, for instance, we find emphasis laid upon appropriate behaviour among practitioners of liberation theology, especially at the popular, unofficial level. In Latin America, where liberation theology originated and has developed, there has been a polarization between the unofficial liberation theology identifying itself with the poor, and the official theology of the Magisterium, identified with the Vatican. The latter insists upon the conversion of individual souls and rejects any co-operation with non-Catholic secular organizations, while the practitioners of liberation theology are often forced into increasing partnership with secularist (often Marxist-oriented) organizations where behaviour is based upon co-operation towards a common goal for society. And this behaviour when properly reoriented is regarded by the practitioners of this theology as 'conversion' (*conversio*).[16] This is 'conversion' by behaviour which is rejected by official Catholicism, which still regards conversion as the saving of the individual soul.

A similar dichotomy between official and unofficial religion is to be found in Islam. Though Islam is not as centralized as Catholicism and its Magisterium emanating from the Vatican, Islam's official position is mainly to be found (among the Sunni) in the body of its learned clerics – the *ulama* – that exists in most Westernized Islamic nation states. The unofficial position, often championing the poor, at the popular level, is very often taken up by those groups which used to be called fundamentalists, but which now prefer the name of political Islam.[17] The practitioners of political Islam expect everyone to behave in the same way as they do, which they believe is the proper way for Muslims in a properly ordered Islamic society. So as long as everyone 'behaves' as a Muslim (i.e. women wear the veil, men grow beards and wear turbans, etc.) everyone is a true convert to Islam. This of course is behavioural conversion by duress, since no one is allowed to oppose the trend, and non-Muslim behaviour can bring severe punishment.

Inter-religious interaction, on the other hand, for both liberation theology Catholics and Political Islamists still resorts to 'conversion' of individuals, not by behaviour, but by ritual. Thus Catholics in Latin America would expect a Protestant to undergo appropriate

47

rituals before being accepted as a convert, and the same would be expected of a Catholic being received into the Protestant pentecostal fold. Similarly, political Islamists in Egypt, for instance, would expect a conversion by ritual of a Coptic Christian in political Islam, and the same expectation would be present for the acceptance of a political Islamist into the Christian Coptic Church. But these exchanges would be very rare – if not indeed dangerous for the individual concerned.

Conclusion

The foregoing paragraph has shown that in spite of the lack of restriction within divisions of most religions, where no rituals are performed to mark the transfer from one division to another, the transfer of allegiance from one religion to another is normally officially sanctioned and marked by ritual. Inter-religious interaction is official and important. It is regarded as conversion, with its attendant overtones.

However, there exists a wealth of inter-religious interaction which cannot be regarded as 'conversion' as such, but which I have labelled as 'awkward conversion' which could also be called 'awkward-in-between traffic'. This traffic occurs at a popular, unofficial level and is not marked by any ritual. And it consists mainly in the participation of members of one religion in the festivals, pilgrimages and even worship of another religion. Although purists know that this traffic exists, they do not approve, and even condemn it.

It is the existence of this latter interaction that gives rise to acknowledging the importance of religious behaviour. For many, to behave in an appropriate manner of a religious tradition is sufficient for that person to be accepted within the tradition. This seems to be true not only of Hinduism, but of Protestantism, Catholicism, Islam and Judaism. But that someone is only unofficially accepted, and is rejected by the traditionalists who have control of the official levels of the religion. Even though we may find a few rare examples of 'conversion' by behaviour, they remain on the periphery.

However, in spite of the rigidity of the official traditionalist, there seems to be a trend, in Western-style liberal democracies, towards inter-religious interaction where the boundary walls between religions are becoming increasingly porous. True, this is happening at the unofficial, popular level, where we are beginning to see the emergence of 'multifaith' individuals who spurn the idea of 'conversion', but welcome the idea of liberal inter-religious behaviour. Perhaps the celebration of Christmas in these Western style societies where everyone seems to acknowledge some Judaeo-Christian values (interspersed with the values of secular consumerism) without wanting to 'become' a Christian, is a foretaste of this trend.

Notes

1. L. Wittgenstein, *Philosophical Investigations* (Oxford: Basil Blackwell, 1953), par 43, pp. 20f.
2. In the following sentences, and throughout this chapter, though the masculine personal pronoun 'he' (and its cognate forms) is used, the word is intended to include the feminine forms of 'she' and 'her' as well.
3. The *Shahada*, or Word of Witness, is as follows: 'I witness that there is no God but Allah, and that Muhammad is His Prophet'. (The word rendered Prophet is *Rasul* in Arabic which strictly means Messenger or Apostle.)
4. See Jean-Loup Amselle, 'A Case of Fundamentalism in West Africa: Wahabism in Bamako', in L. Caplan (ed.), *Studies in Religious Fundamentalism* (London: Macmillan, 1988), (translated by Donald Taylor).
5. This is not to say that Sikhism is a syncresis of Islam and Hinduism. Sikhs maintain that Sikhism is a new revelation granted to Guru Nanak, their founder.
6. The expressions 'Great Tradition' and 'Lesser Tradition' applied to Hinduism were first used by the American anthropologist, Robert Redfield. See David L. Shills (ed.), *International Encyclopaedia of Social Sciences* (London: Collier Macmillan, 1968), vol. 13, p. 352.
7. For instance, the Vaisnava sects Swaminarayan and the Vallabha; or the Caitanya followers of Krishna.
8. See Donald Taylor, 'Charismatic Authority in the Sathya Sai Baba Movement', in Richard Burghart (ed.), *Hinduism in Great Britain: The Perpetuation of Religion in an Alien Cultural Milieu* (London: Tavistock Publications, 1987), pp. 119–33.
9. See Louis Dumont, *Homo Hierarchicus* (London: Granada Publishing, 1972).
10. R. B. Pandey, *Hindu Samskara: A Socio-religious Study of Hindu Sacraments* (Delhi: Motilal Barnarsidas, 1972).

11. The *sannyasin* is the fourth stage of the idealized life of the devout Hindu. Ideally he should end his life as a wandering ascetic, having renounced all caste ties.

12. See B. Pfaffenberger, 'The Kataragama Pilgrimage: Hindu-Buddhist interaction in Sri Lanka's Polyethnic Social System', *Journal of Asian Studies*, 38:2 (1979), pp. 253–70.

13. See Donald Taylor, 'The Symbolic Construction of the Sri Lanka Hindu Tamil Community in Britain', unpublished PhD thesis presented to the School of Oriental and African Studies, London University, 1994, p. 145.

14. For instance, in 1987 the head of the Hare Krishna movement in Britain was an American who was regarded as a Guru, and assumed the title of His Divine Grace Srila Bhagavan Goswami Maharaja. The founder of the Hare Krishna movement, Bhaktivedanta Swami, also conferred Brahman priestly status and bestowed the sacred Brahman thread on his close American and British disciples. See Sean Carey, 'The Hare Krishna Movement in Britain', in Burghart (ed.), *Hinduism in Great Britain*.

15. See Robert Wuthnow, *The Restructuring of American Religion: Society and Faith since World War II* (Princeton, NJ: Princeton University Press, 1988).

16. See Frederick Lawrence, 'Political Theology' in M. Eliade (ed.), *Encyclopedia of Religion* (London and New York: Macmillan, 1987, vol. XI, p. 405).

17. See Olivier Roy, *The Failure of Political Islam* (London: I.B. Tauris, 1994).

3. Conversion: up from evangelicalism or the pentecostal and charismatic experience

Frank K. Flinn

Conversion in the Western and Eastern religious traditions is as common as baked bread. And it has come in just about as many varieties. One can point to the celebrated individual conversions of Augustine of Hippo, Siddartha Gautama and Thomas Merton, as well as the mass conversions of whole peoples: the Slavs, missionized by Saints Cyril and Methodius, the Chinese by Buddhist missionaries, and Africans by Muslim imams. Nonetheless, conversion has become very controversial in recent history. The rush of Western youth into the new religions brought charges that these 'conversions' were the result of some form of 'brainwashing' (Bromley and Richardson, 1983). By extension the same sort of charges have been laid at the doorstep of those entering upon the paths of evangelicalism and pentecostalism. But this is getting ahead of the story. Before discussing the special nuance that the pentecostal and charismatic movements have put upon the story of conversion, I want first to examine the general character of religious conversion and the competing interpretations of conversion from the perspectives of theology, psychology and sociology.

The phenomenon of conversion

The word 'conversion' is derived from the Latin *convertere* which means 'to revolve, turn around' or 'head in a different direction'.

This basic meaning also holds for the biblical Hebrew word *shub* ('to turn, return') and the Greek terms *strepho* and *epistrepho*. Two other Greek words in the New Testament associated with the phenomenon of conversion convey overtones of repentance and regret. The first *metamelomai* ('to be anxious, regretful') describes the state of the subject undergoing a conversion experience. The second *metanoia* ('change of mind') describes the positive state or attitude of one who has undergone a conversion.

Closely related to, but distinguishable from, the phenomenon of conversion is the experience of vocation or calling. Although people commonly refer to the conversion of Saul (Acts 9:1–30), Paul himself never refers to himself as one converted but as one called – in Greek *kletos* (Romans 1:1; 1 Corinthians 1:1) – to be an apostle of the gospel. Paul models his calling on the classic pattern of the calling of the prophets in the Old Testament (Isaiah 49:1; Jeremiah 1:5). In contrast with conversion, which stresses the introspective aspects of consciousness, calling puts the emphasis on divine appointment and election along with a mission to the community at large (Stendahl, 1976: 7–23).

Conversion in contemporary parlance is almost exclusively restricted to religious phenomena. However, Plato recounts a story of the conversion of the philosopher in Book VII of his *Republic* (515a–516b). In this passage Socrates narrates how the lover of wisdom or philosopher must be dragged from the Cave of images, shadows and fleeting opinions, undergo a 'turn around' (in Greek, *periagoge*) and be led up to the light of the Sun where truth, beauty and goodness abide. The conversion is from the changing to the unchanged, from the temporal to the eternal, and from becoming to being. The philosopher's turn illustrates the intellectual or cognitive aspect of conversion.

While it is common to separate the cognitive aspect from the religious and emotional aspects of conversion, such rigid divisions appear false to experience. Plato's account of the philosopher's turn is coloured with language adapted from the initiation of neophytes into the Greek mystery religions, such as the mysteries at Eleusis. In every conversion there seems to be a cognitive aspect, a religious aspect, a moral aspect and an emotional aspect.

Popular accounts of conversion experiences such as the one recounted in *Seven Storey Mountain* by Thomas Merton leave the impression that modern conversions are distinctly private and solitary affairs. The common experience, however, is that conversion is undergone in the context of wider communities. Even the US Great Awakening in the late 1730s and early 1740s, often held up as the example *par excellence* of the individualistic interpretation of conversion by William James, was more like a social phenomenon. William Scheick (1974) has pointed out that the family, not the individual, is the central motif of Jonathan Edward's *A Faithful Narrative of the Surprising Work of God in the Conversion of Many Hundred Souls in Northampton* (1737). Edwards wrote:

> There were remarkable tokens of God's presence almost in every house. It was a time of joy in families on account of salvation being brought unto them; parents rejoicing over their children as new born, and husbands over their wives, and wives over their husbands. The doings of God were then seen in his sanctuary; God's day was a delight, and his tabernacles were amiable. (Edwards, 1966: 101)

Beginning with William James's *The Varieties of Religious Experience* (1902), psychologists consistently have neglected the social factors in the conversion experience. Josiah Royce, James's colleague and mentor at Harvard, remarked that James limited religious experience to 'the experience of an individual who feels himself "to be alone with the divine"' (Royce, 1969 II: 1029). Royce himself spent the last phase of his thinking demonstrating that conversion to faith is a spiritual reality that takes place within communities of interpretation (Royce, 1968). Indeed, conversion, following upon atonement, is conversion into community. Following the lead of James, American psychologists and even theologians have tended to see conversion in atomistic, individualistic and positivistic terms. While the 'sense of personal sinfulness' cannot be excluded from any account of the conversion experience, Royce argued with equal force in a celebrated essay 'Individual Experience and Social Experience as Sources of Religious Insight' that the meaning of intensely private experience depends upon the interpretation of faith in the 'wider vision' of a community (Royce, 1969 II: 1015–37).

The conversion of Saul of Tarsus in Acts 9 is a perfect illustration of Royce's insight on the reciprocity of individual and social religious experience. The flash of light, the voice lamenting 'Saul, why do you persecute me?' and his bewildering blindness were traumatic experiences which drove Saul into the inner sanctuary of the private self. What could all this mean? The interpretation of Saul's experience, however, did not come from himself but from

Ananias, 'a disciple in Damascus'. It is the latter who received a vision from God (in close parallel to the calling of the prophet Samuel in 1 Samuel 3:1–8) that interpreted to Saul his future mission as the Lord's chosen vessel to bear his name before the nations, the kings and the people of Israel (Acts 9:15). The significance of Saul's individual experience depended upon the interpretation of the community of faith in Damascus.

Models of conversion

The terms for conversion in the Western tradition tell us that it is some kind of turning but do not tell us a lot about the character of the turning. There have been two models used to interpret conversion. Both have to do with arguments about the nature of the human soul (H. Richardson, 1977: xlvii–xlviii).

The first model is based on the idea of Plato and the neo-Platonic Augustine that the soul is something like a spiritual eye which attains perfection by turning away from the images and shadows of temporal life toward the eternal and unchanging realities ('Ideas', 'God'). This understanding of the soul lends itself to an interpretation of conversion as a sudden event and an escape from time. This model lies behind many accounts of being suddenly 'born again' and many psychological models of conversion as a climatic event resulting from some sort of life crisis.

The second model follows Aristotle's and Thomas of Aquinas's understanding that the soul is the principle of growth in all living things by which they attain completion and fruition. In this view all living things have souls, even the lowly acorn within which resides a green 'fuse' that gives rise to the whole oak tree. The soul is not a Archimedian lever for hoisting oneself out of time but the life-fulfilling meaning of time itself. Conversion in this light is not a sudden event but a turn toward the next stage in the cycle of growth; it is a process of ordered stages.

Both these models of conversion contain a partial truth. On the one hand, in the heat of the experience conversion seems, to subject and observer alike, a sudden turning away from one's past life and behaviour, a momentous event marked by emotional upheaval and a radical crisis in thinking, values and norms. On the other hand, conversion in the long stretch of a full life-cycle seems a stage of growth toward maturity, a transition from one status to another, a turning toward a fuller and more complete commitment to the wholeness of life and its ultimate meaning. The immediate temptation is to opt for an either / or solution to the problem – either it is an event or it is a process. A both / and approach seems to give a fuller account of all the aspects of the phenomenon.

The case of St Augustine of Hippo is instructive. In Book VIII of his *Confessions* he recounts the immediate circumstances surrounding his decision to become a Christian. He found himself in inner turmoil with his divided will struggling against himself until, sitting in a garden, he heard a child chanting over and over *Tolle, lege* ('Take up and read'). Thereupon he took up Paul's Epistle to the Romans and read chapter 13 verse 13. 'Instantly,' Augustine continues, 'there was infused in my heart something like the light of full certainty and all the gloom of doubt vanished away' (*Confessions* VIII. xii). To someone who has read only Book VIII Augustine's conversion would appear as sudden, rapid and radical. Augustine himself gives this impression in that Book. But if we behold the full amplitude of Augustine's rich narrative, the event in the garden may be likened to the Garden of Gethsemane. In two other places Augustine speaks of gardens. When he was 16 years. old he once stole some fruit from a garden. This experience made him conscious of his sinfulness: 'And I become a wasteland unto myself' (II. x – whence the title of Eliot's famous poem). He likens his sin with Adam and Eve's sin and expulsion from the Garden of Eden (II. ii). The other garden scene takes place long after the garden conversion event. Here he is with Monica, his mother, shortly before her departure and death. They are overlooking a garden in Ostia, conversing about celestial things and the Garden of Paradise (IX. x). The recurring theme of the garden scene in the *Confessions* provides the dense background and context of the stages in Augustine's spiritual journey: remorse over sin; surrender to God's will; and foretaste of celestial bliss. Augustine's dramatic conversion experience in Book VIII is both a momentous event and a stage on life's way.

Contemporary theory of life development lends support to the reconciliation of the Plato–Augustine and Aristotle–Aquinas models of conversion. In his celebrated essay 'Eight Ages of Man' (1963: 247–74) and more recently in *The Life Cycle Completed* (1982), Erik Erikson notes that the human life cycle unfolds in ages or stages, beginning with the child's basic trust vs. mistrust and ending with the older person's ego-identity vs. despair. However, the transition to young adulthood (identity vs. role confusion) is particularly marked by a call to 'ideological' commitments and conversion-related orientations. The conversion experience required for the transition into young adulthood was the subject of Erikson's *Young Man Luther*. Conversion can be both maturational or a stage in the unfolding of life's dialectic and / or a critical or crucial event like Luther's *Turmerlebnis* (tower experience) that shapes the fundamental orientation of a person toward life.

Uniting Erikson's psycho-sexual stages with Lawrence Kohlberg's stages of moral development, James Fowler has derived six possible relations between stage development and conversional change in his seminal *Stages of Faith*. Fowler builds on Lewis Rambo's definition of conversion as 'a significant sudden transformation of a person's loyalties, patterns of life, and focus of energy' (Rambo, 1980: 22). (Rambo's definition is obviously a James derivative.) According to Fowler, conversion entails 'significant changes in the contents of faith'. But the relation between stage and conversion is not one-to-one. There can be (1) a stage change without conversion, (2) a conversion without a stage change, (3) a conversion that precipitates a stage change, (4) a stage change that precipitates a conversion, (5) a conversion that goes hand in hand with a stage change (the example of Luther), and (6) a conversion that either blocks or helps a stage change (Fowler, 1981: 285–6). Fowler fails to mention a seventh possibility: a stage change that either blocks or helps a conversion. Fowler's contribution to the conversion debate has been to demonstrate that the phenomenon of conversion is amazingly complex. This complexity is pushed aside by those who would see religious conversion as a type of 'ego reversion' or 'infantile regression' or blockage to maturational growth.

The phases of conversion

Drawing together the many strands sketched above, we can now see that conversion is an extremely complex phenomenon. It is both event and process. It is a state and a dialectical movement. That dialectic can be broken down into three moments: (1) a turning away or separation; (2) a state of suspension; and (3) a turning toward. Below I will discuss these three aspects in detail.

TURNING AWAY

Those who experience a conversion seem to undergo something akin to 'spiritual dissonance'. The horizon that the person is living within is now perceived, for one reason or another, as limited and unfulfilling. This perception of a limited and unsatisfactory horizon is experienced on several distinct planes which are nonetheless interconnected. Psychologically the convert may appear to suffer from 'mental disturbances'. Such phenomena did not upset William James in the slightest. To James such disturbances signalled a shift of peripheral ideas to the centre of consciousness: 'To say that a man is "converted" means, in these terms that religious ideas, previously peripheral in his consciousness, now take a central place, and that religious aims form the habitual centre of his energy' (James, 1902: 183). Emotionally, the about-face can be described as 'losing one's grip'. Intellectually, conversion is akin to a 'radical clarification' that induces a paradigm shift such as the celebrated 'Copernican revolution' noted by Immanuel Kant in the *Critique of Pure Reason*. From the viewpoint of religious experience, the turning away can be described as 'finding oneself a sinner' (Christianity) or as being 'entangled in the threads of existence' (Buddhism). Theologically, conversion can be described as the workings of the Holy Spirit on the affections (Edwards, 1966: 184–95). Morally, there may be 'pangs of conscience' experienced in the conflict between self-satisfaction and universal norms. Sociologically, the phenomenon may perceived as a discrepancy between stated public ideals and the real status quo, leading to disillusionment and the formation of new religious groups such as the Quakers or Mormons. Politically, a group turning away can form the nucleus of a revolution leading to the formation of new groups such as the founding of the people of Israel by Moses or the establishment of new political orders.

It is imperative to note that all of the above factors – psychological, intellectual, religious, moral, sociological and political – are latent in any conversion experience (Gelpi, 1976; Lonergan, 1972: 237–44). Although each factor has its specific function, all potentially can resonate with one another as wave peaks in a single continuum. Restricting our scope of analysis to the psycho-emotional aspect of conversion arbitrary neglects the other factors that accompany each and every conversion experience. Such restriction is very common in modern treatments of conversion and religion. Alfred North Whitehead, following upon James' restrictive definition of religious experience, defined religion as 'what the individual does with his own solitariness' (1974: 16). In reality, religious conversion takes place in communities and through the interaction of the public and private realms. Moreover, such conversions partake of a much broader realm of social phenomena which include such events as 'scientific revolutions' (Kuhn, 1970). Paradigm shifts occur in the field of art, perhaps best exemplified by the shift from the aspectival, bifocal rule of construction in Gothic painting to the perspectival, monofocal rule in the Renaissance (Gadol, 1969: 22–37). Conversion invites us into the interconnectedness of all human phenomena. The turning away that initiates the conversion experience is one species of a genus which, in general terms, may be called a change in worldview, a paradigm shift or the discovery of an unforeseen horizon (McGowan, 1982). Turning away is an about-face resulting from fundamental conflicts which are overcome only by an intellectual, moral, religious or social conversion to a new set of ideas and behavioural norms that will make sense of the whole.

SUSPENSION

The middle phase in the conversion process is very difficult to describe. It has suffered from considerable inattention, mostly stemming from the view that conversion is an instantaneous event. This gap is now being filled. I use the term 'suspension', though this may not be the best term. This phase also can be described as a state of indecision, of a divided mind (James), or of dwelling in what Plato called the 'in-between' (Greek, *metaxu*), or of standing on the threshold (Latin, *limen*) where the convert is not all the way out of one room ('the old man') and not all the way into the next ('the new man'). This last notion refers to the 'liminal phase' in rites of passage during which initiates are statusless, anonymous, and secluded from ordinary society (Van Gennep, 1960; Turner, 1969: 94–130; 1970: 93–111). Although we are tempted to restrict rites of passage to primal societies, liminal transitions still occur in modern industrial society but they are diffuse and fragmented (the 'teen years') rather than compact and intense as they are in tribal societies (Melton and Moore, 1982: 47–59).

Recent investigations into the genetic and structural aspects of development have increased our understanding of the transitional state of suspension. E. D. Starbuck in his classic study of adolescent conversion *Psychology of Religion* (1899) noted the psychological features of the transition state as a 'sense of incompleteness and imperfection; brooding, depression, morbid introspection, and sense of sin; anxiety about the hereafter, distress over doubts and the like' (quoted in James, 1902: 185). These descriptions have often been used to bolster the charge that the conversion experience is some kind of mental illness rather than a transitional shift to a pattern of knowing, construing and committing oneself to a wider horizon of ultimate concern. Starbuck and James carefully pointed out: 'Conversion is in its essence a normal adolescent phenomenon, incidental to the passage from the child's small universe to the wider universe and spiritual life of maturity' (ibid.). Indeed, James felt that the great converts of history were those who experienced the greatest extremities of emotion. Genetic and structural studies of paradigm shifts have lowered the emotional charge attached to purely psychological descriptions of conversion. Jean Piaget speaks of the transitional states between phases of learning as 'cognitive disequilibrium' (1970: 45–6). Lawrence Kohlberg talks about 'cognitive conflict' between moral states (1981: 47). Thomas Kuhn refers to the unsettling perception of an anomaly preceding a paradigm shift (1970: 52–65). Bernard Lonergan speaks of an 'inverse insight' leading to a reinterpretation of phenomena (1958: 19–25). Erik Erikson notes that transitions in general and the passage to identity in particular are signalled by a 'psychological moratorium' (1963: 262–3). William James depicted this phase as the 'divided self' or *homo duplex* who stands in need of being twice-born (1902: 156–76).

Another feature of the state of transition between stages is that it is often accompanied by what developmental psychologists describe as a temporary 'ego regression' to an earlier stage. Erikson sees this as a 'regression in service of the ego' through which the person picks up the loose ends of unassimilated experience before moving on to the next stage (1982). Fowler notes that this is a normal 'recapitulation in service of faith development' (1981: 288). Anti-conversionists often highlight this phenomenon in their allegations that religions 'infantilize' their young converts. Developmentalists see the period of suspension as normal, transitory, and even beneficial to maturational development. This does not mean that

59

there cannot be pathological regressions among converts – or among the general population for that matter. Melton and Moore have discovered some incidence of 'chronic liminality' among converts to new religions (1982: 59–60), but to date there have been no solid studies of permanent ego regression or chronic liminality as related to religious conversion in general.

In sum, the transitional state of suspension can be compared to what L. S. Vygotsky called the 'zone of proximal development' during which the developmental process lags behind the learning process (1978: 84–91). Each of us experiences this phenomenon when we know that our old patterns of construing and knowing no longer work but when we do not yet sense the wider horizon in which the parts hold together again. Vygotsky likened this state to the 'buds' and 'flowers' as opposed to the 'fruits' in biological development.

TURNING TOWARD

Many theories of conversion stop with the *terminus a quo* of the conversion experience. The experiences accompanying the 'turning away' phase are often colourful, dramatic and even traumatic. The modern temper is well suited to finding causes and origins and less suited to tracking down ends and purposes. That conversions have long-term effects is without question. Moses turned away from the luxury of the Egyptian court and founded a people of faith. Gautama's abnegation of royal life led to the foundation of a monkhood and eventually one of the greatest missionary religions of all time. Augustine's conversion led to a lifetime as leader of the Catholic Church in North Africa and pre-eminent theologian of Western Christianity. I once heard a psychiatrist compare the conversion experience to an alcoholic bender: something all right once in a while but best got over quickly. William James, though he is the father of psychological interpretations of conversion, never fell into such quick-fix similes. That is why over half of his masterful *The Varieties of Religious Experience* is devoted not to the 'turning away' and 'suspension' phases of conversion but to the 'turning toward' results.

James characterized the third phase of the conversion experience with terms like commitment, revitalization, renewal, regeneration, a sense of sanctification, holiness or blessedness (1902: 239–341). If the first two phases of the process can be said to be inner-directed, the third is other-directed in the sense that the convert dedicates himself or herself to new ideals, new codes of behaviour, new spiritual disciplines such as prayer, fasting and meditation, works of charity or evangelization. The social impact of conversion is felt through the public expression of new modes of life. That impact is publicly felt even when the stated aim of the conversion is to 'withdraw from the world'. Here we can point to the example of monks and hermits during the Byzantine era, the most notable instance of whom was Simeon Stylites who from his anchorite's pillar near Aleppo exerted enormous theological and political power.

The third phase is also the seedbed of religious innovation. The turn toward the goals and ideals of sanctification and regeneration often flows into the revitalization of a traditional belief (Moses), the founding of a new religion based on an earlier religion (Christianity, Islam, Mormon), the founding of new types of religious orders (St Francis of Assisi, St Dominic, St Ignatius of Loyola, the Muslim Sufi orders), the reformation or reformulation of an established religion (Martin Luther, John Wesley, John Calvin), the generation of religious renewals within traditional religions (pentecostalism, charismatics), or the creation of religious 'blends' from native and missionary elements (Handsome Lake among the Iroquois, Simon Kimbangu in Africa). It is hard to underestimate the innovative impulse which religious conversion nurtures and motivates. Yet this innovative impulse is what makes conversion controversial and questionable to the majority who abide with self-satisfaction in their comfortable pews. What a new discovery is to scientific theory, conversion is to religion. It unsettles the perception of sacred reality, not only for individuals but also for entire civilizations. Conversion is also a response to the different needs of history. As the late Roman empire with its state religion became weighed down with its own earthly concerns, religious seekers turned to the contemplative life with its guarantees of a blessed hereafter in Christianity. This was the age of the rise of the great monasteries in southern Gaul. When the contemplative life itself became jaded with benefices and indulgences, the Protestant reformers legitimated the active life of the tailor and the tinker as the proper arena for sanctification. Today many people speak of the meaninglessness which has inflicted itself on post-industrial societies. Conversion now is often a conversion to the ultimate meaning of life.

Cycles of conversion, cycles of awakening in America

The rise of the pentecostal and charismatic movements in the United States cannot be understood apart from the cycles of conversion which have accompanied the four major awakenings in American history.

The first awakening is called the Great Awakening (CE 1735 ff.). It perhaps ought to be called the Primal Awakening, for it has shaped the character of American religion ever after. The awakening followed upon the compromises of the Half-way Covenant under which children of non-practising parents were allowed to be baptized. The big names associated with this first 'outpouring of the Spirit' on America were Jonathan Edwards, the Congregational pastor in Northampton, Massachusetts, and the British Anglican divine George Whitefield, who preached the length of the American colonies. At first the awakening was a spontaneous event, but it soon gave way to crusades of preaching and revivalist gatherings. The fact that the great lights were from two different denominations marked one of the chief characteristics of this first awakening: it was interdenominational. Presbyterians, Dutch Reformed, Lutherans, Anglicans and, later, Methodists all contributed. The awakening was also international, for it spread to the English-speaking world, and even to the Continent. Likewise it was interracial, for in the Southern States blacks began to participate and the Great Awakening contributed to the formation of the distinctive character of American black Christianity. Theologically and religiously, the Great Awakening set the pattern for American religious revival: (1) the 'outpouring of the Spirit' shaped the fundamental consciousness of the United States as a 'Redeemer Nation', and (2) the 'born-again' experience entered the American Protestant religious credo. The Great Awakening introduced a democracy of the Spirit into American religious life, thereby setting the stage for the American Revolution (Bumstead, 1970).

The Second Awakening (1820s ff.) might best be called the Revivalist Awakening or even the Frontier Evangelical Awakening, for it set the pattern of tent revivals which still take place in the southern and western states. The triggering event was the Cane Ridge Revival in Kentucky (1805), during which there was rampant emotionalism including 'barking', 'dancing', 'falling' and mass singing (Cleveland, 1916: 86–127). The 'falling' phenomenon later came to be known as 'being slain in the Spirit'. Later, the key theoretician was Charles Finney, who taught that revivals were not miraculous events but humanly contrived means ('new measures') for winning souls to Christ (Finney, 1960: 12–17). This revival stressed the freedom of slackers to convert back to God on the pattern of the Book of Judges. The 'new measures' included sustained prayer, pressure for immediate conversion, and the 'anxious bench' where repentants prayed before the altar call. This pattern of revival, with a few changes, is still in effect today and describes perfectly Billy Graham's worldwide crusades (Graham, 1965; Ferm, 1958). (It is also the pattern critiqued in the Sinclair Lewis novel *Elmer Gantry*.) The conversions resulting from the Revivalist Awakening are properly called evangelical: salvation comes solely through the cross of Christ. While reliance on the Bible was upheld, the principal stress was and is on repentance of sins and 'standing up for Christ'. Many luminaries of the Second Awakening, including Finney himself, were much influenced by the Methodist Holiness movement.

The Second Awakening, like the first, was post-millennial in its belief. Adherents believed that the 'surprising work of God' had begun in America and that Christ would return at the end of the millennium spoken of in Revelation 20 and 21 to crown the work of the Spirit. Hence, both awakenings contributed the progressive and reformist spirit which marked much of the nineteenth century: prison reform, abolition, temperance and the suffragist movement. The next two awakenings were pre-millennialist, that is, believers felt that Christ would have to come before the millennium in order to rescue a sinking world. The dividing line marks what we today call theological 'liberals' vs. 'conservatives'. Late nineteenth-century evangelical revivalism often is perceived as a rural phenomenon but from the beginning it was urban. It is only in the twentieth century that certain forms of revivalism have retained a toe-hold in rural America, especially Appalachia.

The third awakening can be called the Populist or Fundamentalist Revival (1880s ff.). The fundamentalist movement has its roots in the post-Civil War period of failed hopes. The key figures were Dwight Moody, founder of the Moody Bible Institute in Chicago, A. J. Gordon of Boston and James Hall Brookes of St Louis. All three were shaped by the vision of Irishman John Nelson Darby, erstwhile divine of the Church of Ireland and eventual founder of the

Plymouth Brethren (Marsden, 1980). Darby taught that God dealt with humans in seven 'dispensations', beginning with the Age of Innocence in the Garden of Eden. Humans failed each and every task set before them by God. Christ would have to come to the rescue. Darbyites expect Christ to come 'at any moment' before the millennium and snatch away the church of true believers in a secret rapture. Thereupon the events of the Last Days will begin to unfold according to the plot in Revelation: the Anti-Christ, Armageddon, the loosening of Satan for a little while, the restoration of Israel, the Last Judgement, and finally the creation of a new heaven and new earth (Darby, 1900). The intensity of the expectation of the end drove Moody and his cohorts to world evangelization efforts. Over time the Populist Revival took on strict doctrines (literal interpretation of the Bible, the Virgin birth of Christ, sacrificial atonement, miracles) which served as a picket fence around the traditional evangelical conversion experience. This paved the road into what we now call fundamentalism. Oftentimes fundamentalism took on unsavoury elements of nativist anti-Catholicism (the Papacy as the 'Whore of Babylon') and anti-Semitism (the conspiracy between 'Bolshevism and Jewish Bankers'). While attacking theological 'liberals' like Harry Emerson Fosdick, the popular pastor of Riverside Church in New York, the early fundamentalists, especially after the public disaster of the Scopes trial, tended to withdraw from direct political life. The world was after all the 'wrecked vessel' Darby painted it to be. No use in saving it, just the souls in it. Conversion was away from the world. Forms of the Populist Revival prevail throughout rural Appalachia in the United States up to this day (Dickinson and Benziger, 1974).

While the Fundamentalist Revival was gathering steam on the East Coast and in the South, another spark took fire on the West Coast – Pentecostalism. But I will say more about this below.

Today the United States and the world are experiencing something like a Fourth Awakening. It is a multifaceted awakening, ranging from the rise of new religions, the introduction and spread of various forms of Eastern religion and blends of Buddhism, Hinduism, Confucianism and Christianity, to the rise of the Religious 'Right'. The Religious 'Right' movements may be called a Neo-Fundamentalist Awakening. It is manifested in public movements like the Moral Majority, the Christian Coalition, Focus on the Family and the, Promise Keepers (Martin, 1996). Promise

Keepers especially has become a conversionist crusade, appealing to Christian men and upholding a traditional view of the family. The Neo-Fundamentalist Awakening does not share the world-pessimism of the first fundamentalist wave, but it still upholds many of its traditionalist, and often conservative, values. And, unlike the first wave, the neo-fundamentalists seem to be abandoning the pre-millennialist agenda of Darby. Instead of expecting the Second Coming at any moment, they are entering the political fray (almost exclusively on the Republican side) in order to make their views a part of the social policy of the nation. A side effect is that some neo-fundamentalists are beginning to abandon the religious chauvinism and racism that marked the Populist Revival. In brief, they are showing signs of beginning to look like the reformist (and 'liberal'!) Second Awakening. Another, and perhaps more significant, part of this Fourth Awakening is centred on the pentecostal movement which has spread from a tiny cell in Los Angeles to the four corners of the earth.

Pentecostal conversion

Although pentecostalism today had its origins in the western United States, there have been various manifestations of pentecostal tides throughout the history of Christianity, such as the Montanists of the second century, varieties of Joachimites in the Middle Ages, and the Doukhaboors in Russia. Most varieties of pentecostalism have placed unusual emphasis on a second baptism in the Spirit which bestows the nine gifts of the Spirit listed in 1 Corinthians 12 and 14, including speaking in tongues (*glossalalia*) and healing of physical ailments. The nine gifts are: wisdom, prophecy, knowledge, discernment of spirits, faith, speaking in diverse tongues, healing, interpretation of tongues, working of miracles.

Pentecostalism finds its primary biblical foundation in the events surrounding the outpouring of the Spirit at the first Pentecost as recounted in Acts 2. This is also called sometimes the Baptism of Fire.

Pentecostalism is a very diverse phenomenon composed of many strands. One strand reaches back to mainline evangelical Protestant-ism. Its content is the necessity for conversion and gaining a personal relation to Jesus as saviour. Another strand finds its root in the

Methodist-inspired Holiness movement. Holiness teachers in the early nineteenth century believed that evangelical conversion would lead eventually to full perfection or 'entire perfection' (Wesley) both of the individual and of society. It is this perfectionist possibility that opened up the first pentecostals to the full range of the gifts of the Spirit. Significantly, the key founders of the pentecostal movement, Charles F. Parham and William J. Seymour, both came from a Methodist Holiness tradition. Not all pentecostal traditions, however, have Holiness tendencies. Another thread leads to the Keswick movement which stressed 'living victoriously in the Spirit' and which also had a great impact on Dwight L. Moody. Finally another thread embraced the pre-millennial dispensationalism of Darby with its on-the-edge teaching of the 'any moment' return of Christ.

The first recorded evidence of pentecostal conversion took place when Agnes Ozman began speaking in tongues at Charles F. Parham's Bible school in Topeka, Kansas, on New Year's Day, 1901. But the catalytic event for the spread of pentecostal conversion throughout the United States took place in a home at 210 North Bonnie Brae Street in Los Angeles on 9 April 1906. While Brother William Seymour was preaching, seven persons received the 'Holy Spirit' and began to speak in tongues (Golder, 1973: 27–8). Members shouted and prayed for three nights, creating a stir in the neighbourhood and eventually the whole city. New quarters were found at 312 Azusa Street in a former Methodist church. This was renamed the Azusa Street Mission and rapidly became the Mecca for the pentecostal movement in the United States and the world. A remarkable feature of the early pentecostal assemblies is that they were multinational and interracial from the very start in an era when the intermixing of blacks, orientals, American whites, Scandinavians and European immigrants in any venue was socially taboo. By 1924 outside social pressures led to a split between white and black wings of the movement, but today they are coming back together.

The pentecostal denominations are the fastest-growing churches in the Christian world. They are spreading rapidly into Latin America, the South East Pacific, Korea and Africa, where they are blending in with traditional African animism and Baptismal cults. The volatility of the conversion experience, especially the conviction to let the congregation be led by the Spirit, has led to radical 'schismaticization' resulting in over 300 pentecostal denominations in the world. The schisms have occurred over such issues as sudden vs. gradual sanctification, organized vs. Spirit-led worship, baptism in the name of Jesus Only vs. the traditional Trinitarian formula, Holiness (Wesleyan) vs. non-Holiness (non-Wesleyan) affiliations. The main denominations are the Church of God (Cleveland, Tenn.), the Pentecostal Holiness Church, the Church of God in Christ (COGIC), Assemblies of God (Jimmy Swaggert's original affiliation), the Pentecostal Assemblies of the World, the United Pentecostal Church, and the International Church of the Foursquare Gospel (founded by Aimee Semple McPherson in Los Angeles). More recently the non-denominational Full Gospel Business Men's Fellowship International, founded by Demos Shakarian with the aid of Oral Roberts in 1951 as the Full Gospel Business Men's Association, has become a spark for the spread of the charismatic movement to mainline denominations. A famous pentecostal leader is Pat Robertson, who, along with Oral Roberts, Rex Humbard, Jim Bakker and Jimmy Swaggart, brought the pentecostal experience to TV. Robertson has gone on to found the Christian Coalition which is now having profound impact on the American Congress (Martin, 1996: 299–326). (Robertson avoided political involvement in the earlier days of his ministry. But in the mid-1980s he did a turnabout and even ran for the presidency of the United States.) Some scholars estimate there are as many as 300 million pentecostals throughout the world.

The pentecostal experience is marked first by a conversion phase (repentance, a conviction of salvation in Jesus' Name), to be followed by the baptism in the Spirit (including speaking in tongues, divine healing and the laying-on of hands, and attestations of Christ's imminent return). Many pentecostals reduce these teachings to the 'four-square' plan of the Heavenly Jerusalem as related in Revelation 21:16. This is the origin of the 'Four-Square Gospel': the Saviour, the Great Physician, the Baptiser with the Spirit, and the Coming King (McPherson, n. d.). The end-time expectation had led many pentecostal believers to see themselves as heralds of the Second Coming and recipients of the 'latter rain' (Joel 2:28), the 'first rain' being the Day of Pentecost recounted in Acts 2.

Until the late 1970s most pentecostals adhered to a stern code of behaviour as a result of conversion: banning gum-chewing, wearing neckties, short-sleeves, trousers or shorts on women, soft drinks, alcohol, tobacco, and movies. While some denominations still adhere to this stern code, many have relaxed several of the above provisions. Pentecostal worship, when compared to mainline denominations, is boisterous and free-wheeling, bespeaking the fundamental belief in the gifts of the Spirit.

In the early days the pentecostal experience had the patina of belonging to the uneducated rural poor. In fact, most members were blue-collar workers and of modest means. In the 1960s pentecost-alism started to become upwardly mobile (Synan, 1975). As they gain greater clout in society at large, pentecostals begin to abandon their pre-millennial world rejection and take on post-millennial social and political activism. Their anti-abortion activism is an illustration of this ideological turn.

Charismatic conversion

The spread of pentecostalism to the mainline denominations is now generally called the charismatic movement. A chief catalyst in the spread of pentecostal conversion into the mainline denominations was the Full Gospel Business Men's Association. One of the great religious ironies of our time is that the pentecostal movement, historically splintered into factions and schisms, has become a magnet for the unification of mainline denominations. The meetings of the FGBMA, which are growing at present, are attended by traditional pentecostals, Baptists, Presbyterians, Episcopalians, Methodists, Lutherans and Catholics.

The first noteworthy mainline flame seen around the world was the baptism in the Spirit and speaking in tongues in 1959 by the Rev. Dennis Bennet, pastor of St Mark's Episcopal Church, Van Nuys, California. His experience was soon followed by that of the Catholic Dominican priest Francis McNutt. Soon leaders of other denominations were quick to follow. Often independent charismatic movements have grown up within mainline denominations as a result of contact with pentecostals. Noteworthy here is the Women's Aglow movement among various Protestant churches and FIRE SHARE LAMP, Life in the Spirit seminars and Families in Christ among Catholics. A noted Jesuit theologian Donald Gelpi wrote a theological justification of baptism in the Spirit for Catholics entitled *Pentecostalism: A Theological Viewpoint* (1971).

A new religious phenomenon that accompanied the spread of

pentecostalism into the mainline denominations is pluridenominationality. Although Bennet and McNutt were to drift away from their native congregations, mainline Christians who convert to pentecostalism do not feel they have to abandon their natal congregations. Rather, they feel that the baptism in the Spirit has enriched their natal faith. Many actively partake in the services of their churches and attend Full Gospel meetings at the same time. Some congregations and groups like the Lutheran Church Missouri Synod have fought the encroachment of pentecostalism. This hearkens back to the leading figures of the Reformation who taught that the 'gifts of the Spirit' ceased with the death of the last apostle. Other denominations, especially the Roman Catholic Church in some dioceses, have sought to contain its influence by failing to promote involved priests to higher positions or to marginalize it by treating it a just another option of worship. Often the result is that formerly mainline church members quit their natal congregations and join non-denominational pentecostal and charismatic fellowships.

In an interview with one of the oldest Catholic charismatic groups in the United States, I learned that most reported that their charismatic experience led them to read the Bible regularly for the first time in their lives. All said that they experienced different varieties of the gifts of the Spirit and emphatically stated that any particular gift was for the purpose of building up the whole body of Christ (as Paul says they are for in 1 Cor 12) and not for individual benefit or vanity. In keeping with the charismatic movement, insofar as it can be differentiated from the pentecostal movement, the charismatics I have interviewed put much greater emphasis on the discernment of the Spirit and building up the church. Many express relief from periods of depression, a feeling of closeness to the Lord, and a perception that God is in their hearts. Often these feelings came upon them at a ceremony where they received a laying on of the hands. Some see their natal church as having many gifts, but using them badly. Most noteworthy to me was that, while all attended their home churches regularly and were more than actively involved, their spiritual life was their own, not in conflict with but fully independent of the hierarchical control so typical in traditional Roman Catholicism. For charismatics Jesus is not a lofty King or Judge but a Friend. While experiencing speaking in tongues, tears of joy, healings and other marks of pentecostal conversion, charismatics seem to experience them in a different key from traditional pentecostals.

Many observers of the pentecostal and charismatic movements fault them for resorting so intensely to feeling and emotion. Yet in their favour Jonathan Edwards, the great theoretician of the Great Awakening, argued that religion is centred in the affections and arouses feelings of the excellency of God (Edwards, 1962: 206–54). John Wesley preached that conversion results from a warming of the heart. In Germany the famous theologian Friedrich Schleiermacher found the essence of religion in a *sui generis* feeling of absolute dependence upon God (1963: 12 ff.). Mainline Christianity often has weakened the enthusiasm so characteristic of its beginnings, either by reducing faith to a set of beliefs (propositions to be assented to intellectually) or a moral code of behaviour (ethics). The religion of feeling finds a way to re-balance these reductive tendencies.

The pentecostal and charismatic movements seem to be acting as a new and ever-spreading leavening agent in contemporary Christianity.

References

Augustine of Hippo, St (n. d.) *Confessions* and *Enchiridion*, ed. Albert Outler, Library of Christian Classics VII. London: SCM.

Bromley, David G. and James T. Richardson (eds) (1983) *The Brainwashing/Deprogramming Controversy*. Lewiston, NY: Edwin Mellen Press.

Bumstead, J. M. (ed.) (1970) *The Great Awakening*. Waltham, MA: Blaisdell.

Cleveland, Catherine C. (1916) *The Great Revival in the West 1797–1805*. Chicago: University of Chicago Press.

Darby, John Nelson (1900) *The Collected Works of J. N. Darby*. vol. 11: Prophetic No. 4, ed. William Kelly. Kingston-on-Thames: Stow Hill Bible & Tract Depot.

Dickinson, Eleanor and Barbara Benziger (1974) *Revival*. New York: Harper & Row.

Edwards, Jonathan (1962) *Jonathan Edwards: Representative Selections*, ed. Clarence H. Faust and Thomas H. Johnson. New York: Hill & Wang.

Edwards, Jonathan (1966) *Jonathan Edwards: Basic Writings*, ed. Ola Winslow. New York: New American Library.

Erikson, Erik (1963) *Childhood and Society*, 2nd edn. New York: W. W. Norton.

Erikson, Erik (1982) *The Life Cycle Completed*. New York: W. W. Norton.

Ferm, Robert O. (1958) *Persuaded to Live: Conversion Stories from the Billy Graham Crusades*. Westwood, NJ: Revell.

Finney, Charles G. (1960) *Lectures on the Revival of Religion*, ed. W. G. McGoughlin. Cambridge, MA: Harvard University Press.

Fowler, James. (1981) *Stages of Faith*. San Francisco: Harper & Row.

Gadol, Joan (1969) *Leon Battista Alberti*. Chicago: University of Chicago Press.

Gelpi, Donald L. (1971) *Pentecostalism: A Theological Viewpoint*. New York: Paulist Press.

Gelpi, Donald L. (1976) *Charism and Sacrament: A Theology of Christian Conversion*. New York: Paulist Press.

Golder, Morris E. (1973) *History of the Pentecostal Assemblies of the World*. Indianapolis: Pentecostal Assemblies of the World.

Graham, Billy (1965) *World Aflame*. New York: Doubleday.

James, William (1902) *The Varieties of Religious Experience*. London: Longman.

Kohlberg, Lawrence (1981) *Essays on Moral Development, Vol. 1: The Philosophy of Moral Development*. San Francisco: Harper & Row.

Kuhn, Thomas S. (1970) *The Structure of Scientific Revolutions*, 2nd edn. Chicago: University of Chicago Press.

Lonergan, Bernard (1958, rev. edn) *Insight: A Study in Human Understanding*. London: Longmans, Green & Co.

Lonergan, Bernard (1972) *Method in Theology*. New York: Herder & Herder.

Marsden, George M. (1980) *Fundamentalism in American Culture*. New York: Oxford University Press.

Martin, William (1996) *With God on Our Side: The Rise of the Religious Right in America*. New York: Broadway.

McGowan, Thomas (1982) 'Conversion: A Movie Version', *New ERA Newsletter* 2/1: 5, 4.

McPherson, Aimee Semple (n. d.) *This We Believe*. Los Angeles: International Church of the Foursquare Gospel.

Melton, J. G. and Moore, R. L. (1982) *The Cult Experience*. New York: Pilgrim.

Piaget, Jean (1970) *Main Trends in Psychology*. New York: Harper & Row.

Rambo, Lewis (1980) 'Psychological Perspectives on Conversion', *Pacific Theological Review* 13/2: 22 ff.

Richardson, Herbert W. (1977) *New Religions and Mental Health*. Lewiston, NY: Edwin Mellen Press.

Royce, Josiah (1968) *The Problem of Christianity*, ed. John E. Smith: Chicago: University of Chicago Press.

Royce, Josiah (1969) *The Basic Writings of Josiah Royce*, ed. John J. McDermott. Chicago: University of Chicago Press.

Scheick, William (1974). 'Family, Conversion, and the Self in Jonathan Edwards' *A Faithful Narrative of the Surprising Work of God*', *Tennessee Studies in Literature* 19: 29–89.

Schleiermacher, Friedrich (1963) *The Christian Faith*, vol. 1. New York: Harper Torchbook.

Stendahl, Krister (1976) *Paul Among Jews and Gentiles*. Philadelphia: Fortress Press.

Synan, Vinson (ed.) (1975) *Aspects of Pentecostal-Charismatic Origins*. Plainfield: Logos International.

Turner, Victor (1969) *The Ritual Process*. Chicago: Aldine.

Turner, Victor (1970) *The Forest of Symbols*. Ithaca: Cornell University Press.

Van Gennep, A. (1960) *The Rites of Passage*. Chicago: University of Chicago Press.

Vygostsky, L. S. (1978) *Mind and Society*. Cambridge, MA: Harvard University Press.

Whitehead, Alfred North (1974) *The Making of Religion*. New York: New American Library.

Part II
Conversion in the world's religions

4. Conversion as a process leading to enlightenment: the Buddhist perspective

Christopher Lamb

At its beginning every religion is marked by a conversion. Conversion provides the experience that marks a threshold between one state of life and another. It is only usually referred to as a conversion when an irreversible decision has been made to cross a threshold into a new religion. Something similar happened when the future Buddha, then known as Siddhartha Gautama Sakya, left his wife and new-born child to become one of the many religious seekers or *sramanas*, wandering around the roads and by-ways of India in the 500s BCE. They had left all family and worldly commitment to take up the homeless life, clearing the way to devote themselves to the life of the spirit and the pursuit of liberation.

Buddhism arose among the Renouncer movements in the period that Karl Jaspers called the Axial Age.[1] This period of seminal religious thought produced such people as Pythagoras, Socrates, the Greek tragedians, the prophets of Israel, Lao Tzu and Confucius in China, some say Zarathustra in Persia, and Mahavira and the Buddha in India. The old sacrificial religion of the brahmins was undergoing review or challenge from the seekers who composed the Upanisads and others who rejected the Vedic authority altogether. It was during this period that codes of ethical conduct began to emerge, free of ancient ideas of purity and taboo. Mary Douglas has effectively analysed these in *Purity and Danger*.[2] An exchange of benefits between humans and the gods through minutely performed sacrifice brought protection and favour. While some Renouncers rejected the value of the Vedic ritual sacrifice altogether, a reaction among the orthodox Renouncers elevated the rite to cosmic significance.

The set of experiences that caused Siddhartha to take up homelessness is known as the 'Four Sights'. Three of these sights are perfectly normal experiences that punctuate life. The story goes that Siddhartha's father had tried to protect him from the harsh realities of old age, sickness and death, but in the end at the age of 29 years, the young man, on excursions outside the palace, glimpsed not only the effects of time and circumstance on the human being, but also met a sadhu, a holy man who had given up the worldly life to pursue a transcendent goal. The Four Sights are not a revelation in quite the way the monotheistic religions understand it. They were ordinary external events that triggered in someone whose mind was receptive an intense internal conviction.

In narrative form and rudimentary terms the whole Buddhist problem and its (religious) solution are intimated by the Four Sights. The events of the Buddha's Enlightenment show that they were a preview of the religio-philosophical analysis of the Four Noble Truths,[3] upon which the whole Buddhist religion is based. In any event, the Sights set Siddhartha off on his quest. A further six years passed, until, at 35 years of age, he had the experience known as the Awakening or the Enlightenment. This brought about a radical change in self-perception and worldview. No longer to be addressed merely as the Venerable Gautama, the new Buddha points out in the prelude to the first sermon: 'Do not address the Tathagata by name or by the title "venerable"; I am an Arhat, a Tathagata (the One Who Has Gone Beyond), a fully awakened one.'[4] In that night under the Bodhi Tree he saw his previous existences, the death and rebirth of all beings everywhere and the process, sometimes called a law, of ethical causality – *karma* – in operation. He realized the Four Noble Truths and attained *nirvana*. Soon after these momentous events he perceived the principle of Dependent Origination – *pratityasamut-pada* – which explains the process of causation:

> This being, that becomes, from the arising of this, that arises;
> this not becoming, that does not become;
> from the ceasing of this, that ceases.[5]

Conversion in the early scriptures

The transition from a personal experience to the birth of a new religion was said to have been made when the new Buddha decided to accede to the god Brahma Sahampati's request to teach the world. So he went in pursuit of his ascetic companions. They had left him earlier when he accepted a dish of creamed rice from the young woman Sujata, so ending a six-year period of ascetic practice. He caught up with them again in the deer park at Sarnath on the outskirts of Varanasi where he launched the Middle Way with the *Sermon on Turning the Wheel of the Dharma – Dhammacakkappavattanasutta*. One of their number, Kondañña, attained the knowledge that everything subject to origination is subject to cessation and received the *pabbajja* ceremony for leaving the world and the *upasampada* ceremony of ordination. The Buddha admitted him with the words 'ehi, bhikkhu – come, monk, well proclaimed is the doctrine; lead a religious life for making a complete end of pain'.[6] The others followed soon after and so formed the first *sangha* or monastic community.

These ascetics became the first monks, but they were not the first disciples of the Buddha. That honour goes to two merchants bringing rice cakes and honeycomb to him in the week following his enlightenment while he was still in the vicinity of the Bodhi Tree at Bodh Gaya. They took refuge 'in the Blessed One and in the Dharma'. The Vinaya says these were the first in the world to become lay-disciples or *upasakas* by the formula which contained (only) the dyad, that is, 'I take refuge in the Buddha; I take refuge in the Dharma'.[7] The third refuge 'I take refuge in the Sangha' was added after the *sangha* was formed.

Much of the rest of the Buddha's career, some 45 years, was occupied with spreading the doctrine and so making converts. Soon after the First Sermon he preached the *Sermon on the Marks of Non-Soul – Anattalakkhanasutta*[8] – and for the first time used the Threefold Refuge to receive the layman Yasa. Soon after that Yasa's mother and former wife took Refuge. Eventually the numbers wishing to join the Order became so numerous that the Buddha began to allow the monks joining to use a kind of self-ordination. They did this by shaving their heads, putting on the yellow robe and reciting the Triple Refuge. This second form of admission or ordination to the Order is no longer used. The third form given in the Vinaya is the one in use today and has probably been used from the time following the Buddha's death. It has variants for use in different places and with a double rite for nuns.[9]

A delightful story of the conversion of the fire worshippers, culminating in the *Fire Sermon*,[10] is worth recounting because it includes (not unlike Elijah's contest with the priests of Baal on Mount Carmel[11]) persuasion through the use of miraculous power. The conversion of the fire-worshipper happened only after the Buddha had performed some 3500 miracles, but ultimately these did not clinch it. At Uruvela, the texts tell us, lived a matt-haired fire-worshipper named Uruvela Kassapa with five hundred disciples, whilst further down the river lived his brother Nadi Kassapa with three hundred disciples, and further down still at Gaya lived their brother Gaya Kassapa with two hundred disciples. Despite the performance of miracles Kassapa remained convinced of his own spiritual superiority. He thought 'the great hermit has great magical power but he is not an Arhat (one who has reached the penultimate stage of perfection before Buddhahood) like me'. Miracle-working was not rated very highly as a mark of spiritual advancement in India at that time. The Vinaya rules count boasting of such powers along with carnal knowledge of any living thing, murder and theft as the four 'defeats' incurring irreversible excommunication from the Order.

At last the Buddha challenged Kassapa's spiritual smugness and confidence in the efficacy of ritual. He told him he was not as spiritually advanced as he thought: by itself ritual fire-worship was useless. The Buddha's words had more effect than all the miracles. Kassapa cut off his dreadlocks and threw them together with all the implements for the fire sacrifice into the river. He and his disciples asked for ordination. Further downstream the disciples of Nadi Kassapa when they saw the items floating past wondered why. Soon they followed suit and cut off their dreadlocks and took ordination. Further down the river at Gaya the disciples of Gaya Kassapa seeing all the floating implements asked the same question. Then all two hundred of them took ordination. On the hill outside the town of Gaya (where today the footprint of Visnu is the centre of a great pilgrimage) the Buddha preached the *Fire Sermon*. Far from having a ritual or sacred significance fire is taken to mean the voracious appetite which consumes everything it wants: 'everything is burning with the fires of lust, hatred and delusion'. T. S. Eliot named the third section of *The Waste Land* after it, rating it as corresponding in importance with Jesus's Sermon on the Mount.[12]

A less extravagant conversion story in the early scriptures is that of the two chief disciples Sariputra and Maudgalyayana. These men were friends from childhood. While they were living near Rajagrha they decided they would become wandering mendicants and follow the teacher Sañjaya, one of the many heterodox teachers in India then. While on his alms-round, Sariputra met Assaji, who had also been there when the Buddha preached the First Sermon. His noble bearing impressed Sariputra, so when he was asked about his master and his teaching the young monk said that as he was only newly ordained he could only give a very brief outline. This is what he said:

> Of things that proceed from a cause
> Their cause the Tathagata has told,
> And also their cessation;
> This is the teaching of the great Hermit.[13]

This verse, carved on rock walls as a *mantra* all over North India, and occurring once in the Pali Canon, persuaded Sariputra and Maudgalyayana and 150 other followers to follow the Middle Way and to go to the Veluvana Park where the Buddha was staying, to seek admission to the Order.

The threefold refuge

The threefold 'Going for Refuge' – *Tri-sarara-gamana* – is the ceremony used by all Buddhists, monks and laity alike, regardless of the tradition they belong to, to mark their allegiance to the Buddha's teachings. Its most common use is as a rite of veneration of the Three Jewels – *Tri-ratna* – the Buddha, the Dharma and the Sangha. But it is also the primary initiation rite by which a person enters the Middle Way and embarks on the stages of sanctification. Thereafter he or she ceasing to be a *prthagjana* or 'common person', becomes a 'member of the family' – *gotrabhu* – of 'noble persons' – *arya pudgalas*, eliminating all defilements on the Path to enlightenment. Buddhism represented a new departure – only by ethical conduct, not ritual observance or avoidance of taboo, could a person be considered pure or noble.

After recitation of the Refuge formula a person may seek to establish himself as an *upasaka* (male) or *upasika* (female) by vowing to observe the Five Precepts. Going for Refuge is also the rite of introduction to the ceremonies of monastic ordination and it is recited before *bodhisattva* vows are taken. In tantric ceremonies a Fourth Refuge in the *guru* prefaces the other three.

The most spectacular performance of the Refuge ceremony must have been when the Founders of the Theosophical Society, Madame Blavatsky and Colonel Olcott arrived in Sri Lanka in 1890 and took the Three Refuges and the Five Precepts. H. P. Blavatsky was a Russian aristocrat and Olcott was an American colonel and a judge. Though they formally espoused Buddhism on this occasion they were really theosophists and heralds of the New Age. Their act can be seen to be as much political as devotional, indicating their solidarity with the Buddhists of Sri Lanka against the perceived Christian imperialism of the missionaries. In some respects as an act it was more Christian in spirit than Buddhist. Olcott's *Buddhist Catechism*[14] published in 1881 and many times since, while attempting to formulate the basic tenets for Buddhists everywhere, had as one of its purposes the strengthening of Buddhist resolve against missionary endeavour. When the missionaries first arrived in Sri Lanka the monks had invited them to preach in their temples, but it was not long before they realized that the invitations would never be reciprocated, at least, until the advent of the contemporary interfaith movement.

The Emperor Asoka

Buddhism has its counterpart to Constantine in the emperor Asoka who inherited the Mauryan kingdom in 269 BCE. For two generations the throne of Magadha had conquered most of India. One remaining area, Kalinga, had held out against the imperial ambitions, so in 260 BCE Asoka started out like any other military conqueror to annex it by force. After the event Asoka was so horrified by the carnage that his campaign had brought about that he became a follower of Buddhism. He renounced the use of force and set about inculcating the principles of compassion for all things and tolerance for other religions.

At the outset of his conversion he made a pilgrimage to the most important sites in Buddhism. He visited Bodh Gaya where the Buddha achieved enlightenment, Sarnath where he preached his First Sermon and established the monastic community, and Kusinagara where he was cremated. The emperor put up *stupas* or memorial mounds in these places and also built what is probably the most beautiful complex of *stupas* at Sañci.

Eight years after his consecration he proclaimed fourteen edicts and had them engraved on rock pillars and rock faces all over his empire. Thirteen years later an additional seven edicts were proclaimed and set on polished stone pillars. He wished to take care of all his subjects and sought to make the administration humane. He gave up military conquest in the name of *ahimsa*, the principle of non-harming which underlies the whole of the Buddhist ethical code. Inspired by the precept against killing, he banned animal sacrifices, regulated the slaughter of animals for food, and even protected certain species of birds and animals. He forbade the royal hunt and put pilgrimage in its place. He himself gave up meat-eating and advocated vegetarianism in the royal palaces. He was not a complete pacifist but he tried as far as possible to civilize the wild tribespeople by persuasion through the principle of Dharma-conquest rather than military might. He did not renounce the use of the death penalty but he stopped the use of judicial torture. His programme for environmental care was based on compassion for his subjects. He instituted a tree-planting programme so that roads were lined with fruit trees to give rest and shade to weary travellers. He had wells dug at frequent intervals and set up rest houses. He also encouraged the cultivation of medicinal and veterinary herbs to help humans and animals. Dharma officers were appointed to encourage harmonious relations between people. Respect and tolerance were extended to all religions.

The appeal of Buddhism for Asoka seems to have been in its moral and ethical system leading to peace and fellowship. The credit for the original idea of *ahimsa*, probably the greatest idea in the whole of religious thought, is founded on the notion of the kinship of all that lives. The credit for this must belong to India and its Renouncer religions. But such an idea cannot be contained and it arises from time to time throughout the history of later religions as an imperative to peace, ultimately emerging in the secular humanist tradition. Through Asoka Buddhism spread its humanizing influence across the whole of Asia. It was Asoka who made Buddhism a world religion by strengthening the co-operative role between the monkhood and the laity. Eventually in the Mahayana, Buddhism emerged as a universalized religion with the elevation of compassion as the highest ideal. This was enshrined in the *bodhisattva* ideal, whereby the aim was not to leave the world for *nirvana* but to vow to remain in the cycles of *samsara* to help all sentient beings.

Buddhism beyond India

The transmission of Buddhism out of India has a complex and huge history which can only be touched on in this chapter. The conversion of Sri Lanka was instigated by Asoka himself who in 240 BCE sent his son, the monk Mahinda on the first mission. Later Asoka's daughter Sanghamitta followed her brother to found the Order of nuns on the island.

Buddhism spread to China from Central Asia and was introduced there around 50 CE. What made conversions possible in view of the general Chinese contempt for the barbarity of foreigners? Confucian sensibilities were offended by Buddhist practices that seemed unfilial and unpatriotic. Shaving the head and refusing to marry showed disrespect for one's parents who had given the body, and refusing to bow to the king, as the Son of Heaven, showed disrespect for the social order. This was countered by Buddhists themselves,[15] but it was the resonances between Taoist and Buddhist ideas that must have allowed Buddhism to establish a foothold and eventually develop schools of a specifically Chinese character. We find such in the teachings of Hua Yen, T'ien T'ai and Ch'an. Ch'an (in Japanese Zen) from the Sanskrit dhyana, means 'meditation'. It emphasizes enlightenment as a sudden experience, a direct insight. This was of consequence for the transmission of Buddhism into Tibet.

Buddhism reached Tibet in the so-called First Transmission, c. 640–838 CE, in the period of the three religious kings, Srong-brtsan-sgam-po, Khri-srong-lde-brtsan and Ral-pa-can. It lasted until the persecutions of the next king gLang-dar-ma. The Second Transmission began after the assassination of the king when many translators and scholars brought texts from India. A key event in the conversion of Tibet took place in the reign of Khri-srong-lde-brtsan. This was the Great Debate at bSam-yas. It took place in about 792 under the auspices of the king to establish some kind of coherence and bring order to the activities of Indian and Chinese missionaries. The Indians were teaching that the path to enlightenment was a gradual one by which the bodhisattva achieved liberation by patient application of practice. The Chinese Ch'an teachers, on the other hand, taught that enlightenment was not earned or worked for but came suddenly, in a moment of inspiration. These two paths are respectively termed 'gradualist' and 'suddenist'. The Indian approach was based on the assumption that it was necessary to accumulate a great deal of knowledge and merit through innumerable life-times in order to approach the goal of Buddhahood. This meant there was a necessary place for the monastic and intellectual life in the scheme of salvation. The Chinese case rested on the absolute notion of Buddhahood, that everything has the Buddha-nature which once it is realized it is attained. Whatever the reasons, political or theological, the victory was officially given to the Indians and the Chinese told to pack up and leave.[16]

Buddhism returns to the land of its birth – conversion from untouchability

In recent times a clear example of Refuge as a rite of separation[17] is the case of the Untouchables of Pune, many thousands of whom in the 1950s were led out of caste-Hinduism by Dr Bhimrao Ramji Ambedkar, himself an Untouchable. He became the first Law Minister in Nehru's cabinet of the post-colonial Republic of India. Though the new constitution outlawed discrimination on the grounds of caste, Ambedkar came to realize that religion itself sanctified it by teaching that people were born with different degrees of purity according their caste status. One's ritual purity could be infected by contact with someone of a lower caste. Beyond the caste system were the outcastes or Untouchables. They were frequently not even allowed into the temples because of their polluting presence. The Untouchables were condemned by this system to poverty and ignorance; they were normally only permitted to do the vilest jobs. Gandhi himself, though wishing to alleviate the lot of the *harijans* or 'children of God' as he preferred to call them, was actually opposed to the abolition of caste and he resisted the idea that anyone could change his religion.

Ambedkar had come to the conclusion that the only way for the Untouchables to liberate themselves was to change their religion. Liberation or *moksa* is a key idea in Indian religions, but for him it had a political and social rather than a transcendent significance. He had been looking for a suitable religion and eventually found in Buddhism something that would meet his needs, or, at least, could be remodelled to meet them. The conversion of thousands, eventually millions of people to Buddhism would not involve a repudiation of their Indian roots, nor would it destabilize the Hindu majority the way that mass conversion to Islam or Christianity might do.

Buddhism had redefined the notion of nobility. The word 'Aryan', meaning 'the noble people', was how the Sanskrit-speaking people who brought the Vedic religion to India referred to themselves. The redefinition is from a racial, national or social distinction to a spiritual quality that could be attained by anyone, however humble his social origins might be. The Buddha, born into the *ksatriya* or warrior caste, condemned caste-structural segregation, asserting that, as we have already said, purity was not a matter of birth but of ethical conduct – living according to the Noble (Aryan) Eightfold Path. In his view a high-caste brahmin would not be polluted if the shadow of an Untouchable should fall on him. Deliberate breaking of the principle of *ahimsa* as codified in the Precepts, was the only way a person could incur pollution and this would have karmic rather than ritual consequences.

On 14 October 1956, in the year of the 2500th anniversary of the *parinirvana* of the Buddha and on the same day as Asoka's conversion twenty-three centuries earlier, Ambedkar and his wife took Refuge and the Five Precepts from Chandramani Maha Thera, so formally converting from Hinduism to Buddhism. The following day he administered the Refuges and the Precepts and twenty-two vows he drafted himself concerned with avoiding the beliefs and practices of Hinduism to nearly half a million people, thereby initiating possibly the largest single mass conversion of the twentieth century. The number of Ambedkarite Buddhists was given as 3 250 277 in the 1961 census, but current estimates give between 6 and 7 millions.[18]

Unfortunately Ambedkar died six weeks later, leaving the fledgling Buddhists without a leader. The English monk Sangharakshita, who some years later was to found the Friends of the Western Buddhist Order in Britain,[19] had known Ambedkar and decided to continue his work among the ex-Untouchables. This work is being continued by members of the Western Buddhist Order in collaboration with the Trailokya Bauddha Mahasangha.

Conversion 'to' has sometimes entailed conversion 'of'. Both Ambedkar and Sangharakshita made a selection from traditional Buddhism to meet the needs of their particular situations. In Ambedkar's case he makes clear in his posthumously published *The Buddha and His Dhamma* that first and foremost he perceived Buddhism as a social teaching.

'The center of his Dhamma is man and the relation of man to man in his life on earth.'[20]

Sangharakshita has said that commitment is more important than lifestyle. Many of his followers take a post-modern 'non-realist' view about much of the supernaturalism of traditional Buddhist teaching. This is perhaps not so revolutionary when put alongside Nagarjuna's second-century teachings about *nirvana* in his *Memorial Verses on the Middle Way*:

> *Samsara* has nothing that distinguishes it from *nirvana*; *nirvana* has nothing that distinguishes it from *samsara*. The limit of nirvana is the limit of *samsara*; there is not even the subtlest something separating the two.[21]

Christopher Queen points out the tendency throughout the development of Buddhism: 'Great shifts in Buddhist thought have typically entailed assertions that appeared at first to negate or compromise the original teaching ... a famous utterance of the ideological and practical shifts ... is found in ... the Heart Sutra that conclude[s] "There is no suffering, no origin, no cessation, no path, no exalted wisdom, no attainment, and also no non-attainment".'[22]

Conversion in the West

Conversion to Buddhism in the West has only very partially been the result of deliberate proselytizing, despite the fact that Buddhism is said to be a missionary religion. The history of this has been traced by such writers as Christmas Humphreys in *Sixty Years of Buddhism in England*,[23] Stephen Batchelor in *The Awakening of the West*[24] and Rick Fields in *How the Swans Came to the Lake*.[25]

In the West conversion is rarely marked explicitly in the way that a convert to Christianity would pass through a liminal stage of formal instruction culminating in baptism or a reception ceremony. Many of the people who attend Dharma centres of varying traditions, Theravada, Tibetan, Zen or even the FWBO (Friends of the Western Buddhist Order) are not separated between those who have gone for Refuge against those who have not. They may find in attending the *pujas* or liturgies that they have already chanted the Refuges and the Precepts. Conversion to Buddhism seems to be an interior and gradual change of mind set which need not be revealed to anyone else.

In ancient Buddhist texts there is the rather odd category of *pratyekabuddha*, the 'solitary realizer' who became enlightened completely on his own account without any contact with other people. This idea is superseded in the Mahayana by the idea that the person you pass in the street might be a bodhisattva on his or her way to buddhahood. Everything that lives has the Buddha-nature, so there are myriads of beings who have already achieved Buddhahood throughout the cosmos.

Within the Tibetan tradition an important part of current practice is the taking of tantric *abhisekas, dbangs* or empowerments. One might expect that the devotee, wishing to take such a step, had already taken the Refuges, the Precepts and the *bodhisattva* vows and be therefore a confirmed Buddhist. But this was surely not so in the case of a Benedictine monk, the late Dom Sylvester Houédard of Prinknash Abbey, Gloucestershire, whom I saw, dressed in his Christian monastic habit, take a *dbang* from the Dalai Lama himself.

It is certainly extraordinary how readily the highest tantric empowerments are given, considering that in Old Tibet the tantric path was a secret one and no lama would have given initiation to anyone who was not judged to be spiritually ready and fully prepared. In recent times in the West the highest tantric initiations, among them the Kalacakra, have been given in such public places at Central Park New York by the Dalai Lama himself, with thousands of people in attendance. It is as if the Pope were to give a mass priestly ordination to the crowds in St Peter's Square below his window without ascertaining whether they were prepared or had received the preliminary sacraments such as baptism. The Tibetans explain this by suggesting that one receives what one is ready to receive; at the simplest level for the non-Buddhist or neo-Buddhist the *abhiseka* would not be an empowerment to practise the tantric path but a blessing (and a prophecy of future Buddhahood). A seed is planted which may come to fruition in this life or a later one. This acceptance arises from the sense of kinship between all sentient beings. The idea of rebirth takes the pressure off; though concerned with post-death states, Buddhism has no real eschatology, no Four Last Things to be contemplated before one's eternal fate is sealed for ever.

The Theravada is similar in its approach. Conversion by assimilation means that people who attend a Dharma centre to learn meditation may eventually define themselves as Buddhists but on the other hand they may attend a Dharma centre as Christians or Jews to learn the spiritual techniques of meditation or yoga which they then take back 'home'.

In the FWBO the arrangements are more structured. The ordinary person who goes along to a centre may eventually informally become a 'Friend'. If he or she makes a commitment he becomes a 'mitra', Sanskrit for 'friend', and so the relationship to the Order is formalized. But he is still not a member. To become an Order member requires a long period of application, followed by periods of retreat and selection procedures, only after which the applicant may be ordained. The ordination used is not the monastic ordination but the *upasaka* ordination of the lay Buddhist, which is widespread in traditional Buddhism. In the FWBO it has been given a new function. A higher status is conferred on the ordinand. His transition is marked with a new Sanskrit name and permission to wear a ceremonial *kesa* or stole, in origin a Japanese adaptation of the monastic robe. He is inducted into a tantric method of visual meditation and given a meditation Buddha in pacific or wrathful form.

The Buddha-nature and conversion

The universalist ideas of the Mahayana that everything that lives will eventually reach enlightenment is worked out in the *Tathagata-garbha* theory. According to this, everything that lives has the Buddha-nature, human and non-human alike. *Garbha* means either the womb or its contents, that is, the embryo. At first it was understood as the place where the enlightened being is produced, but in later tradition it came to be understood as the seed or essence of Buddhahood which is present as a luminous, pure, eternal characteristic of all beings, but clouded by adventitious defilements. These become partially removed in the bodhisattvas and entirely so in the Buddhas. The *garbha* itself is intrinsically pure and synonymous with suchness, innate in all beings.

The effect of this teaching is that if everyone has the Buddha-nature, there is no need to strive officiously for their conversion. This will inevitably happen when the seed ripens.

Notes

1. Karl Jaspers, *The Origin and God of History* (New Haven, CT: Yale University Press, 1953), pp. 1–77
2. Mary Douglas, *Purity and Danger: An Analysis of the Concepts of Pollution and Taboo* (London and New York: Routledge, 1966).

3. These define the condition of existence and liberation from it, in terms of (1) its suffering; (2) the cause of that suffering; (3) the release from suffering (*nirvana*); and (4) the path leading to the release from suffering (the Noble Eightfold Path).
4. *Majjhima Nikaya* I 171.
5. *Majjhima Nikaya* II. 32.
6. *Samyutta Nikaya* v 420.
7. *Vinaya* Mahavagga I 4, 5.
8. *Samyutta Nikaya* iii 66.
9. See Christopher Lamb, 'Buddhism', in *Rites of Passage*, ed. Jean Holm and John Bowker (London and New York: Pinter 1994), pp. 18–22.
10. *Vinaya* Mahavagga I 20, 21.
11. 1 Kings 18: 20–40.
12. T. S. Eliot, *Collected Poems 1909–1962* (London: Faber, 1963), p. 84.
13. *Vinaya* Mahavagga 1.23.5.
14. Richard Gombrich, *Theravada Buddhism* (London and New York: Routledge, 1988), p. 186.
15. Mou Tzu's 'Disposition of Error' and Hui Yüan's 'A Monk Does Not Bow Down Before a King', in *Sources of Chinese Tradition*, vol. I compiled by Wm. Theodore de Bary, Wing-Tsit Chan and Burton Watson (New York: Columbia University Press, 1960), pp. 274–86.
16. See D. Snellgrove and H. Richardson, *A Cultural History of Tibet* (Boulder, CO: Prajna Press, 1980), pp. 78–80.
17. See Van Gennep in *The Rites of Passage* (London: Routledge & Kegan Paul, 1960), p. 103.
18. Alan Sponberg, 'TBMSG' in *Engaged Buddhism*, ed. Christopher S. Queen and Sallie B. King (Albany, NY: State University of New York Press, 1996), p. 113 n. 6.
19. For an account see Alex Kennedy (Dh. Subhuti), *Buddhism for Today: A Portrait of a New Buddhist Movement* (Salisbury: Element Books, 1983).
20. Cited in Christopher S. Queen, 'Dr. Ambedkar and the Hermeneutics of Buddhist Liberation', in *Engaged Buddhism*, ed. Christopher S. Queen and Sallie B. King, p. 56.
21. *Mulamadhyamakakarika* 25:19–20.
22. Queen, 'Dr. Ambedkar and the Hermeneutics of Buddhist Liberation', p. 61.
23. Christmas Humphreys, *Sixty Years of Buddhism in England* (London: The Buddhist Society, 1968).
24. Stephen Batchelor, *The Awakening of the West: The Encounter of Buddhism and Western Culture* (Northampton: Aquarian, 1994).
25. Rick Fields, *How the Swans Came to the Lake: A Narrative History of Buddhism in America* (Boston and London: Shambhala/Random House, 1986).

5. Conversion to Judaism: a tale of the good, the bad and the ungrateful

Rodney Mariner

Slanderers or saviours?

Three times a day, during the morning, afternoon and evening service, the *Orthoprax* Jew recites the nineteen benedictions of the weekday *Amidah* (the standing prayer, the focus of all statutory acts of Jewish worship). This finely wrought liturgical compilation originated in Israel with the men of the Great Assembly (fourth century BCE) and achieved its ultimate form under the guidance of the patriarch Gamliel II around 100 CE. In considering the Jewish attitude to conversion, *berachot* (benedictions) twelve and thirteen are essential reading.

The first of these *berachot*, with a harshness uncharacteristic of either the prayer or the prayerbook states:

> As for the *malshinim* (lit. slanderers) let there be no hope, and let all wickedness perish in an instant; may all Your enemies be swiftly cut off. May You swiftly uproot, smash, cast down and humble the dominion of arrogance – swiftly, in our days. We praise You Eternal, who breaks enemies and humbles the arrogant.

The second returns from what would be more accurately termed a malediction to a benediction which states:

> For the righteous and the pious, the elders of Your people the House of Israel, for the remnant of their scribes, for the *geirei tzedek* (lit. righteous strangers) and for us too, may Your compassion be aroused, Eternal our

God. Grant a good reward to all who faithfully trust in Your name; may our lot be ever with theirs, so that we may not be put to shame, for we trust in You. We praise You Eternal, support and assurance of the righteous.

Significantly, the malediction was the last of the *berachot* to be added to the nineteen and it is reasonable to suggest that few of those who read it in prayer today would be conscious that *slanderers* refers in the main to heretics, apostates (namely Jews who converted to Christianity) and informers (former Jews). Yet, in times past, this portion of the liturgy was grist for the calumny that claimed that Judaism actively prayed for the destruction of all non-Jews. The text, indeed its very aggression (despite attempts to tone it down across the centuries), is clearly directed against those who, in an attempt to demonstrate the extent of their loyalty to the Romans (or any subsequent oppressor) were prepared to inform against their erstwhile co-religionists. However, if not overtly, at least subliminally, the sub-text of this prayer must have read for some, 'If a born Jew cannot be trusted when they convert to another faith, how much less can a member of another faith be trusted when they convert to Judaism?' Indeed Josephus (*Against Apion* 2:123) sadly confirms such a view with regard to the Greeks while the period of the Hadrianic persecutions provided even greater evidence of former proselytes who were prepared to clear their skirts by turning state's evidence.

Love with the proper stranger

Cheek by jowl with the malediction lies a benediction, that not only places the *ger tzedek* (proselyte) on the highest level of piety, but makes of such an individual a lens through which God's compassion may be focused on Israel. Further, given the ambivalence with which the process of conversion to Judaism is viewed in certain quarters today, it should be stated that the high regard the *Amidah* accords the proselyte, is neither unique or even rare in classical Jewish literature.

Abraham, traditionally (albeit anachronistically), the father of the Jewish people, is the first convert to Judaism, in that he chooses God and through both belief and reason, seeks sanctuary *tachat kanfei hashechinah* (beneath the wings of the divine presence), an expression used by Boaz to Ruth and still applied to proselytes. Not only the first proselyte, Abraham is the first proselytizer for the one God, gaining, according to rabbinic legend, countless converts by his example of righteous living, as well as actively converting his own slaves, according to the Torah. Sarah too, we are taught, was, as a geriatric wet nurse, able to transmit the faith to every infant that imbibed her miraculous milk (Pesikta Rabbati).

Moses converted Jethro the priest of Midian, his father-in-law (enabling the rabbis to avoid the conclusion that the great lawgiver 'married out'), instead of journeying to the Promised Land, he returned home to bring the revealed light of the new faith to his own benighted people.

Ruth, of course, became the paradigm of proselytes. Her plea to her mother-in-law Naomi still stands as the exemplar of the convert's credo:

> Do not press me to leave you, to return and not follow you. Wherever you go, I will go and wherever you stay, I will stay; your people are my people and your God is my God; where you die I will die and there I will be buried. Indeed, may the Eternal do this to me and more if anything but death separates me from you. (Ruth 1: 16–17)

This proselyte's marriage to Boaz not only ensures that two dysfunctional genealogies are redeemed: Ruth's, who as a Moabite came from the union between Lot and his older daughter, and Boaz's which originated in the union between Judah and his daughter-in-law Tamar; it also establishes the line that will produce of King David, who in turn is the progenitor of the Messiah, thus, the paradigm proselyte is a pivotal figure in the unfolding destiny of the Jewish people.

The Esther story concludes with the claim that 'many of the peoples of the land [of Susa] converted to Judaism, because fear of the Jews had seized them'. While the Talmud rejects the validity of fear as a motive for conversion, history gives credence to Scripture in the well-documented forced conversions of the Idumeans (Edomites) and the Itureans by John Hyrcanus during the Hasmonean period – though few would not consider the provision of Herod with a Jewish lineage by this means, as a outcome, dubious in the extreme.

Rabbinic literature abounds with proof texts for the high esteem in which proselytes and proselytization were held up to and including the first centuries of the church's establishment. By turns we are taught that the hand of welcome should be extended to the proselyte 'that he may be brought under the wings of the *Shechinah*' (Levitucus Rabbah). Israel is portrayed as only being exiled in order to increase its numbers through proselytism (Talmud Pes87b), while its own status is even described as inferior in the sight of its own God, as Israel required the revelation of Sinai to compel its acceptance of *ol malchut hashamayim* (lit. The yoke of the kingdom of heaven), but the proselyte does so from love alone (Tanchumah, Lech Lecha). One who befriends a proselyte is considered as if he created him (Genesis Rabbah). Rabbi Acha teaches that even God is prepared to take on the role of proselytizer, telling the nations that they should repent, so that 'He might bring them under His wings' (Song of Songs R.). A more pragmatic basis for conversion is found in the story of Timnah, whom the Talmud describes as a princess. She wanted to become a proselyte but Abraham, Isaac and Jacob would not receive her. Even so she became a concubine of Eliphaz, son of Esau, saying, 'Better to become a handmaid of this nation than a princess of any other.' Her son was Amalek, who brought great evil to Israel [when the slaves left Egypt]. Why? Because they ought not to have rejected her (Talmud Sanhedrin).

That conversion or descent from a convert was seen as no slur in ancient times is supported by references to the proselyte origins of such famous rabbis as Shemiah, Abtalion, Akiba and Meir. It was even claimed that they were descendants of such infamous enemies of Israel as Sisera, Sennacherib, Haman and Nero (Talmud Git. 56a, 57b; San. 96b). The ancient world produced such notable converts as the Royal family of Adiabene, Onkelos (a first century Parthian Kingdom), Flavius Clemens (the nephew of Vespasian), and Fulvia, the wife of Saturninus (a Roman senator). Even the Emperor Antoninus was claimed as a convert (see *Enc. Judaica* 'Proselytes').

His Majesty's loyal opposition

That conversion to Judaism at the beginning of the Christian era was both welcomed and promoted is beyond question. Indeed, it is estimated that in this period of religious experimentation as many as 10 per cent of the Roman empire had placed themselves under the protection of the God of Israel, many of whom of course subsequently became Christians. However, normative Judaism, with the notable exception of the Greek Jews, was far from being a missionary faith and there are sufficiently potent proof texts to be found in rabbinic literature to indicate hostility to both converts and conversion. Further, while such texts may be claimed to be the result of historical circumstances and not born of a biological or an intrinsic ideological racism, their presence cannot be ignored, especially as they are adduced at times (particularly our own), to support the view that Judaism was and is opposed to conversion.

In its mildest form, this opposition is to be found in the rabbinic dictum (derived from the Book of Job), that requires that the prospective proselyte be 'repelled with the left hand and brought near with the right hand' (Ruth R.). The same source requires (on the basis of the Ruth and Naomi story), that the candidate be rejected three times before acceptance. Both of these responses, in form at least, are still common practice today. This represents the normative response by rabbis to an approach for conversion, to be, at best, cautiously welcoming.

There are other classical sources that offer far less encouragement for the would-be proselyte. The proselyte is described as a sort of 'fair-weather' friend who despite taking on the outward appearances of Jewish observance will in times of trouble jettison both Jewish observance and Judaism (Talmud Av. Zar 3b). More explicitly, we are taught that 'evil after evil comes upon those who receive proselytes' (Yev. 109b) and that the advent of the Messiah is delayed by the very presence of proselytes (Nid. 13b). R. Judah son of R. Ila'i who is described as a 'son of proselytes', is said to have denounced R. Jose and R. Simeon b. Yochai to the Romans to disastrous effect. While in no less than four places in the Talmud proselytes are deemed to be as injurious to Israel as a leprous skin lesion, even though scriptural support for such a view is itself derived from such a positive prophetic statement that speaks of a time when, 'the Lord will show compassion for Jacob and once again choose Israel, settling them on their own soil so that strangers will come to join them and *attach themselves* to Jacob' (Isaiah 14:1, 2). Rashi describes the proselyte as an irritant because their lax observance of Jewish precepts sets a bad example for born Jews. An additional commentary affirms that proselytes are an irritant inasmuch as they expose the laxity of born Jews!

Indeed this 'fondly–fearful' nexus is expressed in the actual ritual of conversion as described in the Talmud, which can be read to reflect ambivalence to both proselytes and conversion:

> If anyone comes nowadays and desires to become a proselyte, they say to him; 'Why do you wish to become a proselyte? [Lit. What have you seen?]. Do you not know that the Israelites are nowadays harried, driven about, persecuted and harassed and that sufferings befall them?' If he says, 'I know it and I am not worthy,' they receive him at once and is given instruction in some of the minor and some of the major commandments. He is also told of the punishment for the transgression of the commandments ... [and of the reward for their fulfilment] ... He is not, however, to be persuaded or dissuaded too much. If he is accepted, he is circumcised forthwith ... As soon as he is healed, arrangements are made for his ritual immersion ... When he surfaces after his immersion he is deemed to be an Israelite in all respects. (Yeb. 47b)

Indeed, it is the particularly brutal nature of that 'nowadays' and the bitter experience of proselytes who subsequently apostatized (even though from a Jewish perspective an apostate who was converted to Judaism remained forever a Jew) that for many explains not only the malediction of the *malshenim*, but the particular animosity of some of the teachings of the ancient rabbis.

Fondly fearful becomes fearfully fixated

If Judaism entered the first centuries of the Christian era fondly fearful of proselytes and the act of conversion, the choice of finding a resolution to this paradox was, however, soon taken out of their hands. From the time of Constantine (fourth century) conversion to Judaism was a capital offence for both converter and converted. Wherever and whenever Christianity became established, legislation promising the most dire punishments for apostasy to Judaism were not only promulgated but enacted, be it the Councils of Orleans in the sixth century or the edicts of Alfonso X in the thirteenth. The same pattern prevailed under Islam. While Jews enjoyed the status of *dhimmi* (protected), their protection did not extend to a tolerance of proselytization, so that conversion from Islam to Judaism incurred the death penalty and continues to be the case today, at least in terms of the letter of Moslem law. It is not difficult to imagine the effect of these Christian and Islamic bans on Jewish communities who were fearful of collective punishment. Conversion to Judaism for most of the last sixteen hundred years has varied between being virtually non-existent to rare. As recently as the beginning of the twentieth century, a popular compilation of Jewish law instructs the reader to consider the laws of conversion as only applying to 'days of old' as today, 'it is forbidden by the law of the land for us to accept proselytes' (Aruch Hashulchan Y.D. 268). There are few things in Judaism that are more permanent than the temporary, that is to say, attitudes and responses to changing circumstances endure long after the circumstances no longer prevail. It is certainly the case with the issue of the proselyte, having commenced with a substantially welcoming stance and then by degrees being forced to adopt a more suspicious response, almost in direct proportion to the physical threat the converted Christian or Muslim represented to the community, Judaism for the past sixteen hundred years can be characterized as being both non-proselytizing and relatively unwelcoming to approaches for conversion. Indeed, making a virtue of a necessity, some sections of Judaism today, in a time when Christian and Muslim restrictions no longer apply outside of any but the most benighted communities, still choose to apply the minority, negative teachings of the classic rabbinic with respect to proselytes rather than return to what was clearly normative practice in ancient times.

Khazars and falashas, exceptions that prove the rule

Of course there have been exceptions across the millennia, most notably the eighth-century conversion of the kingdom of Kuzaria which lay between the Black Sea and the Caspian Sea, which endured for more than two hundred years and at its height occupied territory hundreds of times greater than that of the modern state of Israel. Unfortunately, few details of this fascinating people, who were probably descendants of the Huns but who eventually claimed descent from the tribe of Simeon, have entered the domain of scholarship. Arthur Koestler's book *The Thirteenth Tribe* which claimed that the converted Khazars were the progenitors of today's Ashkenazi Jews, has been largely rejected by serious scholars. However, the disputed theory that the stereotypical European Jew is descended from an Eastern European nation of Jewish converts, has been sufficiently unwelcome as to render study of the Khazars an area of research largely off limits for Jewish as well as Russian archaeologists, the Russians being as unhappy with the prospect that their empire was initially ruled by Jewish kings as the Ashkenazim were that they might not have a genetic connection with the freed slaves who met with God at Sinai. The only people who seem generally happy with the phenomenon of the Khazars are those Arab countries who are eager to repudiate Jewish claims to an historical connection with the land of Israel.

The conversion of the Khazars, which despite the theories as to their ultimate fate, is undoubtedly true, serves as a useful contrast to the so-called 'Falashas', the Jews of Ethiopia who in the popular imagination must represent a similar phenomenon. Yet all available evidence would suggest that this is not the case. Ethiopian Jews, who claim descent from the tribe of Dan, leapt into prominence with the spectacular airlifts of Operation Moses and Operation Solomon in 1985 and 1991, respectively, that brought to Israel so many of the *Beta Yisrael* (House of Israel), a term used in preference to the derogatory *Falashah* which means exile or stranger. Yet it is beyond question that they had existed as a Jewish community for at least two thousand years, and may well lay claim to the veracity of the story that the issue of a union between Solomon and the Queen of Sheba figures prominently in their heritage. One scholarly opinion would place them among the Israelite slaves in Egypt. Far from being an example of mass conversion, Ethiopian Jews are a contemporary reminder of how ancient and how pervasive was both the desire and willingness of the Jewish people to include in their number any who were willing to throw in their lot with them and that this preparedness to value conviction over colour or any other divisive distinction, remained the hallmark of Judaism until conversion became a capital crime and a danger to the very survival of diaspora Jewish communities. It must be noted, however, that Ashkenazi rabbis in present-day Israel have not been whole-hearted in their recognition of the Jewish status of the *Beta Yisrael* and, shamefully they have attempted by subterfuge to force them to undergo elements of the conversion ritual. Fortunately, this proud people, who because of their isolation believed that they were the only Jews left in the world, have quickly become politicized and rejected the need to come up to the standards of those who by their estimate, cannot boast of a Jewish lineage of equivalent antiquity. After some unpleasant false starts, it is clear that Ethiopian Jews have a permanent place in the destiny of the State of Israel and that their homecoming will enrich the Jewish people immeasurably.

From capital offence to power politics

The issue of Israel's absorption of Ethiopian Jews has been just another episode in the long-running saga that is usually entitled the, 'Who is a Jew?' question, which in part, continues to have a significant impact on the issue of conversion both there and in diaspora communities.

In 1950 Israel's first Knesset (parliament) enacted the 'Law of Return' which, subject to the usual limitations on public health and the security of the state, stated that every Jew had the right to immigrate to Israel. A Jew had only to enter the country to take up citizenship and all its rights and benefits. Just what constituted Jewish identity was left undefined at the time, naively, as subsequent history has shown, it seems that everyone thought they knew what a Jew was. For Israel's Rabbinate, it was someone born of a Jewish mother or someone who had converted to Judaism, for the Ministry of the Interior, 'anyone who professes in good faith that they are a Jew shall be registered as a Jew. No additional proof shall be required.' Thus, in the first decade of the State, two definitions prevailed, one defining the basis of religious identity and the other the basis of citizenship, it was not surprising that such a disparity would lead to conflict. A number of landmark cases over the last thirty years have seen Israel's legislature and judiciary struggling to define the nature of Jewish identity. The first and most bizarre was that of Oswald Refeisen or Brother Daniel, a Carmelite monk who in 1962 was unsuccessful in being accepted as an immigrant under the Law of Return and being registered as a Jew by nationality and not religion. The Supreme Court of Israel, by a vote of four to one, rejected Refeisen's claim to be a Jew of the Catholic religion. The state thus amended the definition of Jew to read: born of a Jewish mother or converted to Judaism *and not a member of another religion*. The case was bizarre not only because Brother Daniel had been born of a Jewish mother and had been a fighter in the Jewish resistance in Poland but on the basis of *Halachah* (Rabbinic law), even as an apostate, he was in fact still a Jew – 'a Jew who sins is still a Jew albeit a sinful one', secular law had thus overridden religious law and had been able to say, 'This Jew is not a Jew'.

It was not long, however, before a challenge was made to the validity of conversions that were not performed under Orthodox auspices. Following the Yom Kippur war in 1973, Golda Meir resigned. In the elections that followed *Mapai* (the Labour Party) lost so many seats that it desperately needed to bring the NRP (National Religious Party) into the coalition if it was to remain in power. Realizing the leverage it now possessed, the NRP threatened to leave the coalition unless the phrase 'converted according to *Halacha*' was included in the Law of Return's definition of a Jew. Rabin's government of the time was successfully able to resist the pressure for change and thus forestall the disastrous consequences that would ensue, if all diaspora non-Orthodox conversions were deemed to be invalid. Successive governments have, often in a time of crisis, been subject to the same pressure for change in the definition by Orthodox coalition partners. As the political power of the religious right-wing has increased, so too the frequency and the intensity of these demands.

In the interim there has been a *modus vivendi* which has allowed Reform and Conservative diaspora conversions to be recognized by the Ministry of the Interior for the purpose of citizenship, while the Ministry of Religion continues to reject their validity for all matters of religious status. In 1995 the Supreme Court ruled that conversions performed in Israel by the Reform and Liberal rabbis were valid, but to date, the Knesset has not enacted the ruling and does not appear likely to do so under the Netanyahu government. Further, at the time of writing, with the portfolio of the Ministry of the Interior in the hands of the Orthodox, a fresh attempt has been made to invalidate all non-Orthodox conversions by making them subject to the scrutiny of the Orthodox Rabbinate. Ironically such an invalidation would render the second wife of the Prime Minister not Jewish and thereby nullify their marriage!

The Orthodox insistence on having the 'sole agency' for conversion in Israel would not be so troubling if they were prepared to exercise it, particularly in respect of a large proportion of Jews from the former Soviet Union (as many as 150,000) whose *Halachic* status is questionable. Of an estimated 10,000 candidates in 1997 only 400 were accepted. The prospect of a 'status' timebomb in Israel remains very real.

Even when an individual is able to push past the rejecting 'left hand' and undergo the rigorous demands of an Orthodox conversion in Israel, the results may be less than satisfactory. The case of Brother Daniel, the 'Jew who was not a Jew' has its equally bizarre counterpart in the case of Paula Cohen the 'convert who was not a convert'. In 1981 Paula Cohen was converted by Israel's then Ashkenazi Chief

Rabbi Shlomo Goren but when she subsequently returned to England, neither she nor her three children were accepted by the London *Beit Din* (Rabbinic Court) as Jewish. Her children were in fact excluded from religious services at the Jewish primary school they attended. Certainly, by Orthodox standards the marriage of a convert to a *cohen* is not sanctioned, but this is no more than a Jew behaving improperly as a Jew. Mrs Cohen's problem was even more intractable, her conversion certificate contained the words, 'not valid outside of Israel', thus the moment she and her children passed beyond the borders of Israel they ceased to be Jewish. Despite appeals to both the courts of England and Israel the matter has not been satisfactorily resolved.

Born Jews and Jews by choice

While Israel's struggles with the, 'Who is a Jew?' question have spilled over into diaspora communities, there remains a core of truth in the assertion that a Jew is someone who professes to be one. Even born Jews, regardless of blood, are only Jews *in potentia*, that is to say, that until a Jew chooses to claim his or her heritage through one or more of the components of religious observance, peoplehood and Jewish culture they remain in breach of the "Trades Descriptions Act" in defining themselves as a Jew. For one not born as a Jew, there remains only one point of entry, as unfair as it may seem. A born Jew may choose to identify through peoplehood or culture, the proselyte may only enter through the door of religion. That they continue to knock on that door despite the obstacles that are placed in their path, is as much a mystery to the many Jews who experience their Judaism as their fate rather than their faith, as it is a vindication of the enduring power of Judaism and its worldview, to speak with relevance to the questions of the age. Indeed, the question that should be asked of the intending proselyte is less, 'Why should we accept you?' than, as it is expressed in the Talmud, 'What have you seen [of Jews and Judaism] that would make you want to be part of this harried and despised people?' To do so, is frequently to be privileged to be reminded of the glory of a faith too often taken for granted and largely forgotten by those who remain insistent that 'Jews are born and not made'. Proselytes frequently remind us of what being Jewish really is, rather than what for too many it has become.

Undoubtedly, the motive for many to convert in our time is

marriage and while Orthodoxy would question the sincerity of a candidate whose motives were not altruistic, most Reform and Conservative rabbis see marriage as a realistic starting-point for a process that ultimately, must be about the individual's conversion for themselves and not for the sake of their spouse or for their children. In rabbinic terms, all conversions must be *leshem shamayim* (lit. for the sake of Heaven) if they are realistically to serve both the needs of the individual and the Jewish people.

From slanderer to saviour?

Today in non-Orthodox congregations, after convincing the Rabbi that they are serious (which usually means a period of regular attendance at synagogue), the proselyte will undergo a course of studies involving learning to read (vocalize) Hebrew, ritual observances, familiarization with the liturgy, the festivals and Jewish history. At the end of the course the candidate will appear before a *Beit Din*, Rabbinic Board or similar tribunal that will satisfy itself that the proposed conversion is in the interests of both Judaism and the proselyte. Those who say it is not possible to convert someone to Judaism are at least partially correct, in so far as the *Beit Din* or equivalent accrediting body, cannot effect a change but only recognize through questioning, that such a change has truly taken place. The candidate takes on the *ol malchut hashamayim* and is welcomed as a brother or sister who can claim Abraham and Sarah as spiritual parents. While specifics of the ritual of acceptance may vary, it is usual that the candidate if male will have been circumcised and that both male and female candidates will undergo *tevillah* (ritual immersion) in a *mikveh* (a pool constructed to precise specifications).

While each Rabbi can list 'failed' converts, those who having done all that was required of them (including dazzling the *Beit Din* with their sincerity), nevertheless fail to integrate effectively with their Jewish community and remain in what must be the most tangible form of a Jewish Hell, the 'failure' is more often to be attributed to the 'schizophrenia' of the Jewish spouse and not the proselyte. Further, for every 'failure' there are the most sublime 'successes', new Jews, who bring with them not only an awesome devotion to being Jews but an enthusiasm and hunger for the lifelong process of study and learning that is the secret mechanism that ensures Jewish survival.

Fortunately, all the modern manifestations of Judaism are positive in their desire to fulfil the *mitzvah* of *Keruv* (the command to enable the proselyte to 'draw near'). Though the call by some of the leadership of the American Reform movement to return to active proselytizing has not been met with widespread enthusiasm, the recognition that on a minimal level that conversion is the means by which a mixed marriage may be 'redeemed', has not escaped the notice of many in a post-Holocaust era in which intermarriage and assimilation continue to deplete the numbers of those who identify themselves as Jews. For others, proselytes represent not only a new influx of enthusiasm but a welcome addition to a gradually depleting gene pool (the legacy of those who made a virtue of the necessity of a policy of non-conversion).

What remains clear to all but the most self-blind Jews, a condition that paradoxically can be shared by both the ignorant and the myopically learned, is that maintaining an open stance towards proselytes is not a concession to modernity but a return to the very essence of Judaism as a universal faith. The *malshinim* should remain in the liturgy as a reminder of a tragic past when even believing the *wrong* belief or encouraging others to share one's *wrong* belief was a capital crime that imperilled not only individuals but whole communities. There are other prayers, however, such as the *Aleinu Leshabeiach* (it is our duty to praise) which concludes every statutory service. For a people that has been taught that the eyes are placed in the head in a position that encourages us to look forward and not backward, it offers the clearest response to the proselyte and the question of proselytism:

> All who inhabit this world shall meet in understanding and know that to You alone each one shall submit and every tongue pledge loyalty. In Your presence, Ever-present, our God, they shall bow down and be humble, accepting the glory of Your being. Then all shall accept the duty of establishing Your rule, so that Your reign of goodness shall come and last forever.

That some who have been captivated by the millennial faith of the Jewish people will choose to walk towards this Messianic age as Jews and in the company of Jews, should remain for all a cause for joy and sublime wonderment for the enduring grace of the God of Israel.

6. Conversion from within and without in Chinese religion

Jordan Paper

Prologue

Chinese religion is typical of ethnic religions, as compared to 'universal' or 'proselytizing' religions, in that it is inseparable from the culture in which it is found. Such religions provide both the ideological basis and the ritual practices that define and continue the socio-cultural matrix. Being the foundation of the culture as a whole they are inseparable from the given culture and, hence, usually have no name, other than the culture itself. Such religions tend to be flexible, and alternate modes of religiosity within the general framework may be present as additional options to the normative practices.

Chinese religion encompasses an understanding of society at all levels as modelled on a patrilineal, extended family, a family that includes the dead and those yet to be born. The living on death become ancestral spirits to whom sustenance is offered by the living and who, in turn, have a degree of power to assist the living members of the family. Religious rituals centre on banquets offered to the dead and eaten by the living. Individuals understand themselves primarily as member of social units, particularly the family. One's religious duty is to continue the family by producing male progeny and, to the best of one's abilities, enhance the fortunes of the family. Communication between the living and the dead is facilitated by mediums (spirit possession specialists) who function at all levels of society, as well as at the court in the past, and other, non-ecstatic methods of divination.[1]

By two thousand years ago, as Chinese culture both spread from present-day northern China and amalgamated with related cultures elsewhere in eastern Asia, this religious construct had disseminated over all of the area of contemporary China proper (the area that is culturally Chinese, an area smaller than the present boundaries which maintains that of the previous Manchu Empire), excepting small pockets of indigenous cultures which remain to today. In addition, the religion had spread throughout all levels of society, from the Emperor and Empress, whose offerings to the dead of the imperial family were state rituals, to the peasant farmers.

There is little to suggest that this spread was due to conscious conversion. Rather, as Chinese culture was deemed desirable to emulate and, due to the vicissitudes of invasion, as Chinese emigrated to southern parts of eastern Asia, this pattern was slowly adopted throughout the area. It was probably not substantially different from the religions already present; for example, the aboriginal religions of Taiwan indicate that religions oriented towards the family dead were also quite widespread in Pacific oceanic cultures. As the rulers of Japan and Korea later voluntarily adopted Chinese governmental patterns, so too they accepted the attached ideological and ritual frameworks. These formal patterns also became ubiquitous in these countries, coexisting with the indigenous religious modalities.

Because of the relatively extensive written records in China, particularly over the last 2,200 years, it is possible to trace and comprehend the interactions of new religious movements, both from within and without, with the normative Chinese pattern. Hence, the history of Chinese religion provides us with the ability to understand the nature of conversion in ethnic religions over a long period of time.

Conversion from within

Empires are not permanent. Chinese religion, culture and society became homogeneous and widespread with the first major Chinese Empire, the Han, whose dates are approximately similar to those of the Roman Empire. As the Han regime stultified and decayed towards the end of its fourth century of rule, a religio-political movement, often termed the Five Pecks of Rice, swept through much of China, its sacred text named the *Taiping jing* (Classic of Great Peace). Perhaps led by court exorcists and mediums, who had been ousted during a period of repeated reform and counter-reform movements, and almost certainly stimulated by new ideas from Buddhism beginning to be present in China (perhaps the earliest meaningful impact of Buddhism on China), the movement fostered an ordered society with a communal economy. Opposed, of course, by a dynasty struggling to remain viable, the clashes between the peasant armies and those of the government led to widespread destruction. Although the Han dynasty retained the upper hand, the effort to put down the rebellion led to the dynasty's ultimate collapse. The son of the commander-in-chief of the Han army became the emperor of the succeeding dynasty in the third century (CE).

Stripped of its military and political roles, the defeated movement did not disappear but became the core of a new, auxiliary mode of religion in China. This development consisted of institutions separate from but legitimated by the government that supplied priests (male and female) and rituals auxiliary to but understood to enhance the normative family and community-centred religious practices, in which the eldest of the families and clans functioned as priests. These Daoist (*daojiao*) churches developed in parallel with Buddhist monastic institutions, which originally served communities of foreign merchants but, in this time of political–cultural flux, were making considerable inroads among the Chinese people. (Daoist monasticism did not appear until the twelfth century CE.)

Buddhism (*fojiao*) was not originally understood to be a foreign religion by the majority of Chinese. Because of a translation process using what were understood to be matching terms (similar to the earlier European practice of translating Sanskrit words in the *Upanishads* with Christian equivalents: e.g., 'soul' for *atman* and 'God' for *brahman*), Buddhism was viewed as similar to Daoism and also as an adjunct to normative Chinese religion.

In the several hundred years of relative chaos that followed the collapse of the Han in the southern part of China, Buddhist monasteries filled the stability vacuum by becoming centres of economic wealth protected by armed and martially trained monks (both practices in contravention of the traditional *vinaya* [monastic rules]). At times it was more advantageous for farmers to donate their land to monasteries and become their tenants, monastic land being tax exempt, than to pay land and labour taxes. Governments exacerbated their long-term financial problems by raising money through selling certificates of Buddhist ordination, which exempted the bearers from tax obligations for life. In the north, foreign conquerors, already Buddhist, instituted state-controlled Buddhism as a means to control their newly conquered Chinese populations.

When China was reunified under a native regime fourteen hundred years ago, Chinese culture slowly reasserted itself in a period of increasing stability. The formation of the Tang dynasty (seventh century CE) led to the reopening of the overland trade route to west and south Asia. Chinese monks travelled to India, became well versed in Sanskrit, and retranslated Buddhist sutras with greater accuracy. These two developments led to a counter-Buddhist movement, the nativistic Chinese critiques of Buddhism charging Buddhism with being un-Chinese, particularly because of the monastic practices of voiding family ties and celibacy. This ultimately led to the last of a series of economic and political suppressions (there was no concern over individual beliefs) of Buddhism twelve hundred years ago from which Buddhism did not recover until the twentieth century.

Consequently, Buddhism became wholly sinified in China. The religion since has functioned, in conjunction with Daoism, primarily as an adjunct to the family-centred religion. Daoist priests specialized in funeral rituals, as well as community renewal rituals, and Buddhist monks and nuns offered memorial masses for the dead. The Pure Land, initially in India a temporary spiritual abode to enhance meditation to enable exiting from the 'wheel of life', amalgamated with indigenous beliefs to become the Western Paradise. The Pure Land became a permanent heaven where offerings of food, houses, servants and other features of the good life can be sent (via burning paper representations) for the enjoyment of the families' dead.

Buddhist monks and nuns tended to either be those from elite backgrounds, who for a variety of reasons, retired to monasteries after raising families, or orphans without families raised in the monasteries. Only monks and nuns were outside the normative family-centred religion; lay persons, even the most devout, amalgamated their Buddhist practices with Chinese religion. And even for monks and nuns, their primary priestly functions were in support of normative Chinese religion, in their reciting masses for the dead on behalf of families.

From that time to the present, periods of dynastic decay, replete with massive corruption, government ineptness, and widespread suffering, have led to new religio-political movements. The most successful was the Taiping movement of the nineteenth century. It is this movement, for which we have a wealth of data, including government and Taiping documents, as well as reports by Westerners, on which the analysis of internal conversion will focus.

In the mid-nineteenth century, the last dynasty was in a period of decay. The West, in a period of imperialistic expansion, took advantage of this weakness to engage China in a brief war in southernmost China (the capital was in the far north) over the right to push opium on the Chinese people, although Chinese law made the sale and distribution, other than for medical use, illegal. After a few lost skirmishes, the Chinese government caved in and granted European (and by extension, American) powers extraordinary rights. Particularly coveted and gained were rights for Christian missionaries (the history of these missions will be briefly dealt with in the next section) to reside in China.

Shortly after the cessation of hostilities, Protestant and Catholic missionaries established themselves in Canton and began translation activities. One educated individual, Hung Xiuqian, on becoming aware of a Protestant Christian tract in Chinese, interpreted an earlier vision as indicating he was the younger brother of Christ, the Christian tripartite, singular deity understood by him as a divine family. Soon a small circle gathered about him, including one who was possessed by God, the Heavenly Father, and another by Christ, who both (Chinese polytheism did not encourage an understanding of the Christian Trinity as a single deity) testified to Hung's identity.

Using language in part taken from the above mentioned Chinese language Christian tract and from the Five Pecks of Rice Movement seventeen hundred years previous, Hung developed and led a rapidly growing religio-revolutionary movement to establish the *Taiping-tianguo* (Heavenly Kingdom of Great Peace). This geometrically expanding army rapidly swept through much of southern and central China. On capturing Nanjing, the Chinese capital previous to its being moved to Beijing in the fifteenth century, now understood as the New Jerusalem, the Taiping-tianguo was proclaimed, with Hung as the Heavenly King.

The short-lived regime instituted a translation of the Bible as the basis of the civil service examinations in place of the Classics and required conversion to a sinified version of Christianity. This mode of Christianity continued Chinese practices but replaced the sacrifices to the family dead with those to God and his family. Also borrowed from Christianity was the Christian intolerance for non-Christian religions; there was widespread destruction of religious structures.

Western Christians considered a Chinese messiah an anathema, and Western imperialism required the continuation of a weak Chinese government. The two motivations led the Western powers to assist the Manchu regime in putting down the new nation which covered China's heartland and 'breadbasket'. As nearly two thousand years before, conquering the Taiping-tianguo led to massive, widespread destruction, followed by the collapse in all but name (until 1911) of the Manchu dynasty. The Western powers, after a second 'Opium War,' took over the administration of China's finances and obtained extraterritoriality over much of China.

The collapse of the Taiping-tianguo was followed by a century of turmoil until the success of the Chinese Communist Party. Similar to Hung's movement in relation to Christianity, the Chinese Communist Party utilized the rhetoric of Marxist–Leninist–Stalinist 'communism' but with an indigenous understanding. Similar to the Taiping movement, there was decreasing tolerance for alternative religious understanding (here, the interpretation of Communism as an outgrowth of Protestantism is being followed).

When Mao feared a backsliding away from his understanding of Communism after a generation in power, he launched the 'Cultural Revolution'. Intended to be a massive revitalization of Communism among the new generation of youth, the movement quickly became a pawn in a power struggle and instigated the virtual destruction of all things 'Chinese'. All old buildings, including temples, suffered considerable devastation; the attempt was to force a new religion on the old. (The destruction equalled the devastation consequent to the Taiping movement.) Within a decade, the movement failed, and its failure spawned a new awakening of traditional religion. When students again threatened to take control in the 'Tiananmen Incident', there was great fear of a renewed Cultural Revolution. In response, the revival of traditional religion accelerated.

In Chinese communities outside of China, Buddhism, also modelling itself on Christian institutions, is enjoying an interesting resurgence. Many Chinese living in Christian cultures are made to feel uncomfortable in not being part of a 'religion', religion understood as institutions outside of the state, seemingly separate from culture *per se*, and having a name. Since, as will be discussed in the next section, conversion to Christianity meant converting from being Chinese, an alternative was sought. The early part of the twentieth century, in the British colony of Hong Kong, saw the development of Chinese Buddhist institutions modelled on Protestant ones, in particular, on the YMCA. It was perceived that Buddhism could offer all that Christianity did while maintaining a Chinese identity.

Recently an enormous growth of these institutions has taken place in Taiwan. When the Nationalist government relocated in Taiwan after the success of the Communist Party, it not only brought its connections with Christianity with it, but tolerated, if not fostered, both Catholic and Protestant missionary activities. In part, this policy was directed towards encouraging the understanding in the American Congress that the Nationalist government was the legitimate (i.e. Christian) Chinese government opposed to godless communists.

The approximately two million refugees from the mainland were cut off from their families, family homes, clan temples and gravesites. This made continuity of the family rituals difficult. While Christianity was an alternative for the families from the mainland, so was Buddhism which offered not only an enhancement of rituals towards the family dead but the traditional Buddhist individualistic spirituality as well.

When martial law, imposed since the reversion of Taiwan to China after the end of World War II, was lifted in 1987, there was a rapid growth of Buddhist institutions in reaction to the previous promotion of Christianity, along with many new indigenous religious movements and a rapid expansion and modernization of traditional modes of religiosity. The decade since has witnessed the growth of Buddhist universities, publishing houses, hospitals and other charitable institutions, as well as monasteries. This renewed growth has been exported to countries with rapidly growing Chinese populations, such as Canada and the United States. Buddhist organizations in these countries function more as churches than monasteries, offering the new immigrants religious rituals parallel to Christian ones that allow full maintenance of Chinese identity.

Conversion from without

There is a long tradition of Western religions in China. Beginning about twelve hundred years ago, Islam, Judaism and Nestorian

Christianity arrived with foreign merchants and experienced the typical Chinese tolerance of different customs and religions so long as they were not seen to be disruptive of Chinese society or a threat to the government, as well as a modicum of government support. Their descendants blended into the Chinese population save for maintaining special dietary practices, rituals, sacred texts, skullcaps, and so forth. Islam remains a religion of many millions of Chinese, as well as being the dominant religion in several western autonomous regions. Jewish communities continued to be viable until the turmoil consequent to the Taiping movement discussed above. None of these traditions seemed to have actively proselytized in China proper, or, at least, not for a long time.

This situation changed four centuries ago with the arrival of Jesuit missionaries. The Jesuits went to China, as they did elsewhere, with but a single purpose: to convert China to Christianity. Their method was to work from the top down. They sought to convert the most powerful figures in the government. To this end, they underwent an elite Chinese education, including the texts on sacrificial rituals, and accepted government positions, which required them to take part in state sacrifices.

In order to not be charged with heresy for so doing, especially during the period of the Inquisition, they deliberately skewed the understanding of Chinese religion in their reports ('Relations') back to Europe. For example, they translated the *sanjiao* ('three teachings' – the ideological bases of Buddhism, Daoism and 'Confucianism', understood in China as three aspects of a single macro-ideology) as 'three religions' (starting a confused understanding of Chinese religion that continues into the present).

To render Christianity palatable to the Chinese elite, they deliberately turned a blind eye to normative Chinese religious practices, deeming them to not be religion. Given that the Christianity they presented could function, like Buddhism, as an adjunct to Chinese religion, Jesuit missionaries 'converted' several princes and high officials.

Dominican and Franciscan rivals, who later arrived on the scene and ministered to ordinary people, insisted that Chinese religion indeed was religion. Those who converted from Chinese religion must cease to practise the normative family-centred rituals; in other words, those who became Christians could not remain culturally and socially Chinese. Hence, if officials converted, they would have to give up their offices, elite social status, and economic perquisites.

This battle, known as the 'Rites Controversy', was fought out in the Vatican for a century. When the Jesuit political position ebbed in the early eighteenth century, the decision went against them. The Chinese emperor, then the most powerful political figure in the world, on hearing of the Vatican's decision, which went against his own determination, subsequently threw all Christian missionaries out of China.

Not until China lost the two 'Opium Wars' in the mid-nineteenth century, were Christian missionaries, preceded by European guns, to be found in China. The second treaty granted extraterritoriality not only to Europeans but to Christian converts. Murderers and rapists who converted were released from prison; converts automatically won civil litigations. Missionaries could confiscate land from Chinese at will, backed by European soldiers. In famines, food was offered only to those who took Christian instruction. Money forced from the financially-strapped government as reparations was used to support missionary endeavours.

Needless to point out, as evidenced by the periodic popular uprisings against missionaries and converts, Christians were hated by the general populace. Converts were not only detested for lording it over non-converts, while protected by Western armies, but also because they were seen as *diguo zhuyi zougou* ('dogs trotting after imperialist [masters]') long before Communism developed in China.

In the early twentieth century, Western educational institutions were founded by missionary societies, and conversion was a requirement for receiving a Western education. (This phenomenon was so ingrained in the Chinese cultural memory that when the Cultural Revolution ended in the 1970s, young Chinese flocked to the few extant Christian churches expecting to be taught contemporary science; of course, this phenomenon was short-lived.) When the Chinese Communist Party came to power, the missionaries, saving those few friendly to the new regime, were again thrown out of China, being understood as the advance soldiers of Western imperialism. Christianity has been remarkably unsuccessful in China in spite of or, indeed, because its missionary activities were zealously fostered by Western governments intent on colonizing China.

In the renewed Christian missions in China since the mid-nineteenth century, missionaries taught that the indigenous religion was devil worship. Worship and offerings to not only the deities but the ancestral spirits themselves were taught to be wicked and to lead to eternal damnation. But these teachings were tempered by a stress on the commandment to honour one's parents and to do good in society. Hence, the more evangelical missionaries taught converts to detest all concepts and things Chinese; the more benign missionaries taught confused converts that Christianity was but a more modern version of the *rujia* ('Confucian') teachings. It was not until the decisions of Vatican II effectively reached Taiwan, which took place nearly two decades after the fact due to the elderly, reactionary cardinal resident in Taiwan, did one begin to see family altars in Chinese Catholic Christian homes, a phenomenon not to be found in the homes of Protestant Christian converts.

Kenneth Scott Latourette, in his still standard history of Christian missions in China,[2] presciently concluded in the 1920s that Christianity could succeed in China only under one of two scenarios. On the one hand, Christianity would have to radically change in its rigidity towards other cultures, a change that took place in Roman Catholicism with Vatican II (now seemingly a short-lived reform) but too late to influence (mainland) China. On the other hand, Chinese culture would have to radically change; that is, no longer be Chinese. Such change did take place during the Cultural Revolution, but as seen in the aftermath of forced conversions to Christianity (as on Canadian and United States reservations for indigenous peoples until the relatively recent revitalization movements), the consequences are frequently a moral vacuum. For the outcome of the Cultural Revolution was an entire generation bereft of culture, with no sense of a past, no promise of a future, and no codes of social and personal behaviour.

Conclusions

In ethnic religions, such as Chinese religion, there are two possible modes of conversion: (1) conversion *to* with no lessening of previous modes of religiosity, and (2) conversion *from*, requiring the individual to adopt a new, to varying degrees, cultural foundation. The first mode is additive; the second, substitutive. One could argue that the first mode is not conversion at all, for the normative understanding of 'conversion' assumes a *change* in religious understanding; that is, the term is commonly only applied to the second mode, not the first. If a male Protestant Christian becomes a Mason, one does not use the terminology of conversion, for the person has added new rituals to his practices without dropping any of the old. Similarly, when Jesuits converted some Manchu princes in seventeenth-century China, these individuals would have added Christian rituals to their normative ritual mix of Chinese religion combined with Lamaistic (Central Asian) Buddhism, adopted by the court partially for diplomacy, and their own indigenous Manchurian shamanism.

When the second mode occurred, even as indigenized foreign religions, it led to major social turmoil and considerable death and destruction, as took place with the mid-nineteenth-century Taiping movement and the more recent Cultural Revolution. Non-indigenized modes could only succeed through external military force or the complete collapse of the culture; in mainland China, Christian missions disappeared with the end of European imperialism. In Taiwan, although the two leading contenders in the recent (1996) presidential election were Christians, with the end of martial law, Christianity is giving place to revitalized and new modes of indigenous religion. These patterns can be also be seen in the history of native North American and sub-Saharan African traditions, accepting that the imposition of colonial control was successful in the Americas and temporarily successful in Africa.

A subsidiary issue is the depth of conversion. For example, the economy in 1950s' Taiwan was weak. Christian missionaries, as earlier on the mainland, offered food and used clothing from the West to converts. Christianity was locally called in Taiwan at that time (in translation) the 'Butter-Milk Religion', after those foods being offered which were particularly foreign in Chinese eyes. (China is a non-dairy culture, while the 'barbarian' cultures to its north and west are dairy cultures.) Other motives for conversion included the desire to study at Western universities; it was assumed that converting to Christianity would greatly enhance the opportunity to do so. Also, Christianity was considered fashionable in that to be considered modern and progressive meant to be perceived as following Western customs, not only in dress, but in religion. Because of the family orientation of Chinese culture, when one member of the family converted, especially a senior member, all others would often automatically convert, although there may have been no personal interest in doing so and no more than minimal adherence to the new practices. The question is whether, to use an old Western term, the majority of 'Rice-bowl Christians' had converted in any other than a formal institutional sense. If this be the case, then what is the meaning of conversion in this regard?

A major difference between ethnic religions and proselytizing ones is the latter have an ideological basis, often leading to a creed. Ethnic traditions are based on practices, ritual patterns, that imply an understanding of reality, of the world about one, but are not tied to ideological systems. Hence, they are very flexible and can continue in spite of changing ideology, as evidenced today in Taiwan, Hong Kong and Singapore, all post-industrial societies witnessing a remarkable resurgence of traditional modes of religion with increasing generalized wealth.

Ethnic traditions also do not have a concept of belief (nor an indigenous term for it). Religious practices are understood to be valuable for their own sake and require no belief system to justify them. For example, Chinese people feel good about offering food to their dead parents or grandparents and enjoy sitting down to a feast, without worrying about whether or not the spirits of the dead truly exist. A common attitude towards making offerings to deities at temples is that it cannot hurt and may be beneficial. In any case, the religion is utterly pragmatic. Only deities perceived to be beneficial for worldly ends (success in business, passing examinations, healing illness) have their temples refurbished and new temples constructed.

Furthermore, ethnic religions (throughout Asia, Africa and the indigenous traditions of the Americas) perceive religious truths experientially – either mediumistically or shamanistically – rather than through creeds. Belief in the Christian sense is inapplicable (although pentecostal Christianity is also primarily experiential) to such traditions.

On the contrary, proselytizing traditions tend to have acceptance of an oral formula, a creed, as a sign of conversion. In Buddhism, this is but adherence to the *triratna* (Three Jewels: Buddha, Dharma, Sangha), and Islam requires but a simple statement. Christianity usually demands acceptance of a complex doctrinal statement, and different modes of Christianity literally fight to the death over subtle differences in the wording of these statements. Islam and Christianity, being monotheistic, have notions of a singular 'Truth' that is either accepted or rejected in its entirety, and it is these particular traditions that have wed religion to imperialistic expansion.

Ethnic religions, by their nature, do not proselytize, except in cases of conquering new territories and requiring the population to adopt, not convert, to the culture of the dominating people. Such was the situation in Manchuria, when the Japanese wrested that part of East Asia from China. In schools, the language of instruction was Japanese and the students were expected to adhere to the revised Shinto rituals of the military-dominated government. But the Japanese had little if any concern for the religious practices of the population outside of their own institutions or those they directly controlled.

Similarly, when China informally colonized Taiwan in the sixteenth century, a few persons unsuccessfully tried to teach the indigenous population *rujia* ethics, from the perspective of the colonizers, to try to stop them from defending their farmlands by killing Chinese. Eventually, the native population retreated to the mountains, where they retained their traditions until the Nationalist government encouraged Christian missionary activities, and tacit control, among the reservations on which the aboriginal population was located after 1949. The purpose of the practice was to 'pacify' the aboriginal villages (a practice very similar to that of the American and Canadian governments which, for many decades, put Native American reservations under the control of Christian missionaries for the same purpose).

In conclusion, one must ask whether the term and the connected concepts relevant to 'conversion' are applicable to ethnic religious traditions. Perhaps conversion is only meaningful to and within the proselytizing traditions – Buddhism, Christianity (and its offshoot, Communism) and Islam (with offshoots such as Baha'i) – in which conversion is an ethical imperative.

Notes

1. For general and more advanced introductions to Chinese religion as expressed here, see Lawrence Thompson, *Chinese Religion: An Introduction* (6th edn, Belmont, CA: Wadsworth, 1995); and Jordan Paper, *The Spirits Are Drunk: Comparative Approaches to Chinese Religion* (Albany, NY: State University of New York Press, 1995).
2. Kenneth Scott Latourette, *A History of Christian Missions in China* (London: SPCK, 1929).

7. Contra conversion: the case of the Zoroastrians of India

Homi B. Dhalla

The question of conversion has been the cause of controversies in the Zoroastrian or Parsi community of India since the beginning of the twentieth century. It assumes a peculiar poignancy as conversion seems to be the only answer to those Parsis who see their diminishing numbers as a threat to the survival of their community. However, there are few instances of Parsis advocating conversion from other religions to their faith. More troubling within the Parsi community is the issue of converting a non-Parsi spouse of a Parsi. This chapter examines both types of conversion.

Conversion among Indian Christians

Since the Parsis have not sought to convert persons from other religious communities in India, a look at the Christian community which has pursued this strategy might prove illustrative. It offers several cautionary lessons. First of all, it helps us to see that conversion cannot be seen in isolation. It is not only a religious issue – it has social, cultural, economic, legal and political repercussions. Christian missionary activity in India was linked to European colonization from the sixteenth to the early twentieth centuries. To minister to the 'heathen', to offer 'salvation' through Jesus Christ, to extol their religion as the only one 'revealed by God', was the missionaries' credo.[1] But Harvey Cox of Harvard University saw the link between conversion and colonization when he wrote:

> Empires must always deal with the religions of those societies they dominate. Sometimes they simply destroy them. Christians and Muslims seem to have favoured this strategy. Sometimes they use the religions of

their satraps for the purpose of dividing and dominating, as England did so adroitly for so long in India, or they may try to emulate as the Romans did the Greeks. Always they distort indigenous faiths in one way or another. Eventually the colonizers begin to realize the enormity of what they have done, and the guilt begins to tincture hope and engender fear.[2]

ANTI-CONVERSION LAWS

When Christian missionaries put forward their exclusivist claims, Indian religious and political leaders were at first bewildered, then outraged. The Hindu sensibility was deeply stirred when the missionaries began converting tribals. With the escalating tension, the *rajahs* (rulers) of some Indian states took exception to conversion. This led them to enact anti-conversion laws. The first was known as the Rajgarh State Conversion Act of 1936. The reason for these laws, given in the preamble to the Act, was that 'some recent mass conversions have fanned the communal flame in the State to such an undesirable extent that serious communal riots might break out at any time'.

The second anti-conversion law was the Surguja State Hindu Apostacy Act of 1945 and the third was the Udaipur State Conversion Act of 1946. The preamble to this Act stated that 'a fair number of *Adivasis* (tribals) changed their religion and such conversions are creating an atmosphere which might disturb the public peace'.[3]

Later, Dr Kailash Nath Katju, Home Minister, declared on the floor of Parliament in 1953, that 'It had been made clear to all foreign missionaries working in the country that if they were engaged in social welfare work, medical work and education, they were welcome, but if they indulged in proselytisation it would be undesirable.'[4] Basically, this came to be the government's attitude.

THE NIYOGI COMMITTEE REPORT

As representations were continually being made to the government of Madhya Pradesh regarding 'forced conversions' as well as charges of 'fraudulent' methods adopted by the Christian missionaries, the

Government appointed the Niyogi Committee on 14 April 1956. Justice Niyogi was the Chairman of this Christian Missionary Activities Enquiry Committee. Before making its recommendations the Committee interviewed 11,360 persons and received 375 written statements from 700 villages. The findings of this Committee reveal the social, political and psychological problems that were generated by the policy of proselytism, due to which the people exploded into open rebellion a number of times.[5] The Committee declared that most conversions had taken place because of economic considerations, that the missionaries instilled an idea of a separate nationality to enable them to demand a separate state for themselves, and that all the philanthropic acts were a mask for carrying on their proselytizing activities, sometimes through intimidation and at times by tempting the simple and illiterate.

In India, Christianity has often been seen the spirit of domination and identified with Western imperialism. These and other allegations have created hostility and ill-will towards the Christians in India.[6] On the other hand, Christians have denied all these charges and contend that it was their spiritual zeal that moved them to organize various social activities.[7]

THE ARYA SAMAJ

Although Gandhi stated that 'there is no such thing as proselytism in Hinduism',[8] it must be acknowledged that the Arya Samaj founded by Dayanand Saraswati (1824–83) introduced the *Shuddhi* movement, that is, the re-conversion of Indians and tribals to Hinduism, especially the recent proselytes, who had embraced Islam or Christianity. It was the Arya Samaj which introduced proselytism into Hinduism and this is what brought about hostility towards other proselytizing religions.[9]

ENACTMENT OF ANTI-CONVERSION LAWS BY SOME STATES AFTER INDEPENDENCE

Article Twenty-five of the Indian Constitution guarantees freedom of religious conscience, that is, the right 'to practise, profess and propagate one's religion subject to public health, public morality and public order'. But this does not include the right to convert any person to one's own religion. The Supreme Court of India has ruled that what is freedom for one is freedom for others, in equal measure; and there can be no such thing as a fundamental right to convert any person to one's own religion.[10]

For the purpose of preventing forcible conversions the following Acts were passed in three states of India: the Freedom of Religion Act of Orissa (1967), the Freedom of Religion Act of Madhya Pradesh (1968), and the Freedom of Religion Act of Arunachal Pradesh (1978). Clause Three of the last Act reads: 'No person shall convert or attempt to convert, either directly or otherwise any person from an indigenous faith by use of force or by inducement or by any fraudulent means nor shall any person abet any such conversion.'[11]

HINDU OPINIONS CONCERNING CONVERSION AND PROSELYTIZATION

Mahatma Gandhi believed that conversion in the sense of self-purification and self-realization was a crying need of the times,[12] but he opposed proselytization. (See the essay on Gandhi by S. Rao in this volume.) He felt that organized programmes of proselytization meant little or no peace for the world. Indeed, he said that he would personally like to stop conversions growing out of proselytizing as they did more harm than good.[13] Similarly, Dr Radhakrishnan, India's first president, states that Hinduism declares that all religions have a right to express themselves. But he condemned religious fanaticism and argued that,

> the supersession of the different religious traditions would make this world into a poorer place. Have we the right to destroy what we have not learnt to appreciate? To drag into the dust what is precious to the soul of a people, what has been laboriously built up by the wisdom of the ages, is spiritual vandalism.[14]

These opinions from earlier in the twentieth century led me to ask two contemporary Indians, prominent in their fields, the question, 'What if the Parsis had promoted conversion over the years?' I asked this question in September 1996 of Mr Justice Madhukar Kania, the retired Chief Justice of the Supreme Court of India. He replied as follows:

> The tension between Hindus and Christians in some parts of the country is due to conversion. If the Parsis had converted members of other

communities to their faith, there would certainly have been resentment against them. If they had proselytised, they may not have been allowed to live peacefully with the other communities.

I then approached Dr Usha Mehta, a Gandhian who is a national figure. Like Justice Kania he is not a Zoroastrian. Dr Mehta remarked:

> It is the wisest policy that the Parsis adopted – not to convert. This has helped them to live harmoniously with all other communities. To not proselytise is the right spirit in religion. You have identified with the country that has offered you sanctuary. Indeed, you are an ideal minority – a model for other communities in India.[15]

CONVERSION AS AN OBSTACLE TO DIALOGUE

Following the Second Vatican Council, there has been a new openness in the attitude of the Roman Catholic Church towards other religious traditions. This outlook resulted in Pope Paul VI instituting the Papal Secretariat for non-Christian Religions in 1964. This Secretariat has been assiduously encouraging dialogue with other religions at the regional as well as at the international level. It has contributed much to inter-religious dialogue. And yet Cardinal Francis Arinze, head of the Pontifical Council for Inter-religious Dialogue, in his lecture at Harvard University in October, 1985, said, 'The tension between the missionary thrust of Christianity to convert everyone and the call to respect the religious views of others has led some Christians into untenable positions.' He adds that, 'Some non-Christians are not sure of the Christian motives of dialogue. They suspect that it is conversion. They are afraid that dialogue is a Trojan horse which Christians want to bring into the fortified cities of the non-Christians.'[16] The former Archbishop of Canterbury, the Most Reverend Dr Robert Runcie, speaking at Bangalore in 1986, urged Christians in India to give up their 'superiority hang-ups' and to be respectful of other faiths.[17]

Proselytism has posed problems in India and in many parts of the world. This issue was discussed at the Parliament of the World's Religions held at Chicago in 1993. The Summary Report from the Assembly of Religious and Spiritual Leaders refers to the problems with conversion / missionary activities. Those activities create social tension and it is very widespread.[18] In 1995, a series of workshops and seminars took place involving different religious groups where the question of conversion came up. Christians at a workshop on 'Issues on Hindu–Christian Relations' at Madurai Kamaraj University in October, 1995, felt that the Hindu fear of conversion was pervasive[19] and everyone agreed that enticement to convert is wrong.[20] Moreover, 'the Hindus found the traditional methods of missionary activity very offensive'.[21] At another Hindu-Christian Dialogue on 'Working for Harmony in the Contemporary World' in New Delhi in October, 1995, the final report stressed that 'dialogue aimed at "converting" the other to one's own religious faith and tradition is dishonest and unethical; it is not the way of harmony'.[22] A similar view was expressed at a meeting of religious leaders of five Central Asian Republics held at Tashkent (Uzbekistan) entitled 'Living Together under one Sky' in 1995. The final report states:

> Much of the Tashkent meeting was spent discussing the arrival of new religious groups and sects in the region, both Christian and non-Christian. The participants appealed to the World Council of Churches to assist them in dealing with the alarming problems raised by the active proselytism of these groups, including the threat they pose to interreligious harmony.[23]

THREAT TO INTER-COMMUNAL HARMONY

In India in recent decades we have seen a growing fundamentalism aggravated by communalism.[24] Political advantage has been taken of these tensions to foment trouble, chiefly between Hindus and Muslims. In 1981, a stormy controversy spread all over the country when some Harijans were converted to Islam at Meenakshipura, South India. It led to considerable tension between Hindus and Muslims.[25] On 1 March 1982 clashes took place between Christians and Hindus over conversions at Mandaikadu in Kanyakumari district. The Justice Venugopal Commission which inquired into the clashes suggested enactment of legislation to curb conversion.[26] An article entitled 'Are These Men Dangerous?', in December 1985, stated that expulsion notices had been served on six Christian missionaries who had been converting tribals in the Surguja district of Madhya Pradesh.[27] Tension had mounted when about 25,000 Hindus were converted to Buddhism in Patna in December 1993.[28] Harmony between Hindus and Christians in Mundakkayom, Kerala, was disturbed when 800 persons who had been converted to Christianity were reconverted to Hinduism under the auspices of the Hindu Aikya Vedi in July 1995.[29] In January 1996, a Belgian priest, Rev. Louis Birje and Sister Vriddhi Ekka were sentenced to six months' rigorous imprisonment in Bhopal. The case dates back to 1988 when they had converted tribals in Surguja district. They have appealed against the judgment.[30]

The President of the Vishwa Hindu Parishad recently wrote to Cardinal Simon Pimenta of Bombay that Christians should apologize for what they had done to the Hindus during British rule. The Catholic Church has responded by saying that as a number of priests have been murdered and attacked in the recent past, an apology, on the contrary, is due to the Church.[31]

In August 1996, Mr M. Lodha, a member of the Legislative Assembly of the Bharatiya Janata Party in Bombay, drafted a Bill which seeks to jail those resorting to religious conversion. A notice of the Bill has been given to the Speaker of the Assembly so it could be introduced shortly.[32] In this context it is pertinent to note that similar Bills have already been passed in Orissa, Arunachal Pradesh and Madhya Pradesh.

LESSONS

It is imperative that the handful of Parsis who advocate conversion from other faiths should know these facts and so understand the serious problems between religious communities that conversion has created in India today.

Following Muslim oppression in Iran in the ninth century, Zoroastrians fled the country; they became a scattered people, having neither a land, nor a central religious or political authority. Those who came to India were afforded shelter by the Hindu ruler, Jadav Rana. To him they gave an assurance as recorded in the *Kisse-i-Sanjan* (K.S. 164) that, 'We shall be the friends of all India'. They have kept their promise. Kulke emphasizes this by saying:

> The Parsis were able to live within their environment without conflicts as both they and their environment did not attempt any assimilation or mutual conversion, which prevented, from the very beginning, any aggressive reactions or frustrations, which might have resulted from a rejection on the part of the minority or the majority.[33]

As a microscopic minority the Parsis ought to heed the warning of the Niyogi Committee which examined the problem of proselytism in Madhya Pradesh. It states, 'In the present secular state of India, the best safeguard any minority could have is the goodwill of the majority community.' And the majority community of India has shown a sustained sense of goodwill. This is precisely what Pandit Nehru, the first Prime Minister of India, meant when he referred to the Parsis as those 'following their faith and their customs without being interfered with and without interfering with others'.[34]

Parsi advocates of conversion have to ask whom they seek to convert. Do not they see that the communal violence caused by 'conversion' would also pose a threat to their own community? They have to be made to see that active proselytizing and conversion would deal a death-blow both physically and psychologically to the less than 100,000 Parsis in India.[35]

The Parsis of India have aligned themselves with the cause of the nation. Prior to the Independence of India in 1947, the President of the Bombay Parsi Panchayat, Sir Shapurji Billimoria stated, 'we will continue to give our best to the country and the Government'.[36] Now on the threshold of the twenty-first century, I would like to express the hope that the Parsis will continue to live harmoniously and contribute positively to this great nation.

Intermarriage and spousal conversion among Parsis

The questions that have troubled the consciousness of the Parsi community in India for decades are intermarriage and spousal conversion. Until today, there has been no resolution of these issues.

For over a millennium, till about the beginning of the twentieth century, Zoroastrians in India lived in closed societies. Exogamous marriages were discouraged as they were seen as a threat to the religio-ethnic group; in fact, a threat to the survival of the religion over a long period of time. When Zoroastrians migrated to India, the practice of intra-marriage was already regarded as a sacred duty: it was etched in the communal psyche. Having come to a socio-cultural environment where the Hindu caste system was already entrenched, the Zoroastrian custom found acceptance. They were looked upon as a distinct caste. Marriage within one's caste was wholly in accordance with the normal practice of the Hindus.

However, in recent years the rate of exogamous marriages has increased. As the non-Zoroastrian spouse is ineligible to take part in religious ceremonies and communal matters, the question has become even more troubled. In India the majority of Zoroastrian priests refuse to officiate at a marriage ceremony where the woman is a non-Parsi. The question has become more and more complex. Perhaps it would help to look at the chronological events over the past century.

On 8 January 1903, Ratan Dadabhai Tata, a member of a prominent industrial family, married a Frenchwoman, Suzanne Briere. This triggered successive events significant for the future of the Zoroastrians in India. After his marriage in Paris, Mr Tata on his return to India had his bride's *navjote* ceremony (investiture to the faith) performed. He then went through the Zoroastrian marriage ritual with her. Thereafter, he announced that she was now a Parsi Zoroastrian. This was the first time in the history of the community that such an induction had been attempted. Because of this 'conversion', Mrs Tata could claim to have access to all the religious institutions of the Parsis. She could thus enter the fire-temples and have her body consigned to the *dakhmas* (Towers of Silence) if she so wished.

This unprecedented event led to a series of meetings. Finally on 2 August 1903, a committee was appointed to deliberate on the controversial question whether *juddins* (literally 'of alien faith', but meaning a non-Zoroastrian) should be initiated into the faith. While the community was still faced with this conundrum, a Rajput woman who lived with a Parsi and had three children by him, had her *navjote* performed on 18 March 1904.[37] She was ailing, and desired to be placed in the *dakhma* at her death.

A meeting of the Zoroastrian *Anjuman* (assembly of the community) was held in Bombay on 2 March 1905, under the chairmanship of Sir Jamsetji Jeejeebhai. It sought to pass certain Resolutions on the Report submitted to the Trustees of the Bombay Parsi Panchayat by the Committee appointed on 2 August 1903, on the crucial question: 'Whether non-Zoroastrians should be converted to the Zoroastrian faith'.

This public meeting declared:

Resolution 1:
This Anjuman meeting resolves that in the interest of the community, and looking to the religious and social conditions of the Parsi

community, it will be incorrect to convert people from other religions, as such a move would be damaging to the community, and shatter its ancestry and unity.

Resolution 2:

(a) This Anjuman meeting resolves that such non-Zoroastrians who profess themselves as Zoroastrians, and have entered the Parsi Zoroastrian community by any means, that they enjoy no rights and privileges over the funds and institutions of the Parsi Zoroastrian community in Bombay or in any other place, such as Atash Behrams, Adarians, Daremihrs, Dakhmas, Dharamsalas, etc.

(b) This meeting dislikes the act of any Parsi priest who performs the initiation of a non-Zoroastrian for converting such an individual to the Zoroastrian religion. It further resolves that Trustees of all Parsi Zoroastrian charities and Institutions should boycott such priests, and to make public the names and addresses of such priests and to show their total disregard for such priests. It also requests the Trustees of Parsi Zoroastrian Institutions not to allow such priests to perform religious ceremonies in places under their jurisdiction and requesting further the entire community not to get religious ceremonies of their household to be performed through such priests, and also to boycott such places of worship or trusts which would allow the initiation of non-Zoroastrians.

Resolution 3:

This Anjuman meeting resolves that the above 2 Resolutions are also applicable to children of Parsi fathers and non-Parsi mothers or mistresses, that they have no rights or privileges over the Parsi Zoroastrian funds, charities and institutions, as they would be prejudicial to the community. However, children by such marriages who have already been initiated into the Zoroastrian religion are not to be affected by this Resolution as a special case.[38]

THE PARSI PANCHAYAT CASE

As a result of these Resolutions, the ground was prepared for the historic 'Parsi Panchayat Case' (PPC), Suit No. 689 of 1906. The battle lines were drawn between the elite of the community in this legal drama which was to cast its shadow on communal events for the rest of the century. The two judges of the Bombay High Court who presided over this suit were Justice Davar, a Parsi, and Justice Beaman, an Englishman and a leading theosophist. The two fundamental issues which were dealt with in the suit were:

1. Whether the Defendants are validly appointed Trustees of the Properties and Funds of the Parsi Panchayat, and Whether, in the event of death or resignation of one or more of them, they have the right of filling such vacancy or vacancies as they occur; and

2. Whether a person born in another faith and subsequently converted to Zoroastrianism and admitted into that Religion is entitled to the benefit of the religious Institutions and Funds mentioned in the plaint and now in the possession and under the management of the Defendants.

For the purpose of this chapter, it is only the second issue which is relevant to our discussion.

The plaintiffs averred that Zoroastrianism not merely permitted but also enjoined the conversion of others to that faith. And hence once they were initiated into the faith by the *navjote* ceremony, they became not only Zoroastrians but Parsis. They were then entitled to all the rights and privileges of a born Parsi Zoroastrian. They could thereafter have access to all the charitable and religious institutions of the Parsi communiy. The plaintiffs asserted that it was customary for Parsis to admit *juddins* into the faith (PPC, 735–36). Mr R. D. Tata held that as his wife had been initiated, she had become a Parsi (PPC, 759). On the other hand, the defendants maintained that although it might be construed that Zoroastrianism permitted conversion, ever since their arrival in India the Parsis had not admitted a *juddin* into their faith. Because of this, this practice that was understood as favouring conversion had fallen into disuse. They, however, admit that children born of a Zoroastrian father by a non-Zoroastrian mother have been allowed to enter the fold by the performance of the *navjote* ceremony. But no person born of non-Zoroastrian parents, has ever been admitted into the fold (PPC, 736).

An expert committee of scholars had also been appointed to express their views on a number of issues and they had also submitted a report. Scholars from this committee as well as other witnesses were examined in great detail by the Court. A few relevant observations were made by the Court, some of which were based on the Persian *Rivayats*.[39]

• That though the Zoroastrian religion enjoins the conversion of a person born in another religion, the Zoroastrians ever since their advent to India 1200 years ago, have never attempted to convert anyone into their religion. Moreover, there is not a single instance proved before the Court of a person born of both non-Zoroasrian parents ever having been admitted into the Zoroastrian religion professed by the Parsis in India.

- That the Parsi community of Bombay, at a public meeting held on April 16, 1905, expressed its disapproval of any conversions being allowed.
- Concessions could be made for anyone of Zoroastrian origin wanting to revert to the faith of his forefathers. There would of course be the strictly enjoined proviso that such a person seeking conversion does so from religious convictions, not from any other considerations.
- That he should in all other respects be fit to be admitted to the Zoroastrian faith.
- That such an admission is only permissible if 'no harm of any kind would be done to the Zarthosti Mazdyasnans themselves'.
- That the candidate for admission would have to undergo certain religious ceremonies. (PPC, 757–58).

On the question of conversion, Justice Davar further emphasizes that

> No one had for twelve centuries ever made an attempt to convert persons professing other religions. Proselytizing was wholly unknown amongst the Parsis. No one preached the religion or attempted to teach it to an alien. There was not an instance known either in modern or ancient times in India of anybody but a Parsi who professed the Zoroastrian religion. (PPC, 760)

Davar also states:

> If they did attempt anything of the kind, the chances would have been that they would have to go in search of another place of refuge ... that any such attempt would have been so seriously resented that it would have resulted in ruin to the community, whose further continuance in the country depended on the goodwill of the ruling classes, the Hindus. (PPC, 751)

As a large part of the case dealt with the rights and privileges of natural born members of the Parsi community, which would preclude *juddins* converted to Zoroastrianism, Justice Davar tackled this issue in depth. The critical issue was whether a *juddin* who is admitted to the Zoroastrian religion is entitled to participate in the benefits of the Charitable Funds of the Parsi community and be admitted to the benefits of the Religious and Charitable Institutions of the Parsis (PPC, 750). As several trusts had been established many years before this case, this question was of utmost concern. On this issue Justice Davar declared:

> that a *juddin* converted to Zoroastrianism could not possibly have been within the contemplation of the donors and founders. It would be a most violent presumption to make ... a presumption utterly unjustified by the circumstances existing at the time when these institutions were founded ... that the possibility of a *juddin* convert to Zoroastrianism was ever present in the minds of these founders and that they intended to include him. (PPC, 766)

The Judgment further stated that:

> For the reasons I have recorded above, I come to the conclusion that even if an entire alien — a *juddin* — is duly admitted into the Zoroastrian religion after satisfying all conditions and undergoing all necessary ceremonies, he or she would not, as a matter of right, be entitled to the use and benefits of the Funds and Institutions now under the defendants' management and control; that these were founded and endowed only for the members of the Parsi community; and that the Parsi Community consists of Parsis who are descended from the original Persian emigrants, and who are born of both Zoroastrian parents, and who profess the Zoroastrian religion, the Iranians from Persia professing the Zoroastrian religion, who came to India, either temporarily or permanently, and the children of Parsi fathers by alien mothers who have been duly and properly admitted into the religion. (PPC, 773)

In this context it is pertinent to note that there have been Resolutions passed by the community, very much before this case was filed, to show its disapproval of admitting children born of non-Parsi mothers. Such Resolutions were passed in the years 1818, 1830, 1836 and 1850.

The learned jurist also elucidated the terms 'Parsi' and 'Zoroastrian'. 'The word Parsi has only a racial significance and has nothing whatever to do with his religious professions'. The word Parsi is derived from Pars, a province of Iran, from which the inhabitants fled to India. Hence these people from Pars were called Parsis. 'The word Zoroastrian simply denotes the religion of the individual: the word Parsi denotes his nationality or community, and has no religious significance whatever attached to it' (PPC, 759).

The bulk of this one hundred and sixty-four page judgment was written by Justice Davar. Justice Beaman agreed with the main conclusion, although he was not in concurrence with every aspect of this complicated case (PPC, 776).

After years of toil in the Court, this judgment could not bind Mrs Suzanne Tata who had intentionally and deliberately abstained from the Court throughout the proceedings. And Justice Beaman states that part of the judgment is *obiter* (PPC, 782). In legal terms, the Parsi Panchayat Case cannot be deemed to be a law enacted by a legislative body. The practice followed by the Parsi community rests solely on the legal opinion of Justice Davar. And in spite of this it is seen as 'Community Law'. Several issues have been dealt with in this case which have had a resonant impact on the community.

THE ORTHODOX AND REFORMISTS

By the second decade of the twentieth century the positions on both sides had become quite hardened. The community was divided on the question of conversion between the 'orthodox' and the 'reformists'. To the orthodox the importance of preserving racial and religious identity was of the utmost urgency and this could be maintained only though exclusivity. For the reformists, religion could not be confused with race. Jehangir Vimadalal was the person who championed the cause of the orthodox. In several articles and lectures he emphasized the importance of preserving the identity as well as the racial characteristics of the community. He opined that there was no justification for a non-Zoroastrian spouse in an intermarriage to convert to Zoroastrianism. Dastur Dr M. Dhalla who was a scholar and high-priest of Karachi favoured conversion. He interpreted Zoroastrianism as a proselytizing faith. Of the many who disagreed with Dr Dhalla, one who needs to be mentioned is Phiroze Masani, an advocate of the Bombay High Court. He wrote a very detailed tome, *Zoroastrianism, Ancient and Modern*, refuting the stand of Dr Dhalla. He dedicated this work to Justice Davar.

SAKLAT VS. BELLA 1925

Another incident which rocked the community took place in Rangoon in 1915. It related to a child of a Parsi mother and a

128

non-Parsi father. The girl child, Bella, was the orphaned daughter of a Goanese Christian father and a Parsi mother. She grew up in a Zoroastrian home in Rangoon. After her *navjote* was performed, Bella was taken to the Rangoon fire-temple by her adoptive father (a Parsi) on 21 March 1915. After ten days, three Parsis of Rangoon filed a suit against Bella and her adoptive father, claiming that they had 'not only wounded the religious feelings entertained by religiously inclined Parsis, but also caused the desecration of the said sacred temple (Privy Council Judgment)'. The case was thrown out in the preliminary judgment, and the chief court of Lower Burma was in agreement with the initial judgment. An appeal was made before the Privy Council. They ruled that Bella was 'not entitled as of right to use the temple, or to attend or to participate in any of the religious ceremonies performed (Privy Council Judgment)'.

Hence, the right to grant permission to converts to enter a fire-temple is the sole prerogative of the trustees. This is the case to this day. Almost all trusts nowadays controlling fire-temples and towers of silence in India, require the beneficiaries to be both Parsis and Zoroastrians.

REVERTING TO THE ANCESTRAL FAITH

Another incident which once again raked up the conversion controversy took place in recent years. Octogenarian Neville Wadia, the head of the philanthropic Wadia family expressed his long cherished dream of reverting to his ancestral faith. His father who was born a Parsi, had become a Christian and married a non-Parsi. Neville Wadia sought guidance from the high-priests of the community. Before his initiation into the Zoroastrian fold, on 24 September 1994, he wrote to them, clarifying his background:

> In spite of my being brought up in the Church of England, I have all my life, and particularly latterly, been a strong believer in the teachings of Lord Zoroaster, particularly because of its positive attitude and its emphasis on good thoughts, good words, and charity. My own roots are purely Zoroastrian, and under certain circumstances which were beyond my control, this deviation has come into my life. So my desire is to come back into the original Zoroastrian fold. I have always tried to follow the teaching of Zoroaster and act accordingly ...[40]

The four high-priests opined that this reversion to his ancestral religion was possible, if he underwent specified ceremonies. There was an uproar from certain sections of the orthodoxy who felt that this was validating an act of conversion, which should not be allowed. As the high-priests have meticulously laid down their opinions about conversion it is imperative to quote verbatim.

The Principle

The principle is: Zoroastrianism does not accept conversion. According to this principle, if a non-Zoroastrian is converted to Zoroastrianism, that conversion is illegal and invalid. This may be termed 'inward-conversion'. The same principle also lays down that if a Zoroastrian is converted to an alien religion, that conversion is also illegal and invalid. This can be termed 'outward-conversion'. Hence, the principle works both ways.

Zoroastrian Groups

The present Zoroastrian community may broadly be divided into the following groups:

1. Those who lead a good life of virtue, observe religious rites and lead a benevolent life according to circumstances.

2. Those who lead a good life of virtue but neglect religious rites. Still they are considered Zoroastrians in every respect.

3. A Zoroastrian may be a thief, criminal or sinner, even a murderer, still he is regarded as a Zoroastrian enjoying all rights in the community. Such a person is free to attend religious ceremonies and visit places of worship. After death, too, *dokhmenashini* is allowed and all ceremonies are performed without any criticism, objection and opposition, leaving everything to divine justice. He is still considered a Zoroastrian.

4. There might be Zoroastrians who are married to non-Zoroastrian women or who have kept non-Zoroastrian mistresses; such persons enjoy every right as Zoroastrians in the community.

5. There are some Zoroastrians who are attracted to alien rites, philosophy and even to an alien religion. Till only a decade ago, non-Zoroastrian religious ceremonies were openly performed by some Zoroastrians in various places including Nargol, Udvada, Navsari and Surat. The Zoroastrians involved in these alien ceremonies were not regarded as non-Zoroastrians. They have not been debarred from any Zoroastrian institutions or ceremonies. Some Zoroastrians might have formally adopted an alien faith only a generation ago. Such Zoroastrians may be called Zoroastrians who have gone astray. If such Zoroastrians realize their mistake in later life, sincerely repent their past action and express their honest desire to revert to their ancestral religion, without

any ulterior motive, then they are allowed to revert to the ancestral religion after ceremonial repentance (*nahan* and *patet*). Even if the *navjote* is not performed at the proper age, it can be performed after expressions of a genuine desire and sincere repentance.[41]

JUDDIN

Since Parsis live in a pluralistic society, it is imperative to understand what the term *juddin* means to them. It is not at all used in a derogatory sense. Justice Davar explains this explicitly:

> When a Parsi uses the word '*juddin*' when designating a person professing religion other than his own, he does it in no offensive sense. Some of the greatest admirers of the Zoroastrian religion have been *juddins*. Some very learned men of Europe have studied Zoroastrian scriptures, as few Parsis have studied them. They have expounded the scriptural writings of the Zoroastrians, translated them, and written most learned treatises on them. These are all *juddins*, but they are *juddins* whom the Parsis revere, whose friendships while living were most prized by the learned men of the Parsi community, and whose memories are reverently cherished by all Zoroastrians. The religion of Zoroaster teaches its followers to look upon all religions ... with veneration. Therefore, when I refer to these two ladies, the French wife of the 6th plaintiff and the Rajput lady as *juddins*, I mean not the slightest disrespect to them. The word merely signifies born in a religion other than the religion of Zoroaster. (PPC, 750)

'ACCEPTANCE'

Perhaps the issue that most perplexes the Zoroastrians of North America and Canada is the question of conversion. One small group amongst them have introduced the practice of 'acceptance' of aliens into their fold. Those who favour this practice point to the American and Canadian legal and constitutional guarantees regarding the equality of all. They are in favour of 'accepting' the children of a Zoroastrian and a non-Zoroastrian union, irrespective of the fact whether the mother or father is a Zoroastrian. A semi-missionary movement to introduce the faith to non-Zoroastrians may gradually commence. The traditional system of disposal of the dead will give way to burial and cremation.[42] These are among the main features of 'acceptance'. With very few exceptions, mainstream Zoroastrians do not subscribe to this; they consider 'acceptance' a heresy.

Three high-priests of Bombay, Dasturji Dr Mirza, Dasturji Dr Jamaspasa and Dasturji Dr Kotwal wrote *Conversion: A Myth Exploded* in 1983. Dr Kersey Antia of Chicago published *The Argument for Acceptance* in 1985. The three High-Priests refuted his arguments in *Antia's 'Acceptance': A Zoroastrian 'Ahrmogih'* (heresy) (1985). Another earlier work on the subject is *Conversion Caucus* by Dasturji Dr Mirza.[43]

Conclusion

Hence the conversion debate goes on and at times becomes acrimonious. There seems to be no solution which is acceptable to the two sides of this controversy. Aspects of both sides of that controversy may be summarized here. The conservatives justify the ethnic exclusivity of their faith. Besides the reasons already pointed out, there is the belief that all religions are based on truth and a believer should seek that truth in his own faith, the religion of their birth. If he cannot find it in his own religion, how will he find it elsewhere? Moreover, God in his infinite wisdom has given him birth in a particular religion with a definite purpose. Should one question this by opting for another religion? Today, the Parsi population of India is a mere drop in the ocean of this vast subcontinent. We are respected by all the other communities as we have lived in harmony, not treading on the religious susceptibilities of the others. Why should we endanger this goodwill after so many centuries by resorting to the practice of conversion?

In spite of our microscopic population, Parsis have created several charitable trusts which are purely cosmopolitan in nature. There are other trusts which are communal. It is common knowledge that there are instances where persons have converted to another faith for material gains. Many Parsis believe that once the doors are thrown open to converts, the community will be inundated with claims to various charities; whereas genuine converts would only be a handful.

It is further pointed out that Zoroastrianism as a religion is part of an ancient culture. This culture comprises of a way of life, a distinctive language, literature, food, songs, poetry, festivals and humour. These are salient features of a culture. This heritage has been preserved for thousands of years and every attempt should be made to conserve it. After the Arab conquest, when Zoroastrians fled Iran, a group migrated to China. They have been totally wiped out, probably because of intermarriage. We know about them only from certain historians and the fire-temples that lie there in ruins.

On the other hand, the liberal reformists notice that the community is diminishing at an alarming rate and, if this trend continues there will hardly be any Parsis by the middle of the next century. Conversion, they believe, can reverse this trend. There is no doubt that the community is shrinking and it is a cause for grave concern for all thinking Parsis.

Moreover, the liberal reformists declare that Zoroastrianism has been a proselytizing religion and there is ample evidence from Iranian history to prove this. If this was not so, how could the religion have spread to various countries of the ancient world? Besides this, they argue that the *Gathas* which are the hymns of Zarathushtra speak of conversion. Dastur Dr Mirza and others have refuted these arguments in their works quoted here. The traditionalists maintain that there is no perfect translation of the *Gathas*. In fact, there are several translations of these hymns and there is no unanimity among scholars regarding their content. Moreover, the conversion that Zarathushtra speaks about is moral or inner conversion.

Perhaps we need to initiate a healthy dialogue within the community in which all participants listen to one another and attempt to discern what should be done. Perhaps then a referendum could be held among the Parsis of India. Till then, there does not seem to be any solution to the question of conversion facing the Parsis of India.

Notes

1. The missionary impulse is rooted in the command to the disciples to 'Go therefore and make disciples of all nations ...' (Matt 28:19).
2. Harvey Cox, *Turning East* (Harmondsworth: Penguin, 1979), p. 154.
3. Brojendra Banerjee, *Religious Conversions in India* (New Delhi: Harnam Publications, 1982), pp. 193–9.
4. Ibid., p. 229.
5. *Report of the Christian Missionary Activities Enquiry Committee*, Madhya Pradesh, vol. 1 (1956), pp. 7, 9.

6. Banerjee, *Religious Conversions in India*, pp. 219–21, 228–9.
7. Cited in ibid., p. 24.
8. D. Smith, *India as a Secular State* (Princeton, NJ: Princeton University Press, 1963), p. 171.
9. Dhirendra Srivastava, *Religious Freedom in India* (Delhi: Deep & Deep Publications, 1982), p. 157.
10. *All India Reporter*, Nagpur, 1977, p. 908.
11. Banerjee, *Religious Conversions in India*, pp. 260–1.
12. *Young India*, 23 April 1931.
13. Ibid., 29 May 1924.
14. In S. Radhakrishnan, *Eastern Religions and Western Thought* (2nd edn, Oxford: Clarendon Press, 1940), pp. 335, 330.
15. Swami Vivekananda, *Hinduism* (Madras: Sri Ramakrishna Math, 1976), p. 16.
16. Francis Cardinal Arinze, 'Interreligious Dialogue: A Roman Catholic Perspective', *The CSWR Bulletin*, Harvard University, Silver Jubilee Issue, 1960–85 (1985), pp. 14–15.
17. 'Be Humble, Runcie tells Christians', *The Times of India*, Bombay, 21 February 1986, p. 23.
18. *Summary Report From The Assembly of Religious and Spiritual Leaders*, 1993 Parliament of the World's Religions, 28 August–5 September 1993, Chicago, p. 5.
19. *Current Dialogue* 29 (Geneva: World Council of Churches, January 1996), p. 4.
20. Ibid., p. 5.
21. Ibid., p. 11.
22. Ibid., p. 19.
23. Ibid. p. 34.
24. *IRFWP Newsletter*, vol. IV, no. 1 (New York, Spring 1996), p. 3.
25. S. Shahbuddin, 'Conversions: A Quest for Equality or a Challenge to Hindu India', *Indian Express*, Bombay, 6 Sept. 1981, p. 2.
26. 'Curb Conversion by Law: Panel', *The Times of India*, Bombay, 13 May 1986, p. 12.
27. S. Abdi, 'Are These Men Dangerous?', *The Illustrated Weekly of India*, Bombay, 22 December 1985.
28. 'Thousands Convert to Buddhism', *The Times of India*, Bombay, 7 December 1993, p. 7.
29. 'Hindu Group's Bid to Reconvert Christians', *The Times of India*, Bombay, 7 August 1995, p. 9.
30. N. Mishra, 'Missionaries get RI for Converting Tribals', *Indian Express*, Pune, 31 January 1996, p. 13.
31. 'VHP Demands Apology from Christians', *Communalism Combat*, Bombay, June 1996, p. 7.

32. V. Date, 'BJP MLA Seeks to Make Conversion an Offence', *The Times of India*, Bombay, 5 August 1996, p. 3.
33. E. Kulke, *The Parsis in India* (Bombay: Vikas Publishing House, 1974), p. 239.
34. J. Nehru, *The Discovery of India* (Bombay: Asia Publishing House, 1960), p. 138.
35. *Iran League Quarterly*, Bombay, October 1947–January 1948, p. 162.
36. Ibid. p. 161.
37. Shapur Desai, *History of the Bombay Parsi Panchayet, 1860–1960* (Bombay, 1977), p. 15.
38. *Parsi Prakash*, vol. IV, Bombay, 16 April 1905, p. 14.
39. Persian *Rivayat*. From the fifteenth to the seventeenth centuries, the Parsi priests of India addressed a number of questions to their co-religionists in Iran on scripture, religion, customs and practices. Lengthy answers were received on these matters and this entire literature was termed as '*Rivayats*'.
40. *Parsiana*, Bombay, October 1994, p. 31.
41. Ibid., November 1995, pp. 29–32.
42. Ibid., February–March, 1995, p. 86.
43. Dastur Dr Hormazdyar Mirza, *Conversion Caucus* (Udava, Bombay: Dastur Kayoji Mirza Institute, 1971).

8. Conversion: a Hindu / Gandhian perspective

K. L. Seshagiri Rao

In this chapter I shall discuss a representative Hindu approach to the theme of 'conversion' as crystallized in the life, thought and experience of Mahatma Gandhi. Because of historical and biographical considerations, I have, for the major part, dealt with the topic in the context of Gandhi's relations with Christianity, though the principles involved are applicable to other world religions also.

Rarely perhaps has any religious personality in modern times experienced so keen a struggle within himself regarding the momentous issues of religion and faith as has Mahatma Gandhi. His whole life was one unceasing endeavour 'to see God face to face'. It was his religious motivation that made his life a compelling example and the centre of attention of peoples throughout the world. Though he did not yield to the persistent efforts made to convert him to a religion other than his own, he could open himself to and benefit by the insights of other religions in his lifelong pilgrimage towards the realization of Truth and non-violence.

Family background

In the life of the Gandhi family, religion played a vital part. In Kathiawar, on the west coast of India, Jainism exercised an enduring influence along with Vaishnavism. Gandhi's non-violence, vegetarianism, and many other traits of his religious personality date from his early years. He seems to have received a bent of mind towards personal piety and honesty from his parents. His father had friends in all faiths and they visited him frequently for religious discussions.

Young Mohandas, while attending on his father, listened to these discussions with Hindus, Muslims, Parsis, Jains and adherents of other religions. All these made him very tolerant in his religious ideas and non-sectarian in nature. He later wrote:

> In Rajkot, I got an early grounding in toleration for all branches of Hinduism and sister religions. For my father and mother would visit the Haveli as also Shiva and Rama temples, and would take or send us youngsters there. Jain monks also would pay frequent visits to my father, and would even go out of their way to accept food from us non-Jains.

But his earliest impressions of Christianity were disturbing. 'In those days, Christian missionaries used to stand in a corner near the high school and hold forth pouring abuse on Hindus and their gods', and many Hindus converted to Christianity 'ate beef and drank liquor'.[1]

During this period, he read Hindu religious texts such as the *Ramayan*, the *Bhagavata* and the *Manu Smriti* from his father's library. He was especially impressed by the Indian play *Harischandra*, in which the hero had a profound passion for honesty and truth and had to suffer many ordeals for maintaining his integrity. The young Gandhi wanted to be like this hero. Gandhi never received any vedic, theological or philosophical training. And the roots of his emotional and intellectual activity seem to have remained in popular Hindu literature and devotional hymns.

In England

Gandhi left for England in 1888 to qualify himself as a barrister. He spent a large part of his time in London cultivating the acquaintances of personalities who had made their mark in the fields of religion and ethics – theosophists, Christians, even atheists. In his teen years, Gandhi was for a brief period drawn toward atheism. His doubts were not adequately answered by the religious writings that came his way. But, he later on recalls that even then he had a regard for morality as the basis of all things, and truth as the substance of morality: 'Truth became my sole objective. It began to grow in magnitude everyday, and my definition of it has also been ever widening.'[2]

The literature of theosophists introduced him to the religious movement for the unity of religions. Edwin Arnold's *The Light of*

Asia, about the life of the Buddha, made a lasting impression on him, and his version of the Bhagavadgita, *The Song Celestial*, stirred him so deeply that for the rest of his life it became his constant guide. He was also much moved by the teachings of the New Testament, and especially by the Sermon on the Mount. The verses, 'But I say unto you that ye resist not evil; but whosoever shall smite thee on thy right cheek, turn to him the other also', went straight to his heart. He wrote later about this experience: 'My young mind tried to unify the teaching of the *Gita*, *The Light of Asia* and the *Sermon on the Mount*. That renunciation was the highest form of religion appealed to me greatly.' Further, from Carlyle's *Heroes and Hero Worship*, he learned of Mohammed's 'greatness, bravery and austere living'. He also read Washington Irving's *Life of Mohammed and His Successors*. These books raised Mohammad in his estimation. Thus he gained more and more knowledge of different religious traditions. They gave him some of the basic principles of his life, and he became inclined towards a life of acceptance and assimilation of the spiritual truths of the Eastern and Western traditions.

In South Africa

Gandhi's life in South Africa presented him with direct experience of good as well as terrible aspects of religion. He witnessed many cruelties and inhumanities, practised in the name of 'religion'. He had hardly set foot in South Africa in the spring of 1891, when he became involved in the racial and colour conflict. One experience, especially, changed the course of his life. He was travelling in a train with a first class ticket, but was turned out of his compartment to make way for a white passenger. In the midnight cold of Maritzburg, he was not allowed even to enter a waiting room, because of the colour of his skin. Then the moment of decision came: should he go back to India or stay in South Africa and start a lifelong struggle for human justice? He decided to stay and fight injustice.

During one of his journeys from Johannesburg to Durban, Gandhi read John Ruskin's *Unto This Last*. It made a tremendous impact on him: 'The book was impossible to lay aside; once I had begun, it gripped me. I could not get any sleep that night. I determined to change my life in accordance with the ideals of that book.'[3] He realized that 'a life of labour, i.e., the life of the tiller of the soil and the handicraft man is the life worth living'.[4] He got up at dawn that morning and resolved to give up his career as a successful lawyer in order to become an Indian peasant; he decided to transform his whole mode of existence, his profession and even his private life.

To realize the new way life, he established an *ashram,* an experimental spiritual community, the Phoenix settlement near Durban. The a*shram* was a kind of 'moral laboratory', where his experiments in truth and non-violence were conducted in the living of daily life. The inmates of the *ashram* belonged to different religions and races. There were no dividing lines of class, creed or nationality. They lived a life of voluntary poverty, purity and self-restraint. In the community life of the *ashram,* Gandhi gave first priority to the culture of the heart. To him, to develop the spirit was to develop character. He encouraged members to keep their respective religious observances. For example, Muslims observed their *ramadan* fast, Hindus their *pradosha* (fast until evening) and Christians their Lent. The value of the experiment was that all the inmates became convinced of the value of fasting and the practice of self-denial.

A passion for simplicity and service took hold of Gandhi; he volunteered to become a compounder and a nurse in a charitable hospital and gave two hours of his time in the morning to this work. When Boer War began in 1899, Gandhi organized an Indian Ambulance Corps and offered its services to the authorities. In 1904, when plague broke out in Johannesburg, he closed his law office and devoted himself to sanitary work and the evacuation and nursing of victims. In 1906, when the Zulu rebellion occurred in Natal, he organized from among the Indian community a stretcher bearer company and offered its services to the government.

One of the persons who exercised a most decisive influence on Gandhi during this period was Count Leo Tolstoy; in his first year in Africa, in Pretoria, Gandhi read *The Kingdom of God is Within You.* In Durban, he read some other later works of Tolstoy such as *Gospels in Brief* and *What to Do.* Tolstoy furnished a reasoned basis for Gandhi's non-violence. Gandhi developed a new political tool for the masses, *satyagraha.* The South African Indians, under the leadership of Gandhi, launched a non-violent struggle against the discrimination to which the Transvaal Government had subjected them. The method he chose to adopt in his fight was that of insistence on truth without violence – *satyagraha* – a method inspired by Tolstoy's writings, by the New Testament and by Thoreau's *Essay on Civil Disobedience*. In the course of this eventful and protracted struggle, the basic outlines of his religious and moral philosophy were drawn in the light of his spiritual and practical experience.

Gandhi and Christian missionaries

At the beginning of the twentieth century, the attitude frequently adopted by Christian missionaries in relation to Hinduism was to dismiss it as a religion of superstition and crass idolatry. They did not think it worth taking seriously. They had an implicit belief that the Western nations possessed a superior religion and culture. They went out to give and not to receive; their aim was to spread Christianity. The technique often adopted was to exaggerate the so-called vulnerable points in Hindu thought and practice, with little appreciation of the good elements in them. The missionaries' works of philanthropy and educational services were often used as means for winning converts.

Gandhi came in contact with the adherents of a variety of Christian sects. A good deal of efforts were made to convert Gandhi to Christianity. It was thought that he was too good not to be a Christian. A fellow lawyer in South Africa, A. W. Baker led Gandhi to his own private prayer meeting where the latter joined a group of devout Christians in prayer. A prayer was made for Gandhi's welfare: 'Lord, show the path to the new brother, who has come amongst us. May the Lord Jesus who has saved us save him too. We ask all this in the name of Jesus.'[5]

Another lawyer, Mr Coates, a Quaker, gave Gandhi selected books on Christianity and took evening walks with him in the hope that the latter would see the light through his discourses. Once Coates noticed around Gandhi's neck a Vaishnava necklace of *Tulsi* beads. He thought that it was an evidence of Hindu superstition, and he was pained:

'This superstition does not become you,' he said, 'Come let me break this necklace.'
'No. It is a sacred gift from my mother.'
'But you believe in it?'
'I do not know its mysterious significance. I do not think I should come

to harm if I do not wear it. But I cannot without sufficient reason give up a necklace that she put round my neck out of love. When with the passage of time, it wears away, I shall have no desire to get a new one. But this necklace cannot be broken.'[6]

Coates believed that Gandhi could not be saved until he embraced Christianity. His sins could not be washed away except by the intervention of Jesus. So Coates continued his efforts, and introduced Gandhi to a family of Plymouth Brethren, another Christian sect. One of them took Gandhi by surprise by saying: 'It appears you must be brooding over your transgressions every moment of your life, always mending them and atoning for them. How can this ceaseless cycle of action bring you redemption? ... How can we bear the burden of sin? We can but throw it on Jesus.' To this Gandhi replied: 'I do not seek redemption from the consequences of my sin. I seek to be redeemed from sin itself or from the very thought of sin.'[7]

Gandhi enjoyed the close friendship of many Christian missionaries. They had awakened his religious quest, for which he was thankful. But he was their constructive critic as well. He commended their humanitarian work. Their insistence on service to society as well as their preference for the poor and the humble made a strong appeal to him.

Religion and culture

Religious faith, according to Gandhi, is the strongest force by which many people are sustained in the conduct of their life, and anything that tended to weaken that faith would be a disservice to religion itself. He, therefore, maintained that no one should be induced to reject his own tradition outright. Just as a man cannot renounce his own body, his family and his kin, similarly one cannot renounce the cultural and religious heritage into which one is born.

Gandhi believed that all people should be firmly rooted in their respective traditions, and then purify them if and where necessary. He was emphatically against proselytization. He wrote: 'Religion is a matter of life and death. A man does not change his religion as he changes his garments. He takes it with him beyond the grave. Nor does a man profess his religion to oblige others. He professes a religion because he cannot do otherwise.'[8] Gandhi believed that all religions are branches of one and the same tree – the tree of Truth. The shape and size of the branches may vary, but the same vital juice runs through them all. At the same time he held that all religions are imperfect, because truth comes to human beings through human channels. He thought that there was no point in tearing away a man from the natural surroundings of his own religion and putting him inside an alien religion. He was against uprooting from anybody's mind, and especially from the minds of innocent and simple people, the faith in their respective religions. He deprecated the attempts of missionaries to change people's religions all of a sudden with no effective realization of the interplay between the individual and his cultural environment. For example, many Harijan ('untouchable') converts to Christianity became apathetic and morally and spiritually lost ground after having lost their 'gods'. He felt keenly about such conversions.

A person usually prefers that particular tradition in which he is born, lives and acts; but such a preference does not mean that other religions are false or inadequate. For example, the attitude that Christians alone are the chosen people, that the Christian Church is the only church of God and that Christianity is the only true religion is not acceptable. Such an attitude, firstly, disables people from comprehending the growing fullness of truth; and second, controversies over dogmas and doctrines of different religions can never be settled. In the heat and dust of dogmatic controversies, there is the danger of the denial of religion itself. To consider one's own religion as superior to others' religions is a travesty of true religion.

Gandhi's own approach to the subject was very different. He advocated firmness of faith. He could no more think of asking a Christian or a Muslim to change his religion than he could think of changing his own. As he explained:

> Here is Miraben.[9] I would have her find all the spiritual comfort she needs from Christianity, and I should not dream of converting her to Hinduism, even if she wanted to do so. Today it is the case of a grown-up woman like her; tomorrow it may be that of a European child entrusted to my care by a friend. Take the case of Khan Saheb's daughter entrusted to my care by her father. I should jealously educate her in her own faith and should strive my utmost against her being lured away from it, even if ever she was so inclined. I have had the privilege of having children and grown-

up persons of other faiths with me. I was thankful to find them better Christians, Muslims, Parsis, or Jews by their contact with me ... Let my missionary friends remember that it was none but that most Christ-like of all Christians, Albert Schweitzer, who gave Christianity a unique interpretation when he himself resolved "not to preach any more, not to lecture any more" but to bury himself in Equatorial Africa simply with a view to fulfil somewhat the debt that Europe owes to Africa.[10]

It is not doing justice to the love of God to restrict his love to any group, nation, church or creed. God, being the Father of all, is concerned with each human being, whether Hindu, Muslim or Christian. The entire human race relies on his power and grace. Everyone should pursue salvation by the light of his or her own faith and experience. 'The hour is coming, when neither on this mountain nor in Jerusalem will you worship the Father' (John 4:21). 'God is spirit and those who worship him must worship him in spirit and truth' (John 4:25).

The impact of Christianity

In the supreme sacrifice of Jesus Christ on the cross, Gandhi saw an unfailing source of inspiration for mankind. The Sermon on the Mount impressed his mind and became a dominant factor which moulded his life. While Christian theology did not attract him, Christ's life and example reached the depths of his heart. He understood that the cross was not something to be believed in and to be subscribed to as a dogma but as something to be lived and borne in life and experience.

The New Testament symbol of the Kingdom of God impressed Gandhi profoundly, both in its individual and social aspects. It revealed to him the inner truths of the Christian message in its moral aspect. He was deeply moved as he read that the 'Kingdom' belonged to the humble and the poor, that the 'persecuted and the meek' are its citizens, that the 'pure in heart' see it, that to 'love one's enemies' is to be perfect, that the 'Kingdom of God is within you', and that the Kingdom is not meat or drink, but righteousness, peace and joy in the Holy Spirit; it is a present possibility of goodness hidden in every person. Gandhi wrote: 'I have no desire for the perishable

Kingdom of earth; I am striving for the Kingdom of heaven which is spiritual deliverance. For me the road to salvation lies through incessant toil for the service of my country and humanity.' Gandhi thus absorbed the New Testament's teaching, but found no reason to change his religious allegiance. The cause of God's Kingdom has other advocates besides those we find within the Christian Church.

Gandhi acknowledged his deep debt to Christianity and to other faiths. He developed a capacity for assimilating insights from other traditions. But he insisted that 'while we should throw open our windows for fresh breezes from different directions, we should refuse to be swept off our feet'.[11] In a revealing conversation, Gandhi told Mrs Henry Polak in South Africa: 'The gentle figure of Christ, so patient, so kind, so loving, so full of forgiveness that he taught his followers not to retaliate when abused or struck, but to turn the other cheek. I thought it was a beautiful example of a perfect man.' 'But you did not embrace Christianity, did you?,' she asked. 'No,' replied Gandhi thoughtfully. 'I studied your scriptures for some time and thought earnestly about them ... but eventually, I came to the conclusion that there was no need for me to join your creed to be a believer in the beauty of the teaching of Jesus or to try to follow his example.'[12]

Proselytization

Gandhi deprecated the offering of material advantages like money, educational facilities and medical service to secure religious conversion. He thought conversions secured through secular aids to be degrading; he doubted whether they commanded the respect of and did honour to any religion. He observed:

> I hold that proselytizing under the cloak of humanitarian work is, to say the least, unhealthy. It is most certainly resented by the people here. Religion, after all, is a deeply personal matter; it touches the heart. Why should I change my religion because a doctor who professes Christianity has cured me of some disease or why should the doctor expect or suggest such a change whilst I am under his influence? Or why should I in a missionary educational institution have Christian teaching thrust upon me? In my opinion, these practices are not uplifting and give rise to suspicion if not even secret hostility.[13]

Elsewhere he observed, 'Conversion and service go ill together.'[14]

People should help one another to rise to higher heights of moral and spiritual life, potential in their respective religious traditions. There should be no attempt to 'wean out' anyone from his or her religious affiliation. Gandhi gave his considered opinion on conversion thus:

> I believe that there is no such thing as conversion from one faith to another in the accepted sense of the term. It is a highly personal matter for the individual and his God. I may not have any design upon my neighbour as to his faith, which I must honour even as I honour my own. For I regard all the great religions as true, at any rate for the people professing them, as mine is true for me ... And seeing that it takes all my resources in trying to bring my practice to the level of my faith and in preaching the same to my co-religionists, I do not dream of preaching to the followers of other faiths. 'Judge not lest you be judged' is a sound maxim for one's conduct. It is a conviction daily growing upon me that the great and rich Christian missions will render true service to India if they can persuade themselves to confine their activities to humanitarian service without the ulterior motive of converting India, or at least her unsophisticated villagers, to Christianity and destroying their social superstructure which notwithstanding its many defects has withstood from time immemorial the onslaughts on it from within and from without.[15]

Nevertheless, Gandhi tried to understand the urge behind the missionary motive. He welcomed the sharing of one's experience of truth with others. But he pointed out that this could not be in one direction only. Further, he maintained that religion is best propagated through the noble lives led by its followers; no other propaganda could match that:

> To live the Gospel is the most effective way ... most effective in the beginning, in the middle, and in the end. Preaching jars on me and makes no appeal to me, and I get suspicious of missionaries who preach; but I love those who never preach but live the life according to their lights. There lives are a silent and yet most effective testimony. Therefore I cannot say what to preach, but I can say that a life of service and uttermost simplicity is the best preaching. A rose does not need to preach. It simply spreads its fragrance. The fragrance is its own sermon. If it had human understanding and if it could engage a number of preachers, the preachers would not be able to sell more roses than the fragrance itself could do. The fragrance of religious and spiritual life is much finer and subtler than that of the rose.[16]

In the spiritual transformation of life, one may draw inspiration from every available source. It is not necessary to discard one's own religion to benefit by the teachings of other great religions.

> If a person wants to believe in the Bible let him say so; but why should he discard his own religion? This proselytisation will mean no peace in the world. Religion is a very personal matter. We should by living the life according to our lights share the best with one another, thus adding to the sum total of human effort to reach God.[17]

Further, 'It is tragic to see that religion is dragged down to the low level of crude materialism, to lure people into which the most cherished sentiments of millions of human beings are trodden underfoot.'[18]

Vertical conversion

At the same time, Gandhi maintained that conversion in the sense of self-purification and self-realization was the crying need of our day. It is a normal need in humanity's moral development. This phenomenon occurs when people are made aware of a higher truth or universal value than that within which they are living, and at the same time become conscious that the higher value is one which they ought to realize. There is a crisis in their moral life, and life takes on a new aspect; the mind turns in criticism upon the life that is past. It is at such times that the inner life becomes prominent. Gandhi suggested:

> Conversion should mean a definite giving up of the evil of the old, adoption of all the good of the new, and a scrupulous avoidance of everything evil in the new. Conversion should therefore mean a life of greater dedication to one's own country, greater surrender to God, and greater self purification.[19]

But the modern methods of conversion rarely focus on the quality of inner life. 'Conversion nowadays has become a matter of business. I remember having read a missionary report saying how much it cost per head to convert and then presenting a budget for "the next harvest".'[20]

In the psychological sense, real conversion, or inner change of heart, with corresponding differences in outward ways of life, is recognized as the birth of true religion in man. But real conversion or rebirth in spirit takes place in the lives of very few persons. Without the wonderful blessing of conversion a God-centred life is impossible. When such a new life begins, there is a new quickening of the spirit, a stronger attachment to God, and a new discipline to strengthen one's life. It is the incursion of purity; it is a new birth. He is the truly regenerate person who has been reborn and whose face is now turned towards God. Such alone realize God. 'Except one is born anew, he cannot see the kingdom of God' (John 3:3). In such conversions, the ethical and spiritual life of the person concerned is raised to a higher level and the heart is uplifted. One begins a new life which establishes the kingdom of God in the heart, bringing the joy of spiritual fulfilment. To be born of the spirit is indeed the real conversion. In the words of Gandhi, 'Real conversion springs from the heart and at the prompting of God not of a stranger. The voice of God can always be distinguished from the voice of Man.'[21]

Conversion is from the Latin verb *convertere* meaning to turn or change. Hence conversion means turning about or changing. True conversion is an actual overturning of the inner life. It opens up a new vision to morality and spirituality. In the words of Evelyn Underhill:

> Conversion then is the larger world consciousness now pressing on the individual consciousness. Often it breaks in suddenly and becomes a great new revelation. This is the first aspect of conversion; the person emerges from a smaller limited world of existence into a world of being. His life becomes swallowed up in a large world of being, in a larger whole.[22]

Conversion in this sense within the context of one's own religion is the first necessity of our times, not just changing of religious labels. As a matter of fact,

> Nothing wonderful will happen to the world if the entire mankind be converted to Hinduism, Christianity, Buddhism, or Islam or to any other religion, but assuredly something marvellous will happen if a dozen of men and women pierce the thick walls of the church, temple, synagogue, and realize the Truth.[23]

A person with the infectious fervour of creative religion must first of all work with his own religious group to kindle the fire of spirituality among his co-religionists. But to force the belief in one's own prophet as the only saviour on all others is unacceptable.

Salvation

The aim of all great religions is the spiritual salvation of human
beings. Each spiritual tradition has sustained the hearts and minds of
millions of people down the ages. Each of them has an individuality
and a message. Each has attempted to solve life's problems in its own
way. All of them have supplied answers to the persisting questions of
the mysteries of existence. They have enlightened humanity on the
path of right conduct and have given solace in the face of suffering
and death. Every religion extols human kindness and charity. If any
religion claims a monopoly of truth and salvation or elevates itself
over all other traditions ignoring the spiritual values in other
religions, then religious conflict, scepticism and materialism become
inevitable. For example, Wilfred Cantwell Smith considers that it is
unchristian to think that Christianity is the only true religion and the
others are either false or insufficient. He fervently appeals:

> May I plead that we abandon, as utterly unworthy, the traditional notion
> that if Christianity is true, then it must follow that other faiths are false –
> or at least inadequate. This entire formulation seems to me inept; the ideas
> juxtaposed just do not cohere ... For the moment, let me point out some
> ways in which such a position gets one tied up in unchristian knots. For
> example, there is danger of the converse proposition; that if anyone else's
> faith turns out to be valid or adequate, then it would follow that
> Christianity must be false – a form of logic that has, in fact, driven many
> from their own faiths, and indeed from any faith at all. If one's chances of
> getting to Heaven – or to use a now-a-days more acceptable metaphor, of
> coming into God's presence – are dependent upon other people's not
> getting there, then one becomes walled up within the quite intolerable
> position that the Christian has a vested interest in other men's damnation.
> It is shocking to admit it, but this actually takes place. When an observer
> comes back from Asia, or from a study of Asian religious traditions, and
> reports that contrary to accepted theory some Hindus and Buddhists and
> some Muslims lead a pious and moral life and seem very near to God by
> any possible standard, so that as one can see in these particular cases at
> least, faith is as 'adequate' as Christian faith, then presumably a Christian
> should be overjoyed, enthusiastically hopeful that this be true, even though
> he may be permitted a fear lest it be not so. Instead, I have sometimes
> witnessed just the opposite: an emotional resistance to the news, one
> hoping firmly that it is not so though perhaps with a covert fear that it
> might be. Whatever the rights and wrongs of the situation theoretically, I
> submit that this is just not Christian, and is indeed not tolerable. It will not

do, to have a faith that can be undermined by God's saving one's neighbour; or to be afraid lest other men turn out to be closer to God than one has been led to suppose.[24]

Religious harmony

Conversion programmes of today lie directly in the path of religious harmony; they are exercising the minds of many thinking people all over the world. There is a need to understand the urge behind such programmes and to point out a way of reconciliation between different religions. Gandhi insisted that whatever is high and noble in any religious tradition should be accepted, and whatever separates man from man should be rejected. Humanity's best spiritual resources are to be rallied to help resolve the crisis of our times. What religions are called upon to undertake at this time, when the world has become one, is an adventure in faith, a fuller sharing of the deepest and the best within them, in a joint endeavour to achieve a just and peaceful world order in the religious field as in others. The integrity of each religious tradition is to be safeguarded. This has now become the very condition not only of human welfare but of human survival.

The time is ripe for a reorientation of the religious outlook on a worldwide scale. Modern scientific achievements have annihilated distances and brought peoples and religions of the world nearer to one another than ever before. Truthful and unreserved intercourse with other great cultures and religions has become an urgent necessity in the context of the modern world order. Gandhi held that each religion must bring its individual contribution to humanity's understanding of the spiritual world. He believed that all the world's religions are God-given, and that they were necessary for the people to whom these religions were revealed. Therefore, while religions confront one another on a worldwide front, if they do not co-operate in friendly fellowship, it will only lead to a general decay of the religious spirit. Gandhi cautioned that it is dangerous to humankind as a whole to overemphasize the parochial. If religious peace and harmony are to be achieved, worldly competition in the field of religion must be avoided. The resources of all the great religions of the world are needed to eradicate evil and injustice in human society and to work for the greater glory of God and the greater happiness of humankind.

Notes

1. M. K. Gandhi, *An Autobiography* [1927] (Boston: Beacon Press, 1966), p. 4
2. Ibid., p. 34.
3. Ibid., p. 288.
4. Ibid., p. 289.
5. Ibid., p. 153.
6. Ibid., p. 154.
7. Ibid., p. 156.
8. *Harijan*, 17 January 1937.
9. An English woman who became a disciple of Gandhi, who wanted at one time to become a Hindu.
10. *Harijan*, 25 January 1935.
11. See Seshagiri Rao, *Mahatma Gandhi and Comparative Religion* (Delhi: Motilal Banarsidass, 1978), p. 153.
12. Krishna Kripalani, *Gandhi: A Life* (London: George Allen and Unwin, 1970), p. 23.
13. *Young India*, 23 April 1931.
14. *Young India*, 19 January 1928.
15. *Harijan*, 28 September 1935.
16. *Harijan*, 29 March 1935.
17. *Young India*, 23 September 1926.
18. *Harijan*, 8 August 1936.
19. *Young India*, 20 August 1925.
20. *Young India*, 23 April 1931.
21. *Harijan*, 25 September 1937.
22. E. Underhill, *Mysticism* [1911] (New York: Meridian Books, 1960), p. 214.
23. Swami Nikhilanada, *The Mandukya Upanishad with Gandapada's Karika* (Mysore: Sri Ramakrishna Math, n.d.), p. xxxv.
24. Wilfred Cantwell Smith, *Occasional Papers* (London: Department of Missionary Studies) No. 5, April 1960.

9. Conversion to Islam: the Qur'anic paradigm

Yasin Dutton

Introduction

Islam is based on the Qur'an, which is accepted by Muslims as the final revelation from God to man through the medium of His final Messenger Muhammad, whose life is in turn seen as the best example of how this Qur'anic message was and should be put into practice. Thus the two main sources of Islam, whether for matters of belief or practice, are firstly the Qur'an and, secondly, the *sunna*, or normative model, of the Prophet Muhammad, as recorded by those around him and transmitted to those after them down to the present day. In this chapter we look at the phenomenon of conversion to Islam, basing our remarks primarily on what is said about it in the Qur'an and on how this Qur'anic picture was reflected in the lives of the Prophet and the first community of Muslims.

Conversion as 'submission'

There is no word in Arabic for 'conversion' *per se*. Rather, there is the idea of 'becoming a Muslim', for which the verb *aslama* (literally, 'to submit') is used. It is from this verb that the words 'Muslim', which is, grammatically, the active participle and means 'one who submits, a submitter', and 'Islam', which is the verbal noun – equivalent to the gerund in English – and means 'submitting, submission', are derived. Thus it could be said that to understand conversion to Islam, one need go no further than understanding the name 'Islam' itself.

Since the word *islam* is, grammatically speaking, a verbal noun, it has a distinct verbal force behind it. Thus 'Islam' is not simply the name of a religion in the way that, for example, 'Christianity', 'Hinduism' and 'Buddhism' are, but actually denotes an action – in this case predominantly of the heart, although also of the limbs – that should be the hallmark of this religion, namely, 'submission'. It is in this way that the word *islam* and its associated forms are invariably used in the Qur'an.

Beyond this 'verbal', or active, quality of the word *islam*, the first point to note about the Qur'anic usage of the term is that this activity of submission is associated with all the prophets and not just the Prophet Muhammad. Thus Noah – the archetypal 'early', or pre-Abrahamic, prophet in Qur'anic terms – tells his people that he has been ordered to be 'one of those who submit / one of the Muslims' (Ar. *min al-muslimin*; Q. 10:72). Abraham is associated with *islam* on many occasions: he is ordered by God to 'submit' and he does so (Q. 2:131); he asks God that both he and his son be 'submitters' to Him, as also his descendants (Q. 2:128), and he tells his sons not to die in any state other than one of 'submission' to God (Q. 2:132). Most importantly, he is described as having been neither a Jew nor a Christian, but rather a 'pure worshipper of God (*hanif*) and a submitter (*muslim*)' and one who 'was not an idolater' (Q. 3:67). Indeed, according to one interpretation, it is Abraham who is credited with adopting the term 'submitter' (*muslim*) to describe the pure worshippers of God (Q. 22:78). Joseph, one of Abraham's great-grandsons, asks God to make him die in a state of submission (i.e. 'as a *muslim*'; Q. 12:101). Bilqis, the Queen of Sheba, accepts Solomon's prophetic authority and 'submits' with him to God, the Lord of the Worlds (Q. 27:44). Moses encourages his people to be 'submitters' (Q. 10:84), while Pharaoh's magicians, after witnessing the signs of divine authority in Moses' actions, accept that Moses has superior knowledge and, like Joseph, ask God that they be allowed to die as 'submitters' to Him (Q. 7:126). Even Pharaoh himself, when he is about to drown, claims to be a 'submitter', although by then it is too late (Q. 10:90). Later in time, the followers of Jesus acknowledge that they are 'submitters' (Q. 3:52, 5:11), and, in more general terms, the People of the Book (i.e. the Jews and the Christians) who accept the message of the Qur'an acknowledge that they were already 'submitters' beforehand (Q. 28:53). Indeed, all the prophets of the People of the Book are among 'those who have submitted' (Q. 5:44). It is, perhaps, needless to say that there are numerous references to the Prophet Muhammad and his followers being encouraged, if not ordered, to take exactly the same attitude as the former prophets and to 'submit' themselves to God, the Lord of the Worlds, and not to die except in a state of *islam*, or submission, to Him (e.g. Q. 2:133, 136; 3:20, 64, 84, 102; 4:125; 11:14, 16:81; 21:108; 22:34; 29:46; 39:54).

All of these references make it clear that what is being envisaged here by *islam*, or 'becoming a Muslim', is not simply the acceptance of the outward forms of any one particular prophet's practice, not even that of the 'Seal of the Prophets', Muhammad. Rather, the word represents that pure worship of, and obedience to, the Divine that is exemplified in the lives of all of these prophets, from Noah, through Abraham, Moses and Jesus, to the Seal of the Prophets, Muhammad. Thus Islam is, to use the Qur'anic idiom, that one 'submits one's face to God, and acts correctly, and follows the way of Abraham as a pure worshipper [of God]' (Q. 4:124); and whoever takes this path 'will have a great reward with his Lord; – there is no fear on them, neither shall they grieve' (Q. 2:112). It is in this context that the Qur'anic statements that 'the [true] religion in the sight of Allah is *islam*' (Q. 3:19), that 'whoever seeks other than *islam* as a religion [will find that] it is not accepted from him, and in the Next World he will be one of the losers' (Q. 3:85), and that God is pleased with *islam* as the way for people to behave (Q. 5:3), must be understood. Thus to take on Islam, to 'become a Muslim', is in essence to take on the ancient, Abrahamic, way of worship, albeit given the specific detailed requirements reflected in the outward practice of the Seal of the Prophets, Muhammad.

What does becoming a Muslim involve?

In historical terms, becoming a Muslim meant – and still means today – accepting God as Lord and accepting the Prophet Muhammad as the final prophet and messenger of this Lord. This two-fold acceptance is enshrined in the double declaration of faith, 'I bear witness that there is no god but God, and I bear witness that Muhammad is the Messenger of God', which, when said in front of witnesses, marks the formal entry of someone into the community of Muslims. (A fuller definition of this acceptance would include the six elements of belief, namely, belief in Allah, the angels, the divinely revealed books, the prophets, the Last Day, and the Decree, both the sweet of it and the bitter of it.) From the earliest period until now there has been discussion as to whether this declaration is enough as a sign of genuine belief or whether it should also be accompanied by the correct outward practices detailed by Islamic law that form part and parcel of the practice of Islam. Reports from the Prophet indicate that as long as one makes this declaration with sincerity, one is promised at least eventual entry into the Garden (the Muslim term for Paradise) regardless of one's wrong actions – for which one may or may not be punished – as long as one is not guilty of having associated anyone or anything else with God. Indeed, despite the above-mentioned dispute about what constitutes the true belief assumed behind this statement, its actual declaration is enough to protect someone in a legal sense from the accusation of being a *kafir* (non-believer) and, in conditions of war, from being fought. There is an incident recorded from the lifetime of the Prophet when one of the Companions was fighting in a battle and about to kill one of the enemy when his opponent declared 'There is no god but God and Muhammad is His Messenger'. The Companion nevertheless went ahead and killed him, on the assumption that the man had only said the words in order to save his life. On being told about this, the Prophet made his famous reply, 'How did you know what was in his heart?', thereby making it clear that the words are the minimum requirement and actual belief is a matter between the person and his Lord.

It can thus be seen that in one sense it is very easy to become a Muslim, the only formal requirement being that this dual declaration of faith, known as the *shahada*, is said publicly, that is, in front of witnesses. Nevertheless, there is the assumption that in declaring this statement, the person doing so is prepared to live by its implications, the most obvious being to live by what Allah and His Messenger have decreed for mankind in both the Qur'an – the divine revelation as transmitted by the Prophet Muhammad – and the *sunna*, or normative practice, of the Prophet, which, as mentioned above, together form the basis of Islam and its law, or *shari'a*. In other words, anyone who openly states that he believes in and accepts Allah and His Messenger is expected to live by the dictates of Allah and His Messenger as preserved in the Qur'an and the records of how the Prophet put this Qur'anic message into practice in practical, everyday terms, that is, his *sunna*.

However, the Qur'an itself states 'Have fear of Allah as far as you are able' (Q. 64:16), thus allowing for at least the possibility that not everyone will be able to do everything in terms of a practical expression of the law. More importantly, in terms of minimum requirements, is the Qur'anic statement that 'Allah will not forgive that anything should be associated with Him, but will forgive everything short of that for whoever He wills' (Q. 4:48 and 116), thus allowing the possibility of forgiveness for any wrong action short of the mental, or spiritual, sin of idolatry (shirk), that is, associating anyone or anything else with Allah, whether this be a physical or a conceptual idol. This verse, in addition to hadiths (Prophetic sayings) indicating that the statement 'There is no god but God' is a protection from the Fire, and that it is the best thing that Muhammad or any of the other prophets before him had said, was the basis for the arguments of the early theologians over what constituted correct belief and who was, therefore, a genuine Muslim.

Two main tendencies emerged. There were those who, following the literal meaning of the hadiths referred to above, considered the mere statement of belief to be enough to include someone in the fold of Islam. Others, however, considered it a travesty of the word 'belief' for it to be on the tongue and not appear also as outward action. Indeed, some extremist elements (e.g. the Khawarij, or Kharijites, of the early Islamic period) even considered the commitment of a major wrong action (i.e. in particular, the ones for which serious penalties exist in the law, such as drinking alcohol, stealing, fornication and / or adultery, and murder) to be a clear indication of unbelief and treated such people accordingly, considering it lawful to fight them as unbelievers. However, the dominant position was soon established – and has remained ever since – that although one cannot deny that a person is a Muslim if he says the shahada, nevertheless his belief is not complete without action by the limbs, that is, the outward practice of the dictates of the shari'a, at least in public. Thus in practice it is expected that, having said the shahada, which is the First Pillar of Islam, the new Muslim will pray the ritual prayer five times a day (the Second Pillar), pay the annual alms-tax of zakat if he has the required basic sum of money (the Third Pillar), fast the month of Ramadan (the Fourth Pillar), and go on the hajj, or pilgrimage, to Mecca at least once in a lifetime if he is able (the Fifth Pillar). Similarly, it is expected that anyone entering Islam will neither drink alcohol nor eat pork or meat of any incorrectly slaughtered animal, and will respect the basic prohibitions relating to such matters as stealing, committing adultery and/or fornication, murder, and so on.

It should, however, be noted that even commission of these offences does not, in the view of the main body of the Muslims, take someone out of Islam. Rather, the punishment prescribed for them in this world is considered sufficient expiation and the offender is considered free from any further punishment for that offence in the Next World. Furthermore, even the most serious offences are not punishable if committed privately, because witnesses are needed to establish them and it is considered an unacceptable invasion of privacy to try to 'catch someone out' in their own home. Thus, for instance, the story is told of the second Caliph 'Umar going at night into the house of someone he knew to be drinking, only to be told by the man, who had indeed been drinking, 'What right do you have you to go into a man's house without his permission?', at which point 'Umar, acknowledging the correctness of the man's reply, withdrew his accusations and left.

It is also usual for people to take on an overtly 'Islamic' name on becoming Muslim, though not obligatory: this practice dates back to the time of the Prophet who would change people's names if they overtly reflected unacceptable pre-Islamic beliefs or practices. There is also an expectation in some quarters that males should undergo circumcision, should this be necessary, but again, although recommended, this is not considered obligatory, and older people becoming Muslim may well decide not to go ahead with this operation. In fact, circumcision is one of the five *sunan al-fitra*, or 'practices of the natural state of man', that are recommended for any Muslim, the other four being to keep the nails pared, to trim the moustache and let the beard grow, to remove under-arm hair, and to shave the pubic area.

Ways of becoming Muslim

At the risk of over-simplifying, it could be said that there are two basic ways of becoming Muslim, the way of light and the way of power. The way of light is when someone becomes Muslim by individual personal conviction and certainty, regardless of the external difficulties this may bring. The way of power is when someone becomes Muslim by virtue of external circumstances which make it difficult not to do so. Both these types of 'conversion' are illustrated by the early history of Islam and exemplified in particular by the Meccan and Madinan periods of the Prophet's life, respectively: in the Meccan period, that is, before the Emigration (*Hijra*) of the Prophet from Mecca to Madina, people became Muslim through strong individual conviction of the truth of the Prophet's message, despite the ensuing problems in terms of rejection by the rest of society and even, in some cases, physical torture, that this brought; whereas in the Madinan phase people frequently became Muslim because the leaders of their group had become Muslim: it was, in effect, 'the thing to do', regardless of the depth of individual motive. Thus we see almost the entire population of Mecca accepting Islam at the time of the 'Conquest' of Mecca in the year AH 8 / CE 630 when the Prophet entered Mecca at the head of a large armed force, although there is no record of any 'forced' conversion – indeed, there was practically no blood spilt during the whole enterprise.

At this juncture we should also mention the growing presence of the 'hypocrites' (*munafiqun*) in the new community in Madina – a sure sign that there were also people who were becoming Muslim outwardly but had no Islam in their hearts. The size and seriousness of this phenomenon are indicated by the Qur'anic reference to them as 'the [real] enemy' (Q. 63:4). It is also stated in the Qur'an that they will be in the lowest level of the Fire (Q. 4:145), that is, that they will receive the worst form of punishment in the Next World, because of the heinousness of them saying one thing – of so serious a nature – on the surface and holding another in the heart, and indeed in most instances taking every opportunity to actually work against the believers where at all possible. The threat is severe, but not everyone of course is prepared to listen to threats that they do not accept as having divine authority. On which note the third Caliph 'Uthman is recorded to have said: 'People are restrained by the sword in a way that they are not restrained by the Qur'an', which brings us to the matter of Islam and the sword.

Islam and the sword

The claim has often been made – even if only to counter it – that Islam spread by the sword, and yet we have noted that in the Muslim sources it is forbidden for someone to force another to become a

Muslim, that is, to make him do so 'under the sword', as the expression goes. Nevertheless, it is clear that there was considerable military activity associated with the spread of Islam, both within the Arabian peninsula at the time of the Prophet, and in what were later to become the heartlands of Islam in Syria, Egypt, Iraq and Iran, in the time of the Rightly-Guided Caliphs immediately after him.

Perhaps the simplest answer to this question is that Islam spread not so much *by* the sword as *with*, that is, alongside, the sword. For the purpose of the Muslim armies was not so much to make everybody Muslim as to establish Islam, which meant, primarily, establishing Muslim rule. That the people of the conquered territories were not forced to become Muslims is evident from the fact that the majority of the inhabitants of the 'heartland' areas outside Arabia did not become Muslim until many decades, even centuries, after the conquests. (Bulliet, for instance, has suggested on the basis of name-studies that it was not until the fourth century AH that over 80 per cent of the people had become Muslim in Iran, and the same seems to apply to other areas.)[1] It is also well known that some of the main administrators of the early Damascus-based Umayyad dynasty (AH 41–132 / CE 661–750), for instance, were Christians, not to mention the fact that there are sizeable Christian and Jewish minorities in Syria, Iraq and Egypt even to this day. If there were mass forced conversions, it is hard to imagine firstly, how people could have taken so long to become Muslim, and, secondly, how in many cases they could have failed to do so even by today! Rather, what seems evident is that the early Muslims were intent on making Islam 'dominant' in the sense of establishing Muslim rule: the longer-term goal of people becoming Muslim could then be left to take its natural course.

Motives for conversion

Much has been written about the motives for conversion. It will be apparent from the above that to a certain extent this is not a problem in Islam. That is to say, once outward 'conversion' has taken place, and been seen to take place, the rest is more or less left up to a person's conscience. Furthermore, different degrees of sincerity are possible. In one of the most famous *hadiths* of the Prophet, and the one which begins the most famous collection of *hadiths*, that of al-Bukhari, we are told:

> Actions are by intentions, and everyone will get what he intends.
> Whoever emigrates for the sake of Allah and His Messenger, has
> emigrated for the sake of Allah and His Messenger; while whoever
> emigrates for the sake of some worldly thing that he wants to get or
> some woman he wants to marry, has emigrated for whatever it is that he
> has emigrated for.[2]

In the same way a person's conversion to Islam may be for very
varied reasons, and not necessarily from a deep, spiritual motive, but
it is still Islam.

One of the characteristics of Islam spreading is that it is generally
a one-way traffic. That is, once people have got into Islam – by
whatever means – they tend to stay in it and, moreover, deepen their
attachment to it. We find this reflected in numerous stories from the
early period of Islamic history. Among these is the story of how Abu
Sufyan ibn Harb, one of the chief nobles of Quraysh, was on a
trading journey to Gaza at around the time the Byzantine emperor
Heraclius recovered the Holy Cross from the Persians in the year CE
628 (AH 6). The Emperor, having had a dream, called Abu Sufyan to
him to ask him about this man that he had heard about who had
appeared in Mecca claiming to be a prophet. In particular he asked
him whether his followers followed him with love and loyalty or
were prone to leaving him. When he was told that none of them left
him, he said, 'This is the sweetness of faith: it does not enter the
heart and then leave.'[3]

A further observation of Abu Sufyan in this exchange was that
Muhammad's followers were mainly 'the weak and poor and young
slaves and young women; not one of the elders and nobles of his
people followed him', thus reflecting the situation of Noah in the
Qur'an ('We see only the most abject among us following you'; Q.
11:27) and indicating that it was easier for the less privileged to leave
their forefathers' ways and take on the new religion than it was for
the more privileged with their strong vested interest in maintaining
the *status quo* for reasons of personal wealth and prestige. It was
only later, as the Prophet became more successful in a political and
military sense, that the leaders also accepted Islam, particularly, as
we have seen, at the so-called 'Conquest' of Mecca, when
comparatively large numbers of people accepted not only the
political but also the religious dominance of Islam and the Prophet
Muhammad. Indeed, by the time of the Prophet's death in AH 11 / CE
632 the whole of the Arabian peninsula had at least outwardly

accepted this dominance, thus illustrating the second of the two main modes of becoming Muslim outlined above, namely, that of Islam by power.

The early sources depict many variations on these two modes. With regard to Islam by light, we find the early Muslims being impressed not only by the Prophet's Qur'anic message of creation, death and ultimate accountability, but also by the excellence of his personal behaviour as manifested, for example, in his exceptional patience, generosity, clemency and courage, the like of which they had never seen before. Particularly impressive for many was his knowledge, not only of the seen world but also of unseen matters: many examples are told of people becoming Muslim when realizing that the only way the Prophet could have known of a particular thing or event was through some divine means (thus reflecting the Qur'anic picture of Pharaoh's magicians accepting and submitting to the authority of the Prophet Moses). We also hear of individual seekers of the truth, sometimes guided by dreams, rejecting idol-worship and eventually finding their heart's desire in the company of the Prophet.

Once people had started accepting Islam, they in turn became a model for others, particularly close associates. It is noteworthy that several of the earliest Muslims were friends of Abu Bakr, the first to become Muslim outside the Prophet's immediate household and himself a close friend of the Prophet. Likewise Mus'ab, the man appointed by the Prophet to call people to Islam in Madina before the Emigration, was the cause of many people becoming Muslim there: they were as much impressed by his qualities of character as they were by the message he had to pass on. Similarly, we hear of leaders of tribes accepting Islam and this leading in turn to the acceptance of Islam by the rest of their tribe.

This latter could be considered an example of Islam by power. Another variant of this mode is that of Islam through marriage. By Islamic law, a Muslim man is allowed to marry a Muslim, Christian or Jewish woman but a Muslim woman may only marry a Muslim man; that is, a man must be Muslim before he may marry a Muslim woman. Thus in the early sources we hear of individuals becoming Muslim because the women they wanted to marry, or were already married to, had become Muslim and would not accept them unless they too became Muslim. This situation continues to be a source of new Muslims to the present day. A corollary of the marriage laws is that, even where only the father is Muslim, the children will generally be brought up as Muslims, thus furthering the gradual 'Islamization' of society. Another stimulus to this process – or at least a deterrent to its opposite – is the existence of the penalty of death, in certain circumstances, for apostasy, which is balanced by the strong feeling among Muslims that Islam is the final and complete version of the true Abrahamic religion ordained by God for all mankind: what, then, could be better?

Modern theories of conversion to Islam

Modern theories of conversion tend to differ somewhat from what one finds in the classical sources. Most obviously, there is a marked absence of any acknowledgement of either the miraculous or the world of dreams as a cause of conversion. Instead, one finds the general assumption that the vast majority of those who became Muslim either did so because of some material benefit that would accrue to them or some material harm that they would avoid. To an extent, of course, this assumption has some truth in it: power (rather than 'force'), for example, certainly played its part in setting up a situation whereby many people quickly became Muslim, as in the example of the 'Conquest' of Mecca mentioned above. It also seems clear that many people became Muslim in order to avoid some harm that they feared might come to them, as was presumably the case, for example, with the 'hypocrites' in Madina referred to above. But although this might help to explain some aspects of the situation, it does not explain why many people, once they had become Muslim, not only chose to stay in it but also became staunch stalwarts of its cause. Furthermore, as indicated above, recent research has suggested that mass conversion even in the heartlands did not occur until relatively late in the region's history (and even now is not complete): force, if at all applied for this purpose, seems to have been remarkably unsuccessful in getting people to change their religious identity. Perhaps even more importantly, some researchers have shown an *inverse* relationship between the degree of political penetration in certain areas and the degree of conversion to Islam. Eaton, for instance, speaking of the specific case of India, has argued that if conversion to Islam had ever been the function of military or political force, one would have expected the areas of heaviest conversion to correspond with those areas exposed most intensely and over the longest period to rule by Muslim dynasties. Yet the opposite seems to have been the case, with the regions lying on the fringes of Indian Muslim rule, such as Eastern Bengal or Western Punjab, showing the most dramatic conversion of the population, whereas in the heartland of that rule, the Indo-Gangetic plain, there was a much lower incidence of conversion.[4]

The idea that people became Muslim *en masse* because of expected worldly gains, particularly a rise in political or social status (the theories of 'political patronage' and 'social liberation', respectively), is also shown by the Indian experience to be an inadequate explanation. Though the 'political patronage' theory may possibly account for the relatively light incidence of conversion in the Delhi heartland, it does not account for the massive conversions that took place along the political fringe where the influence of the government was much weaker. (The presence in the early Muslim caliphate of numerous non-Muslim officials, as noted above, also suggests that becoming a Muslim was by no means a necessary prerequisite for political advancement in Muslim society.) Similarly, although much has been said about former caste-structured societies being 'liberated' by Islam, there is considerable evidence that in the Indian instance such stratification often existed as much after the society had become Muslim as it had before. Indeed, it would seem that the Muslims were not at the time overly concerned with this issue: contemporary sources suggest that those who were engaged in presenting Islam to Indians did not stress any ideal of social equality as opposed to Hindu caste, but rather Islamic monotheism as opposed to Hindu polytheism. And again, speaking in geographical terms, the greatest incidence of Muslim conversions occurred among groups that were not fully Hindu in the first place. Thus it seems that, for the vast majority of South Asian Muslims at any rate, the question of 'liberation' from an 'oppressive' Hindu social order was simply not an issue.[5]

The dominant picture that emerges from these studies is that Islam may spread as the result of both militant and peaceful activity. Where there is military activity, the establishment of Muslim political power allows the establishment of Islamic institutions – mosques, courts, etc. – which in turn creates an Islamic ambience which is conducive to more people becoming Muslim. On the edges of the Muslim domains traders, if not warriors, pave the way for men of religion, perhaps marrying also into the local populace. Once Muslim institutions begin to be set up the process is speeded up by the influence of the respective functionaries, whether judges or *imams* ('prayer-leaders') or, increasingly in later days, Sufi *shaykhs* (men of knowledge). The ensuing conversions may be either individual or communal. Individual conversions generally show greater commitment to the new cause and less 'carry-over' from the past, but the numbers involved are usually small. Communal conversions, on the other hand, involve large numbers of people, but the resulting society often exhibits much less of a break with pre-Islamic patterns and practices. These frequently remain, albeit in a modified form, until reform movements spring up later with the aim of bringing the newly Islamized – or partially Islamized – society into conformity with the greater world of 'orthodox' Islam beyond. Thus the society eventually becomes fully Islamized and finds itself integrated into the greater Islamic society elsewhere.

Brief mention should be made at this point of the role of the Sufis, whose influence in spreading Islam is generally accepted to have been very great. Indeed, it has been stated that it was only with the growth of the Sufi movement in the tenth century that Islam spread beyond the frontiers of the Muslim states; before that conversion had occurred only within the Muslim dominions.[6] It remains true today that Sufism, with its emphasis on a universal, non-intellectual but very real *tawhid*, or science of God's unity, is still one of the main points of entry into Islam for contemporary Europeans.

Contrary to this tendency is the claim by certain Muslims – especially those of a 'modernist', anti-Sufi outlook – that Islam appeals by its 'rationality' and that an unbiased study of the texts will – or should in theory – lead to the reader becoming Muslim. However, this view not only denies – or at least severely restricts – the intervention of the Divine (i.e. the miraculous) in such matters, but also assumes that there is only an intellectual recognition of truth and no other. A careful reading of the sources would suggest that becoming a Muslim is not a question of being convinced by rational means but rather by a recognition of the heart (the seat of the 'intellect' ['*aql*] in Qur'anic terminology), whether on an individual or communal basis, that is, whether by recognition of light or power, to use the distinction outlined above. If it were by intellect, one would have expected the majority of people – supposedly rational – to have become Muslim by now, but this is not the case, nor was it in

163

the early period. By all accounts it would seem that when the first Muslims left Arabia they did not – and did not need to – present 'rational' arguments for Islam; for the most part they did not even know the languages of the people whose lands they conquered. Rather, they declared their Islam and embodied it and sought to impose the *shari'a* as a governing structure when and where they could and to the best of their ability.

However, there seems to be a universal tendency – especially among scholars – to rationalize even what cannot be rationalized, and once a rational argument has been put to the scholastic mind it is often hard for that type of mind to affirm what seems to be a non-rational position. And yet the original event, and the revelation resulting from that event, defy complete rationalization, and cannot have been accepted by the first Muslims on that basis. As one of the early scholars of Islam, Malik (d. AH 179 / CE 795), said, when someone insisted on delving into the meaning of the Qur'anic expression that God had 'settled' on the throne (Q. 20:5): 'You have asked about what is not unknown (*ghayr majhul*) and have spoken about what cannot be encompassed by the intellect (*ghayr ma'qul*). I think you are a man of no good. Get him out of here!'[7] Indeed, as has been said, anyone who can argue themselves into Islam can argue themselves out of it again.

Given the infinite possibilities of motive, or combination of motives, it is, ultimately, impossible to explain why people become Muslims and, more especially, why they should remain so. One could speak of the natural appeal of the ancient religion of Abraham that offers freedom from creation in slavery to the Real. Or one could speak of the justice and tolerance of the Muslims in comparison with the oppression of others (as seems to have been the case, for instance, with the Byzantine dominions at the time of the initial Muslim conquests). One could even posit a desire on the part of some to achieve a higher status for themselves in society. These are just some of the possibilities. Muslims are called to invite others to Islam, that is, to submit themselves to God, but the results are not guaranteed, either by the intellect or any other means: some will become Muslims and others will not, and for differing reasons. More importantly, once people have formally accepted Islam, their attachment tends to grow stronger and deeper with time – often within a very short space of time – regardless of the means by which they made the initial move. Perhaps in time researchers will find that the most convincing 'explanation' of the phenomenon is that referred to in the Qur'an itself: 'You do not guide whoever you like, but Allah guides whoever He wants; and He knows best those who are guided' (Q. 28:56).

A note on sources

In addition to the sources referred to in the text, the following compilations of essays contain a wealth of further information on the subject:

Gervers, M. and Bikhazi, R. J. (eds), *Continuity and Change: Indigenous Christian Communities in Islamic Lands, Eighth to Eighteenth Centuries* (Toronto: Pontifical Institute of Mediaeval Studies, 1990)
Levtzion, N. (ed.), *Conversion to Islam* (New York: Holmes & Meier, 1979).

Notes

1. See R. W. Bulliet, 'Conversion to Islam and the Emergence of a Muslim Society in Iran', in N. Levtzion (ed.), *Conversion to Islam* (New York: Holmes & Meier, 1979), p. 31.
2. M. M. Khan (trans.), *The Translation of the Meanings of Sahih al-Bukhari* (Ankara: Hilal Yayinlari, 1974), vol. i, p. 1.
3. A. Guillaume (trans.), *The Life of Muhammad: A Translation of Ibn Ishaq's Sirat Rasul Allah* (Oxford: Oxford University Press, 1955), p. 655.
4. See R. M. Eaton, 'Approaches to the Study of Conversion to Islam in India', in *Approaches to Islam in Religious Studies*, ed. R. C. Martin (Tucson, AR: University of Arizona Press, 1985), pp. 107–8.
5. Ibid., pp. 108–11.
6. See N. Levtzion, 'Toward a Comparative Study of Islamization', in Levtzion (ed.), *Conversion to Islam*, p. 17.
7. See Ibn Rushd (al-Jadd), *al-Bayan wa-l-tahsil* (Beirut: Dar al-Gharb al-Islami, 1987), vol. 16, pp. 367–8.

10. Conversion in the Sikh tradition

Doris R. Jakobsh

Sikhism is not a religion known for its proselytizing activities. It has primarily been understood and presented as a regional faith, originating in Northern India and transplanted to virtually all areas of the globe by its adherents. As such, women from the Punjab attired in their traditional Punjabi dresses, the *salvar kameez* and turbaned and bearded Sikh males are a familiar sight in nearly every major city in the world. While the Sikh presence is clearly a global phenomenon, this has not been translated into a major expansion of Sikhism beyond its Punjab-based adherents. And yet, the ideals and tenets of Sikhism from its inception are universal, going beyond a particular cultural milieu. Tradition has Guru Nanak, the founder of Sikhism, wandering from Punjab as far as Mecca to spread his message of Truth and internal purity. Further, the message of Nanak attracted adherents who were both Hindus and Muslims. Mardana, the musician who accompanied Guru Nanak on his travels was a Muslim. An oft-quoted line from the *Puratan Janam-sakhi* insists that: 'There is neither Hindu nor Muslim', giving a distinct impression that one aspect of Guru Nanak's mission was to draw Muslims and Hindus nearer.[1] A significant feature of the *Adi Granth*, the Sikh sacred scripture is that it is composed of the writings of the Sikh Gurus as well as including contributions by both Muslim and Hindu saints.

To come to an understanding of conversion from the vantage point of the Sikh tradition, it is important to also understand aspects of the historical development of Sikhism. Guru Nanak, the first Guru in the lineage of ten Gurus preached a message of interiority, stressing that the route to liberation was not by way of ritual, pilgrimage, temple or icon, but through meditation on the Name and devotion to the Guru. As the fledgling Sikh community grew in numbers and extended over space, devotees simply could not have the personal contact with the Guru which had earlier been possible. Institutionalization became the obvious alternative. Sacred spaces were built; important doctrines such as compulsory interdining, known as *langar*, were institutionalized; the words of the Gurus were collected and codified; deputies called *masands* were put in place to preach the message of the Gurus as well as to oversee the administrative aspects of the growing movement; pilgrimages to important shrines played a part in connecting devotees to the historical and sacred development of their tradition.

It would appear that despite the itinerant activities of the first Guru, the initial core of *Nanak-panthis* (followers of the teachings of Guru Nanak) were of the Khatri caste group. This was the caste of all the ten Sikh Gurus and their wives, and it was within this community that Sikhism was born and began to flourish. It was during the time period of the fifth Guru, Guru Arjan (1563–1606), that there was a significant shift in the development of the Sikh movement. Alongside the increasing institutionalization of Sikhism came a politicization as well; the execution of Guru Arjan at the hands of the Mughals, who viewed this development with growing distrust, is indicative of this evolution. Further, historians have pointed to an influx of a different caste group, the Jats, as crucial in this developmental process. From the time of the sixth Guru, Guru Hargobind, the Sikhs, due in part to the growing hostilities of the Mughal government but also to the militaristic tendencies of the Punjabi Jats who had overtaken the Khatris in terms of leadership, became increasingly characterized as a militarized religious and political movement.[2] This culminated in the actual institutionalization of militarism during the guruship of Guru Gobind Singh, the tenth and last Guru in the Sikh Guru lineage. Understood primarily as a reaction to the increasingly corrupt practices of the *masands*, the Guru called upon all Sikhs to disassociate themselves from these now powerful rival leaders and enter into a direct relationship with their Guru, regardless of caste or region. Guru Gobind Singh then introduced a novel initiation rite known as *khande ki pahul* or baptism of the sword, which afforded clear distinction between the Khalsa of the Guru (the 'pure ones' as the new initiates were called) and those who did not heed his call. The initiation rite was prepared by a bowl of sugar and water (*amrit* or 'nectar of immortality') being stirred with a two-edged sword, which was then drunk by the initiates. This initiation practice has continued to the present day. A new ethical code outlining Khalsa conduct was also introduced which included clear identity markings to distinguish this new Khalsa brotherhood. The well-known five Ks of the Sikh tradition stem from this crucial time in the development of Sikh identity.[3] They refer to five items of external appearance which all Khalsa Sikhs must follow, each beginning with the letter 'K': *kes*, uncut hair; *kangha*, a wooden comb worn in the hair, *kara*, steel bangle, *kirpan*, sword or dagger, and *kachh*, a type of undergarment. As already noted, many Sikhs of the day enthusiastically followed and upheld the vision of Guru Gobind Singh. Many others did not. A large number of Sikhs were content to remain associated with what they understood as Guru Nanak's radically opposite message of interiority.

While many historians have defined the development of Sikhism and a corresponding Sikh *identity* as easily distinct from the wider social, religious and cultural milieu, Harjot Oberoi in his influential *The Construction of Religious Boundaries* insists that Sikh history is not nearly as simple as textbook classifications would have us believe. Oberoi notes that early Sikhism

> had shown little enthusiasm for distinguishing its constituents from members of other religious traditions, or for establishing a pan-Indian community. Sikh notions of time, space, corporeality, holiness, mythology, kinship, social distinction, purity and pollution, gender, sexuality and commensality were firmly rooted in Indic cultural thinking.[4]

There was a certain affinity towards a fluidity of religious, social and cultural identities; rites of passage, namely birth, marriage and death rituals were easily shared between Hindus and Sikhs for the majority of the developmental process of the Sikh tradition. Individuals within this world-view could claim adherence to a varied religious cosmology. An example of this can be seen as late as the nineteenth century, where it was common practice for Hindu families to dedicate their first-born son to the Sikh Khalsa brotherhood. This wide-boundaried, fluid understanding of religious identity is essential in attempting to ferret out the meaning of the conversion phenomena in the Sikh tradition, specifically from a Western perspective.

A major shift in the development of Sikh identity came after the annexation of Punjab by the British in 1849. Following the conversion of a number of Sikh youths to Christianity and fearing a continued loss in numbers, Sikh males who had access to British education organized themselves into a reform group called the Singh Sabha and began a thorough process of re-evaluating their religious beliefs and practices.[5] Convinced that the fluid cosmology which permeated their tradition was detrimental to what they believed to be the very *essence* of Sikhism, they sought to purify those aspects of their religious traditions which bound them to the larger Hindu worldview. Stressing their tradition's avowedly monotheistic nature, Hindu deities which had been placed within the Golden Temple precincts were removed in 1905. Whereas Hindus and Sikhs had shared ritual components, new 'Sikh' rituals and regulations were ordained and implemented. The rite of initiation and injunctions which Guru Gobind Singh had created for his Khalsa were stressed as normative for *all* Sikhs, a development which had not taken extensive root in the wider Sikh culture. Proselytizing teams and preachers actively set out to reclaim those who had left the Sikh fold and further spread the message of a reformed and 'pure' Sikhism. Given their elite status within the political framework, the Singh Sabha leaders had access to and control of the newly developed print culture in India. Thus armed they were capable of constructing and developing a Sikh identity which has for the most part become normative for Sikhs the world over to the present day.

Nonetheless, despite the efforts of the Singh Sabha reformers to construct a homogeneous Sikh identity, it is still extremely problematic to clearly delineate 'who is a Sikh' to this very day. While the injunctions known as the Five Ks are followed by some, many do not view these identity markers as essential to their being 'good' Sikhs. While orthodox Sikhism views the Guru lineage as ending with Guru Gobind Singh, numerous groups who count themselves as within the Sikh fold follow the teachings of a living guru *as well* as the tenets and rituals of Sikhism.[6] There appears to be an in-built tolerance of diversity within Sikhism which must be kept in mind when speaking of this context of conversion, particularly from a Western perspective.

As stated earlier, Sikhism has largely been defined and composed of Indians of Punjabi heritage. While there have been occasional conversions of non-Indians to the Sikh way of life, they have indeed been rare. This changed during the 1960s in the United States where Harbhajan Singh Puri, a Khatri Sikh who took on the name Yogi Bhajan and began to attract American students. He later established an ashram in the United States. One year later he initiated the 'Healthy, Happy, Holy Organization' (3HO), which had as its focus Kundalini Yoga, and in an indirect manner the Sikh way of life. Increasingly, Yogi Bhajan began to stress Sikh doctrine, and in 1971 he accompanied 84 North American converts to the Golden Temple in Amritsar. At this time the Yogi was honoured by Sikh authorities for his missionary work in the context of North America. Reflecting his changed focus from a primarily yogic to a Sikh identity, Yogi Bhajan changed his name to Siri Singh Sahib.[7] Siri Singh Sahib at this point introduced Sikh initiation ceremonies to his religious teachings and Sikh identity markers (five Ks) to his North American followers. Whereas many Punjabi Sikhs immigrating to new host countries often shed their traditional identity markers, wishing to blend in more effectively with the majority culture of these societies, members of the 3HO clearly deem their identity markers as essential to their new-found religious sensibilities. Both women and men are easily identifiable in their white Indian clothes and turbans; their communal living arrangements and Indian names accentuate their difference, as do the flowing beards of 3HO males. 3HO members 'have asserted their right to a full public expression of their version of Sikh orthopraxy and have sought aggressively to have their "religious rights" recognized by the North American public'.[8] Correspondingly, the media has responded to these 'exotic' Sikhs and praised them for their 'good deeds' (free kitchens and drug rehabilitation programs).

[W]hat media exposure they have received has been uncritical in accepting the converts' claim to represent orthodox Sikhism in North America. All of this activity has made the converts known beyond what their numbers might otherwise warrant. Punjabi Sikhs in North America, in particular, have been made well aware of the existence of the gora Sikhs, even if they have personally had little or no interaction with them.[9]

Responses to these *Gora* (white) Sikhs has largely been shaped by the way Punjabi Sikhs respond to their own internal diversity and what it means to be a Sikh. Dusenbery notes that in general, feelings are mixed toward these converts. While their strict Sikh ritual discipline is admired, they disapprove of the uniformization which has taken place; both women and men wear similar white garb (traditionally the colour of mourning in Punjabi culture) and the degenderization of the turban which has taken place within the 3HO membership, both males and females proudly covering their uncut hair with a turban (a strictly male identity marker among Punjabis). While Punjabi Sikhs insist that both men and women are equal in their own religious tradition, *Gora* women wearing turbans and insisting unabashedly on their equality with men as result of their Khalsa initiation cause some Punjabis a good deal of discomfort. Similarly, in terms of reaction to the followers of Siri Singh Sahib, many question the combination of Sikh rituals and practices with yogic exercises. Further, 3HO members insist on a rigid vegetarian diet, a notion which many Jat Sikhs in particular spurn. Most significantly, the veneration of the living guru, Siri Singh Sahib, leads many to view the organization as a deviant cult and its leader as a false guru. Dusenbery points out, however, that more commonly the *Goras* are referred to as 'good' Sikhs as opposed to non-Sikhs and admired for their resounding heralding of the Sikh tradition as a message of truth and timelessness for the entire human race. Nonetheless, while recognized as 'good Sikhs' they are still people who 'bear the alienating stigma of being *gora*. This, in turn, affects the way that Punjabi Sikhs interact with them.'[10]

The *Gora* attitude toward Punjabi Sikhs is largely based on their own understanding of what it means to be 'religious' in Western society. Highly enshrined Western notions of individual rights pave the way for an insistence that members of the 3HO Organization as *Sikhs* be given the rights of full religious expression in North America, including a choice of religious naming practices, religious garb and head covering. In terms of coming to an understanding of their own place in the wider Sikh Panth, converts tend to characterize a sense of superiority with regard to their own 'pure' version of Sikhism as opposed to the more fluid practices of Punjabi Sikhs. Verne Dusenbery has aptly defined the North American converts' understanding of Sikhism as 'radical egalitarianism' as opposed to the Punjabi Sikh approach to 'unity in diversity', in coming to terms with their seemingly contrary frameworks.[11] Converts are quick to point out the lack of equality between males and females in Punjabi gender roles, and the continued emphasis on caste, issues which they hold as unequivocally contrary to the teachings of the Sikh Gurus.[12] Further, given the central place accorded to the Khalsa initiation ceremony of the 3HO members, it becomes quite simple for these converts to identify who *is* and who *is not* a Sikh. Only one who lives according to the Sikh code of ethics and who wears the corresponding five Ks is a Sikh. Needless to say, the irony is manifest given the converts' own ambiguous position in light of their continued veneration of Siri Singh Sahib, a living guru, and orthodox Sikh theology. The complex interplay of tolerance toward diversity *central* to the Punjabi Sikh community since its very inception does not easily concur with the high ideals or the cultural impulses and expectations of many of these Western Sikh converts.

Notes

1. Bhai Vir Singh (ed.), *Puratan Janam-sakhi* (5th edn, Amritsar: Khalsa Samachar, 1959), p. 16, as quoted in W. H. McLeod, *The Sikhs: History, Religion and Society* (New York: Columbia University Press, 1989), p. 21.

   Janam-sakhi literature refers to a genre of traditional narratives of the life and times of Guru Nanak. W. H. McLeod has done extensive research on this collection and insists that '[t]he janam-sakhis are properly understood as hagiography; and their appropriate context is not the lifetime of the first Guru but the later period within which they actually developed.' Thus, they correspond more to the needs of a later faith community than of the actual historical events. W. H. McLeod, *Who is a Sikh? The Problem of Sikh Identity* (Oxford: Clarendon Press, 1992), p. 15.

2. W. H. McLeod has written extensively on what has become known as the 'Jat Theory'. See his *The Evolution of the Sikh Community: Five Essays* (Oxford: Clarendon Press, 1976), pp. 9–12. It must be noted that McLeod's insistence on the significance of the Jats in the increasingly militaristic development of Sikhism has been hotly contested. Jagjit Singh argues that it is Sikh ideology, divinely ordained, not the Jat ascendancy which is responsible for what he calls the 'Sikh social and political revolution'. See Singh's 'Sikh Militancy and the Jats', *Advanced Studies in Sikhism*, ed. J. S. Mann and H. S. Saraon (Irvine, CA: Sikh Community of North America, 1989), p. 215.

3. Whether the number of these five injunctions were complete during the time of Guru Gobind Singh is a matter of debate. Certainly, tradition has the 5 Ks originating with Guru Gobind Singh.

4. Harjot Oberoi, *The Construction of Religious Boundaries: Culture, Identity and Diversity in the Sikh Tradition* (Delhi: Oxford University Press, 1994), pp. 47–8.

5. The first Singh Sabha was established in Amritsar in 1873. In subsequent years over a hundred Singh Sabha associations were formed in Sikh communities. It is essential to note that the spirit of reform affected all Indian religious communities during this time.

6. The Namdhari and Nirankari Sikhs espouse a guru lineage dating back to the nineteenth century. The North American group of Western converts, the 'Healthy, Happy, Holy Organization' or 3HO also falls into this category.

7. One of the injunctions of Guru Gobind Singh stated that all initiated Sikh males were to take on the surname Singh. Clearly, the name change from Yogi Bhajan to Siri Singh Sahib reflected his increasing emphasis on his Sikh roots.

8. Verne A. Dusenbery, 'Punjabi Sikhs and Gora Sikhs: Conflicting Assertions of Sikh Identity in North America', in *Sikh History and Religion in the Twentieth Century*, ed. J. T. O'Connell, M. Israel, W. G. Oxtaby, W. H. McLeod and J. S. Grewal (South Asian Studies Papers, Toronto: University of Toronto, Centre for South Asian Studies, 1990), p. 345.

9. Ibid., p. 345.

10. Ibid., p. 345.

11. Ibid., p. 353.

12. The issue of caste has been a matter of a good deal of discomfort within the Sikh Panth. Certainly Guru Nanak's attitude toward caste is often repeated:

> Worthless is caste and worthless an exalted name.
> For all mankind there is but a single refuge. (A.G., P. 83)

Nonetheless, it is clear that the Guru lineage did not stray beyond his own Khatri caste boundary. All the wives of the Gurus were also Khatris. Yet, the Sikh Gurus insisted that caste can be no barrier to liberation. Only the discipline of *nam simaran* or 'remembering the name' and veneration of the Guru bring one in accord with the divine order. The distribution of *karah prasad* (sanctified food), known as *langar*, to all persons regardless of their caste when present in the gurdwara (the place where Sikhs gather in community), also points to the 'casteless' nature of Sikhism, given that pollution laws have typically been associated with eating and community. W. H. McLeod notes that 'whereas [the Gurus] were vigorously opposed to the *vertical* distinctions of caste they were content to accept it in terms of its *horizontal* linkages'. In other words, the Sikh Gurus were willing to observe the marriage conventions of their society, yet were 'opposed to the discriminatory aspects of the vertical relationship', in reference to caste as barrier to liberation, *The Evolution of the Sikh Community: Five Essays*, pp. 88, 90. Nonetheless, caste is still a major issue within the Sikh community. A number of gurdwaras in North America are built on caste lines as the Western Sikh converts critique; this applies to some Indian gurdwaras as well. J. S. Neki, a respected Sikh scholar, adds:

> But we, in contravention of the guru's ordinance, have become caste-proud. The Jats are proud for being Jats, the Khatris for being Khatris. The Ahluwalias consider themselves the cream of all. The Ramgarhias reckon themselves inferior to none ... As a result of the Singh Sabha and Akali Movements, we had dropped caste-designations from our names ... [t]oday , we have begun to re-affix caste-designations after our names. This retrograde step has pushed us back into a Brahmanical practice. ('Fifth Annual Raghbir Singh Bir Memorial Lecture', *The Sikhs: Tenets and Tremors*, ed. Harkishen Singh: Harkishen Singh, n.d.), pp. 157–8.

Part III
Conversion in Christianity

11. Conversion in Christianity: from without and from within

M. Darrol Bryant

Conversion in Christianity: an overview

Conversion looms large in the story of Christianity since Christianity is, along with Buddhism and Islam, a missionary religion. Beginning from its emergence within the Jewish tradition and its missionary activity among the Gentiles intiated by the Apostle Paul, one of the early and most important converts, it seeks to bring people from all 'tribes and nations' to share the Christian faith and life. During the first three centuries of the Christian era, the early Christian community moved from its origins as a Jewish sect to an outlawed religion in the Roman Empire to its status as the 'official religion of the Empire' under the Emperor Constantine in CE 325. Christianity also went south into Africa (Egypt and Ethiopia) and east into the Middle East and perhaps as far east as India. But our account will be mainly confined to Christianity in the West.

After CE 325 Christianity was, in the West, linked to the state and its imperial ambitions. Thus after the 'internal' conversion of Roman society, largely through female converts to Christianity, and the 'external' conversion of Constantine in his successful battle at the Milvian Bridge, the 'conversion' of European peoples was partly through missionary efforts (Ireland) and partly through conquest (Germanic peoples).[1]

In medieval Christianity, when Christianity was the dominant religion in Europe, conversion was centred on efforts to convert the Jews and 'infidels' (usually Muslims) and the spiritual process of 'conversio' in the monasteries. Thus conversion came in the Christian tradition to have an ambiguous meaning. It meant, in some contexts, a spiritual process of turning one's life to God in Jesus Christ and, in others, a formal confession of the Christian faith and participation in the sacramental life of the Christian Church. At the time of the Reformation, the rhetoric of conversion again loomed large as Western Christianity splintered and the new Protestant churches sought converts from Catholicism. Here, 'conversion' became part of intra-Christian polemics. Lutherans and Calvinists sought the 'conversion' of Catholics, Anabaptists sought to convert cultural Christians, Catholics sought to restore the wayward to the Holy Church. For Lutherans, Calvinists, and Catholics, conversion could be accomplished by force if necessary.

The sixteenth and seventeenth centuries saw the extension of the missionary movement to the New World of North and South America. Catholic and Protestant missionaries sought the conversion of the indigenous peoples. Bartolomé de Las Casas wrote a moving critique of the enforced 'conversion' of the aboriginal peoples, but his voice went unheeded. The contact with European peoples devastated the indigenous peoples of the Americas, partly through new diseases, partly through conquest, partly through enforced conversions. Later in the eighteenth and nineteenth centuries, the missionary movements focused on Africa and Asia, where they were often linked to imperial ambitions and to Western cultural values. How did one distinguish genuine conversion – the New Testament term was *metanoia*, to be turned around – from compliance with a new dominant political power or Western culture or the promise of a full bowl of rice?

Within more recent Christian history, 'conversion' has become a controversial topic, especially in relation to Protestant Christianity.[2] Beginning with the Reformation, we saw the emergence of a unique context for conversion, namely, 'conversion' within the Christian tradition. That is, Luther experienced a profound 'conversion' – Luther referred to it as his *Turmerlebnis* or 'tower experience' – from his Catholic Christianity to his 'Pauline' Christianity centred on justification by faith. John Wesley, already an Anglican, spoke of his 'heart strangely warmed' in response to a Moravian sermon on Luther. The Methodist Way that then emerged in relation to Wesley often emphasized conversion as crucial to the achievement of what Wesley called 'Christian perfection'. And within Puritan Christianity, we had already seen the emergence of a view of the Christian life that centred on 'new birth' as the mark of the Christian. These streams of Christian religious life were especially developed in American Christianity, where 'new birth' and 'conversion in the spirit' became distinctive marks of being a Christian.

It was then in the early twentieth century that we saw the emergence in the USA of 'pentecostal' Christianity which also emphasized the 'conversion' experience or 'baptism in the spirit' often associated with 'tongue speaking'. Thus within contemporary evangelical Protestant and pentecostal Christianity 'conversion' is central. And pentecostal Christianity is growing phenomenally around the world.[3]

Conversion is largely a first-generation process and event that has to do with becoming a Christian. But curiously, conversion continues to be an issue for those who are born into and educated in the Christian community. Here, it is not linked to being a Christian as opposed to something else, but rather it is linked to the process of becoming a God-centred person, a deepening and revitalizing of their Christian faith. But how precisely is that 'conversion' to be understood? For some streams of Christianity, conversion has been an inward turning of the spirit towards God, for others it has been outward conformity to the sacraments and the authority of the Church, for still others it has been conformity to dominant cultural values, and for some it has been allegiance to their own version of Christianity. Certainly, the meaning of 'conversion' has varied within the history of Christian thought and life.

The conversion of Paul

The beginnings of Christianity are obviously linked to Jesus of Nazareth, whom Christians affirm to be the Messiah, the anointed one of God. But those beginnings are also importantly linked to Saul of Tarsus, more familiarly know as the Apostle Paul, who was the first missionary to the Gentiles. It was Paul who took the Christian message to the non-Jewish world. And Saul / Paul is, in many ways, the most important 'convert' to Christianity. It is Paul's letters to the churches in Galatia, Rome and Corinth that are the earliest Christian literature to become part of the Christian Scripture. And those scriptures include the dramatic story of Saul who became with his conversion, Paul, the Apostle to the Gentiles.[4]

The dramatic version of Saul's conversion to the Christian faith is not told in the Apostle Paul's writings, but in the book of the Acts of the Apostles, written by Luke. Saul was not an original disciple of Jesus; indeed, he did not know Jesus during his ministry. Saul was a devout Jew who, according to Acts, was present at the stoning of Stephen (Acts 7:58) and who 'laid waste the church ... entering house after house, he dragged off men and women and committed them to prison' (Acts 8:3). Saul, the story continues, was on his way to Damascus looking for those 'belonging to the Way' that he 'might bring them bound to Jerusalem' (Acts 9:2). But as he approached Damascus, 'suddenly a light from heaven flashed about him. And he fell to the ground and heard a voice saying to him, "Saul, Saul, why do you persecute me?" And he said, "Who are you, Lord?" And he said, "I am Jesus, whom you are persecuting; but rise and enter the city, and you will be told what you are to do"' (Acts 9:3b–6).

His companions hear the voice, but do not see anyone. And Saul when he arises cannot see, and he is led to Damascus. For three days he is 'without sight, and neither ate nor drank' (Acts 9:9). Ananias, a Christian in Damascus, is urged in a vision to go to Saul, but he initially resists since Saul is known for the 'evil he has done to thy saints at Jerusalem' (Acts 9:13). But his objections are overturned, and Ananias is commanded, 'Go, for he is a chosen instrument of mine to carry my name before the Gentiles and kings and the sons of Israel; for I will show him how much he must suffer for the sake of my name' (Acts 9:15–16). Thus Saul is approached by Ananias who blesses and baptizes him. So Saul becomes Paul and the story of his conversion enters into the fundamentals of the Christian story.

Contemporary scholarship has pointed out that the account we have in Acts reflects the growing hostility between the early Christian community and the Jewish community. In this it varies from Paul's own accounts which contain neither the dramatic and miraculous dimensions found in Acts nor the hostility towards the Jewish community. Indeed, Paul is proud of his Jewishness, even asserting in his letter to the Philippians that he is 'blameless' before the law (Phil. 3:6). Moreover, his comments concerning his conversion are more restrained, emphasizing his 'revelation' rather than the dramatic experience of conversion we find in Luke, the author of the Acts of the Apostles. In his letter to the Galatians, Paul speaks of himself as a Jew who now knows 'that a man is not justified by works of the law but through faith in Jesus Christ' (Gal 2:16). And in his letter to the community in Corinth, Paul emphasizes his role as an 'apostle' though 'the least of the apostles' (1 Cor. 15:9). The noted New Testament scholar Krister Stendhal thus speaks of Paul's 'call' rather than his 'conversion'. This view may go too far, but it does point to the link between conversion and vocation: Paul's conversion to Christ is also the beginning of his ministry.

For Paul, his conversion was a call to faith in Christ and a ministry to the Gentiles. For other New Testament writers, his conversion was the model of the dramatic conversion we might see among the Gentiles.

It is, then, Luke's dramatic account of Paul's conversion that looms large at the outset of Christianity. Paul's conversion is characterized by the basic metaphor of an old and new life, a radical disjunction between the past and the present that (1) involves changes in Paul's religious beliefs; (2) moves Paul from his Pharisaic Jewish world into the emerging Gentile Jewish Christian community; and (3) gives to Paul a sense of vocation to carry the Christian message to the non-Christian or Gentile world. But in the hands of Luke, the story of Paul gives a model of conversion as sudden, dramatic, ecstatic, and due to external divine intervention that is to remain front and centre in Christian thinking about conversion.

The conversion of Augustine: the Christian classic

Although the story of Paul's conversion lies at the foundation of the Christian way, it is the fourth-century story of Augustine's conversion that emerges as the classic case. Augustine was born in North Africa in 354, fewer than thirty years after Christianity had become the official religion of the Roman Empire. His home was religiously mixed: his father, Patricius, was a pagan, and his mother, Monica, a Christian. Augustine's story of his journey to the Christian faith is told in his famous religious autobiography *Confessions*, probably written in 397–98, a decade after his conversion and baptism.

The *Confessions* is not a straightforward narrative of Augustine's life. It is written from a religious point of view, with Augustine looking back on his life from the vantage point of his conversion and under the conviction that 'we are made for God' and 'that our souls are restless until they rest in God'.[5] Thus when Augustine looks back on the stages of his life – his infancy, his childhood, his youth, and his young adulthood – he sees there a restlessness that is an inchoate searching for God. Thus, in retrospect, Augustine sees that God is present to one's life at every point, but that the consequence of human sin is that we 'turn away from God'. While God made us and is 'the source of all good' and everywhere preserves us (*Confessions*, p. 25), Augustine is also aware of the disorder in the human soul that turns humanity away from God.

Many interpreters of Augustine focus all their attention on the dramatic moment of Augustine's conversion in the garden in Milan in 386. It is the moment in Augustine's *Confessions* when, Augustine writes, 'my inner self was a house divided against itself ...' (p. 170):

> When I was trying to reach a decision about serving the Lord my God, as I had long intended to do, it was I who willed to take this course and again it was I who willed not to take it. It was I and I alone. But I neither willed to do it nor refused to do it with my full will. So I was at odds with myself. I was throwing myself into confusion. (p. 173)

When Augustine is in this state, he leaves his friend Alypius 'so that I might weep and cry to my heart's content' and while weeping hears 'the sing-song voice of a child in a nearby house' saying 'Take it and read, take it and read' (p. 177). Then, 'telling myself that this could only be a divine command to open my book of Scripture', Augustine returned to his friend Alypius and picked up Paul's Epistles,

> opened it, and in silence I read the first passage on which my eyes fell: *Not in revelling and drunkenness, not in lust and wantonness, not in quarrels and rivalries. Rather, arm yourselves with the Lord Jesus Christ; spend no more thought on nature and nature's appetites.* I had no wish to read more and no need to do so. For in an instant ... it was as though the light of confidence flooded into my heart and all the darkness of doubt was dispelled. (p. 178)

Thus was Augustine converted.

However, a reading of the whole *Confessions* also yields another way of seeing Augustine's story, namely, that his conversion was a process that unfolded over his whole lifetime and reaches its culmination at the moment described above. Other significant moments along the way are, for example, when he reads Cicero's *Hortensius*. Augustine says that Hortensius 'altered my outlook on life ... It changed my prayers to you ... and provided me with new hopes and aspirations' (p. 58). This happened when Augustine was nineteen and studying rhetoric in Carthage. It was a time when, Augustine says, 'I found myself in the midst of a hissing cauldron of love ... for although my real need was for you, my God ... I was not aware of this hunger' (p. 55). Apparently, it was Cicero's *Hortensius* that led Augustine to an awareness of that hunger for God, since he writes that upon reading Cicero, 'all my empty dreams suddenly lost their charm and my heart began to throb with a bewildering passion for the wisdom of eternal truth' (pp. 58–9).

In these words from Augustine's *Confessions*, we encounter not only Augustine the young man but also Augustine the master of rhetoric. He shapes his account of his quest for God through the stages of his life in moving and dramatic terms. In retrospect, he realizes that he has always been searching for God, even as a jealous infant, a rebellious school boy, an adolescent stealing pears from the neighbour's garden, a young man caught in the 'filth of lewdness' and 'hell's black river of lust' (p. 55). But now Augustine says that Cicero persuaded him 'to love wisdom itself, whatever it might be, and to search for it, pursue it, hold it, and embrace it firmly' (p. 59).

This passion for wisdom led Augustine to explore a number of different philosophies, including the Manichaean and neo-Platonic views then current, over the next fourteen years. These philosophies were not merely abstractions for Augustine; they were existential options. And here again the story is two-sided. On the one hand, Augustine's retrospective account tells us how he moved through the Manichaean and neo-Platonic options in his quest for wisdom and, simultaneously, how important they were in, for example, finally realizing that God was not material. In a word, these moments in Augustine's life are also part of the process of conversion.

In his rhetorical effort to persuade the reader that all the credit for his conversion goes to God, Augustine emphasizes his own failures. 'From the nineteenth to the twenty-eighth year of my life,' Augustine writes, 'I was led astray myself and led others astray in my turn' (p. 71). Yet in the midst of this, Augustine also describes his growing intellectual conversion – he had become a Manichee and was struggling with the problem of evil, but moves beyond it to neo-Platonism as he realizes the spiritual nature of things – as he moves towards the final stage of his conversion to Christianity. As Augustine says, he was 'on the road to conversion' (p. 115).

Augustine was obviously a gifted teacher, for by the end of his twenties, he had managed to secure an important position in Milan, through the Prefect of Rome, as a 'teacher of literature and elocution' (p. 107). And his quest continues, for it was in Milan that Augustine encountered Bishop Ambrose, initially to see if 'the reports of his powers as a speaker were accurate' (p. 107). He tells us in his *Confessions* how he was struggling with two issues: the nature of God and the origin of evil. He was making his way towards an awareness of God as the Creator and an understanding of evil as rooted in the will. Augustine would come to understand sin as the tendency of the self to curve in upon itself rather than open out to God, its true source and end.

These theoretical insights were also related to Augustine's own personal struggle. Augustine realized that he was caught in the conflict of his own will. 'This', he says, 'was the nature of my sickness. I was in torment, reproaching myself more bitterly than ever as I twisted and turned in my chain' (p. 175). It took, for Augustine, an act of grace to lift him beyond the chains of habit born of his own will to finally 'rest in God', the hidden goal of his twisting and turning.

Augustine's story, so powerfully articulated in the *Confessions*, becomes an archetypal account, one in which subsequent generations of Christians saw, again and again, their own story. It is a story of humans being drawn to God, often despite their own surface will, until they are finally turned towards God in whom they realize the deepest object of their longing and striving. While Augustine's story makes clear the intensely personal character of conversion, it also provides a model of conversion that was to prove significant in the story of Christianity. Many would find themselves mirrored in Augustine's story. For example, Teresa of Avila (1515–82), more than a thousand years later, would read Augustine's *Confessions* and so identify with his story that she would write:

> When I started reading the *Confessions* it seemed to me that I was seeing my own self right there. When I got as far as his conversion and read how he heard that voice in the garden, it was just as if the Lord gave it to me, too, to judge from the grief that filled my heart. For a long time I was wholly undone by my weeping, and with Augustine's very same love and anguish within my own self, too ...[6]

Augustine's story thus shaped Christian thinking concerning conversion. The movement of the heart towards God involved an intense personal struggle – Poewe in her contribution to this volume centres that struggle on the issue of lust versus continence – and active saving grace. For, as Augustine emphasized in his controveries with the Pelagians, sinful humanity is unable to turn towards God without the presence of transforming grace.

Conversion: the Reformers and Protestant Christianity

Conversion within medieval Christianity was seen within two distinct contexts. There were the efforts to convert Jews and Muslims to Christianity, but the more familiar context was the gradual conversion of one's life to God that took place in the context of monastic life. With the eruption of the Reformation, new understandings of conversion began to emerge. These were centred on 'intra-Christian' conversions, often dramatic and intense and resulting in a shift from one brand of Christianity to another brand of Christianity, from one denomination to another.

The story of Luther (1483–1546), the unwitting initiator of the Protestant reforms, is an example of this change. Luther was an Augustinian monk and a biblical scholar at the University of Wittenberg when he experienced a profound change – the so-called *Turmerlebnis* or 'tower experience' – that led him to believe that the heart of the Christian gospel was Paul's teaching on 'justification by faith alone'. We now know that these events in Luther's life were preceded by more than a decade of deep unhappiness and an inability to find a resolution to his existential despair within the context of his Catholic faith. It was through his study of Scripture that Luther won his insight into the Good News: that it is not human effort but God's gracious act towards humankind in Jesus Christ that grounds one's relationship with God. Heretofore, Luther had felt that he was condemned and liable to judgement, but he came to believe that the Christian life is one of trusting in the promise of God that we are justified and made right with God through grace.[7]

These changes in Luther's own life lay behind his famous 'Ninety-five Theses' and his subsequent break with the Catholic tradition. Initially, Luther seems to have believed that the Catholic Church would respond positively to his critique of the practice of 'indulgences'. But that was not to be the case. The consequence was that Luther became increasingly hostile to the Catholic tradition, calling it 'the whore of Babylon'. This in part led to the intra-Christian polemics that were to mark Protestant–Catholic relations until the more ecumenical age of the twentieth century. In this context, 'conversion' came to signal a change from a Roman Catholic view of justification – Luther called it the 'way of works – to another or Protestant way of understanding the Christian gospel – Luther again called it the 'way of faith'. From the vantage point of a later age, we can now see that these were differing, indeed competing, schemes within the Christian world. Those diverse schemes came to be reflected in the different denominations – Lutheran, Calvinist, Anabaptist, Anglican, and later Puritan, Presbyterian, Methodist, Congregational, Baptist, Quaker – that emerged out of the Protestant Reformation and beyond.

These intra-Christian conversions are reflected in the stories of figures in the Reformation period and beyond. We have already described Luther's conversion from a Catholic Christianity to an evangelical or Protestant Christianity. We see a similar pattern in other Reformers as well. For example, Menno Simons (1496–1561), who was to become the pastor and leader of those Anabaptists known as 'Mennonites', was originally a Catholic priest in Holland who was deeply moved by the stories he heard of the Anabaptist martyrs. He then began to investigate the Anabaptist claims concerning their rejection of infant baptism. He thus became 'converted' to the Anabaptist way and left the Catholic Church. For Simons, and the Anabaptists, the Christians were those 'called out of the world' to live in community with others who have likewise become disciples of Christ. Calvin (1509–64), the French-born reform leader in Geneva, is reticent in the details of his conversion, but he too speaks of his 'sudden conversion' when God 'subdued and made teachable' his hardened heart, a heart he describes as 'addicted to the superstitions of the Papacy'. Originally a Catholic, Calvin became one of the most important of the Protestant reformers.[8] John Wesley (1703–91), the founder of the Methodists more than two hundred years after the Reformation, spoke of his heart being 'strangely warmed' in response to a Moravian sermon in 1738 on Luther's doctrine of justification by faith alone. Wesley then went on to preach a form of Christianity in which the true believer is one 'who has "the love of God shed abroad in his heart by the Holy Ghost given unto him", one who "loves the Lord his God with all his heart, and with all his soul, and with all his mind, and with all his strength" ... is inwardly and outwardly conformed to the will of God ..."[9] For Wesley, Christianity is not the mere acceptance of doctrine, nor mere attendance of the Christian Church and participation in its rituals, it is a life sanctified by the Holy Spirit and marked by 'Christian perfection'. In these forms of Christianity, much emphasis is placed on the experiential dimension of the Christian faith, beginning with conversion and justification and issuing in a sanctified life.

While these forms of denominational Christianity emerged in Europe, it was in the New World, especially the American colonies, that they really flourished. From the reform movements in Puritan England of the 1600s and in the American colonies of the 1700s, there emerged the classic form of conversion in Protestant Christian life, a conversion that is often linked to changing one's denominational affiliation as well as changing one's orientation to God. The stages were (1) a conviction of sin; (2) a recognition of one's need for a redeemer; (3) an experience of redeeming love or assurance of salvation; and (4) and the living of a Christian life. While the person may have been baptized into the Christian faith, it was really this experience – often called 'the conversion experience' or 'the experience of new birth' – that made one a 'real Christian'. A similar conversion pattern, though named in varying ways, was to be found across the reform movements within Protestant Christianity: Puritan, Pietist, Wesleyan and Baptist. Often the older Reformation traditions were critical of these new innovations, seeing them as too emotional and unstable.

Nevertheless, in the evangelical and sectarian traditions of post-Reformation Protestant Christianity, 'conversion' and 'new birth' became part of the standard Christian vocabulary of the Christian life. One's life in the Christian community was marked by the experience of 'conversion' or 'new birth'. Unlike the earlier understanding of conversion as involving the movement from outside to within the Christian world, here the language of conversion and new birth signalled the emotional and psychological experience of appropriating redemption – that one is redeemed by Christ – and sanctification – inwardly transformed by the Holy Spirit. This continues into the twentieth century, especially in the evangelical, charismatic and pentecostal streams of the Christian tradition. The charismatic and pentecostal traditions are dealt with in the chapters by Frank Flinn and Karla Poewe elsewhere in this volume.

Conversion of native peoples in the Americas

Perhaps the most disturbing chapter in the history of Christianity and conversion surrounds the missionary efforts of the Christian denominations in relation to the indigenous peoples of the New World, the Americas. With the arrival of Columbus in the new world came Christian missions, the efforts of Christians to convert the indigenous people to Christianity. While differences are to be found in the missionary styles and strategies employed by different missionaries throughout the Americas, there was a shared conviction that these peoples should be converted. The assumption was that such peoples – often called 'pagans' and / or 'infidels' – were outside God's grace and they must be brought into the Christian fold by any means necessary, including in some instances by force. Here conversion was seldom, if ever, understood as an inward spiritual process in which one's life was turned to God in Jesus Christ. Instead, conversion was mostly seen as a rejection of traditional practices and beliefs and an outward assent to Christian beliefs, ritual forms and ecclesiastical authority.

One of the few critical voices to be raised in this situation was that of the Spaniard, Bartolomé de Las Casas (1484–1566). Before becoming a priest in 1507, Bartolomé had already spent five years in the New World, on family lands in Hispaniola (Cuba). He returned to the New World in 1510. In addition to his priestly duties, he also presided over family lands. He became deeply distressed by the enslavement of the indigenous peoples and the ways that conversion was enforced. Later he was to write his *Only Way* which sharply and incisively critiqued the 'war of conversion' and argued from scriptural and historical theological sources that the only way to evangelize and seek appropriately the conversion of the native people was through exemplary lives, love and gentle reasoning.

According to Las Casas,[10] 'One way, one way only, of teaching a living faith to everyone, everywhere, always, was set by Divine Providence: the way that wins the mind with reasons, that wins the will with gentleness' (p. 68) '... the form Christ fixed for ... drawing people to a living faith ... is remarkably kind, gentle, peaceable, sensible ... lovable ... it is suffused with compassion' (p. 80).

But is this the way observed in relation to the non-Christians? Las Casas sees that instead of a way marked by love and compassion, Christians have engaged in 'wars for conversion'. He writes, 'the practice of subjecting pagans to Christian political power by the awful engines of war and thus make them willing to hear the gospel and to become Christians, is the utter opposite of the ... pre-established way' (p. 121).

As a landholder, Las Casas had been part of the way that he had rejected and was now criticizing. Indeed, he had come to recognize that 'there exist extraordinary kingdoms among our Indians' and that 'their society is equal to that of many nations ... they surpass many another ... they are inferior to none' (p. 65). This did not mean that Las Casas rejected the idea of conversion – of Indians coming to 'a living faith, to Christianity' (p. 71). But as he remarked in his discussion of the ideal missionary, 'non-Christians ... must sense that the preachers want no power over them' and that preachers 'are not really itching after their wealth' (p. 103). Moreover, Las Casas rejected the belief that those outside the Catholic Church were outside God's grace, he refused to demonize the non-Christian. Indeed, there are some suggestions in his writings that Las Casas believed the indigenous peoples of the Americas to be 'blameless infidels'.

Conversion in an age of dialogue

The issue of conversion of non-Christian peoples has become exceedingly controversial within contemporary Christianity. In large part this has to do with a sea change in the attitudes of some Christians towards non-Christian people. Until recently, most Christians held that one is only truly related to God in and through the Christian faith. Thus, it was obvious that all other people must be brought to share that faith. But in the twentieth century, more and more Christians have come to realize that God is not circumscribed by the Christian faith, indeed, there is a growing acknowledgment of the authenticity of men and women of other faiths – Jewish, Muslim, Hindu, Buddhist, etc. Thus Christianity in general and missionary Christianity in particular are struggling to find a more differentiated attitude towards people of other faiths. This does not mean that Christianity abandons its missionary impulse to share the good news of the Gospel with all peoples since Christians are persuaded that the Good News is for the whole of humanity. But in an increasingly pluralistic situation, the missionary impulse will have to unfold with an awareness of other faiths and that God is present to other faiths and peoples before the arrival of the Christian missionary and evangelist. In the midst of the post-Christian West we now encounter missionaries of other faiths – Muslim, Buddhist, and Hindu for example, inviting men and women to share their faith. And as well as the continuing conversion of peoples to the Christian faith, we are also witnessing conversion from Christianity to other faiths. This is proving to be profoundly disturbing to a Christianity that long believed it was the only authentic religious option for humankind.

Though conversion, as the work of the Spirit in turning the heart and mind towards God in Christ Jesus, continues to be central to certain streams of the Christian faith, the legacy concerning conversion is ambiguous. While Christians continue to affirm that the Spirit of God seeks the *metanoia* of all humanity, some wonder if we can continue to identify that spiritual work of *conversion* as only a turning to the Christian faith.

Notes

1. See W. H. C. Frend, *The Rise of Christianity* (Philadelphia: Fortress Press, 1984) for the history of conversion through the first six hundred years of Christianity.
2. It is worth noting that the *Oxford Dictionary of the Christian Church*, ed. F. L. Cross and E. A. Livingstone (3rd edn, Oxford: Oxford University Press, 1997) does not include an entry on 'conversion'. For certain strands of Christianity, conversion is not emphasized.
3. See Harvey Cox, *Fire From Heaven: The Rise of Pentecostal Spirituality and the Reshaping of Religion in the Twenty-First Century* (Reading, MA: Addison-Wesley, 1995).
4. For the best contemporary study of Paul's conversion see Alan F. Segal, *Paul the Convert: The Apostolate and Apostasy of Saul the Pharisee* (New Haven, CT: Yale University Press, 1990).
5. Augustine, *Confessions*, trans. R. S. Pine-Coffin (Harmondsworth: Penguin, 1961). Subsequent references are in brackets in the text.
6. *Life*, ch. 9, quoted in Victoria Lincoln, *Teresa: A Woman* (New York: Paragon House, 1984), p. 40.
7. See Erik Erikson's classic study *Young Man Luther* (New York: W. W. Norton & Co., 1962) and for a sample of Luther's writings see John Dillenberger (ed.), *Martin Luther: Selections from his Writings* (Garden City, NY: Anchor Books, 1961).
8. See François Wendel, *Calvin, The Origins and Development of His Religious Thought*, (London: Collins, 1965), p. 37.
9. As quoted in Hugh Kerr (ed.), *Readings in the History of Christian Thought* (Nashville, TN: Abingdon Press, 1978), p. 193.
10. Bartholomé de Las Casas, *Only Way*, ed. Helen Rand Parish (Mahwah, NJ: Paulist Press, 1992). Subsequent references are in brackets in the text.

12. Charismatic conversion in the light of Augustine's *Confessions*

Karla Poewe

Introduction

To scholars, Augustine is one of their own. He and his works are classics, the subject of theses, scholarly papers and learned symposia. When Augustine converted from academia to ecclesia it surprised no one that he should produce sophisticated theological works. After all, he was a scholar before conversion and would remain one thereafter, except that his subject-matter had its source in a new inspiration. What is surprising, however, is that a scholar should 'bare' or reveal himself by relating his human failings and growth in relatively simple, experientially based stories.

Augustine did not so much resolve as transpose his pre-conversion conflict from 'his heart' to the 'written page', for no one can deny that there is a tension between experience and analytical thought. In the hierarchy of the sciences and scholarship, personal experiences, the telling of them, and the conversion of them into written knowledge, maintain their largely untouchable and pariah status.

It may be for this reason, that the worldwide upsurge of experiential forms of Christianity, namely, pentecostalism, neo-pentecostalism, and charismaticism, have only recently received some attention from serious scholars. Among them are the works of Walter Hollenweger, David Martin, David Stoll, Stephen Glazier, Harvey Cox and Karla Poewe.[1] Enriching too has been the survey work of David Barrett and John Padwick and the dictionary by Stanley Burgess, Gary McGee and Patrick Alexander.[2]

Only one respectable academic has produced a serious work about a major existential Christian figure of our time.[3] No one has yet produced a serious study of Demos Shakarian (1919–93), for example, the founder of the Full Gospel Businessmen's Fellowship International (FGBMFI). Shakarian was a millionaire dairy farmer from California whose ethnic background was Armenian. In my interview with him, he emphasized that Armenian spirituality inspired him to bring men into churches that were then (following World War II) primarily attended by women. Over the last five decades he has inspired, affected, indeed, turned around hundreds of thousands of lives, often of prominent people, in 94 countries. In terms of sheer numbers, his lay Christian organization with its more than four thousand chapters across the world can even be respectably compared to the Roman Catholic empire rooted in Rome. Yet Shakarian remains largely unknown and unstudied, while academics have written uncountable pages about Augustine who, in his lifetime, had nowhere near the impact of the 'simple' dairy farmer, telling and soliciting 'simple' stories about life-changing Christian experiences.

And yet in one thing the converted scholar and converted dairy farmer are alike. Both told – one in written, the other in oral form – those personal, human and superhuman, experiences that reflect 'God's image' in the 'naked man', or, more importantly, that persuade men, even scholars, to 'undress' themselves in public so that 'God's image' may be reflected in 'the looking glass' of their human nakedness.

It is not my intention to answer why Christian conversion is so closely associated with the impulse of human learning. Rather, the topic is mentioned because most scholars find it difficult to look directly at the 'innocent' nakedness of Augustine's *Confessions*, despite the fact that Augustine's exposure has been partially draped by the cloak of time. If that is a problem, scholars find it even more problematic to look at, and know what to do with, present-day charismatic Christians – people in the process of experiencing God – who far from draping themselves are quite deliberately shedding their cultural garb in public places. Why are oral *confessions* popular among charismatic Christians? Do they make real the possibility of experiencing a living God? Do people see their own failures and potentials reflected in these stories? Are these stories peculiarly believable when so much else is not? In short, this chapter looks at

Augustine's act of 'baring' himself in the *Confessions* because we hope to find in it something that explains the persistence of the tradition in today's charismatic community.[4]

Priorities

It may well be true, to quote a critic, that 'conventional scholarship' sees Augustine's conversion as more involved than that of a sudden shift from Manichaeism to Christianity, recognizing rather that he passed 'first through Skepticism, then Stoicism, and finally Neoplatonism'. But in the *Confessions*,[5] Augustine does not see his conversion in that light. He does what every interviewed charismatic Christian does, namely, to speak from and speak about a dramatic shift in state of being from one condition to another. In the case of Augustine that shift is from being an academic and Manichaeist to being a Catholic bishop.

It is wise here to observe several things. First, in speaking about his conversion, Augustine condenses individual events, thoughts, and emotions by way of selective omissions or inclusions into dominant symbols which derive their meaning from dominant symbolic frameworks, one having informed the dominant symbols before conversion, the other following it.[6] Thus, a major change of life which may in fact take many years of untidy acting, thinking, and feeling is telescoped into one dramatic event bounded by two sets of dominant and opposite symbols. In the case of Augustine, the symbols that characterize his life before and after conversion are lust and continence, respectively.

Dominant symbols derive their meaning from symbolic frameworks. The latter are more or less well thought out public records of different states of being. As such, they are storehouses of human thought based on different assumptions about the human being, God and the nature of the universe. Different frameworks are not equally good nor equally powerful in affecting or changing individuals when they experience their state of being as empty. Augustine seemed to say as much when he converted. Manichaeism made him aware of the sharp contrast in life between lust and continence but seemingly did not assist him in shifting his priority from the former to the latter, a shift for which he began to long. The progressive experiences that helped him find his way into Christianity also helped him see his life as one wracked by a major conflict – not merely a contrast – between lust and continence. The conflict was experienced as increasingly painful until it became so unbearable as to bring him to his knees at the high point of his conversion process.

We should be aware of some significant events encapsulated in the above paragraph, for Augustine means to distinguish Christianity from other merely intellectual systems. Thus, Manichaeism is such an intellectual system capable of proposing contrasts in thought categories but hardly capable of engineering a change of life, least of all a major one. Intellectual technique and manipulation may make for fine intellectual games, but they are hardly capable of changing the whole man. To deal with the latter, Augustine did what the charismatic community still does, he made room for experience, first ever so human, then uncanny, finally supernatural and divine. We progress from the random, to the more than coincidental, to the divine plan.

And here we have to distinguish as Augustine does the relationship between human being and God from that between human being and human being and the priority of the former over the latter. Let us picture this as human life moving along two axes, one vertical between human being and God, the other horizontal between individual and individual. With the priority of the God–human relationship, it does not make sense to talk of a religious (here specifically Augustine's Christian) conversion as passing through a number of thought systems from Scepticism, to Stoicism, and so on. This kind of shift, primarily intellectual in nature, has significance for academics who seek new homes among new sets of like-thinking academics on the axis of inter-human relationships. This axis that Augustine is intent on abandoning; he mentions the futility of placing too much weight on human ties often enough. Instead, his conversion moves along the axis of the God–man relationship and on this axis intellectual sophistication, especially in the sense of diverse schools of thought, cannot help if for no other reason than that thought is simply not the whole person. The individual is more than thought. He or she is body, that is, feeling, emotion, intuition, sensation, as well as intellect.

If the whole person is to be in relationship to God – and not only in relation to other persons – then the whole person must grow into this relationship. And if relationships among persons call for other than intellectual faculties, how much more so the relationship between a person and God? Furthermore, the human being can experience insights; he cannot think insights into being. A person can have, that is, experience visions, not think visions into being. A person experiences hearing, not thinks hearing into being. In short, to take the human being into the presence of God, to establish that relationship, which is what conversion is, requires experiencing, listening to the experiences of others, and telling one's own experiences to others. And in this telling the human being's capacity to symbolize is more important than rational thought.

To establish or re-establish one's relationship with God, steps clearly highlighted by the experience of conversion and by other peak experiences, theoretical thought is momentarily irrelevant. It comes into play when we have to translate this experience (or these experiences) to communities of others.

A mature charismatic Christian knows what having a vision is. He knows when he 'is in one'. And when he is in one, he is 'seeing' what he would otherwise not see. He is not at that moment thinking. But such visions would be isolating, not relating, if they could not be communicated to other human beings. And here the dialectic between experience and doctrine picks up again. And the more sound the doctrine – the more it has withstood the ravages of time, the attacks of human doubt, the fear of the bizarre – the more sound becomes the experience that is illuminated by it or illuminates it. Doctrine leads to the expectation of such an experience as much as the experience requires doctrinal sanction. Likewise, doctrine may illuminate puzzling experiences as much as an experience may illuminate puzzling doctrinal statements. When these requirements are mutually satisfactory, which they often are not,[7] we are in the presence of a living/vital religion. Of this Augustine became convinced.

I said earlier that in *Confessions* Augustine is intent on describing conversion as a sudden shift from Manichaeism to Christianity. It is just as important to recognize that Augustine spoke about his conversion from his new state of being. He wrote about his past when he was a Christian. This state of being a Christian, that is, a person in relationship with God, informed his reflections about his experiences that brought him there. The fact that the relationship between his experiences and his state of being a Christian is dialectical in nature, in the sense that he reflects upon his experiences in the light of Christian doctrine while also illuminating Christian doctrine in light of his experiences, is at this point irrelevant. To give a personal example, I wrote a book about my childhood after I had become an anthropologist and clearly from within this state of being. The fact that I used a novelistic style to evoke strong images in the reader, rather than deductive logic or whatever else, is irrelevant to the larger fact that I looked upon my early past from within the state of being an anthropologist.

As with *Confessions,* so with charismatic Christians. The individual who *is* (not is becoming) a Christian is encouraged to reflect upon his pre-Christian experiences in light of biblical principles which, having entered the state of being a Christian, it is assumed he is now eager to learn and put to use by constructing his testimony.[8] The fact that his actual thought processes may be dialectical in nature, in the sense of seeing past events from the perspective of biblical principles and enlightening his understanding of the latter in the light of the former (with the help of the Holy Spirit of course) is, as was argued for Augustine, irrelevant to the larger fact of the individual's acceptance of his new state of being and operating from within this new context.

Symbolic methods and conversion as a life-changing experience

Augustine's reflections allow him not only to garner nuggets of wisdom from his experiences on the way to becoming a Christian, they allow him also to portray a major human drama, namely, the drama of conversion. In these endeavours he relies on the human ability to symbolize which, according to Leach, consists of using (1) symbol relationships which are arbitrary but habitual or conventional; and (2) sign relationships which are contiguous but in a relationship of a part to a whole; as well as (3) signal relationships which are causal.[9] In other words, to symbolize the human being relies on his (inborn) ability to recognize and work with something we call metaphor and metonymy. By metaphor is meant simply that A stands for B by arbitrary association. The association can be habitual, conventional, private, or one of planned resemblance as in an icon. Metonymy includes the use of something which Leach calls sign, natural index and signal. In the first or sign case, A stands for B as part for a whole; in the second, A indicates B; in the third or signal case, A triggers B so that the relationship between A and B is mechanical and automatic.[10] So far I have but paraphrased Leach. It is my observation, however, based on fieldwork and numerous interviews with charismatic Christians, that people do not carefully distinguish among sign, index and signal, so that A stands for and indicates B while B is seen to cause A. Augustine did this with 'the voice' episode, for example, and charismatic Christians do this with visions, speaking in tongues, and so on. This is the metonymic process.

If, with the help of Leach's tools, we now look in more detail at the content and structure of Augustine's conversion as he described it, we become aware of a pattern of thought that has, as mentioned, lasted through the ages and is an integral part of this life-changing experience. Thus Augustine describes the telltale signs, emotions, attitudes and thoughts preceding and following the peak experience of his conversion. By peak experience I mean the moment of euphoria, clearly identified by Augustine as having been of divine origin, and as having instantly resolved his life's major conflict.

Let us first look at some of the metonymic aspects of the structure of Augustine's conversion. To begin with, the *timing* of emotional and intellectual events is important. In *Confessions* it is represented by the way Augustine writes using distance between pages to symbolize distance between events.

The experiences that Augustine highlights as signs of God's wondrous hidden ways to aid man, these metonyms, are commonly found in charismatic circles today. One might, for lack of a better term, call them 'heralding events' after Synan.[11] Synan points out that certain 'events are heralded as a demonstration of supernatural power and activity and are linked to biblical types and patterns'.

There is, first, the premonitory curing and conversion of Alypius signifying that God worked through Augustine (*Confessions*, Blaiklock's translation, p. 137) and foreshadowing Augustine's own healing, conversion, and new life or 'ministry'. Such a premonitory healing was likewise noted by many famous modern evangelists, from Bill Branham to Oral Roberts, Kathryn Kuhlman, and Kenneth Hagin, among others. It is usually the first event that sets them on the path of a new life and ministry, usually one involving healing and evangelism.

Second, there is the phenomenon of the 'smiting word'. Again in *Confessions* it happens first to Alypius (with Augustine the instrument) and later to Augustine himself (p. 137). In these 'heralding events', modern charismatics also recognize one or other of what they refer to as the nine spiritual gifts. Thus, one evangelist may have the gift of healing, or of prophecy, or of discernment, but in line with our culture there is considerable gift-specialization. Some charismatic evangelists are specialists in the gift of knowledge, others in that of healing, and so on. Alternatively, an evangelist may shift from the exclusive use of one gift to that of another. As well, we see here the common experience that someone in the congregation is convinced that something said by the minister 'was said on his (the listener's) account alone'.

Third, Augustine, like charismatics today, places events, encounters, and appointments so that they reveal God's plan for the individual. Thus Alypius' arrest by the market-police (p. 139) and later the special meeting between Ambrose and Augustine, are what John Wimber calls 'divine appointments'.[12,13]

Fourth, the charismatic renewal has made explicit the transformation of failure into God's closing some doors in order to open others. We see this again in subtle form in Augustine's *Confessions* with the failure of his mother to find him an appropriate bride (p. 146), with the failure of the commune (p. 147), with the break-up of his common-law marriage (p. 148), and so on. The importance of (a counterbalancing) victory, so common in charismatic circles, is thus also present in Augustine's work.

Fifth, Augustine and present-day charismatics assign equal significance to the listening to testimonies usually prior to conversion and/or to other major ritual milestones.

Important too in the charismatic renewal is the way in which Augustine structured the events of his inner state just before and after his conversion. Examples are the increased inner tension, thematic shifts to those of searching, dying, madness, sickness and the crystallization of inner conflict. Then between the point of 'snapping' and the 'light of confidence' emotions come thick and fast. Despite the great intensity of emotion, however, three intellectual heralding events stand out: (1) the crystallization of reality into two opposing forces (at the point of conversion); (2) the sharp mental concentration at the sound of a voice (at the point of 'divine intervention'); and (3) the instant recognition that the 'smiting words' state his new being (at the point of climax).

If emotion somewhat dominates his state of being just prior to and during the height of conversion, then the intellect dominates his state of being following the climax of conversion. Intellectual surrender follows emotional surrender, increased blessings replace former despair; a sense of wholeness replaces the former sense of conflict; peace and victory replace dread and fear.

In sum, a core element of conversion is listening to other people's testimonies until the listener recognizes in the events of his own life premonitory healing (Augustine, *Confessions*, p. 137), God's closing doors but opening others (pp. 145, 147), an increased inner tension (p. 191), and the longing for its resolution. The shift in perception and the accompanying tension prompt him to describe himself in terms of themes of sickness, 'healthy' madness, a kind of dying, searching, breaking, and dread (pp. 196–7). A snapping point is anticipated (pp. 201–2), followed by a description of emotional crowding (pp. 203–4) that ends in euphoria (p. 204).

Longing and anticipation show that timing too is an important aspect of the structure of conversion. Experiences preceding the actual drama of conversion occur over a number of years; the highlighted emotions preceding the peak experience occur over a number of days. Then follow things of the moment: a storm of tears marking the emotional surrender (p. 203), lamentation (p. 203–4), repentance (p. 204), the voice (p. 204), sharp concentration (p. 204), the biblical passage (p. 204), and euphoric recognition that his conflict is resolved (p. 204).

If emotion predominates in Augustine's description of the period preceding the peak experience of conversion, intellect predominates thereafter (*Confessions*, p. 212). He writes of intellectual surrender accompanied by intense longing to read, think and write (p. 212); an awareness of increased blessings or 'fruits' (p. 216); an awareness of having been made whole (p. 217); intellectual zeal (p. 218), followed by inner peace and the knowledge of having won an important victory (p. 219); awareness of God's plan for humankind's salvation (p. 221); and recognition of signs and wonders (p. 222).[14]

The logic of conversion with its peak experience as climax, and the emphasis on human emotion and intellect respectively preceding and following the climax, is impeccable. Indeed, what makes Augustine's description convincing is that he uses his symbolic faculties as well as logic without losing sight of the existential nature of the conversion experience. As with Heidegger's description of dread or Thackeray's description of a Gros Ventre Indian seeking insight,[15] so the *Confessions* shows an individual living through his dark period, at the cost of existential pain, because he is certain of the light at the end of the tunnel, the rebirth, the emergence from the dark womb into the light of day. The danger of charismatic Christianity, especially when it is practised by immature Christians, is to want to do less than this, to by-pass the existential tunnel, precisely because it is painful and time-consuming. When this happens, charismatic Christians do what Augustine's *Confessions* reminds us not to do, namely, use less than the combination of symbolic and rational faculties and human experiences and rely instead on the sole use of metonymy – the tendency to make concrete and manipulate.

In the positive sense, therefore, Augustine's existentialism is echoed in the charismatic attitude that God is not confined to Scripture, but is found, as Jung said, 'in the storm, in the whirlwind, in the cataclysmic events (of an individual's life and) of history (generally), in the healing presence of his Son (or the Holy Spirit), in the ongoing proclamation of the church'.[16] But it is good to remember that in these life-changing experiences, as in extreme ones, concrete forms of existence tend to predominate and 'symbols tend to actualise'.[17] To quote further Des Pres, 'meaning no longer exists above and beyond the world; it re-enters concrete experiences, becomes immanent and invests each act and moment with urgent depth'.[18]

A later historical perspective: Hamann's proleptic experience as the key to a specific sense of reality

In 1967 Metzke published a prize-winning essay on J. G. Hamann, a charismatic Lutheran pietist, empiricist, philosopher and a compatriot and adversary of Kant, as the man who symbolized and articulated a turning point for philosophy of the eighteenth century.[19] If we look at Hamann here, it is because he can help us with the question why some scientists, even empiricists, do *not* regard conversion to be an illusion. Why instead they see it as the anchor or foundation of knowledge.

According to Metzke, the key to Hamann's thought is a specific happening or proleptic experience. Hamann himself called it his *Bekehrung* or conversion and argued that it gave a permanent direction to his life and outlook. This happening is the source of the peculiar 'constitution' of Hamann's understanding of Being and the world. While some people see Hamann as having deliberately set himself against the Enlightenment for the sake of argument,[20]

Metzke insists that Hamann's outlook is the result of a positive disclosure. His outlook on life, the constitution of his thought, has its source in a specific *Bekehrung*-experience. His intentions cannot be understood as having their source in the thought world of his immediate environment. They have their source, emphasizes Metzke,[21] in the totality of his own new experience.

While the 'atheistic *intellectus*' of the late twentieth century is rooted in the anti-system thinking and the radical relativism of postmodernism,[22] and while this thinking takes place largely within the old categories of being, body, life and metaphor, the source of Hamann's *intellectus* – and of interviewed charismatic Christians who were scientists – is a radical breakthrough to a new experience, perception, and conception of *reality*. But why is the very specific happening of a conversion important? Because Hamann was quite aware that it centred his existence, gave it meaning, and, most important for his thought, provided the key, as said, to his perception of reality, to his ontology.[23]

According to Hamann (here I am loosely translating and paraphrasing Metzke's explication), a *Bekehrung* is not just any happening. It is not a random happening which does not affect the substance of the person's life.[24] Rather, it is a crisis-driven shattering through which a human being becomes another from what he was before. The change is radical. It changes not only the meaning, belief, or dealings of a person, but his very Being. It is becoming a new person. It does not, of course, change the material nature of the person. Instead, it is a turning of one's whole life history and way of life.[25]

Hamann, and the charismatic scientists I interviewed, were convinced that this change is not possible through human effort, will, or wish. It is only possible through divine intervention, through the use, in other words, of metonymic patterns of thought. To them the new life is 'an act of God', precisely because it is a sudden *Umbruch* (radical change) which goes against the will of the person and counter to his developmental tendencies.

Metzke points out that Hamann's thinking,[26] as in my view the thinking of charismatic Christians today, is part of a tradition of German religious and metaphysical thought going back to the Lutheran Pietists Johann Arndt (1555–1621), Philipp Jakob Spener (1635–1705) and August Hermann Francke (1663–1727). In 1687 Francke had a proleptic or assumption-changing experience like that of Hamann in 1758. And like Hamann, Francke's thought too is grounded in this experience.[27] One can also not rule out the more controversial influence from the 'Lutheran mystic' Jakob Boehme (1575–1624) who, in turn, was influenced by Paracelsus (1493–1541) and by another Lutheran mystic, Valentin Weigel (1538–88). Charismatic Christianity is not, therefore, free of serious dangers, among them the flighty pantheistic and theosophical thinking of, for example, the New Age.[28] Consequently, it is important that revelation remain subject to the strictures of science and orthodox Christianity instead of, what usually happens, being excluded from them.

Augustine and Hamann are important because they are witnesses to the fact that conversion is a proleptic experience, an experience that centres one's thought and life. It is not an experience that frees one of the problem of good and evil, nor does it produce instantaneous holiness. This is not always remembered.

Importance of ritual milestones

It is important to keep in mind that Augustine wrote his *Confessions* after his conversion. It serves as a reminder that conversion is merely the beginning of the battle and of the ongoing inner temptations of human beings. There is, however, a significant difference between Augustine's, or for that matter Hamann's, post-conversion concerns and that of charismatic Christians. The latter have turned the ongoing battle with ongoing inner temptations into ritual milestones. Thus in the charismatic renewal the important ritual is no longer conversion but baptism in the Holy Spirit with the evidence of speaking in tongues. The latter ritualized experience moves the person a step beyond conversion to a full commitment of service in the Christian community. Most recently, there is a newer development yet within the charismatic community. I am referring to the 'Signs and Wonders' Movement of John Wimber. The vital ritual is no longer conversion, nor baptism in the Holy Spirit with the evidence of speaking in tongues, but exorcism. The latter provides 'real' deliverance and therefore 'real' entrance into that new life that was formerly thought to have started with conversion.

The above shifts may be said to be paradigmatic: a shift toward a new core ritual which comes to represent a new movement. Thus:

(1) primary emphasis on conversion was associated with the 'born again' movement of fundamentalists (1960s–70s).

(2) primary emphasis on baptism in the Holy Spirit with the evidence of speaking in tongues was associated with the charismatic renewal of the middle classes in mainline churches (1970s–80s).

(3) primary emphasis on deliverance through exorcism and the recognition of all gifts of the spirit is associated with the 'Signs and Wonders' Movement of John Wimber (1980s–90s). Most recently, some charismatics have moved beyond even this to 'laughing'.

Where the popularization of Christian growth and development differs from that portrayed in Augustine's *Confessions* is the expectation today of sudden change and its correlative optimism. Likewise, instead of Augustine's literary confessions one finds today oral testimonies.

The 'Signs And Wonders' movement especially reveals an impatience with time, development and history. For what makes the movement potentially magical is precisely the telescoping of one's past into evil within the present. The person's attitude toward himself and his life is ahistorical, though not anti-traditional. He does not carefully look at his history to see in his past actions bad faith, bad choices and ignorance of heeding God's will. Rather he looks at his present life and sees in it a present evil, that is, his past history is telescoped and reified or objectified.

Conclusion

When Augustine reflects on his life and conversion, he in fact carries out at least two symbolic operations. On the one hand, he examines his mundane actions in order to find in them nuggets of God's wisdom – a metaphoric operation. On the other, he describes the experiential highlights of the conversion drama in order to point beyond them to 'God's plan' – a metonymic operation. The metaphoric operation deals with core theological concepts like sin (*Confessions*, p. 157), humility as the word made flesh (p. 165), evil (p. 172), anti-cultism and anti-magic (p. 186). The metonymic operation deals with the birthing of core charismata out of the womb of tension, conflict, dread, emotional surrender, lamentation, contrition, voices, and so on (pp. 191, 201, 203–4). It is the latter, namely, experiential religion, that currently predominates in charismatic circles.

I stated in the introduction that the major Christian act is that of baring 'the self' in order to restore the individual's relationship with God and to make it the central axis of his or her existence. Thus conversion is the *Urerfahrung*, the original, most basic, or grounding experience that informs the life and thought of the individual thereafter. It is a proleptic or assumption-changing experience. Charismatics are quite aware that it centres their existence, gives them meaning and, importantly, provides the key to their perceptions of reality and to their understanding of being.

If there is a danger, it is the unwillingness of people to endure this baring. Consequently, some Christians, as well as observing scholars, prefer to ignore conversion experiences both in practice and in print. This is the importance of Augustine's *Confessions*. It reminds us that intellectualism has very little to do with the *process* of a person's being made in the image of God. But having achieved that state of being, and after the climax of conversion, the intellect, now inspired by a right source, or simply by a new source – works in full boldness among human beings to manage the affairs of life.

Notes

1. See Walter Hollenweger, *Pentecost between Black and White: Five Case Studies on Pentecost and Politics* (Belfast: Christian Journals, 1974); *Erfahrungen der Leibhaftigkeit: Interkulturelle Theologie* [Experiences of Embodiment: Intercultural Theology] (Munich: Chr. Kaiser Verlag, 1979); *The Pentecostals* (1969, 3rd edn Peabody, MA: Hendrickson (1988); *Geist und Materie* [Spirit and Matter] (Munich: Kaiser, 1988); David Martin, *Tongues of Fire: The Explosion of Protestantism in Latin America* (Oxford: Basil Blackwell, 1990); David Stoll, *Is Latin America Turning Protestant? The Politics of Evangelical Growth* (Berkeley, CA: University of California Press, 1990); Stephen Glazier (ed.), *Perspectives on Pentecostalism: Case Studies from the Caribbean and Latin America* (New York: University Press of America, 1980); Harvey Cox, *Fire From Heaven* (New York: Addison-Wesley Publishing Co., 1994); and the study I edited: Karla Poewe, *Charismatic Christianity as a Global Culture* (Columbia, SC: University of South Carolina Press, 1994).
2. David B. Barrett and T. John Padwick, *Rise Up and Walk! Conciliarism and the African Indigenous Churches, 1815–1987: A Sequel to Schism and Renewal in Africa 1968* (Nairobi: Oxford University Press, 1989);

Stanley Burgess, Gary McGee and Patrick Alexander, *Dictionary of Pentecostal and Charismatic Movements* (Grand Rapids, MI: Zondervan, 1988). It should be mentioned that several doctoral students are currently working on pentecostal or charismatic independent churches. An updated dictionary is also being prepared.

3. I am referring to David Edwin Harrell's book *Oral Roberts: An American Life* (San Francisco: Harper & Row, 1985).

4. I have been an observer of the international charismatic community since the beginning of 1984. My research includes life history interviews with over 50 of its leaders in Canada and South Africa and over 150 life history interviews with various charismatic Christians from independent charismatic churches, Christian lay organizations, and charismatic mainline churches. It should be mentioned that interviews were with mature Christians, not the lunatic fringe.

5. For simplicity, in this chapter I use E. M. Blaiklock's translation of *The Confessions of St. Augustine.* (Nashville, TN: Thomas Nelson, 1983).

6. Victor Turner, *The Forest of Symbols* (London: Cornell University Press, 1967).

7. See Irving Hexham and Karla Poewe, *Understanding Cults and New Religions* (Grand Rapids, MI: Eerdmans; 1986); *New Religions as Global Cultures: The Sacralization of the Human* (Boulder, CO: Westview Press, 1997).

8. A. C. Stedman, *Man of Faith* (Portland, OR: Multnomah Press, 1986).

9. Edmund Leach, *Culture and Communication: The Logic by which Symbols are Connected.* (Cambridge: Cambridge University Press, 1976), p. 15. It appears that Leach identifies a deep structure in man's symbolizing activities that is somewhat analogous to grammar in speech.

10. Ibid.

11. Vinson Synan, *Aspects of Pentecostal-Charismatic Origins* (Plainfield, NJ: Logos International, 1975), p. 25.

12. Tim Stafford, 'California's latest "boom church" has power encounters with sin and sickness', *Christianity Today*, 8 August 1986, pp. 17–22.

13. John Wimber, *Power Evangelism: Signs and Wonders Today* (London: Hodder and Stoughton, 1985).

14. The structure is taken from Blaiklock's translation, as mentioned earlier. It should be noted that the distance in terms of pages parallels the timing of events and emotions that make up the conversion process and structure. In that sense, Augustine's *Confessions* is probably the most meticulous and accurate description of the full complexity of the conversion experience in existence.

15. Manda Cesara, *Reflections of a Woman Anthropologist* (London: Academic Press, 1982).

16. Wayne G. Rollins, *Jung and the Bible* (Atlanta: John Knox Press, 1983), p. 96. Recent books have exposed Jung's occult leanings. See here Richard Noll, *The Jung Cult: Origins of a Charismatic Movement* (Princeton, NJ: Princeton University Press, 1994). American Fundamentalists tend to see an affinity between the occult and some charismatics, especially those belonging to the 'laughing church'.
17. Terrence Des Pres, *The Survivor* (New York: Pocket Book, 1977) p. 77.
18. Ibid., p. 77.
19. Erwin Metzke, *J. G. Hamanns Stellung in der Philosophie des 18. Jahrhunderts* [J. G. Hamann and Eighteenth-Century Philosophy] (Darmstadt: Wissenschaftliche Buchgesellschaft, 1967).
20. Rudolf Unger, *Hamann und die Auflkärung* [Hamann and the Enlightenment] (Tübingen: Max Niemeyer Verlag, 1968).
21. Metzke, *J. G. Hamanns*, p. 3.
22. Herbert Richardson, *Toward an American Theology* (New York: Harper & Row, 1967).
23. Metzke, *J. G. Hamanns*, pp. 3, 6.
24. Ibid., pp. 6–7. See Victor Turner, 'Dewey, Dilthey, and Drama: An Essay in the Anthropology of Experience', in *The Anthropology of Experience*, ed. Victor Turner and Edward M. Bruner (Urbana: University of Illinois Press, 1986), pp. 33–44, especially where he distinguishes between *mere* and *an* experience.
25. Poewe, *Charismatic Christianity as a Global Culture*, pp. 243–4.
26. Metzke, *J. G. Hamanns*, p. 4.
27. F. Ernest Stoeffler, *German Pietism during the Eighteenth Century* (Leiden: E. J. Brill, 1973), pp. 5, 11–13.
28. Irving Hexham and Karla Poewe, *New Religions as Global Cultures*.

13. Conversion in an African tradition

Irving Hexham

Introduction

Conversion within the context of African independent / indigenous churches involves many complex cultural factors. Therefore, in this chapter I will examine one particular case to illustrate the dynamics of African conversion. The case in question is that of the conversion, or calling, of the Zulu prophet and church founder Isaiah Shembe (1867?– 1935). But, before we can discuss Shembe in particular it is necessary to know something about African independent churches in general.

African independent churches

The rapid growth of African independent churches is one of the most significant religious developments of the twentieth century. The first recorded development of this kind in Southern Africa is the movement founded by Ntsikana (1780–1821). He was a traditional Xhosa who was regarded by his followers as a 'prophet'. The message he preached was essentially Christian although he did not possess a Bible and appears to have had no contact with Christian missionaries. Exactly what caused him to begin his preaching is unclear. What is certain is that he underwent a conversion experience at a time when he had no contact with whites, missionaries or other Christians. His life changed dramatically and he began an itinerant ministry which involved prophecies, the composition of theistic hymns, and healings.[1]

The traditional Xhosa explanation for Ntsikana's ministry is that he received a message from God by direct revelation and that his teachings were entirely due to the Holy Spirit. In her study of his 'Great Hymn' Janet Hodgson argues that this commonly held belief is wrong because there are oral traditions which indicate that following his conversion Ntsikana had extended contact with missionaries. Although Hodgson makes a good case, her evidence is not conclusive, leaving the possibility that the traditional account of his mission is correct.

What is certain is that Ntsikana developed a theistic theology, compatible with Christianity, which went well beyond the ancestor worship and traditional beliefs of his contemporaries. It is also clear that while he made few lasting converts, many Xhosa flocked to hear his preaching which prepared the way for later missionary activity. Therefore although he did not work for any mission organization and never created a church, there seems little doubt that his teachings prepared the way for Christian missions.[2]

Thirty years later the disaster known as the Xhosa Cattle Killing led to severe disruptions in the traditional societies of the Ciskei and Transkei. The 'Cattle Killing' was prompted by the visions of a young girl, Nongqawuse and the preaching of traditional prophets. According to those preachers, if the Zhosa slaughtered their cattle and destroyed their crops the ancestors would return to drive the whites, whose bullets would turn to water, out of southern Africa. After the great event, when the promised deliverance did not materialize, many Xhosa starved to death while others sought food from the whites who lived to the south in the Cape Province. From the religious viewpoint the cattle killing episode appears to have gained legitimization from a synthesis between traditional beliefs and Christian preaching. Yet, as with Ntsikana's preaching, it left behind no lasting religious movement. Rather, the failure of the prophetic promises made by traditional leaders actually caused many Xhosa to accept Christianity.[3]

The first genuine African independent churches in Southern Africa were created as a result of the work of German missionaries in the Orange Free State and Transvaal. The excellent training their converts received and the German theory of a *Volkskirche* (people's church) led to the development of a spirit of independence which led to the formation of various indigenous movements in the 1860s. Unfortunately, these development have not been studied and are only now the being brought to light by Karla Poewe and Ulrich van der Heyden.

In English language studies, the Methodist preacher Nehemiah Tile is usually credited with creating the first African independent church in 1884. He disagreed with his white supervisors in 1883, resigned from the Methodist Church, and founded his own church in 1884. An essentially Thembu movement, Tile's Church combined Christian teachings with Thembu nationalism. Unfortunately this brave experiment soon disintegrated after Tile's death in 1891.[4]

From the 1880s onwards many African independent churches developed in southern Africa and across the continent. Most of these were small affairs which attracted few followers and soon failed. By the turn of the century African independent churches had finally taken root among blacks in South Africa.[5] Today literally thousands of African independent churches are thriving in South Africa. The majority of these are very small affairs with their own prophet and a handful of members. Others, however, are large well-organized movements which have stood the test of time. The oldest major African independent church is the Nazareth Baptist Church of the amaNazarites founded in 1912 by Isaiah Shembe. Today the largest of these churches is the Zion Christian Church which was founded in 1924 by Ignatious Lekganyane (1885?–1948).[6]

David Chidester estimates that in 1990 'over 30% of the Black population of South Africa' belonged to African independent churches.' This figure represents a doubling of independent church membership in the 30 years since 1960.[8] During the same period, membership of African Traditional religions dropped from 22.6 per cent of the black population to 16 per cent.[9] In other words, African independent churches are growing at the expense of mainline Christian churches. Not surprisingly many mainline Christian writers do their best to minimize the importance of the independent churches which are clearly infringing on their market share.

The life and work of Isaiah Shembe

Isaiah Mdliwamafa Shembe (1867?–1935) was the 'prophet' and founder of the Nazareth Baptist Church, the amaNazaretha, one of Africa's oldest new religious movements, sometimes called an 'independent' or 'indigenous' church. Shembe is perhaps unique among modern religious leaders south of the Sahara because in 1949 his son, Johannes Galilee Shembe (1904–76), commissioned the Rev. Petros M. Dhlomo to collect and record the oral histories of the movement. Dhlomo did this with great diligence thus preserving a record of the life and work of Isaiah Shembe based on eyewitness testimonies. Dhlomo recorded the testimonies of his informants by painstakingly typing them out as the people described their experiences to him. He also provided the names of his informants, but omitted to give any other information about them.

In the late 1960s J. G. Shembe asked the German missionary Dr Hans-Jürgen Becken if he would translate and publish the oral histories in English. But, due to circumstances, including his return to Germany in 1974, Becken was unable to accept the task. After J. G. Shembe's death in 1976 his brother Amos Shembe instructed Dhlomo to expand the project to include the life and work of himself and his brother J. G. Shembe. As a result three large volumes were created, comprising over 250 testimonies and accounts of deeds of the amaNazarite leaders.

Later, in 1989 Becken once more returned to South Africa where he visited Amos Shembe who again requested that he translate the movement's history into English. This time Becken was able to accept the commission. Currently, all three volumes of oral histories have been translated and are to be published by the Edwin Mellen Press, Lewiston, New York in the USA. The following account is based on these texts and other secondary material.

Isaiah Shembe was born on a farm at Ntabamhlophe near Estcourt, in Natal, South Africa. The farm was located near the Drakensberg mountain range known as the Giant's Castle which provided the backdrop for Cy Ranker Endfield's production of the 1964 film *Zulu*. The exact date of Shembe's birth is unknown although he was thought to be about 68 years old when he died in 1935. The family originated in Zululand, but fled to the Drankensberg region after his grandfather, who was a great diviner, became convinced that the Zulu king would kill him. The testimonies are unclear as to whether the king in question was Senzangakhona or his successor Shaka. It is also stated that Shembe's father, Mayekisa, was a 'prophet', although there is no indication that he had any contact with Christianity or Christian missions. Later Shembe's father moved to Ntabazwe near Harrismith in the Orange Free State where the young Shembe grew up.

Many tales are told about the wondrous deeds of the young Shembe. He was married to four wives and had numerous girlfriends. Then, quite suddenly, like John Bunyan (1628–88), in his classic *Grace Abounding to the Chief of Sinners*,[10] and the German Pietist leader,

210

August Herman Francke (1663–1727), Isaiah Shembe was convicted of his sins and sought peace with God after a dramatic conversion.

The story Shembe told about his conversion begins with various prayer experiences during which he felt 'a call' to serve God. But he ignored God's instructions and continued to live a secular life. Then, in the late 1890s a number of his children died in quick succession. Dhlomo records the story[11] as follows:

> 14.1.13 Five days after this burial, another child passed away ... All these children were sick for five days before they left this earth ... (Shembe) asked God: 'What sin did I commit, that you hit me with such a severe whip?' Jehova replied: 'No, I did not bring about this death; it was you ... I told you to separate your wives, for I wanted to speak to you? You said, that it would be better for your wives to die than to allow them to be married to other men ... I have done what you said. But instead of your wives, who are not yet converted, I have taken the children of these women, for they did not yet sin. Today, I tell you: Follow me now. Your wives have now died. I want to do my work through you.' (*Petros M. Dhlomo, Khaya S. Ndelu*, and *Jeslinah Mchunu*)

After this drama, Shembe left his wives to become a wandering seeker. During the next few years he appears to have joined several churches. At first he seems to have been influenced by the Weslyans and may even have been baptized by them. Later he associated with at least two different Baptists groups and was baptized by one of them on 22 July 1906.[12] At this time, like Joseph Smith earlier in the United States and Sun Myung Moon later in Korea, he began to be troubled by the clear divisions and open hostility between members of Christian missionary churches.[13] About the same time that he became aware of disunity among Christians, Shembe came into contact with prophetic traditions within Zulu society through encounters with several independent 'prophets'. One of these men, a former Lutheran catechist, Nkabinde, led Shembe to develop a healing ministry in 1910.

Like Shembe, Nkabinde had experienced a vivid call to serve God. Dhlomo says:

> 18.1.1 Before the war of 1906, Johane Zandile Nkabinde was a preacher of the Lutheran Church at Nquthu ... Then his wife passed away and he remained alone with his children at this home. Then the Word of Jehova came to him ... he refused the call, for he did not know with whom he should leave his children ... the Word of Jehova came to him for a third

time ... This Word said to him: If you will not obey the call, this storm will destroy your houses and kill your children, whom you love so much. (*Daniel Dube*)[14]

Perhaps it was the similarity of their personal experiences which brought the two men together. Whatever the case, it seems that Nkabinde proclaimed the coming of Shembe in his preaching:

Nkabinde said: Listen, you people of Africa. God has told me, that there is a man coming from heaven, who is not like other human beings. I am like John the Baptist to announce his coming to you ...[15] (*Johannes Galilee Shembe*)

With Nkabinde's endorsement Shembe proceeded to preach throughout Natal where he received a very warm welcome and seems to have gathered around him a group of followers. He also initiated baptism in the sea on the Durban beachfront.[16]

Around this time Shembe visited the grave of another Zulu prophet Mfazwe to pay homage. This visit caused the followers of Mfazwe to recognize Shembe as their new prophet and flock to him, thus increasing the strength of his movement.[17] About a year later, in 1912, Shembe founded the iBandla lamaNazaretha or Nazareth Baptist Church.

When Shembe died on 2 May 1935 at Mikhaideni in Northern Natal, his movement seems to have had around 35,000 followers.[18] In 1989 the South African newspaper *The Sunday Tribune* estimated that Amos Shembe's church had over 500,000 members.[19] Another 30,000–75,000 people belonged to the rival branch of the movement headed by J. G. Shembe's son, Londa Shembe.[20]

Isaiah Shembe had established a well-organized religious movement with a rich liturgy based on traditional Zulu ritual and dance. He acquired a farm, close to kwaMashu, near Durban, which became his holy city of Ekuphakameni, and established an annual pilgrimage to the Holy Mountain of Nhlangakazi which was tastefully recorded in the BBC film *Zulu Zion* (1969).

According to the testimonies recorded by Petros M. Dhlomo, Isaiah Shembe was noted for his vivid parables and uncanny insights into people's thoughts. He loved the wilderness and often went to pray on mountains and in lonely places. Animals are said to have understood his commands and dangerous snakes were unable to harm him or his followers. He spoke with spirit beings and on several occasions claimed to see a host of angels or other spiritual creatures which remained invisible to those with him. Most important of all he had the ability to heal people of physical and mental sickness.

Shembe wrote many moving hymns and composed dramatic music which formed the basis for ritual dances. He designed 'sacred' clothing for his followers who were supposed to wear their heavenly garb on festive and other occasions in preparation for life in heaven. The Sabbath replaced Sunday as a day of worship and various food laws, including a ban on alcohol and eating chicken, were instigated. Christmas was also abandoned in favour of New Year and mid-winter (June) ceremonies.

In 1930 Shembe was involved in a serious dispute with the government over his refusal to allow his followers to be vaccinated which he interpreted as evidence of lack of faith in God. Eventually, after many threats and prolonged court action the authorities seem to have given way and allowed the amaNazarites exemption from the vaccination order.

Numerous fantastic stories surround Shembe's death, most of which were concocted by his enemies to discredit the movement. One such story says that he died jumping off a cliff because he thought he could fly like an angel. Actually, his last days seem to have been plagued with illness and exhaustion. From the available records it seems that Shembe simply worked himself to death through continuous travel, preaching, open air baptisms in pools and rivers, and church administration. He died on 2 May 1935 at Mikhaideni in Northern Natal and was buried on 5 May at his beloved Ekhuphakameni.

Following his death there was a short succession dispute which eventually resulted in the son of his third wife, J. G. Shembe, assuming the leadership of the amaNazaretha movement. J. G. Shembe continued the traditions of his father and saw remarkable church growth. When he died in 1975 there was another succession dispute which led to a major split and a division of church properties.[21]

After Johannes Galilee Shembe's death there was a short but bitter leadership dispute which led to lawsuits. Eventually the church divided between the followers of another of Isaiah Shembe's sons, a graduate of Fort Hare and former schoolteacher, Amos Shembe, and one of Johannes Galilee Shembe's sons, a graduate of the university of Zululand and practising lawyer, Londa Shembe. Most older members of the church followed Zulu tradition by recognizing the elderly Amos Shembe as their new leader.

Amos Shembe claimed the right of succession because of Zulu tradition and his birth as a son of Isaiah Shembe. He established a new sacred site on a farm owned by the church about ten miles north of kwaMashu. Although an able administrator, Amos Shembe did not claim to be a 'prophet', nor did he invoke a 'divine call', instead he called himself 'bishop' and assumed a bureaucratic style of leadership.

By contrast, Londa Shembe asserted a charismatic right to inherit his father's mantle. According to him he was content working as a lawyer until he received a vision of his late father's hands drawing him to the spiritual world. This and subsequent visions led him to declare his divine calling and assume the office of a prophet. Many younger, more educated, people joined Londa Shembe, to form a separate movement based on the holy city of Ekuphakameni which was given to him as the result of a lawsuit that divided church property between him and his uncle.

Amos Shembe organized his branch of the church along traditional lines which built on the work of his predecessors and affirmed the biblical basis of their faith. Londa Shembe was a religious innovator who relied on the work of the Spirit and revelations from God and Shembe to uphold his position.[22]

Amos Shembe died in 1995 and the church leadership was taken over by his companions. Thus the switch to a bureaucracy was complete. Londa Shembe was brutally assassinated on 7 April 1989.[23] Today his followers continue his work through a charismatic form of leadership in the midst of what has become a war zone on the outskirts of Durban.

Nevertheless, the prophetic message of Isaiah Shembe delivered by himself, his sons, and grandson lives on in the lives of many black South Africans and will no doubt play an important role in the future religious composition of the new South Africa which is at present undergoing severe birthpangs.

Isaiah Shembe and the tradition of conversion

Whenever one discusses the origins of African independent churches or other indigenous prophetic movements, questions about religious conversion, visions and revelation immediately present themselves. According to traditional accounts, several African prophets, including the Xhosa prophet Ntsikana (1780–1821), Ignatious Lekganyane

(1885?–1948) and Isaiah Shembe (1869?–1935), underwent a conversion experience involving visions prior to contact with Christians or Christian missionaries. Following these initial experiences, these prophets begin a walk with God and over the course of their lifetime receive many revelations from God.

Upon first hearing such stories Europeans are prone to see the African prophet as an exotic being who is uniquely African. As a result barriers are erected between historic Christianity and the new religious movements of Africa. If, however, the experiences of men like Shembe are compared to great Christian leaders in Western society then a different picture emerges. Far from being uniquely African the experiences of Ntsikana, Lekganyane and Shembe fit the pattern of conversion and spiritual life of Christians throughout history. A comparison between the religious experience of Isaiah Shembe and John Bunyan vividly illustrates this fact.

Living centuries apart in very different countries, John Bunyan and Isaiah Shembe ought to have little in common. Yet, surprisingly, their spiritual pilgrimage leading up to their conversions was very similar. Both men were fond of women and, by all accounts, successful lovers.[24] Neither was particularly chaste, but they lived in societies[25] where chastity was not a considered a great virtue.

It is all the more puzzling that both men should be plagued with thoughts of God which created a deep sense of their own sinfulness, especially in sexual matters. Why should a Bedford tinker and a Zulu tradesman be troubled by the life they were living when their social equals admired the manliness of their behaviour? Perhaps Bunyan heard Puritan preaching and came under the conviction of sin. Perhaps Shembe heard a latter-day Puritan repeat the type of message which brought Bunyan to repentance. Both men moved in societies where such preaching was not uncommon. Yet the question remains why they and not others responded to a message which came from a different social and, in Shembe's case, racial group.

Nevertheless, what is certain is that both men did respond and in doing so became leaders of powerful religious movements which challenged the very foundations of their respective societies. Of course, Bunyan's status as the leader of a religious movement can be questioned. His following was never too great during his lifetime, although he was a popular preacher. But in the centuries after his death his writings, particularly The Pilgrim's Progress, drastically shaped the religious consciousness of millions.[26] Similarly, at his death in 1935 Shembe's following remained quite small and almost exclusively Zulu. Yet within fifty years it would spread throughout southern Africa to embrace over half a million people. And the appeal of his teaching shows no sign of diminishing.

My purpose in comparing Bunyan with Shembe is to bring home to Western readers the realization that 'the prophet Isaiah Shembe' is not a isolated figure in religious history. His story is not a curious example of an African living in a very strange society who happened to gather around him a group of ignorant peasants. Rather, behind this unique African story is the story of a man whose experiences were almost identical with those of other men throughout history in many different societies.

Living in a relatively more religiously liberal society than that experienced by Bunyan, Shembe was protected by local magistrates and could build up a living church. Bunyan on the other hand spent over twelve years in gaol forcing him to divert his creative energies into writing.

Of course, it may be objected that Western Christians describe Shembe as 'a prophet' while his followers appear to regard him as something greater than a prophet. Surely, the prophetic element sharply distinguishes a Shembe from a Bunyan, who was, after all, a Calvinist preacher. But there are also prophetic elements in Bunyan's writings. For example, in *The Pilgrim's Progress* when Christian and Faithful approach the Vanity Fair, where Faithful is to lose his life, they are met by Evangelist who encourages their endeavour and is thanked by Christian who says: 'they well knew he was a Prophet, and could tell them things that might happen unto them ...'.[27] Prophets were not unknown in Bunyan's day. The practice of prophecy and recognition of living prophets was associated with the Levellers, Diggers, Quakers and other politically suspect groups.

And in Bunyan's Calvinist tradition there were the words of John Calvin in his *Institutes of the Christian Religion*:

> Those who preside over the government of the church in accordance with Christ's institution are called by Paul as follows: first apostles, then prophets, thirdly evangelists, fourthly pastors, and finally teachers (Eph. 4:11). Of these only the last two have an *ordinary* office in the church; the Lord raised up the first three at the beginning of his Kingdom, and *now and again revives them as the need of the times demands* (italics mine).[28]

Thus Calvin, Bunyan and Shembe all share the belief that although rare, prophets are 'raised up' by God as the need arises. Today thousands of Africans believe that Isaiah Shembe was just such a person raised up by God to speak to them in their own language and cultures thus bringing them to God in a uniquely African way.[29]

Conversion in the African context

How are we to understand conversion in the context of African independent churches? Contrary to various post-colonial and post-modern writers, African conversion is no different than any other Christian conversion. What is important is not the cultural context but absorption into a living tradition. Christian conversion must be viewed within the cultural context of the great tradition known as Christianity. Within this tradition we find common human longings, themes and responses to a divine reality which people entering the tradition claim to encounter. The Christian experience of 'the Holy' forms a basis for Christian conversion which transcends the particularities of human cultures. To the believer this commonality is based on the reality of God. To the unbeliever it can only be explained on the basis of the reality of a common humanity. Thus, for believer and unbeliever alike, Christian conversion in the African context is an important phenomenon which informs contemporary debates by providing evidence of a reality beyond the subjectivity of the individual observer. Whether that reality is understood in terms of God, an external human condition, or a combination of both the divine and the human, does not matter. The fact is, something exists beyond the individual and it is this something which is reflected in the shared cross-cultural experience known as Christian conversion.

Notes

1. Cf. Irving Hexham (ed.), *The Scriptures of the amaNazaretha of Ekuphakameni*, trans. by Londa Shembe and Hans-Jürgen Becken (Calgary: Calgary University Press, 1994), pp. vii–xxii.
2. Cf. Janet Hodgson, *Ntsikana's Great Hymn: A Xhosa Expression of Christianity in the Early 19th Century Eastern Cape* (Cape Town: University of Cape Town Centre for African Studies, 1980).

3. Cf. J. B. Pieres, *The Dead Will Arise: Nongqawuse and the Great Xhosa Cattle-Killing Movement of 1856–7* (Johannesburg: Ravan Press, 1989).

4. C.C. Saunders, 'Tile and the Thembu Church: Politics and Independence on the Cape Eastern Frontier in the Late Nineteenth Century', *Journal of African History*, vol. 11, no. 4 (1970), pp. 553–70.

5. Cf. B. G. M. Sundkler, *Bantu Prophets in South Africa* (2nd edn, London: Oxford University Press, 1961), *Zulu Zion and Some Swazi Zionists* (London: Oxford University Press, 1976); and G. C. Oosthuizen, *The Birth of Christian Zionism in South Africa* (KwaDlangezwa, University of Zululand, 1986).

6. Cf. Elias Khelebeni Lukhaimane, 'The Zion Christian Church of Ignatius (Engenas) Lekganyane, 1924–1948: An African Experiment with Christianity', unpublished MA thesis, University of the North, Pietersburg, 1980. David Chidester, *Religions of South Africa* (London: Routledge), 1992, p. 134, says that the Zion Christian Church was 'founded around 1910'. Here he has confused the earlier evangelistic work of Lekganyane for the Zion Apostolic Church, which he joined in 1912 following a vision and conversion, cf. Lukhaimane, 1980, pp. 13–23.

7. Chidester, *Religions of South Africa*, p. 114.

8. Cf. Human Sciences Research Council, *Religion, Intergroup Relations and Social Change in South Africa* (Pretoria: Human Sciences Research Council, 1985), p. 27.

9. The figure of 16% is an estimate made by Professor Oosthuizen. In terms of available census data, Traditional African religious believers declined from 22.6% in 1960 to 18% in 1980, Cf. Human Sciences Research Council, *Religion, Intergroup Relations and Social Change in South Africa*, p. 27.

10. John Bunyan, *Grace Abounding to the Chief of Sinners* (London: George Larkin, 1666).

11. All of the following sections beginning with a three digit reference number are taken from *The Sacred Books of Africa, First series. South African Scriptures. the Sacred History and Traditions of the amaNazaretha, Volume One, The Story of Isaiah Shembe: History and Traditions Centered on Ekuphakameni and Mount Nhlangakazi*, trans. Hans-Jürgen Becken, ed. Irving Hexham and G. C. Oosthuizen (Lewiston: Edwin Mellen Press, 1996).

12. Ibid., Section 17.

13. Ibid., Section 16.

14. Ibid., Section 18.1.1.

15. Ibid., Section 18.3.1.

16. Ibid., Section 20.

17. Ibid., Section 22.
18. The English magazine *The Illustrated London News*, 8 February 1930, p. 203, carried an article on Shembe in which it stated that he had over 32,000 followers.
19. *The Sunday Tribune*, Durban, 2 August 1987, p. 9.
20. Estimate by Londa Shembe, August 1987.
21. G. C. Oosthuizen, *Succession Conflict within the Church of the Nazarites* (Durban-Westville: Institute for Social and Economic Research, University of Durban-Westville, 1981).
22. These comments are based on interviews with Amos and Londa Shembe in August 1987. Cf. Oosthuizen, *Succession Conflict within the Church of the Nazarites.*
23. *Daily News*, Durban, 8 April 1989.
24. In his MA thesis Absolom Vilakazi puzzles over the question why Shembe should feel guilt for sexual practices which were accepted by his society. See Absolom Vilakazi, 'Isonto Lamanzaretha: The Church of the Nazarites', unpublished MA thesis, Kennedy School of Missions, Hartford Seminary, 1954, pp. 31–6. Similarly, Christopher Hill in his recent biography *A Tinker and a Poor Man: John Bunyan and His Church, 1628–1688* (New York: Alfred A. Knopf, 1989), pp. 41–59, wonders about Bunyan's early life and the events leading up to his conversion.
25. In Bunyan's case this was more likely a segment of society rather than the society as a whole.
26. Cf. Clifford Hill, *Prophecy Past and Present* (Crowborough: Highland Books, 1989), pp. 349–82.
27. John Bunyan, *The Pilgrim's Progress*, [1978] (Burlington: Welch Publishing Company, 1983), p. 96.
28. John Calvin, *Institutes of the Christian Religion* [1559], Book IV. 111.4 trans. Ford Lewis Battles (Philadelphia: Westminster Press; London, SCM Press, 1960), vol. 2, p. 1056.
29. The early life of Shembe and oral histories of his church are being investigated by Professor Hans-Jürgen Becken. Cf. Hans-Jürgen Becken, 'The Deeds of Shembe as Described by his Eyewitnesses', in *Afro-Christian Religion at the Grassroots in Southern Africa*, ed. G. C. Oosthuizen and Irving Hexham (Lewiston: Edwin Mellen Press, 1991).

14. The Benedictine vow 'conversio morum'

Macrina Sitzia

'Without having seen him, you love him; though you do not now see him you believe in him, and rejoice with unutterable and exalted joy.' These words are taken from the first Letter of St Peter (1:8), a letter which in many ways expresses the spirit and perspective which, nearly five centuries further on in the development of the Christian tradition, inspired St Benedict both in his understanding, through his pioneering practice, of the monastic way of life, and in the composition of his Rule for those who wished to follow in the tradition which he himself treasured as a pure and tested way of discipleship. The words quoted are exemplified in him, for whom nothing is to be preferred to the love of Christ, and often find an echo in his teaching; they resonate with the deepest motivation in the hearts of monks and nuns who have undertaken this way as his sons and daughters.

St Peter's Letter speaks of Christ, whom his first disciples had known as they would have known any other, journeying with him, eating with him, listening to him, as a companion, brother and teacher. Christ, who passed from their midst, who was taken from their sight through his death by crucifixion, and whom yet they came to know to be still more truly among them, more powerfully within them, in his manifestation in resurrection. So still they listened to him, in the teaching which he inspired among them, in the illumination of Scripture; still they ate with him, in a foretaste of the marriage feast of heaven, the consummation of ultimate union with God in Christ, at the Eucharistic meal; still they journeyed with him, following him in his Passover from this world to the Father.

St Benedict offers his Rule as a guide for this journey, while strictly emphasizing his dependence on and reference to the Gospel and the tradition.[1] The fundamental, interior structure of his disciple's life is no different from that which in essentials makes itself evident in all those who in whatever age and tradition have sought to respond to the awakening realization of the ultimate in the depths of their being, in whatever way this may be experienced. A Christian looking at this essential structure sees, as it makes itself manifest, the pattern of Christ's death and resurrection. The spiritual awakening is a rebirth into a new, transformed mode of being, which is participation, through union, in the life which is God himself. It is an ever-deepening union because the divine life itself transcends all limits, is beyond all attainment. It is such a union to which St Paul gives expression when he says, 'I have been crucified with Christ; it is no longer I who live, but Christ who lives in me; and the life I now live in the flesh I live by faith in the Son of God, who loved me and gave himself for me' (Galatians 2:20). It is to this union that St Benedict seeks to guide the disciple when he says, 'Through patience we shall undergo what Christ suffered, and thereby be made worthy of sharing his kingdom' (Rule, Prologue 50).

'Through patience ...', St Benedict says. Patience implies a process, and one which is never really fulfilled as long as the awaited, longed-for fruit of labour and endurance is sought as an external reality. The change which brings about the desired resolution is an interior one: it is a change or transformation of mind; it is *metanoia*, repentance.[2] This inner change, therefore, which is effected through patience, is the point of conversion. It signifies the dissolution of the duality which sees suffering as something manufactured externally to oneself, rather than seeing it for what it is, one's own experience, a process within one's own mind; the mind in bondage to suffering imagines that change of external circumstances will bring deliverance, and as long as it clings to this delusion, it remains in bondage, and suffers.

The actual 'change' necessary, as Christ's resurrection most radiantly shows by its transformation of death by the power of the divine life within him, is that of an inner awakening, the arising of that inner dawn of unborn, undying light by which the pain and death of suffering are transformed into unconquered joy. Christ says in St John's Gospel: 'When a woman is in travail she has sorrow, because her hour has come; .., so you have sorrow now, but I will see you again, and your hearts will rejoice, and no one will take your joy from you' (John 16:21–22). The point of transformation, therefore, is the realization of Christ's presence, in a power of being which transcends the life of this world, and death itself. There is an ancient saying handed down from the early monastic Fathers: 'The soul of the monk is like the night of Easter, for it sees Christ rising from the dead.'

St Benedict's emphasis on the practice of patience as the catalyst for this awakening gives the process of conversion or transformation a particular character or perspective. Patience, a humble virtue, is not commonly associated with peak spiritual experience. Yet here this is precisely what is being implied. Christ's teaching on vigilance, found in the Gospels and in particular in certain of his parables, lies at the heart of the monastic tradition and practice, as the above-quoted saying, for example, shows. The bridegroom will come at an unexpected hour[3] at an hour which is not known, for it cannot be known: it is hidden in God, and is not discernible in the temporal realm, only at that point of transcendence between moment and moment. This is the hidden moment, the unknown hour when the bridegroom makes himself known, when through the dissolution of death his light dawns. St Benedict's practice uncovers this unique moment in every moment; the mystery of Christ's dying and rising is realized in every breath.

The monk, or nun's, life, says St Benedict, should be a continual Lent (Rule 49:1). That is, it should be characterized by perpetual vigilance, in accordance with the Gospel precepts outlined above, in which Christ urges his disciples to stay awake, with lamps alight. Such vigilance is marked by purity (49:2) and 'the joy of spiritual longing' (49:7, cf. 4:46) for the Easter dawn. This vigilance kindles in the monk or nun's heart the attitude of mindfulness, which realizes God's presence everywhere,[4] and establishes it in right view, in which, by 'keeping death always before one's eyes' (4:47), one maintains the perspective of ultimate truth.

This orientation towards the dawn, symbolic of the inner awakening, is strongly reinforced by St Benedict's emphasis on the night Office, the service of chanted psalms and Scripture readings performed, according to the Rule, in the early hours of the morning, before first light.[5] In the dormitory, throughout the night, a lamp is to be kept burning and even during sleep, one's mind is to be kept vigilant and ready to wake up, so that the instant the signal is given, one is ready to respond, one's inner eyes open to receive divine illumination.[6]

This illumination is the transforming light of Christ's resurrection, as it is gradually realized in the disciple. All St Benedict's instructions in his Rule are directed to enable this to come about, gradually. The monastic day is oriented towards this dawn, as we have seen, in the prolonged night prayer and the celebration of Lauds at sunrise; the celebration of Sunday, the day of the Lord's resurrection, is the focal point of every week; and the feast of Easter itself is the climax of the year. Life is a continual Lent only up to a point. The light proclaims that Christ is risen. Faith lives according to that light. Love has known its transforming power.

The radiance of Christ's rising pervades the monk's or nun's entire existence. The vow of conversion is taken that this may be so. A scene described by St Benedict in his instructions for the reception of a new member reveals the essence of what is meant by 'conversion' in the Christian monastic tradition. In this text, chapter 58 of his Rule, we have a description of the process whereby one who so desires enters the monastic community and undertakes the monastic discipline. In it, the novice passes through a period of testing and trial, whereby he or she proceeds gradually inwards from the outer circle of the guest quarters, through the intermediate state of dissolution in the novitiate, and so to the threshold of the inner sanctuary, the place of transformation. There the community are gathered, heaven and earth are united in the communion of the holy beings, and the novice comes into God's presence.

According to Christian understanding, this is a presence from which the novice has never been absent. This is the presence of One whom he or she has known, within the consciousness of being known, loved and called. However, this is not a being known or loved or called as another, nor as by another. Rather, a knowing and being known that transcends the dualism of knower and known. And so, the Christian novice enters the presence of God, and finds himself or herself alone : the monk is 'monos', 'one who is alone'.

And yet, never alone. At the heart of the Christian monastery is an altar. On it, the offering is made which, it is believed, gathers all existence into its transforming power and makes all holy. This supreme offering is seen to be the eternal offering of total love which was the manifestation in the temporal realm of the union at the heart of the very being of God. This manifestation is seen to be Christ's incarnation, death and resurrection, in which the marriage of earth and heaven, created and uncreated, temporal and eternal is consummated by the power in Christ of his indissoluble union with the Father in the Holy Spirit. In Christ, therefore, is seen to be the dissolution of all duality, the ultimate realization of that primal, eternal union which is the paradigm and ground of the oneness of all being, and into which one 'returns' by becoming one with Christ's 'return' to the Father.[7]

It is in order to attain to this realization that the novice now approaches the altar and enters by vow into a union with Christ which will precipitate within him or her a participation in and fulfilment of this mystery. What in effect is happening by the making of this vow is that the forces by which this ultimate realization is achieved are located and entered into, rather like a fast-flowing current, in order that the process into which all Christians enter through baptism, the process of Christ's dying and rising,[8] might be actualized as powerfully as possible. These primary forces of realization are twofold: they are love, and death. In Christ, the two are brought together into one power of transformation: death is entered into in the freedom and self-dissolution, or self-emptying[9] of total love, and that very love harnesses the forces of death into itself and so dawns into the unitive realization of transcendence, beyond life and death. It is this quality of transcendence, in practice self-transcendence, that is in essence the union of these two forces of love and death. By vow, the novice enters into the process. That is, he or she receives Christ's empowerment, by means of union with Christ, that the process might be realized. The realization is actualized as the vow is fulfilled, through the practice of self-transcendence in the transformative union of the forces of love and death.

Many of the precepts given by St Benedict in his Rule show how this unification is to be attained. In fact the entire Rule really is an instruction on how the whole of life is to be taken up into this process: eating, sleeping, ordinary actions, no less than liturgy and meditation, are dedicated by means of ritual and their symbolic potential opened up, that there might be nothing which is not transformed into the path of the realization of ultimate union. Again and again his directions for the practice disclose Christ as their origin, inspiration and fulfilment.

In a key passage, for example, 7:35–43, on the 'fourth degree of humility' (there are twelve) he focuses on the experience of one who, like Christ, finds that the path of transcendent love, the path of obedience, leads to seeming annihilation. The way of

224

transformation is to keep loving, to love in free and active self-emptying, to undo death's bonds by this freedom, and to transcend death itself.

Thus the disciple is encouraged by Christ's example not to lose heart in such an ordeal, not to flag or to seek escape, 'for he who endures to the end will be saved' (7:36). The cup of the Lord's suffering has to be drained before it can yield the nectar of immortality. The disciple therefore is instructed to learn how not to be poisoned by the inevitable taste of death in all things: by discerning wisdom and true acceptance, not as if by constraint but by the inner freedom and enlightened knowledge of a heart set on transcendence, the disciple is empowered to make of all experience death's transformation, by the undying power of one who has conquered (7:35, 39). St Benedict therefore describes the attitude of one in whom perfect humility is manifest as one who in his mind knows himself always to be at that threshold between life and death (7:62–70). This vigilance of the purified mind is then joined to the power of love and thereby gains a foretaste of resurrection.

At the heart of this experience is the mind that is 'brought to nothing' (7:50), realizes its own emptiness, and discovers in those very depths union with God; 'yet I am always with you' (7:50). By a symbolic correlation, at the heart of the monastery is the sanctuary, a place set apart and made sacred by the liturgical re-enactment and making-present of Christ's offering. Entering into union with this supreme offering, the monastic neophyte comes to the altar and makes a total dedication. In the climax of the rite of initiation, he or she stands before this altar to pronounce vows of perpetual commitment, and lays upon it the document which testifies to this offering.

'Suscipiendus autem in oratorio coram omnibus promittat de stabilitate sua et conversatione morum quorum et obedientiam coram Deo et sanctis eius ...' – 'The one who is to be received should, in the place of prayer and in the presence of everyone there, make promise of his stability, conversion of life and obedience, in the presence of God and his saints ...'. It would be worthwhile giving some attention at this point to the form which St Benedict gives to this commitment.

First of all, we should note the context. The one about to make the vow is spoken of as 'the one to be received': 'suscipiendus'. This designation reappears in active mode later on, when the newly professed sings the line from the psalm (118 [119]: 116), 'Receive me, Lord, according to your word, and I shall live': 'suscipe me Domine . . .'. Therefore there is a twofold 'reception': the novice is received by the community as a full member, and, by this same act, surrenders himself to being 'received', or 'taken up' by God. This twofold dimension is brought into focus by the parallel setting 'in the presence of everyone there' and 'in the presence of God and his saints'; further on, when the novice is to present the petition embodied in his vow in written form, and so to place it on the altar, it is said that he should draw up the document 'in the names of the saints whose relics are there and of the abbot who is present'.[10] What is envisaged, therefore, is an interpenetration of heavenly reality and earthly: the two realms are seen not as two, but as one, and it is by the reality of this union that the novice's commitment is ratified and from it derives its validity. Actualized in time, it is sealed in eternity.

The novice signs the document, and lays it on the altar. By this act, his or her offering is united to Christ's in his mystery: by this union, the newly-initiated is taken up into the process of transformation which is Christ's Passover from death to new life. This, therefore, is the substance and the purpose of the Benedictine vow: to pass from death to life in union with Christ, to participate in that transformation of life which transfuses the life even of this world with the light of the resurrection.

We should now turn our attention to the formula of the vow itself. The text says 'Let him make promise of his stability, conversion of life and obedience'. This threefold vow is to be understood to be a whole: it is not a matter simply of undertaking to practise three particular precepts. These precepts are not exclusive: they are inclusive of each other, and they are all-inclusive in the sense that they intend a consecration of life in its entirety, embracing all that the tradition to which one has become heir values as essential to this process. Each of the three expressions of this commitment, or each of the three vows, to put it in a way more common in later evolutions of the tradition, brings out a particular aspect of or gives a particular perspective to this total offering. Therefore, obedience is seen to be part of the way of conversion; stability, or perseverance, the strength of obedience; and conversion the power and inner direction making stability and obedience into a force for the transformation of life.

This transformation is the very purpose of the vows and of the way of life shaped by them. It is a process of 'conversion' in that by means of this consecration the ordinary becomes sacred; unenlightened mundane existence is gradually transfigured by the divine light and becomes a participation in and a manifestation of God himself.

It is not, however, as obvious as it may seem that this second of the Benedictine vows actually does mean 'conversion'. Although this is not the place to discuss the matter in detail, it should be noted that in the particular text we are examining (Rule 58:17) as well as in three others in the Rule (1:3, 58:1, 63:1) the manuscript evidence reveals that in the process of transmission scribes thought fit to prefer the reading 'conversio' to the most probably more authentic 'conversatio'. The reason for this would seem to be, understandably enough, that the latter term 'conversatio' can be obscure, requiring to be interpreted and its meaning made more precise: replacement by its cognate 'conversio' was able to achieve this often. That is to say, 'conversatio' was understood to mean 'conversion'. However, it means more than that. Where 'conversion' might imply a single instance, a particular decisive turning-point, 'conversatio' indicates a way of life or a way of being or behaving: the root concept of 'turning' here can be seen to signify not only a 'turning from' or 'turning to' as in 'conversio', but more particularly a 'turning' which takes place 'within' a situation or way of life. It has the nature of a continual choice or response, reinforcing and renewing what might initially have been a change of direction, choice or response.

Thus 'conversatio' in the monastic setting comes to mean not only 'conversion', often signifying in this case the act of entering upon the monastic way of life, but also the monastic life itself, which in turn becomes defined, by a kind of reflex of interpretation, as 'a life of continual conversion'. That is to say, the 'conversion of life' vowed by the novice is a process of continual transformation of life, which in itself constitutes the monastic way of life.

To gain some understanding of this vow, therefore, and of what is meant by conversion in the Christian monastic tradition, we should examine this process of transformation.

As we have seen, when the novice makes his or her commitment to seek God in the monastic way, the document which gives testimony to this vow is placed on the altar. By this act, the offering of one's whole life and being, embodied in the vow, is united to the mystery of Christ. The monk or nun is made one with the mystical Christ, that is to say, with Christ present, always present and given in the 'mysteries' which constitute his work of transformation through his death and resurrection. The epicentre of this transforming process, from which its power emanates, is its continually being made present in symbolic form in the sacred liturgy. The high point of this liturgy, which itself according to the tradition embodied in the Rule encompasses the whole continuum of day and night, is the celebration of the holy Eucharist, the Mass.

This celebration is essentially a re-enactment of the last supper shared by Jesus with his disciples the night before he was crucified; this generally understood to have been a Passover meal, in accordance with the Jewish tradition, but given a transformed significance by Jesus when he took the elements of the meal, bread and wine, and blessed them with a blessing that went beyond the tradition, and thereby, according to Christian understanding, both transcended and fulfilled the tradition. That is, in offering them to God with an invocation of blessing, he made this a total act of self-offering, as a symbol of the surrender of his life in the death which he was about to undergo, and thereby invested the bread and wine with his own being, his life, offered in love to his disciples. Giving the bread, he said 'Take this, eat, this is my body'; and offering the cup he said 'This is my blood'. This 'blessing' signified the making of a new covenant, no longer simply a participation through commemoration in the exodus from Egypt, the 'passing over' of the angel of death sparing the Israelite first-born, or the 'passover' from slavery to the freedom of the promised land, but the fulfilment of all this, the definitive dissolution of death into life, into a new, transformed way of being, the liberation from the moral bondage which causes death, and an entry into true life, the undying life of God's own unoriginate being.

This, therefore is the reality into which the novice enters, radically and absolutely, by the making of the vow. He or she becomes one with Christ in this supreme offering; passes from death to life and is made one with God. Henceforth the whole of life is taken up into this process and is thereby transformed. The altar and the offering which is made there stand as the focal point, bringing all other things, by means of the liturgy which evolves from this central act and leads further into it, into the perspective and transforming power of ultimate reality.

It should be noted, however, that the making of such a vow in such a manner was a relatively late development in the evolution of early Christian monasticism. In the beginnings in the Egyptian desert, two centuries before Benedict, it appears that initiation into the monastic way of life, and therefore, for the Christian, into this particular mode of participation in Christ[11] took place simply by the practice itself: a would-be disciple attached himself to a chosen master, and became like him in manner of life and disposition of heart by learning from what the master did and was himself. The initiation was effected therefore by this coming together of the disciple's commitment and desire to learn and to be changed, on the one hand, and the master's willingness to receive the disciple and to share his life and spirit with him, on the other.

It might seem, therefore, that here we have indicated two distinct and separate means of initiation: the ritual or liturgical, and what might most easily be termed the psychological, that is, an interior process. For St Benedict the point is that the two should become one. Not only in the actual initiation ceremony should the candidate's mind and intention find its truest expression in the ritual which is undergone, and thereby be empowered to transcend itself by being made one with the mystery there enacted, and so be taken to its fulfilment in self-transcendence, into the mystery of Christ's dying and rising, prophesied and proclaimed in the Scriptures. Likewise, as this fundamental process is discerned there and entered into, its power is set free within the individual mind and heart, and works for transformation.

It is in this perspective that the practice of sacred reading should be viewed: St Benedict instructs that several hours a day should be devoted to it, in a manner that continues in the disciple the work begun in the liturgy, which St Benedict calls 'the Work of God'; sacred reading also leads further into this 'Work', preparing the ground for greater understanding and receptivity there.[12] The work being done is the purification of mind and heart. It is therefore not helpful to be careless about what one reads, listens to, sees or in any way becomes involved with.[13] Vigilance, again, is the key: one who seeks God in all things will find God in all things. The realization of sacredness at the heart of life makes of life's journey a process of being made holy.

Notes

1. Cf. Rule of St Benedict, Prologue 21: 'With the Gospel as our guide may we make our way on this Journey, that we may attain to look on him who has called us to his kingdom' and especially the whole of Chapter 73, where he speaks of his instructions as a 'little Rule for beginners', encouraging those who would draw full benefit from it to make use of the teachings from the entire tradition, both sacred Scripture and the writings of the holy Fathers.
2. The Greek word *metanoia*, used in the New Testament to refer to conversion or repentance, literally means a change of mind, or a turning-about of the mind.
3. See Matthew 24:32–36, 42; 25:1–13; Mark 13:32–37.
4. Cf. especially Rule 7:10 and 19:1.
5. Cf. Rule 8:2, 4.
6. Cf. Rule 22: 4, 6; 1:8–9.
7. Cf. John 16:28 : 'I came from the Father, and have come into the world; again, I am leaving the world and going to the Father', and Rule, Prologue 2 : 'By the labour of obedience may you return to him from whom you have fallen away by the lassitude of disobedience'.
8. Cf. Romans 6:3–4: '... all of us who have been baptized into Christ Jesus were baptized into his death ... that as Christ was raised from the dead by the glory of the Father, we too might walk in newness of life'.
9. The archetype of this is seen in Christ, for instance in Philippians 2:1–11, e.g. 5–7-: 'Have this mind among yourselves, which you have in Christ Jesus, who ... emptied himself ...'.
10. McCann's translation.
11. Pachomius drew parallels between monastic initiation and baptism.
12. Cf. Rule chapter 48 and 8:3.
13. Cf. Rule 4:48–55; 43:8; 48: 18; 67:4–5.

Part IV
Contemporary cases of conversion

15. Coming home and coming out Pagan (but not converting)

Graham Harvey

Paganism is not an evangelistic faith but it is among the spiritualities currently enjoying considerable numerical growth. Books and magazines written by Pagans for Pagans are available in 'all good bookshops' but none of them tell the reader 'how to become Pagan'. Celebration, initiation, socializing and therapy are among the many functions of Pagan gatherings, but they are not intended to encourage conversion. Pagans do not expect the world to convert to Paganism, in fact they do not invite conversion at all. It is not that they are apathetic about their spirituality or that they consider it irrelevant to the pressing issues of the contemporary world. Nor is Paganism an exclusive spirituality: Pagans celebrate the increasing number of people who share their way of being in the world. The processes by which people become Pagans are integral to their spirituality and provide the observer of Paganism with useful insights.

Paganism is a spirituality in which the celebration of Nature is central.[1] This is not offered as a credal statement nor as a sufficient definition of Paganism. It merely points to the common ground on which all Pagans stand. A similar one-line pointer to the essence of Christianity might read 'Christianity is a spirituality in which Jesus is central'. Just as Christians and observers of Christianity would require far more detail than this, so too would Pagans. The common ground at the centre of the spirituality is a good place from which to celebrate harmony, but even a brief glance outwards reveals the significant and sometimes painful diversities and differences. Although all forms of Christianity (e.g. Catholicism, Mormonism,

Anglicanism and Unitarianism) celebrate the centrality of Jesus, they do not agree on his significance, nature or role. Although all Pagans celebrate Nature, they do not do so in the same way, at the same time or in the same place. They might not even agree completely on what 'Nature' or 'celebrate' might mean. Some are insistent that every physical body, human or other-than-human, is sacred and to be treated with respect. Others might appear careless of their own body, but demonstrate great reverence for the Earth. Some see tobacco-smoking as an assault on the human body, others drop cigarette butts in ancestral sacred sites without concern. The 'more' which requires saying about Pagan spirituality includes a note that within this broad movement, or 'segmented polycentric integrated network' perhaps,[2] are a variety of 'traditions', for example, Druidry, the Craft (of Witches), Heathenism or Odinism, Goddess or Women's Spirituality, and Magic (sometimes spelt Magick to distinguish it from stage tricks). Happily for the present discussion the distinguishing features of these traditions are not concerned with issues of 'becoming' or 'converting'. The ceremonies by which some groups recognize or welcome new members rarely require renunciation of previous or alternative affiliations, nor do they usually require affirmation of exclusive loyalty to a single deity or pantheon.

Becoming Pagan

Typical responses to the question, 'How did you become a Pagan?' usually assert that at some point the respondent realized that they were Pagan, that the name applied to them, or that they accepted the appropriateness of the name. Narratives of conversion ('testimonies' or 'bearing witness') do not occur in Pagan discourse. Pagans do not speak about realizing the correctness of Pagan beliefs, or of experiences which require rapid changes of world-view. More typically they discover that the name for their existing sort of spirituality is Paganism.[3] They find that they are not alone in the world but that there are books, groups and world wide web sites devoted to the exploration of this spirituality.

For some people the path to Paganism begins with ecology. Participation in direct action to prevent roads being built through complex natural environments encourages them to reject the modern view that Nature is a resource. Instead, a respect for non-human species develops into an acknowledgement that trees or animals are also people and that humanity is just one thread in the 'web of life'. Perhaps increasing intimacy with threatened trees suggests that they are conscious or aware, desire to communicate in some way with their human visitors and have multiple reciprocal relationships. The tree-dweller grows from being a protester against overdevelopment into a celebrant of an animated world. The apparent eccentricity of such celebration leads some people to maintain a silence in human company until they discover that similar views are gaining popularity and that a self-designation is available, Pagan.

Others begin with an interest in ancient monuments. They visit stone circles and burial mounds and read archaeological guide-books. Dissatisfaction with the commodification of once-sacred places by the heritage industry leads to disillusionment with tourist visits and voyeurism. Perhaps a dream or a feeling suggests the presence of ancestors willing to offer different views to the respectful, or mysterious energies requiring careful handling. Rituals expressive of these intuitions might be developed (little things like touching a standing stone, offering a small amount of one's food or drink to 'whoever guards this place', or simple verbal greetings). Then an encounter with other visitors to such a place might lead to the discovery that such actions and attitudes are shared by others.

A walk in a wood may lead to an encounter with elusive beings. What might appear to others to be tricks of light and shade seem rather to be experiential evidence that folk-tales and myths are true. We are not alone in the world, but are surrounded by beings unknown to more secular or sceptical companions. The faery folk still inhabit the wild or semi-natural places at the fringes of the more human-dominated world. Respectful approaches made towards these people might bear fruit in some less equivocal or enigmatic encounter. Candles cast far more light than usual, flutes are heard where there are no human musicians. Some even assert that they have seen 'them' dancing (it is traditional to employ various circumlocutions in this context). A conversation overheard in a pub might confirm that others have heard the music or seen the dance too. Further enquiry reveals that these experiences are celebrated among those who call themselves Pagan.

Adolescent reading of 'occult' books in libraries might lead to nothing more than a brief indulgence in dark clothes and arcane jewellery. Alternatively, it might develop into a life-long practice of ceremonial magic. Not all magicians are Pagan; in fact the elaborate techniques of the Western magical tradition were developed primarily by Christians and Jews. Although many Pagans engage in various forms of magic, from low or kitchen magic (herbalism and potions) to high or ceremonial magic (tantra, kabbalah or thelema), so too do people of other persuasions, religious or otherwise. Attention to the details of a particular magical 'working' can lead to experiences which appear, to the practitioner at least, to be effective. Someone does regain their health, money does arrive, a clearer sense of self-identity or strength of character does develop. Such successes can be interpreted as evidence for the veracity of the techniques employed and encourage exploration of other facets of Paganism.

Enchantment touches some through the medium of fantasy fiction. The works of J. R. R. Tolkien are almost ubiquitous in accounts of books which have influenced Pagans. Pagans are well aware that Tolkien's Roman Catholic spirituality informs his books. However, their elves, dragons, talking trees, effective magic and enthralling story-telling attract Pagans while the dualism (a near-cosmic battle between good and evil) and millennialism are of less significance. Tolkien's books have encouraged a re-evaluation of epic and traditional lore that had almost been obliterated by Victorian 'tweeness'. After Tolkien it became possible to speak about faery folk and faeryland without being thought sentimental. Other fantasy writers have provided books far closer to Pagan yearnings to communicate with 'all our relations' (all that lives) in an interconnected and living world. Alan Garner's re-presentations of Cheshire folklore and *Mabinogion* stories are celebrated by many Pagans. Marion Bradley's *The Mists of Avalon* allows us to see the women who are marginalized in other tellings of the Arthurian cycle. In Robert Holdstock's *Mythago Wood* and its sequels some Pagans recognize the enchanted labyrinth that they have encountered in woodlands and wilderness areas. A thoroughly Pagan world is manifest in Terry Pratchett's Discworld, especially because Pagans take themselves and their activities completely seriously only sometimes (a fact often missed by academics). Fantasy engages readers' imaginations, encourages their own creative story-telling and suggests interesting possibilities for ways of relating to the world. When some readers discover that there are people who take the existence of other worlds and faery folk seriously (and also take great pleasure in this appreciation), they find deep resonances with their own intuitions and identify themselves with such people.

There are several ways in which feminism might act as a introduction to Paganism. The almost global dominance of men can encourage some people to develop alternative spiritualities based in or respectful of female experience or female images of life or the divine. Others desire an egalitarian spirituality in which gender plays no role in determining who will lead or teach others, or who will define the nature or needs of a group or tradition. Not all feminists reject every spirituality as a masculinist 'opiate' or power-game. Some seek a spirituality to match and further empower their political and cultural commitments. If male divinities function as legitimators of male authority and experience, female divinities might challenge them. While some Goddesses may have functioned as nurturers of patriarchs, the feminist spirituality movement finds a different inspiration in its rediscovery of Goddess(es). In her or them, women recognize themselves not only as mothers, lovers, sisters and supporters of men, but as celebrants of female power, authority and beauty.[4] They are not only sexually but also culturally creative. In seeking for or creating such images and roles some women discover Paganism. This is true too for some men who find patriarchy demeaning and immoral, or for those who see a greater cause for celebration in the pluralism of Goddess traditions than in the authoritarianism of male-centred monotheisms.

Some Pagans assert that the realization that this name was applicable to them came from a recognition that they had an affinity for the deities of one Pagan pantheon or another. Celtic, Norse, Saxon and other Northwest European deities are the most popular of these, though Egyptian, Greek, Native American and other polytheistic spiritualities provide inspiration. Many of these deities are first encountered in childhood reading of books of myths and legends – the writers of which might share their reader's delight in such tales, but few if any write to encourage such contemporary veneration. Some writers might even consider their subject-matter to be ancient fantasy, entertaining perhaps but no basis for a serious worldview. However, the recovery of traditional understandings of the world by First Nation peoples is paralleled by Western interest in polytheistic roots indigenous to Europe. The *Hávamál*, for example, offers more than stories of outrageous exploits by macho Gods and heroes. It encourages social virtues and etiquette, offers a rich cosmology and inspires engagement with this world and the Otherworld. The 'Old Gods' have returned not only as Jungian archetypes (though this may be their role in New Age and Jungian-style self-therapies) but as autonomous people in their own right. When the individual's delight in the company of such folk leads to discovery of like-minded devotees, affirmation of Pagan or Heathen identity frequently follows.

Paganism is a spirituality which affirms individual identity, inspiration, intuition, authority, autonomy and imagination. It allows people to bring all their desires and ideas, visions and ideals, and to blend these with existing understandings and celebrations. It does not require repentance or self-negation. Undoubtedly the people who run some Pagan groups are power hungry and attempt to maintain control. However, the existence of formal and informal networks and larger gatherings in pubs or festivals, permits the vibrant exchange of information about alternatives. Pagans quickly form more egalitarian affinity groups in which power-with, or power-from-within is celebrated.[5] In Wiccan language, power is raised from and by the group and is sent out to benefit others. Hierarchical power-over is countered by humour or a 'talking circle' if possible, and explicit rejection if necessary. For many people these group structures and this approach to authority and power are attractive. For those damaged by authoritarian and even abusive relationships and spiritualities, Paganism can be a very welcome relief. Rather than being corrected, people are encouraged to explore their own identity. They are not asked to assent to doctrines or diminished for not sharing an experience, but are encouraged to find their own form of self-expression. While it would be an exaggeration to say that Paganism presents itself as a therapy, it does have this function for many people.[6]

Many Pagan celebrations are private occasions, held in someone's home or in a remote wood. These do not function as opportunities for 'outsiders' to see what Pagans do. Larger gatherings are often held in more public places: ancient stone circles, public parks, at demonstrations against nuclear installations or new multi-lane highways. While some Pagans certainly enjoy media attention and others value the chance to show the world what Paganism is really all about, these gatherings are not intended to attract converts. However, the annual cycles of Pagan festivals (which vary according to the specific tradition) permit people to face a wide range of experiences in supportive environments. All that Paganism is (not just 'is meant to be') is expressed and experienced in these celebrations of nature and life, and this is made clear in most books about Paganism by Pagans. Such books are rarely mentioned when Pagans narrate 'how I became a Pagan', but are not uncommon in their realization that their celebrations of the seasons or their personal life-cycle rituals resonated with those described.

These are some of the experiences referred to by Pagans as significant in their introduction to Paganism. Most often Pagans respond to questions like, 'How did you become a Pagan?' by asserting, 'I have always been one, but I didn't know that was the name for what I was.' Typically, they continue by describing participation in ecology or direct actions, interest in ancient monuments, walks in woods, fascination with occult or fantasy literature, engagement with feminism or polytheism, a desire for self-affirmation or a delight in seasonal celebrations as important steps in the process of becoming Pagan. It is almost universally true, however, that people say that they were doing, feeling, or being these things before they knew there was a name for their spirituality. The discovery of like-minded people (whether through books or at festivals, in media reports or conversations in pubs) leads to a combined sense of 'coming home' and 'coming out'.

Coming home

Pagans are people who 'come home' in two related senses, neither necessarily taking precedence – chronological or ideological – over the other. First, Pagans come home to themselves, second Pagans come home to a sense of belonging with others or within a tradition. (Tanya Luhrmann's 'interpretative drift' and Christel Manning's 'combination' models say less about the experience of Magicians or Pagans and more about assertions of academic 'objectivity', i.e. scepticism and 'knowing better'.)[7]

Coming home to oneself encapsulates the experience of many who discover that their own worldview, experiences, intuitions, preferences and goals can be affirmed. People become Pagans before they know it. This is not usually like turning a corner on a wild winter night and unexpectedly finding yourself outside your home, but more like a gradual realization that you are happy to be where you are. You find woods or hills more spiritual than any 'sanctified' building. You learn more from the four elements than from any sermon or book, of whatever antiquity or beauty. You celebrate the childhood memory of painting trees with smiling faces. You find the company of animals more satisfying than even the thought of a deity's approval. You see divinities manifest in the world around you. You trust your intuition to tell you that a particular place welcomes you and that it is inhabited by 'spirits' (or whatever word you care to use). You want to tell your own story and to hear that of others who share your renewed pleasure and reverence for the land on which you walk and the Earth in which you live. You accept your gut reaction that anger is an appropriate response to many things and that meek acceptance or humbling repentance are often inappropriate. Your spirituality engages all your senses and is not centred on acquiescence to creeds or sermons.

Such experiences are not unique to Pagans, or to those who will become Pagans. Much of the poetry and mysticism of other religions expresses similar ideas. For example, many spiritual experiences occur away from places dominated by humanity (or inhumanity). However, these experiences are usually understood to be supportive of truths already known from more authoritative sources, that is, scriptures or sermons. Conversely, for some religions, being captivated by the beauty of Nature can be perilously close to being ensnared in the pleasures of the flesh and might be condemned rather than commended. It is, in fact, more likely that the celebration of Nature will be noticed more by those who think it is wrong than by those who think it is acceptable. The latter group are only marginally interested in Nature's parroting of lessons already learnt, while the former are opposed to its alleged deceitfulness. In Paganism too, of course, inspiring encounters or spiritual experiences in Nature are neither new nor surprising. They are, however, of inestimable value. What is significant for the current discussion is not the uniqueness or otherwise of these experiences, but their celebration and centrality in the spirituality.

In Paganism the perspective of the individual is not only acknowledged but also vital. Pedantic rationalists might assert that the sun does not rise, but common parlance affirms that from the point of view of every living being each morning begins with sunrise. The centre of each person's world is themselves. Many religions require adherents to adjust their vision so that it agrees with that of a greater being or reality, while scientists and ethicists often allege that there is an objective position from which phenomena can be impartially and completely observed. Paganism asks what the world looks like from where you stand. It encourages affirmation of each person's point of view, each individual's sense of beauty. Instead of insisting on correct belief or complete understanding of objective reality or Truth, it affirms the multiplicity of stories. Paganism hears Keats' phrase 'Beauty is truth, truth beauty, that is all ye know on earth, and all you need to know'[8] as an acknowledgement of the priority of such partialities. Similarly, in a profound and humorous moment in Monty Python's *Quest for the Holy Grail* the quest knights are asked, 'What is your favourite colour?'. To cross the fateful bridge towards their goal requires awareness not only of those things which might be thought through, reasoned out or accepted on greater authority, but more importantly of personal preferences and affinities. These things allow an approach to the Grail because they reveal the individual's loyalties and desires – themselves the subject of two more ancient Grail Questions, 'Who does it serve?' and, 'What do women most desire?'. Another example of this post-modern affirmation of diversity, celebration of being oneself and of seeing the world through one's own eyes is the Womanism of Alice Walker.[9] Beauty is true for each beholder.

Such experiences are deeply personal but they are also shared. An individual who affirms their worldview (including their self-view) and discovers that it is named Paganism has thereby discovered a community. Not all Pagans join small close-knit groups, though plenty of these exist (e.g. Covens, Groves, Hearths or simply groups). Many meet only in occasional pub get-togethers, social events where the conversation ranges widely and people increase their web of friendships rather than listening to a speaker to increase their knowledge. For some the primary contact is through an open festival, probably at a seasonal celebration. However, even when an individual's only contact with other Pagans is through books or magazines, the acceptance of Pagan identity is frequently experienced as a 'coming home' to a community. People discover that they are not alone but there are others who also celebrate Nature, dislike patriarchy, feel that the world is alive, or believe that particular deities are worthy of honour. It can be a great relief to discover that you are not alone.

Those who know anything about Paganism will have anticipated a third sense of the phrase 'coming home'. Becoming Pagan is a homecoming in that Paganism is an ecological affirmation that humanity's home is Earth. It is not a quest for an afterlife or enlightenment above or away from the Earth. It knows no other place in which humans (or trees, hedgehogs, flu viruses, potatoes or any other of Earth's people) can exist. Astronauts do not leave the Earth, they take small packages of Earth with them in the form of air, water, food, fuel and their enveloping spacecraft. Extinct species do not 'leave the Earth', they die. (The phrases 'die out' and 'die away' should be taken as expressions of finality rather than as suggesting there might be somewhere else where they continue to exist and from which they might return.) There are various Pagan understandings of what happens after death,[10] but those who believe in an afterlife do not envisage it as taking place somewhere separated from Earth. The 'Otherworld' is intimately linked to and accessible from 'ordinary' reality.

Paganism is an ecology of souls, it is not only a human religion, nor a human-centred religion. Though it values each individual's world-view and preferences, it encourages the affirmation of the personhood of all living beings, which might include rocks, waves and clouds. Paganism encourages respectful neighbourliness, listening and sharing. It is this recognition of being at home that inspires the pervasive Pagan engagement in ecology and especially in eco-dramas like direct action against destructive road building and quarry digging.

For many of those who realize that they are Pagan, who 'come home' to themselves, to a community and to Earth, there is an allied sense of 'coming out'.

Coming out

Coming home to Pagan identity can be experienced as a 'coming out': recognition, acceptance and affirmation of one's Pagan identity. However, the 'coming out' metaphor allows us to do more than reinforce what has already been said about 'coming home'. Many Pagans feel the need to 'come out' to others, to say, more or less publicly, that they are Pagans. Coming out has a third sense (discussed further in the following section) in that Pagans are often people who have left other religions.

A considerable amount of what Pagans do is invisible but not hidden. Interactions with Nature may look like walks in woods, camping by a lake or vacations at summer camps. Gathering greenery in midwinter or blossom in May is not unique to Pagans and need not attract attention or comment. Some symbols meaningful to Pagans can appear to be merely decorative jewellery. It is not necessary to use elaborate gestures or long speeches to honour the seasons, the sun or the moon. Talking to trees may be eccentric but is far from rare. Participation in direct action or adoption of a more ecological lifestyle do not tend to surprise family and friends but to develop out of attitudes previously expressed. It is more difficult, of course, to read books about Paganism or Magic(k) without attracting some comment. Regular participation in Pagan events, especially in small or close-knit groups, is hard to hide. However, it is only rarely that people now feel the need to hide such activities or Pagan identity itself. My point is not that Paganism is secretive but that it does not encourage, let along demand, proselytism so there is no need for open displays or pious sermons.

While it is perfectly possible to be Pagan without drawing attention to it, Paganism does encourage a sense of community or belonging with other Pagans and 'all our relations'. People join groups to celebrate together or to learn. A first approach to such groups can feel like coming out. Entry into some Pagan traditions includes an initiation or profession in which the individual affirms their affinity with the tradition and group. These rites allow one who has 'come home' to 'come out'. While they are never the first Pagan ceremony that the individual has participated in, they are sometimes the first time they have played an active role. Such events are not considered to convert someone into a Pagan, they acknowledge a kinship between the newly 'out' Pagan and the group or tradition. They do not initiate a change of life or of belief but celebrate the desire of the initiate to associate themselves with others who celebrate Earth's life. The Wiccan tradition is the most explicit form of Mystery tradition within Paganism and its three-level initiatory structure does aim to reveal the nature of reality and the individual's place in the scheme of things.[11] However, revelation of the mysteries entails no surprises for the initiate, except perhaps in their intensity: the facts are well known – they might even be what attracted the person to Paganism in the first place – but in the ritual they are experienced with far more than intellectual power. That is, initiation is not conversion but the affirmation of coming home by coming out. This may develop into even more public roles as Pagans express their respect for the Earth by countering assaults against it.

243

Before exploring conversion from other religions, it is important to note that Paganism itself has 'come out' in recent years. Not only have laws against 'witchcraft' been repealed in most Western countries (although not in Queensland or South Africa), but the central themes of Paganism have gained wider currency. A new confidence among Pagans has led to changes in media portrayals of their spirituality. Pagan ceremonies and eco-dramas are less frequently presented as sinister and silly, and more often as interesting and evocative. Despite continuing opposition from evangelical Christians, Pagans can now hold ceremonies far more openly. That they continue to be fairly private is not due to fear or secrecy but to the intimacy of relationships built up between people. The absence of proselytism and the desire that everyone present at a ceremony engages with it fully as participants rather than as observers contribute to this general privacy. However, completely open and public events do take place, especially those organized by Druid Orders.

Converting from

People do not become Pagans by having a revelatory experience but realize that they have been Pagan for some time, perhaps since they were children, or even in several past lives. Earlier I asserted that 'coming home' should be primarily understood as a sense of acceptance of one's identity. For some, however, 'coming home' *is* like turning a corner on a wild winter night and finding yourself outside your own front door. It is important to the understanding of this metaphor that it asserts that there is a home to which the traveller returns. Some Pagans say that one day they realized that they had ceased to be Christians some time ago and had become something else. They had struggled to create an ecologically sound version of Christianity, or a feminist one, or one in which guilt or hierarchy had no role. They had tried to adjust Christianity to give a significant role to the land in which they live. However, they eventually realized that these attempts were pointless as the goal was impossible. Others assert only that they found that there already was a spirituality like the one they were seeking to create. Rather than struggle, they were greatly relieved to acknowledge that all along they had been mistaken in thinking of themselves as Christians when in reality their true home and identity had been Pagan.

While people do not convert to Paganism, some do convert from Christianity. That this is more to do with Christianity than Paganism is indicated by the fact that Jews who discover they are Pagans tend to see themselves as Pagan Jews or Jewish Pagans (some even adopt the label 'Jewitch' for this identity). Judaism has resources for the celebration of Nature which are alien to Christianity. Revisioning of deity in female forms is also found to be possible within Judaism, albeit of a rather radical nature. Similarly, there are Pagans who combine loyalties to Buddhism and other religions. It is almost only ever Christianity that it spoken of with any anger by Pagans (though they may find elements of other religions disappointing). Some feel the need to make their 'conversion from' Christianity explicit in their 'coming out' ceremonies. Several Heathen or Ásatrú groups reverse the ritual by which Charlemagne forced the Saxons to renounce 'all the devil's deeds and words, Thunar, Woden, Saxnot and all their unholy companions', instead renouncing Christ and Christianity. Though this can be seen as 'Christian-bashing' it is also presented as a powerful psychological mechanism for distancing oneself from the structures of a very different approach to religion and the Earth.

Believing and becoming

Discussions of religions frequently pay considerable attention to beliefs, especially beliefs about deities. It is certainly true that Pagans do believe things that others do not, for example considering Celtic, Norse, Egyptian or other deities to be more than characters in ancient mythological tales. Nonetheless, such beliefs and belief itself are rarely central to the process of becoming Pagan. Neither are they central to Paganism in the sense that belief in a deity is central to the monotheistic religions. The process of becoming Pagan is less like conversion to one of these religions (with the adoption of beliefs that this usually entails) and more like becoming traditional among First Nation or indigenous peoples. In these Nature-centred religions belief, explanations and universal truth are of less importance than experience and the attempt to live respectfully within the reciprocal relationships entailed in sharing a small planet home.

Notes

1. See Graham Harvey, *Listening People, Speaking Earth: Contemporary Paganism* (London: Hurst, 1997). Simultaneously published as *Contemporary Paganism: Listening People, Speaking Earth* (New York: New York University Press, 1997).
2. Michael York, *The Emerging Network: A Sociology of the New Age and Neo-Pagan Networks* (Lanham, MD: Rowman & Littlefield, 1995).
3. Margot Adler, *Drawing Down the Moon* (Boston: Beacon Press, 1986), pp. 14–23.
4. Asphodel Long, 'The Goddess Movement in Britain Today', *Feminist Theology* 5 (1994), pp. 11–39.
5. Starhawk, *Truth or Dare* (New York: Harper & Row, 1990).
6. Shelley Rabinovitch,. ' "An' Ye Harm None, Do What Ye Will'': Neo-Pagans and Witches in Canada' unpublished MA thesis, Carleton University, Ottawa, 1992.
7. Tanya M. Luhrmann, *Persuasions of the Witch's Craft; Ritual Magic in Contemporary England* (Oxford: Blackwell, 1989), p. 312; Christel J. Manning 'Embracing Jesus and the Goddess: Towards a Reconceptualization of Conversion to Syncretistic Religion', in James R. Lewis (ed.), *Magical Religion and Modern Witchcraft* (Albany, NY: State University of New York Press, 1996), pp. 299–326.
8. John Keats, 'Ode on a Grecian Urn', 1819, in Robert Gittings, *Selected Poems and Letters of Keats* (London: Heinemann, 1966), pp. 127–8.
9. Alice Walker, *The Color Purple* (London: Women's Press, 1983); *In Search of Our Mothers' Gardens: Womanist Prose* (London: Women's Press, 1984).
10. Graham Harvey, 'Death and Remembrance in Modern Paganism', in Jon Davies (ed.), *Ritual and Remembrance: Responses to Death in Human Societies* (Sheffield: Sheffield Academic Press, 1994), pp. 103–22.
11. E.g. Vivianne Crowley, *Wicca: the Old Religion in the New Age* (London: Aquarian, 1989).

16. Continuing conversion: a personal journey

Tim Edgar

For many people the whole idea of conversion revolves around a turning away from sin and a returning to God. Essentially, this takes place deep within the individual person and may not have any outward manifestations at all. There is, however, another sort of conversion in which the inward part may still be hidden, but the outward manifestation is all too apparent. This conversion is a move from one communion of the Christian Church to another communion. For me this was from the Church of England to the Catholic Church, a move of such profound consequences that I suspect it will be many years before the full effect can even begin to be realized. Conversion is a strange thing. It is, at once, so simple to describe yet it evades description. Tied to an event in time, it is something that is never ending. For many, conversion implies changing one's religious faith, yet, I think, it is, more a growing into faith, a growing into fullness, a process of becoming.

Michael Mott in his biography of Thomas Merton,[1] entitles his preface 'Continuing Conversion'. That expresses what is, perhaps, the greatest single truth of the phenomena called 'conversion', that it is always and continually a process, though it is characterized as an event. To illustrate this I want to look back over my own 'conversion' (if that is even the right word) from Anglicanism to Catholicism, sparked, in part, by the decision of the Church of England in November 1992 to sanction the ordination of women to the priesthood. I have had to do this so frequently of late, for various television, newspaper and radio interviews, that this 'apologia' has begun to pall with me. There is, however, one thing I feel it is imperative to make clear from the start; I am quite prepared to believe that the priestly ordination of women will be shown to be

God's will for his Church in the fullness of time. What the General Synod voting brought about for me, is not about the ordination of women, but about the self-understanding of the Church of England which the vote demonstrated and the subsequent personal questioning about vocation and what God wanted of me. I wish I could have found the courage to leave for some other 'worthier' reason, for one is now always tarred with the brush of conservatism and misogyny, and treated with a certain amount of reserve by those who have only heard of the 'event' and not the 'process'. Maybe this is a price that has to be paid. No conversion comes without a variety of costs.

From the age of seven I have known that God has called me to be a priest. This 'knowing' is not a knowing of the head, but of the heart. It is an 'unavoidable' knowing, a true knowing; this is what God wants of me and it is something that cannot be ignored. In a very real way priesthood is the only way that I can be fully what God wants me to be. It is, I believe with all my heart, that for which I was made; it is what I was born to be and to do; it is the way I know God most deeply; it is the way God knows me.

From this time too I began regularly attending my local parish church as a choirboy and later as a server. The parish was what used to be called 'Prayer Book Catholic'. The Eucharist was solemnly celebrated on Sundays with priest, deacon and subdeacon, vestments, Reserved Sacrament and, on occasion, incense. No-one in my family was what could be called a practising Christian, other than my grandmother's (second) husband who was a Roman Catholic. He had married my grandmother, who was divorced. This meant that he was barred from receiving the sacraments of the Church but that didn't stop him practising his faith. Sunday Mass (without receiving) with prior confession was the norm; black tea on Good Friday. He was one of the gentlest souls I have ever met. When he died, aged 49, in 1965, I felt his loss very deeply. My grandmother and great-grandmother, inspired by his example, perhaps, began to receive instruction in the faith and, in due time, were received into the Catholic Church. There was, I remember, some talk of me being received too, but my father, I think, put a stop to this. This is a very dim memory and I have no recollection of being involved in any conversations about it, but I guess a 9-year-old shouldn't expect to be consulted. I do remember my father being very anti the local Catholic priest but other than the fact that Father X liked a glass of whisky in the club attached to the church I can't remember why. So,

I continued as an Anglican, for the most part having to get myself to Church on Sundays and later, when I left the choir, serving the early morning Communion on Saturdays. After passing the 11 Plus exam I started attending a grammar school in Southwell, 8 miles away from home. This was a wonderful school for me, quite small, only some 200 or so pupils (all boys). This meant that it was very intimate. Each pupil was known by all the staff. There was no way to become lost and there was a real sense that each member of that small community was highly valued and unique. The school provided the choir for the cathedral which sat next door. During term time the school attended Morning Prayer daily. I didn't appreciate it at the time but I think a foundation was being laid here for a later love of the Divine Office with its quiet rhythm of psalms, readings and prayer.

When I was 14 years old this knowledge of vocation had to be articulated for the first time. 'O' Level options were about to be taken and, so that we could be given appropriate advice in order to match those options taken with possible future careers, we had to call out in class the courses we wanted to take and the reasons for this choice. I remember the sense of silence that descended when I said I wanted to be a priest. I don't recall feeling embarrassed, just thinking, 'It's gone quiet'. Again, as far as I remember, all the staff were totally supportive. No one tried to make me change my mind or see otherwise. It all seemed very natural and right but it meant that my parents had to be told. Priesthood was no longer a secret that could be kept to myself. My parents, most especially my father, strongly disapproved. Maybe this is understandable. I didn't really know what priests did all day, how they really lived, how much money or security they had, and priesthood was far removed from my father's world of the factory shop-floor. Priesthood was something outside his experience and was hard to come to grips with. It didn't promise fame or fortune and seemed like throwing everything away These things were, to me, irrelevant. It is from this time that there was a deterioration in my relationship with him..

After 'O' Levels I entered the 6th Form, took 'A' Levels and gained a place at King's College, London, to read Theology. Throughout my 6th Form time I had toyed with thoughts other than priesthood but whichever way I turned, whatever other choice I made, it seemed as if God closed doors. There was no peace, no rest, until I moved in the direction he was calling. He would not be denied. I loved King's. It was here that I began to be at Mass daily and began to make my confession regularly. It was here too that I met my future wife as she, too, was reading Theology. We decided to marry after I had finished my degree and I would work for a year while she completed hers. We lived in a flat on the top floor of a vicarage near King's Cross and worshipped in a parish that stood at the edge of Anglicanism. Mass was celebrated according to the Roman Rite and the Breviary was used for the Offices. I remember beginning to use the Breviary on the bus as I went to work. It was a wonderful discovery, like a light breaking into a dark place. It made sense in a way that the Prayer Book and its various subsequent 'Series' had never made sense to me. It felt true and real. Instead of being a burden the Office became a delight and a joy and has pretty much remained so.

When both of us had graduated I had a further year's training to do and we both went north, near to Leeds, to a theological college that stood firmly in the Catholic tradition of the Church of England. Here, guided by my spiritual director (himself, now, a convert and Roman Catholic priest), my spirituality moved further Romeward. Daily Mass, Office and Meditation were laid as a firm foundation together with a love of silence. After serving my title in the Diocese of London we moved after two years, to Doncaster, to a small parish that had been built by and grown out of those inspired by the Oxford Movement. From that time The Roman Missal (and the continuing use of the Breviary) became the norm for worship. *Lex orandi, lex credendi.* This wasn't unusual in any way. Many Anglican Priests, especially those of the Society of the Holy Cross, of which I became a member, felt that it was part of our task to make the Church of England more Catholic. Our daily prayer was for reunion with the Holy See, for the work of the Anglican–Roman Catholic International Commission. The Documents of Vatican II were the foundation of our pastoral praxis and theological outlook. Four years later I was offered my own parish in Sheffield on a large housing estate. The parish was in dire straits; few people, huge debts, no heating, a leaking roof. It was very grim. Before I arrived the parish was at the high end of the Church of England, but not Catholic in the way I understood it. From the first day I was there the daily Mass was established, according to the Roman Rite; the Sacrament of Confession was advertised and, from the first time I sat in the makeshift confessional, people came, without any pressure, bullying or cajoling. The knowledge that this sacrament was available seemed to draw them, not only from my own parish but from those around. In due time new heating was installed, along with a statue of

Our Lady, Saint Catherine and the Stations of the Cross. Numbers began to grow and the parish began to pay its way, but it wasn't easy. This was a tough area. Within half an hour of moving into the vicarage we had been burgled and some of the decisions that had to be made for the survival of the parish created a lot of vocal and, at times, violent opposition. Yet, the parish worked; a new ethos began to grow, not, I believe, because anything spectacular was attempted but simply because all of us involved tried to be faithful to what we believed was our Catholic heritage within Anglicanism, to the breaking of bread and the prayers of the universal Church.

After five years as a parish priest, I was asked to consider taking the post of Director of Pastoral Studies at the theological college where I had finished my own formation. This was an offer that came out of the blue. I was happy in parish life. Again, I felt that that was what God had called me to do. The work of a parish priest was very natural and intuitive for me and I knew that there was opposition to my appointment from some who felt that I was too Roman in approach, practice and theology. Nonetheless I was appointed, but was seen as very much the then Principal's appointment, and when he left the Community and the Church of England to test his vocation at Quarr Abbey, a contemplative Benedictine monastery, both Laura and I felt very isolated. His move, and a greater contact with the Church of England than we had had for a very long time, because of the nature of the job I was doing, forced us into deeper reflection, forced us to face the reality of Anglicanism and our place within it in a way that had been avoidable before. The decision of the General Synod in 1992 proved to be the catalyst. What the General Synod voting brought about is, for me, not about the ordination of women, but about the self-understanding of the Church of England which this vote demonstrates. I know many people who welcomed the decision of the Synod and who positively worked for it. There are others, perhaps the majority, who, while being somewhat concerned do not have any strong views as to the principle. There are others, perhaps a small but significant group who were deeply concerned at what had happened. I clearly stood in that third group.

Most of the whole of my life and all my priestly ministry had been built on the belief that the Church of England was an authentic, national expression of the One Holy Catholic and Apostolic Church, founded by Christ himself and bearing his commission. I believed that Church of England bishops were the successors of Saint

Augustine and that through him Anglican roots went down deep into the early years of the Church's life. The sixteenth and seventeenth centuries saw great upheaval and the English Church administered separately, but the English Church consciously retained its claim to be part, a genuine part, of the Catholic Church, with the scriptures, beliefs and ministry of the undivided Church. The ordinals of the Book of Common Prayer and Alternative Service Book set out the unequivocal view that the orders of Anglicanism are not local but universal. Anglican ordinations have always been understood as conveying a grace, which potentially at least, extends to the Church in its wholeness. The Church of England intended to do what the undivided Church had always done.

To reiterate, the problem was not the ordination of women but the change of understanding that went with it. The Synod debate made it absolutely clear that in passing the measure the Church of England would be moving away from the consensus of Scripture and tradition, moving into uncharted waters. That decision is now made, but I do not believe that the Church of England can ever claim again with any confidence, that its ministry is the same as the Apostolic ministry; in stepping outside the consensus of 2000 years of Christian practice the Church of England can no longer assert with any confidence that its ministry is consonant with that which has been handed down from the Apostles. From the time the canons of the Church of England were changed the claim to share in the ministry of the Catholic Church has been dreadfully compromised. At some time in the immediate future, I believe the Church of England will cease to have that special relationship with Rome and the Orthodox by which it has been recognized as a 'sister church', and it will be nothing more than one of the galaxy of reformed bodies whose life and ministry are sustained by their own faith and cannot claim a wider authentication. Signs of this are already beginning to show.

For many, the vote to allow the ordination of women gives a freedom to follow an agenda which they believe is Good News, unconstrained by the tradition of the ancient churches. They can direct the way of the Anglican Church as they feel the Spirit moves them. On the outside I suspect the Church of England will continue much as before. For those of us who were Anglicans because we believed ourselves to be part of the mainstream of the One Holy Catholic and Apostolic Church, the ground had, quite simply, been cut from under our feet; the claim to universality and the hope that one day the catholicity of the English Church would be recognized and that we would return to a place in communion with the great churches of Christendom had been destroyed. However, this is a minor consequence compared with others. The emphasis of Catholic Christians is a sacramental one, and the heart of sacramental life is centred in authority. The sacraments are covenanted means of grace which convey the life of Christ in a true and assured way. At the Mass, it doesn't matter what I feel like for I know, without doubt, that I receive the real body and blood of Christ in a real way. The words and actions of a priest are not personal words and actions when he acts sacramentally, they are words and acts of Jesus who comes to touch our lives where we need him most. The guarantee at the heart of sacramental life has been, I believe, by the Synod's decision, at the very least, compromised. The Church of England can no longer claim that it intends to do at priestly ordination what the rest of the Church intends. In terms of the Eucharist this was and is heart-breaking.

At a more personal level I had the growing feeling that the Church of England was not where I belonged. This wasn't a new feeling but when I had had it before it could be attributed to 'Roman fever' and, by and large, ignored, and part of me had felt the enormous consequences of leaving the Church of one's baptism were, too, the thought that the Church of England was where God had wanted me to be. This was now no longer the case. I had been reading Ian Ker's biography of John Henry Newman[2] and was struck by so many parallels of feelings of not belonging, of feeling, to use Newman's words 'unreal'. I began to feel a fraud when I stood at the altar and I could not, with any integrity, continue, as Director of Pastoral Studies, to prepare candidates for a ministry in which I no longer had any confidence, for a church which I knew, in conscience, that I had to leave. In a very real way the Church of England had become a stumbling block to my following of Jesus. As soon as was practical I made contact with the local Catholic bishop who put us into the gentle and safe hands of a wonderfully wise priest, who listened more than he talked, and loved more than he listened. During college vacations we began to worship in a nearby Catholic parish, even though we were still Anglicans. There had to be a certain discretion about this, to avoid gossip or scandal. Worshipping in a Roman Catholic church felt very natural. People were so welcoming and generous and supportive. It felt authentic and real. The time came when I felt it would be impossible for me to continue in the Church of England, and it became necessary to speak to those to whom I owed responsibility of my decision to seek reception into the Catholic Church as soon as was practicable. This meant that I would have to be released from my contract, which was agreed, provided that I completed that academic year and let no word of what was to happen in the near future escape. This was an enormous difficulty, especially when dealing with students who were preparing for imminent ordination, and yet felt the same as I felt. To offer them any advice would have been impossible. Some began to guess what was likely to occur but were gracious enough to keep their own counsel. This was a period of great uncertainty, of learning to rest in God's providence until the path he wanted us to follow could be discerned. Being received into full communion with the Catholic Church was a wonderful thing and the warmth of our welcome quite overwhelming. It felt, and continues to feel, like a homecoming, a realization that this is where and what God has called me to, this is where we belong, a movement out of unreality into reality. Deep, deep down, I wanted, needed even, to be a Catholic, to be in full communion with the See of Peter, to know that sacramental life was guaranteed. The General Synod vote gave a clarity of vision which, perhaps, one had tended to run away from before.

In 1994 we moved to London with our newly adopted daughter, Rosie. I had been appointed to teach social and political ethics at the Missionary Institute. Laura was also pregnant. Some time after we were married we had been told that we could not have children. We spent a long time thinking about this and decided that we would like to adopt. Within six months of Rosie coming to us Laura was pregnant and Jonathan was born in October 1994, the Feast of S Thérèse of Lisieux, for whom I have always had a deep affection. If ever a sign were needed of the rightness of things, then this was it. After a year at the Missionary Institute I was asked to teach the fundamental moral theology course and I was appointed Assistant Director of Studies.

Initially, I did not feel that I had the right to ask about the possibility of ordination as we came as supplicants, asking for a home. We knew that the Pope had asked the English Catholic Bishops to be generous to convert Anglican clergy, and that generosity has been overflowing. Ordination was a real possibility. Priesthood is, so to speak, necessary for me to be the person God wants me to me, an ontological necessity. Whilst still in Leeds I had undergone a psychological assessment, a fairly standard practice for candidates for the Catholic priesthood and after some four years of discernment by my bishop and those among whom I work, the papers asking for a dispensation from celibacy were prepared and sent to Rome. Three months later a positive answer was received and I, along with three other married candidates, was ordained to the Catholic priesthood by Cardinal Hume on the same day that the Pope celebrated his Golden Jubilee of Priestly Ordination. This was an indescribable day of such joy and such happiness.

I find it hard to believe how good God has been to me. I don't understand it. Many point to the anomaly of convert Anglicans being ordained while Catholic priests who have married are not allowed to exercise their ministry and it is, perhaps, ironic, that I now feel the same joy as those women who were ordained to the Anglican priesthood. What the future holds I do not know. Recent debates about the value of celibacy within and without the Catholic Church have given married Catholic priests more prominence than they deserve. At the moment we are anomalies, exceptions to the norm. Recently I was speaking to an eminent feminist Catholic theologian and, as ever, had to explain how I came to be where and what I was. For a moment a look of distaste (real or imagined?) crossed her face. Maybe this will always be the reaction of some. For the most part people have been so kind and understanding. The parish where I have been attached has been nothing but supportive and encouraging and generous in its care of all the family. In time the novelty of married Catholic priests will fade and we can disappear deep down into the life of the Church, the quicker the better. The path of conversion continues, learning to become what I am, to try and walk with confidence and hope the dark ways of faith, knowing they are illumined by the light of the child Jesus.

Conversion means, for me at least, that I know how loved I am by God and how generous is his mercy. I know the truth of the song of Mary 'the Almighty has done great things for me. Holy his name'.[3]

Notes

1. Michael Mott, *The Seven Mountains of Thomas Merton* (London: Sheldon Press, 1986).
2. Ian Ker, *John Henry Newman: A Biography* (Oxford: Oxford University Press, 1986).
3. Luke 1:49.

17. The story of Darshan Singh, a French convert

Darshan Singh Rudel

When asked how I came in contact with the Sikh faith, and how I became a Sikh myself, I simply reply, it is *Vahiguru da bhana*, or *Vahiguru di kirpa nal*, in other words, thanks to God's will or God's grace.

There are no Sikhs in the south of France where I was brought up. Like most French people, I knew nothing of Sikhism or Sikhs even though many had died in France, during the First World War. I may say I was spiritually minded as a child, but with different ideas that were going to bring me into conflict with my practising Roman Catholic parents. I did not believe Catholics or Christians had a monopoly on truth. I believed Christians should have long hair and beards as Jesus did, and I refused to cut my hair and eat meat, believing 'Thou shalt not kill' should extend to animal life as well. I was 10 when I had these ideas, but I was compelled to eat meat and cut my hair until the age of 15. I was baptized, and remained a church server at the village Catholic church until I was 15 even though I had become more sympathetic to the Reformed Protestant Church. I saw it as closer to the Christian path for its simplicity and more direct approach to God. Members of the Protestant Church (Huguenots), were once persecuted in my region (Languedoc) very much in the same way as Sikhs during and after the time of Guru Gobind Singh. My heroes as a child were (and still are) Garibaldi and St Francis of Assisi, also a French anarchist, Proudhon, who believed religious principles, not politicians, should lead people.

I knew very little about India, except that Buddhism originated there, and that it was the land of Mahatma Gandhi. Ever since I was very young, I had a desire to go to India one day. I was not interested in school studies and in high school I couldn't relate to many youth of my age. I remember having debates with my French teacher, an atheist, about God's presence. I enjoyed being on my own and close to nature while working on my father's farm. Tension with my parents increased to the point that I decided to leave home and school, wishing to learn (mostly agriculture) while travelling around the world. I continued to regard myself as a Christian until I left school at 16. Then I became altogether agnostic and I was often hostile toward organized religion. However, I am grateful to God as strong principles guided me, and despite all my shortcomings, kept me away from wrong, even though I mixed with all sorts of people. Those principles were somehow religious, though my ego didn't want to admit it.

Somehow, my interest in various world faiths never diminished, especially during my first overland visit to India which brought me into contact with many religious communities. Even then I was often critical of their conduct, which was not always religious. It is my encounter with Sikhism which had the greatest impact on me and, I can truly say, restored my faith in God and made me realize that only our ego keeps us away from that reality. I was not yet 19 when I first reached India during the Emergency Rule imposed by Indira Gandhi. Nine months in various parts of that vast land brought me into contact with Sikhs. I wondered if many were only keeping turbans and beards because of tradition rather than because of a vital faith. But I also met some spiritually minded Sikhs. Usually, practising Sikhs are most inspiring people. I felt deeply impressed by their personality and kindness and felt the need to learn about their faith. No one tried to convert me; Sikhs are not known to proselytize. Communication was slow at first as my knowledge of English was almost non-existent in those days and I spoke no Punjabi. I visited Amritsar shortly before leaving India, and was fortunate to spend a few days at the Guru Ramdas Guest House located near the Golden Temple. The discovery of the Golden Temple had a great impact on me. I felt deeply impressed by the beauty, serenity and universal spirit of that temple of God, since the foundations were laid by a Muslim saint, and the four gates welcome all. Also the *Guru ka langar* that provides food to all is a marvellous way of sharing with the less fortunate and a radical way to eradicate barriers between castes and creeds. Listening to *kirtan* (hymns) was also a unique experience, even without understanding the meaning of the *shabads*. *Kirtan* always had a very soothing effect on me.

I left India with a heavy heart, taking with me some literature of

Sikhism and promising myself to return as soon as possible. After working (mostly in agriculture) in Greece, Switzerland and France I did return in 1980. I had long hair then and I wore a turban continuously only after 1980. I revisited Amritsar. I also stopped to see the historical *gurdwara* in Gwalior (related to our sixth Guru) and tried to go to Hemkunt Sahib, where Guru Gobind Singh is said to have meditated during his previous life. I returned to the Punjab in 1983 when tension was high as Sant Jarnail Singh Bhindranwale openly challenged the Indian government. I met him, and also met American and European Sikhs for the first time and tried to meet Harbhajan Singh Yogi, the Sikh who converted them. Harbhajan was regarded as controversial by many Sikhs for mixing tantric yoga with Sikhism. His visit to Amritsar was postponed and I had to leave without meeting him. I left India for New Zealand and Australia where I visited the Sikh community settled there and worked on farms in those countries before going to Japan and Taiwan. I returned to Europe after spending five years abroad in India and the Far East. I finally came to England in 1983 as I had been advised to do by Sardar Dr Trilochan Singh, a Sikh historian whom I met at Sis Ganj gurdwara in Delhi. He said England was the ideal place for a European Sikh since one can live among Sikhs, learn Punjabi and more about Sikhism while listening to *kirtan* as well as having the opportunity to do *seva* (work) at the local *gurdwara* (place of worship). I have been most fortunate since arriving in Southall at the end of 1987, to be able to stay with Sikhs, mostly with an elderly couple that I regard as my second parents. Their only son died ten years ago in a car accident. Some Sikh friends helped me with Punjabi, and I also attended evening classes so I could do Punjabi and English GCSEs while working in a bakery to support myself. Also I joined the British Red Cross as a voluntary member after doing first-aid and nursing courses, since it is an organization doing humanitarian work without discrimination, somehow in the spirit of Sikhism.

I am most grateful to *Vahiguru* for being able to receive *amrit* (initiation) at Anandpur Sahib, realizing one of my dearest wishes. For a long time I knew Sikhism was the right path for me and had started preparing myself to be initiated formally into the Sikh faith. Initiation is for Sikhs a kind of rebirth.

I was finally allowed to return to India and the Punjab in 1991.

The Punjab had been a restricted area for foreigners for several years. Before receiving *amrit*, I visited several historical *gurduaras* spread out in various parts of India, beautiful places mostly related to our Gurus or significant events that took place during their lifetime. It was a kind of pilgrimage meant to gain knowledge and inspiration while helping in the *Guru ka langar* and listening to *kirtan*. I also had the unique experience of spending three weeks at Gurmat College near Patiala in the Punjab, where students practise and learn all aspects of the Sikh faith, but also do comparative studies of all religions.

In 1983 I had visited Anandpur Sahib (the city of peace or bliss) and fallen in love with that peaceful town located in picturesque surroundings, where important events took place. It is the place where Guru Gobind Singhji transformed common people into a casteless community capable of defeating the mighty Mogul and Afghan armies. The initiation ceremony takes place twice a week and on my second visit in 1991 I was able to take *amrit* on Wednesday 10 July, after meeting the head Granthi, a very nice man, who reminded me of my duties as a Sikh. I felt very exalted as I walked to the upper room of Keshgarh Sahib and sat with a group of about thirty Sikhs, all here to reaffirm their faith as Sikhs, some of them taking *amrit* for the second time after breaking the Sikh code of conduct. I recognized a young Sikh, met previously in Mandhi (Himachal Pradesh) where he spent two years doing *seva* at the historical *gurdwara* as a preparation for taking *amrit* (the nectar of immortality, or name given to liquid drunk in the initiation ceremony). We were first reminded of our duties as Sikhs: from that day we were to live according to God's will, recognize Guru Gobind Singhji and Mata Sahib Kaur as our spiritual parents, and seek guidance from *gurbani*. We were requested to always wear the five Ks (see Chapter 10, p. 168), do our daily *nitnem* (Sikh prayers) and keep God in our mind and heart through *nam simran*. We were also requested to abstain for taking any intoxicants, smoking, drinking and to avoid meat. The *amrit* was prepared by the Panj Piare. The five bands and the Ardas were recited before we all drank the *amrit* from the same vessel. It was a thrilling moment. I see it as the greatest moment of my life, in my commitment to my faith, my spiritual rebirth and most of all in the privilege of being initiated at the place where *amrit* was given for the first time to the *panj piare* by Guru Gobind Singhji, who then humbly received it from them on

Vaisakhi, 1699. Before taking *amrit*, I was known as Amarjit Singh, a name originally given by Hindu friends when I visited Sevagram Ashram in 1980, a place where Mahatma Gandhi spent a few years of his life. But I requested the *panj piare* to give me a new name, for I saw that day as a new birth. Darshan Singh was chosen and agreed to by the *panj piare* and the congregation. The *hakam nama* read on that day was a verse from Bhagat Ravidasji and was most appropriate:

When I am, Thou are not: now that thou are (within me), I am not.

A certificate was issued to me from the *gurdwara* to allow me to change my name once back in France.

I realized while living in several countries where very little is known about Sikhism, that to be a Sikh can be quite challenging. But I discovered that it is even more difficult to be a European Sikh since it is so little accepted and understood. Also, over the last few years, Sikhs have been portrayed as a terrorist community, partly due to militants who used terrorism, but mostly due to unfair anti-Sikh media propaganda. Finding work was, at times, difficult in Taiwan (two years) where I learned martial arts and Chinese painting, and in Japan (one year) where I studied Japanese landscape gardening. One can work as a French teacher in those countries since qualifications are not required – to be a native speaker is enough. But with a beard and turban, I obviously didn't look like a stereotypical Frenchman. No school was willing to employ me at first, and some European colleagues said that the only way to get a job would be to shave and remove my turban, something I was not prepared to do.

However, I didn't give up faith and before my savings were exhausted, help came mysteriously from some Japanese and European friends who had once visited Amritsar and were sympathetic to the Sikh faith. They helped me find jobs: gardening for Europeans living in Japan and teaching French in private schools and to private students. I am most grateful to God for their assistance. Since I left school and became an international vagabond, I have been always able to find work to support myself. In India, in 1991, I encountered different types of problems, as on a couple of occasions police tried to obtain money from me while I was travelling by train at night. They assumed I was from the Punjab, but apologized when they realized I was a foreigner. In New Delhi the

CID armed policemen came to pick me up from the Bhai Vir Singh Foundation where I was a guest for a couple of nights. This incident took place shortly after Rajiv Gandhi's assassination. They took me to their headquarters in a van, after searching my room, and kept me for a seven-hour interrogation in which three inspectors tried to establish whether I was a militant, a spy or a human rights activist. They were hostile towards the idea that a European could convert to the Sikh faith, but once more being a foreigner protected me from police brutalities, and I was allowed to go once they realized I was harmless. However, they kept my fingerprints and took my photograph. It was a humiliating experience to be treated as a criminal, but it gave me an insight as to what life can be like for Sikhs living in India.

After taking *amrit* at Anandpur Sahib in 1991, I naturally tried to get my new name recognized officially by the French authorities. In France, a change of name may be permitted only if one has a legitimate reason. Application must be made to the high court, through a solicitor. My father contacted a solicitor at my birthplace (near Montpellier in the south of France) and a request was made to the court. To my dismay, the court dismissed my case as not legitimate, as a change of names for religious reasons is not allowed. The idea was to replace Michel Jean Louis Rudel by Darshan Singh Rudel, wishing to keep my surname since it is not related to caste, would keep my parents happy and would facilitate identification. My solicitor advised me to appeal, but after wasting £650 I didn't want to take that risk as it seemed unlikely that the court would reverse its ruling. To receive a different ruling, French laws would have to change, since they allow one to obtain French, or French-sounding forenames, but are hostile when it is the other way around, as they claim it would marginalize a French citizen. In the name of secularism and integration, French laws are discriminating against people converting to another faith.

My name has been, however, officially recognized in the UK after I signed a statutory declaration. I have finally become a British citizen and renounced my French citizenship.

Relations with my parents have improved greatly over the years and I am most grateful to God for that. My father discovered some positive articles in French about Sikhism and, knowing me, realized that my conversion was a natural thing to happen. Some Roman Catholics and other Christians are somehow hostile towards someone who converts to another faith. When asked why I changed my religion, I usually reply that it is not my religion, but humanity's religion, and that the Sikh Gurus' message is the most universal (catholic) in spirit. Guru Gobind Singh said, 'Recognize the whole human race as one.' Anyone who, while practising his or her faith whatever the label, recognizes God as universal truth, who is humble and surrenders to God's will is a co-religionist. He or she may be better than I, and from such a person I should draw inspiration. Knowledge of and respect for other creeds are essential to promote understanding, spiritual progress and, most of all, peace between religious communities. Relations among French people are not always the best as many French are hostile towards someone practising a different religion. Also a person who is vegetarian and doesn't smoke or drink is often seen as unsociable and often treated as an outcast.

Whatever adversity I face or have faced as a Sikh is insignificant compared to what Sikhs have suffered to defend their faith throughout their history. It has had the effect of testing and reinforcing my faith.

18. Belonging to a cult or new religious movement: act of freewill or form of mind control?

Martin Eggleton

One of the popular myths states that people do not join cults and new religious movements, they are recruited by them. To make such a claim begs the question of the sovereignty of freewill.

Conversion into a new religious movement implies a deliberate decision, an act of free choice, turning to leave behind the old way and join with the new. Recruitment, as the military metaphor might suggest, carries with it the pejorative. People are recruited or drafted into an army. Dragooning is executed through coercion and pressure.

The question raised is whether, on the one hand, some sort of mind control is exercised or, on the other, independent, personal free choice is made. Each potential joiner and each movement have to be considered separately, although movements can be put into clusters or categorized according to some familial resemblance. Circumstances at the point of decision-making are crucial. The context of conversion varies enormously. It is important to elucidate why people move from one major religion to another or why some choose to relinquish agnosticism or indifference and start 'believing'.

In the process of conversion, it has to be recognized that both the intellect and the emotion are involved. Rational argument or strong intellectual dogma can persuade people to enquire further but it has to be alongside that which affects them, that which stirs them emotionally to commit themselves to a group.

Joining a new religious movement has little vogue power (except for the accompanying status that might come with changed name, clothes and lifestyle). Seekers after truth as well as those bewildered by the accelerating pace of change as we reach the last years of the twentieth century, do convert to new religious movements. There is little doubt that the number of cults or new religious movements and their activities will be an obvious phenomenon as we reach the new millennium.

In Great Britain alone, it is estimated that there are over five hundred different new religious movements (NRMs) and it is likely that there is probably twice that number. Professor Eileen Barker thinks it not unreasonable to suggest a figure of around six hundred.[1] Sociologists of religion have differing ways of categorizing them. In terms of 'the world', they can be viewed as 'world-affirming', 'world accommodating', or 'world denying'; or they can be designated according to their roots in one of the major religions or as a 'self-religion' – where the prime purpose is the discovery or the development of the self.

Cults have tended to get a bad press – they are 'dangerous', 'harmful' or 'destructive'. The term 'new religious movement' does not carry the pejorative sense that the word 'cult' carries. Some of the movements can be viewed as 'benign', both in terms of their belief system and their practices. Others, on both accounts, can be construed at least as questionable and at most immoral and destructive.

In making a choice involving a particular value system, a would-be convert can make distinctions between movements. There is a great deal of difference between say, a movement that preaches universal love and practises meditation and yoga and one that preaches the power of Satan and practises child abuse. One can be construed as benign, the other as destructive.

In some movements there appears to be an inseparable link between belief and practice. For example, a belief that the world is to end imminently may cause a disciple to tolerate injustice knowing that the end is nigh or it may spur him to win as many converts as possible before the cataclysmic end. Similarly an unshakeable belief in the teachings of the NRM may lead to abnormal and sometimes bizarre behaviour. An example of this would be Spanish Gnosticism. This is known to have caused sexual disharmony between believers who are partners. Certain tenets of belief are known to prohibit a couple having full coital intercourse.

If we accept that there are people who are genuinely and consciously searching for something (however they define the object

– God, meaning of life, happiness, fulfilment), it follows that new religious movements or cults may be offering answers. Sociologists of religion determine the key factors which condition the rise and fall of the movements. Of the converts they ask such questions as, 'Why do they join?', 'How long do they stay in the organization?', 'Why do they leave?' There are no easy general answers to these questions. Some people, particularly the young and intelligent may be curious, loitering on the edge of the movement, occasionally participating in its activities, continuing to ask questions; others commit themselves wholeheartedly to a new lifestyle, language, outlook and ritual. There are those who, from within the movement, look for ways either to confirm the authenticity of what is happening to them (using external criteria) or to have their experiences confirmed from within the group, as well as responding to their own intuition, reasoning and common sense.

Some of the movements, like the School of Economic Science with its stress on philosophy and syncretist mysticism, appeal to intelligent middle-class, often upwardly mobile, young people; others, like the Jesus Army, include people from the lower socio-economic strata, often disadvantaged black youth. In my experience, I have discovered university students involved in movements like the Central London Church of Christ and the School of Economic Science.

Again, the motivation for joining movements varies. I shall look more closely later at the searches that are embarked upon and the question of recruitment methods will be considered.

Why then do people stay in NRMs – especially those which are demonstrably destructive, fraudulent or apparently contradictory in teaching and practice? One answer to this (as we shall see) is because certain needs, including emotional needs, are being met by the movement.

The length of sojourn in a movement also varies. Children, born into the movements in the 1950s and 1960s, are now taking adult leadership roles in some of the 'new' movements, like the Family of God (formerly Children of God). But membership in a large number of the movements can be short-lived. An average length of stay has been estimated to be about two years.

Again, why people leave any religious community varies. As is experienced in the mainstream churches, some people see obvious discrepancies and hypocrisy between what is preached and what is practised, others question the methods used to raise funds or the disbursement of finances. Still others may question the wisdom of tithing. Again, the conduct of a guru's lifestyle or sexual habits may cause the follower to examine his or her commitment. There is often simply a growing niggle that 'something is not quite right'. For others the construing of reality, or theology or cosmology, somehow does not ring true. The apparent distortion of reality is exposed.

Leadership

Conversion to a new religious movement may be influenced by a gifted and powerful leader. Leaders often carry with them authority which is claimed to have divine backing, as well as effective didactic qualities and charismatic gifts. Given the authoritative nature of a leader, obedience is a natural consequence. Often the guru is charismatic, not only in the sense of exhibiting human personality traits inspiring confidence, but in the sense of having divine properties and gifts. Thus the follower accepts the ability of the leader to pronounce on a wide range of topics – from scriptural interpretation to choice of sexual partner.

The role of leadership is a vital one. The evangelical or charismatic leader of a new Christian movement may be said (by the power of God or the Holy Spirit) to 'convert' people to God or Christ. The converting influence of convincing argument or preaching, the concerted pressure of the group and repeated instructions and mantras can all play their part in a person's decision to convert to a movement. The charismatic leader, as founder, will attract followers but is always subject to causing disappointment or attracting charges of hypocrisy. At their downfall or death or simply with the passage of time, the leadership has to be re-examined and restructured.

A degree of administrative bureaucracy often supplants the more spontaneous charismatic ethos created by the new religious leader. But the myth of the founder and the purity of his teaching might well linger posthumously (as with L. Ron Hubbard and the Church of Scientology).

The leader can have far-reaching control over the followers. The initiated can be totally intimidated and controlled. This may lead to a state where the person begins to love, admire and even sometimes to desire sexually the controllers or captors. There are cases where a convert surrenders herself to the whims of the powerful and authoritative (male) leader. This can include (as in the case of the Branch Davidians or in certain Buddhist groups) sexual submission to the leader. Whereas such behaviour is not uncommon in the old religions, the proximity of the smaller new religious member to the source of control and leadership proves to be more marked. This is particularly true of the more fundamentalist groups with a strong authoritarian leadership.

The searches

Before we turn to look at the actual ways in which new religious movements attract adherents, I want to suggest from my own pastoral work and research that there are three basic searches or quests which NRMs claim to have answers for. The first search young people embark upon is *the search for authority*, for something or someone to live by. The associated question here is, 'Who will tell me what to believe and how to live my life?'

It can be argued that there is a natural developmental model here. An individual breaks away from the heteronomy of the parent or guardian, in the search for autonomy, only to replace the initial heteronomy with another one – sometimes a theonomy where God or the guru takes over the parental role The final stage could be seen as the authority of the self, having finally rejected all external authorities.

Here we often find ironical circumstances. A young person may want to kick over the traces of his or her familial background with its authoritarian, paternalistic or maternalistic structure, only to find a different authoritarian structure in operation. Again, often one familial setting is replaced by another, with an extended family represented by the new organization exercising systemic control of belief and behaviour.

In a climate of insecurity – economic and psychological – where jobs, financial reward, competition and various forms of social malaise are only too prevalent, there is a great temptation to accede readily to those elements which provide security, firmness, shape, structure and conformity. Where the authority claims to have divine or semi-divine sanction – whether it be through a guru

267

or leader who claims to be God or God's representative or whether it be through the demands of an infallible, divinely-inspired Scripture, it carries with it the appropriate unquestionability. Fundamentalism comes into its own where there is widespread insecurity and uncertainty. Besides economic and social insecurity, there is the insecurity which comes from the erosion, breakdown or simply rejection of traditional principles, mores and ethical teaching. In the post-modernist world where 'anything goes', authority which provides not only a comprehensive world-view (if not a universe-view), and a divine plan for every life event and beyond to eternity, has great appeal. If being told what to believe and how to behave serves the purpose of providing security, confidence, assurance and direction for the individual, then authoritarian NRMs answer this search.

The second search is *the search for experience* or experiences. Here the existential question is, 'How can I feel good?', a factor that has gained dominance in economic as well as social circles.

Conversely, where a movement exhibits joy, purpose and meaning and can inspire its followers, then the attraction is obvious. The argument goes that the individual lives within a society largely determined by economic, technological and social forces outside their control. These determine our culture and everything within it including what we are to eat, wear and even think. Image is a key word here. Young people conform to images provided for them by the culture. The external culture preconditions the expectation. It provides reality, both genuine and virtual. If this argument is accepted, then we have an existential problem. How can I experience something which is engendered from within even though externally conditioned? Modern jargon expressed within the youth culture puts it in terms of being 'turned on' or 'having kicks'. Some of the practices of NRMs – meditation, mantra chanting, sleep deprivation – can result in psychotropic states akin to the effects of drugs. 'Trips' or mystical experiences are sometimes claimed by participants. It is not simply a linguistic accident that the experience of ecstasy is testified to not only by a devotee within an NRM but by a follower of the pop rave culture.

Risk is an important factor here. The desire for experience may override the reputed danger of a mind-controlling cult. Risk implies excitement often within an esoteric and dangerous context. New religious movements can offer ecstasy – the ability to stand outside yourself, to have mystical experiences, to practise meditation of the transcendental kind, to feel good, euphoric and even regress to a past life or be transported into a future one.

The third search is *the search for community*. Associated with this search is the quest to find one's identity. The question, is 'Who am I?' or 'Where do I belong?' Breakdown in community and the ensuing isolation, individuation and alienation in modern Western society are not difficult to prove. There are attempts at the restoration of a notion of community (not least among the politicians).

Communitarianism is now a slogan on the political agenda. Concomitant with this is the stressing of a restatement of communal values and morality. These spiritual and moral values are now part of the common curriculum in the British school education system.

Many of the new religious movements provide a sense of community. The disciple is welcomed, accepted, even loved, given an identity and sometimes a new name, reclothed or rebaptized. In addition, the group provides a new way of perceiving reality, a new way of understanding the world, a new way of interpreting historical events. These interpretations are often reinforced daily through the repeating of mantras or prayers or slogans.

Within those movements which are overtly proselytizing in practice, we can see that the community can provide fresh energy. In the clarifying and executing of missional objectives, the disciple finds identity in common with the whole community by embarking on agreed objectives. Some movements, then, stir the adherent to action. Stress is laid upon unstinting zeal and enthusiasm. Returning missioners report on how the latest skirmish has gone, how the battle is faring, how many scalps, so to speak, have been taken.

Thus the religious community provides both vision and mission. The mission is drawn up by the religious community which sets out its objectives. This gives a sense of purpose to the new follower, something, perhaps, which has not been found before in their pre-community life.

So much for the consideration of the would-be convert and the needs that he or she is seeking to be met. We may now turn to look at the way in which new religious movements set out to win their recruits. Within British culture there are advantages and disadvantages for the new religious movements. Traditional religion expressed through the mainstream churches has a declining membership. The exceptions to this tendency are found amongst the fundamentalist, pentecostalist, black-led and house churches where there is evidence of growth.

Recruiting methods

We have suggested, then, that people join new religious movements despite the alternate view that they are recruited through pressure and other forms of mind control. It goes without saying that, for a person to become committed, a particular movement must be available to the individual and operating within that person's social context. Bryan Wilson says 'for the conversion to occur, he must have in his background experience ... the style, promises, or prospects of the movement, or he must be attracted by the example of the members, by the appeal of the association, or the atmosphere as he perceives it'.[2]

There are a number of recruiting techniques used by the new religious movements to attract would-be converts. These techniques vary according to the culture in which the organization wishes to recruit. Religious movements that seek converts want to make personal contacts, door-to-door proselytizing, using mailing lists and other networks and advertising in libraries and colleges. Movements that want to promote self-enlightenment and self-development may advertise more impersonally (e.g. the School of Economic Science regularly advertises philosophy courses on the London Underground hoardings). Some new religious movements (e.g. Transcendental Meditation and Scientology) offer public lectures and meetings open to all (but subject to certain fees). Such courses are promoted as a form of training, leading to some sort of qualification.

A potential recruit (whether seen as a member, client or guest) is invited free of charge but is then offered further sessions progressing to a different level of knowledge or expertise. These sessions are often subject to a particular fee. A number of those who enter a movement this way can find themselves in increasing debt. In their need or aspiration to gain the knowledge or acquire the insight or be accepted within the hierarchy, they are pressurized into making more and more financial commitment. The person may often then feel obliged to stay within the movement, being subject to blackmail and extortion.

Some organizations have perfected the art of rewarding and flattering their potential clients or followers, on the one hand, and threatening or punishing them on the other. The greater the efficiency of the control system, the more the ability to manipulate the client to behave in particular ways to the advantage of the movement.

The promises of eternal life or endless bliss or esoteric teaching that leads to a greater understanding of the mysteries or an encounter with the divine have to be balanced with the threat of enticement by the devil or being cast into outer darkness or not fulfilling one's full potential or letting one's true self down.

Converts who have experienced a sense of the transcendental or a blissful state may be asked to give testimony to those experiences in order to win others to the cause. The born-again convert or grateful customer who has discovered their self for the first time is used to market the organization. Once you have accepted the new teaching or truth then you too will receive this enlightenment, or bliss or spirit or whatever. Again, those who reject such offers of truth and knowledge could be subject to all sorts of mishaps, illness, accidents, even eternal damnation in the fires of hell. (There have been times when large numbers of members of a movement have been expelled and threatened with damnation owing to their lack of zeal.)

Brainwashing or mind control

Integral to this discussion and often seized upon by the media is the question of 'brainwashing' or 'mind control' exercised by the movement and its leaders. I have maintained that there is always the element of freewill in conversion. But to what extent is an individual 'free' to commit himself or herself voluntarily to join the organization?

The truth is, of course, that there is an encounter, a dynamic process going on between recruiter and recruited, salesperson and customer, producer and consumer. Within this process arises the question of logical argument as well as the interplay of emotions. I may or may not be persuaded that the Reverend Sun Myung Moon is actually the Messiah predicted to come, I can equally be influenced or not by the degree of personal attention and concern the community of the Unification Church expresses to me. The former may or may not evoke scepticism and questioning, but the latter may be more decisively persuasive.

Brainwashing is a method first termed when soldiers were subject to strong psychological pressure to adopt a group's views against their own will. In Communist prison camps, brainwashing took place where there was full control over the context of communication. In voluntary conversions, on the other hand, contact is made between recruiter and recruit in an obvious (though sometimes subtle way) without coercing the individual to conform to the group's views. This is not the place to go fully into the origin and history of brainwashing from its context in the Korean War. There is enough evidence, however, to show that in a society characterized by high-pressured propaganda and advertising machines, we are all subject to 'brainwashing' in the popular sense. Selling is based on the conscious and the subconscious, direct and lateral thinking, the literal and the subliminal. Apart from this we are subject to being influenced by flashing lights, body language and gestures, tones of voice and ecological setting.

Bare walls and poor lighting could well affect my response and decision-making in a different way from tasteful decor and strategically placed lighting. The findings of neuro-linguistic programming have shown the importance of the spoken word and the unspoken word, of language and metalanguage.[3]

One of the salient factors here is the question of the authority of the leader or guru. If the person claims to be divine or be speaking on behalf of the divine, or has access to interpretation of holy scriptures and the potential convert respects the validity of that kind of authority, then the possibility for control of the mind is greater. Hypnotism and the techniques of neuro-linguistic programming can be used to influence people. The reinforcement of reality as perceived by the authority figure is a potent way for any advocate to influence a person in a forceful way. It is difficult, however, to test out the validity of saying, 'God told me to join' as opposed to saying, 'I joined of my own free will'.

Some converts would claim, in a sense, that what they are doing is inevitable. There is no alternative, there is some sort of divine compulsion. But this is dangerous, if free and critical decision-making is not made.

In one sense we are all 'brainwashed' – we are the product of determinist factors like genetic make-up and early childhood environment. Following this line, there is little room for freewill. On the other hand, there are those who would claim it is impossible to brainwash anybody, except under extreme conditions where we are reduced to a matter of conditioned reflexes. There is a spectrum of interpretation which varies from brainwashing at one extreme, through mind-control, to strong pressure, to incidental influence.

We have to consider the support for the view that, at least, strong pressure and influence, through particular techniques and methods, is used by a new religious movement to convince possible disciples to join a movement. It is here where we can cite the ecological factors which might substantiate the context of brainwashing or mind control methods.

'Love-bombing' (a technique where the potential convert is showered with warm, complimentary statements – 'strokes' – of a very personal kind), dietary control, physical restriction, repetition, sleep deprivation confusion techniques, trance-induction, sensory deprivation and deception have all been allegedly used by cults and NRMs. There is little doubt that some new movements do employ these techniques.

Brainwashing or mind control, as used in NRMs, has been shown to operate under certain conditions. An exclusive environment, free from outside control, is used. Movements may use a home, a rural retreat, an hotel. During the course of training the potential converts are restricted (limited use of ablutions and toilet facilities). A rigorous schedule involving physical restriction and long working hours leads to physical and mental fatigue, with little time for relaxation and reflection. Some sort of agreement is made between organizers and participants. The potential convert acknowledges that agreements and word-keeping are important values in life and responds by vowing to himself or herself to keep agreements made in the sessions.

There is some intimidation to keep agreements and to remain for the duration of the course. The participants agree to complete their training. They may also agree to obey certain ground rules during the sessions (e.g. no drugs or smoking or restricted food menu or short meal breaks). All this creates an atmosphere of uncertainty, ambiguity and confusion.

The alternation of praising and commending with condemning and blaming induces a feeling of confusion. This technique then renders the person more suggestible and ready to follow authoritative instructions. An instruction to 'abandon yourself – let yourself go completely' means that displacement is followed by replacement.

273

Emptiness can always be filled. Rituals and repetitive patterns are brought in – meditation, chanting, yoga or 'auditing' – at an early stage of induction. The practice of repeating mantras, chanting and the like has reinforcing properties on the potential convert. He or she is being introduced to a new reality, a new world, a new jargon.

Ridiculing the potential convert, playing on guilt feelings, urging the person to share their innermost secrets with other members of the group occurs. In some cults the ridicule extends to the person having to stand in front of an audience being abused by the 'trainer'.

In some sessions people faint, others go into a state of consciousness known as the 'alpha state' where the person is hyper-suggestible. New terms are used – jargon, known only to the insiders, the initiated. Sometimes vicious and abusive language is used to make the person uncomfortable. Characteristic in all these techniques is the distinct lack of humour. The pressure is on until there is some kind of breakthrough and the convert is truly 'found', there is some kind of new birth followed by euphoria and joy. The new converts then become zealots. One slogan runs 'sell it by zealot'.

In some movements, the dynamics of humanistic psychology are used, stressing that a human being has unlimited potential to achieve whatever is desired. The movement often has a good follow-up system to exercise mentoring and monitoring of new converts and to collect them together in some sort of group system. The convert's commitment, initially agreed, is played upon and accountability to the movement and its leadership is demanded.

In this debate about brainwashing or mind control, the terms 'programming' and 'de-programming' are used. Brainwashing or mind control carries with it the idea of programming. Just as a computer is programmed with information and data which can then be manipulated, so too the human brain can be programmed. Thus, stored repetitive mantras, slogans, sayings, commands can all be recalled.

In all this, it is hard to believe that any person is simply a guinea pig subjecting themselves to an environment, both psychologically and ecologically, which they find alien and hostile, exercising no freewill and meekly obeying every suggestion offered.

On the other hand, there are techniques now being widely used (as found, for example, in neuro-linguistic programming) which are reputed to act subliminally and which condition an expectant, suggestible would-be follower to act and conform in particular ways.

Further, the experiences that go with that conditioning can also be brought to present awareness. They can be dealt with in the here and now as they are recalled. It follows that the opposite mechanisms can be exercised. What is programmed can be de-programmed, what is learned, on and after entry into a new religious movement, can be unlearned on exit from it. What has been treated as unquestionable can be treated as questionable.

Just as there is a mode of entry into a NRM so there is a mode of departure. Conversion out of a group may be just as valid as conversion into a group. Departure is often radical and abrupt.

In some countries a de-programmer is hired and the follower kidnapped at the request, say, of anxious parents who have become alienated from their offspring. The concern is for the son or daughter who has changed lifestyle, outlook, even body language and name. Sometimes they have a zombie-like appearance, they talk a different language and they may have been told that their parents and family are 'of the Devil' or belonging to the old world from which the person has now been rescued, liberated or transformed.

Leaving the NRM may cause serious problems – guilt, dissociation, loss of identity, employment problems and the like. During this period between detachment and reattachment to something else, counselling help is sometimes sought. This time brings the dilemma of the person being in a transitional mode, maybe a feeling of liberation accompanied by an ongoing search. This may result in a commitment to another religious group or to none at all.

The journey model

In trying to help this transition, I want to suggest a model which is not as systematic or rigorous as de-programming and can be considered as a form of exit counselling. This model is based upon a truism that everyone is on a journey – they have come from somewhere and are going somewhere. If you like, this is a journey through time, an historical journey. Those who have joined or been recruited by an NRM, are on at least one of a number of journeys.

The first journey, so to speak, is the *journey through life*. Everyone is on a journey through life from birth to death. This journey can be marked by recognized rites of passage from circumcision or baptism or naming ceremony, through nursery and primary education to secondary education, through puberty and adolescence into tertiary education, employment or unemployment, through bonding and broken relationships of various kinds as a mature person, all along being subject to the ageing process, illness, suffering, bereavement and death. Thus Everyman and Everywoman have to take this road.

What we look for at particular stages of this life journey will depend on our age, outlook, need-orientation, values and goals. Life events can be looked back on and they can be projected forward: the client who has come out of a cult or NRM may find it helpful to see the journey they are on in this relative way. Their experience in joining the movement can be viewed as some kind of staging-post.

But the convert may see their commitment to the movement as a *journey of pilgrimage*. There is another journey which is the road travelled as a pilgrim or disciple. Not only can this be taken literally – Mecca, Jerusalem, Rome, Lourdes, Bangalore, Oregon, or Waco as destinations of the journey – but as a spiritual journey. The convert or ex-convert may be able to trace the journey through moments of mystical enlightenment or being born again or receiving the blessing of the Spirit or the guru's visitation. In the counselling situation, the counsellor and disciple can explore together the next stage of the journey. What or who is it you are looking for now? What kind of spiritual insights or wisdom now draw you on?

And, thirdly, the convert may be on a journey of self-discovery. So far the journeys described could be viewed as journeys *along*. In one sense they can be construed as evolutionary or developmental, characterized in terms of stages. Psychologists and educationalists are able to perceive these developmental models through the likes of Piaget and Fowler. Another way of describing the journey is in terms of the journey *downwards* or *within*. This journey has a popular appeal, expressed in the writings of authors like M. Scott Peck, Paulo Coelho and James Redfield.[4] Their works are growing into popular received wisdom, pocket-book bibles by sojourners on the road to self-discovery. Those on such journeys will be attracted to the so-called 'self-religions'. They will be attracted to the Human Potential Movement with the accent on self-discovery, self-realization and self-actualization.

Particularly within parts of the new age movement there lies the possibility to discover oneself rather than discover the god or gods outside oneself. This journey has no limited horizon, it is a journey which takes one on a deep journey downwards within oneself as well as beyond oneself in terms of the transpersonal – the journey *upwards*.

Belonging to a NRM, in terms of journey, can be a staging post on the way. It can be a place to exult in the view, to gasp in awe or dance with delight in, or it can be a place of refuge from familial rectitude. It can be an ashram for renewal, a mission house or a foster home.

However long one stays within a movement will depend on what the total experience adds up to. It may be interpreted as irreality, distortion – a dream-world from which one has to wake up, a prison from which one has to be rescued. Alternatively, it may be a place of enlightenment, joy, bliss where the human and the transcendental meet.

Notes

1. E. Barker, *New Religious Movements: A Practical Introduction* (London: HMSO, 1989; fourth impression (with amendments), 1995, p. 148.
2. See Bryan Wilson's discussion in *Religion in Sociological Perspective* (Oxford: Oxford University Press, 1982), pp. 118–20.
3. For further elaboration of this term see, for example, J. O'Connor and J. Seymour, *Introduction to Neuro-Linguistic Programming* (London: HarperCollins, 1990); R. Bandler, *Using Your Brain* (Moab, Utah: Real People Press, 1985); A. Robbins, *Unlimited Power* (New York: Simon & Schuster, 1989).
4. E.g. M. Scott Peck, *The Road Less Travelled* (London: Century Hutchinson, 1978); Paulo Coelho, *The Alchemist* (London: Harper-Collins, 1988); James Redfield, *The Celestine Prophecy* (London: Bantam, 1994).

19. Being Hindu in North America: the experience of a Western convert

Tamal Krishna Goswami

According to a recent national survey,[1] Indo-Americans have the highest level of education and have the fourth highest family income among all thirty-three population groups in the United States. This fact is all the more striking if we consider their humble beginnings: between 1871 and 1965, only 16,013 Asian Indians were admitted into the US.[2] Now, due to the relaxation of immigration laws, they number more than one million. Between 1980 and 1990, the Indo-American population grew by 126 per cent, an astonishing figure when compared to the total American population growth rate of 9.8 per cent.[3] Assuming that the majority of these South Asian immigrants are Hindus, one would expect Hinduism to be at least a significant minority voice within America's religious marketplace. But if indeed it is, a certain degree of credit must be given to the Western converts of the various Hindu missionaries that have circulated in North America since 1965. Their addition has amplified the Hindu voice to its barely audible level.

The first faint whispers of Hinduism in America came from the eclectic chain-smoking Russian Theosophist Madame Blavatsky. Those whispers were given full voice some twenty years later by an articulate Indian, Swami Vivekananda, only to be drowned out soon thereafter by the din of two World Wars. Not until the 1960s, when a host of gurus came West in response to the *haiku*- and mantra-chanting beats and hippies, did that once faint whisper at last become a great crescendo.

I arrived in San Francisco's Haight during the steaming Summer of Love, a vegetarian, flute-playing, self-taught yoga, with my ear to the ground listening for a truth college had not revealed. A faithful pilgrim from New York's Lower East Side, I searched that Promised Land for what Watts and Ginzberg, and every sacramental psychedelic potion promised. Was it their blessings, or the ritual purification of those sacraments, that led me one morning to a Hare Krishna store-front temple? Or was it the Krishna mantra incantation which seemed to follow me from New York's Lower East Side to the 'Morning Star' commune in Sonoma County, California? Perhaps it was my agnostic Jewish parents who starved me of religion in an already culturally impoverished America? The Vietnam War? So many voices whispered in my ears as I heard for the first time His Divine Grace A. C. Bhaktivedanta Swami Prabhupada, the person who eventually became my guru.

To identify the voices which are responsible for a conversion as radical as mine is no easy task, for mine was a theological, moral, vocational and cultural conversion. More than merely an inner transformation or denominational realignment, my entire existence was fundamentally changed – from shaving my head, to changing my name, to remoulding the habits of heart. This metamorphosis was gradual (begun in a previous lifetime the temple devotees assured me that first morning). And I can still recall repeated dreams as a child – which I shall not repeat here – which might substantiate that claim. The incontestable facts, however, are that I was the only child of a German-born artistic and cultured mother, who shortly after her divorce married a left-wing Brooklyn intellectual and would-be actor of Russian parentage. Though usually away at work, she somehow managed to keep me alive – a lone white child on the streets of Harlem. From the hushed whispers of anti-McCarthy rhetoric and songs of Seeger and Robeson I gathered that I was different from the other white kids from Riverside Drive, and from the Puerto Ricans and blacks on my street. Nevertheless, I was a child of America – a baseball card-flipping, girl hating / loving, naughty New York boy.

Instead of having me *bar mitzvahed* (I had not even once seen the inside of a synagogue), my parents made the economically correct, ethnically select move to a middle-class suburb in Queens. What a dreadful coming of age! Gone was the cultural / ethnic Harlem mix I had learned to 'love' – the Puerto Rican mango carts, the drug dealers, pimps and prostitutes, and black youths scatting me to sleep at night. Compared to this montage of inner city funk, the insipid mediocrity of my new home and neighbours seemed like a cultural wasteland. My parents had emigrated to a new world of possibilities; why had they now migrated to this? They had not consulted me about the move, nor was I savvy enough to appreciate that owning your own home (after 25 years of mortgage payments!) meant you were no longer an immigrant. All I knew was that I wanted out. I carefully plotted my escape. Considering the constraints of my age and meagre resources, I saw only one option – to go within. Through books, music, and dreams, I left that dreary Queens suburb far behind.

It was not long before my consciousness drifted eastward, as if lured by karmic whispers, voices from past lifetimes. By the time I met Prabhupada I was a confirmed vegetarian, an occult practitioner, and aficionado of everything Eastern. I found no ultimate satisfaction nor hope in Western philosophy; the polemics of peace were as uninteresting as war; the Great American Dream, a phantasmagoria. I was searching for a truth which was absolute, which would not be affected by the changing currents of human destiny.

To embrace the Hare Krishna lifestyle was easy, because in many ways I was already living it. The San Francisco temple had an ambience appealing to both the Hindu and the hippie and I fit snugly between the two. The philosophy was not entirely new, though I had never before encountered vedantic personalism, combining biblical monotheism with the richly complex vedic cosmology. Prabhupada's lectures and *kirtanas* provided the final push.

To those gathered in his store-front temple Prabhupada conveyed India in its entirety. It was as if all the mysticism encountered in my readings now sat embodied before me. He seemed to straddle two worlds: singing, his body trembling slightly in ecstasy, he was somewhere else; but when he would speak, his smile reassuring, handing everyone a slice of fruit at the end of the program, he was right there with us in Haight-Ashbury.

Not many Indians visited our temple in those days, but the few who did seemed so different from Prabhupada. Certainly they shared common cultural affinities, but their focus was elsewhere. They were, it seemed, undergoing a similar conversion as we, but in reverse. Now, thirty years later, I see the irony of our joint conversion story, for our conversions, more than individual transformations, are a reorientation toward culture if not a relocation in culture. And it is this swapping of cultures, or more accurately, sharing of cultures, which is at the heart of the Hindu conversion story. When the Indo-American and the Western Hindu convert stand face to face, they cannot conceal the difficulties each experiences in negotiating the present or in anticipating the future. Each recognizes in the other something he or she has tried but failed to leave behind. It can be an uncomfortable meeting, yet is a relationship perhaps neither can do without, holding for each as it does important keys to reappropriating their past.

Issues other than religion have always preoccupied Indian immigrants. The cultural and economic transfusion which is a part of the immigrant experience, while not decoding their Hindu genes, has deeply imprinted their psyche. Shyam has become Sam, Laksmi is now Lucky. Pasta and pizza have replaced their spicy curries. But Sam and Lucky, hiding behind the latest designer garb, cannot conceal their ethnic origins: chillies, not mushrooms, decorate their pizzas.

Those chillies are all that I can recall of a Gujarati Samaj program I attended as a young ISKCON[4] convert in 1968. And those same chillies kept me running through my four-year stint as ISKCON's first Governing Body Commissioner to India from 1970 to 1974. And these were the same chillies that I finally came to love, which gave me the nickname 'Hot Tamali' (I assure you, it had nothing to do with my fiery temper).

A professor recently introduced me to his class on religious cults and sects, 'You have before you a living time capsule; an adherent of an ancient tradition remarkably unaffected by modernity.' If only he knew! For I would still prefer my pizza with plenty of mushrooms, if only they were not so tamasic. Nor do I allow a week to pass without honouring a veggie-burger with chips. And I assure you I am quite Hinduized compared to one of my godbrothers, who prefers peanut butter and jelly and swears that *chaddars* do not stay on our American shoulders as they do on our Indian brethren. In short, we Western converts suffer Sam and Lucky's same crisis of identity. Though we have deeply drunk of India's wisdom, we descendants of Moses and Abraham, like our immigrant Hindu relatives, cannot forget our roots. Our need to reconcile the culturo-religious East and West creates a strong basis for meeting with Indo-American Hindus. Though we approach each other from opposite directions, there is a common resonance to both our needs.

In bonding we have shared our particular strengths. For the nearly 100,000 Asian Indians admitted to the United States between 1965 and 1975, ISKCON temples were perhaps the only ones to which they could make their spiritual pilgrimage. There was a sense of pride in seeing Americans appropriate the various trappings of Hinduism, and for those who came especially close, a genuine appreciation for how deeply we had imbibed the spirit of *sanatana-dharma*. Thrust amidst America's casteless society, they voiced no objection to being lectured by white-skinned Brahmins and women priests. Rather, it enabled them to loosen the age-old halter which had restricted them spiritually, as much as North America's entrepreneurial economy allowed them the freedom of upward mobility.

Yet the marriage of these two peoples has had its difficulties. As the ISKCON lecturers confront their Indian congregation's predilection for worshipping demigods, their warnings against such apparent polytheism echoes the claims of Moses. For Krishna in the Gita clearly pronounces, 'Men of small intelligence worship the demigods, and their fruits are limited and temporary.'[5] While this monotheistic certainty does not exclude the recognition of lesser gods as assistants to the supreme Deity, it still does not sit well with those reared from childhood to worship many gods. As their affluence increases, Indians are erecting their own temples and community centres which better reflect their regional preferences for worship and socializing. For many, ISKCON's monotheistic doctrine with its strong aversion to Shankara's undifferentiated monism confirms their earlier doubt that Westerners are unable to truly embrace Indian thought.[6]

Still, their experience with ISKCON has been educational, especially when in establishing their own temples they had to learn to adjust the closely knit temple and adjoining community structure of their homeland to a new reality of a far-flung congregation. Providing a full-course dinner, ISKCON-style, rather than the traditional sacrament of a *prasadam* token, was just one of the practical lessons borrowed to insure a loyal following.

Yet the proliferation of regional and sectarian temples has not lessened ISKCON's charm and allure. Though most adult Asian Indians find ISKCON *kirtanas* too boisterous, their children love them. It is to this younger generation, both now and in the future, that ISKCON will perhaps be most meaningful. Without their parents' cultural backgrounds, Hindu spirituality is difficult to assimilate. Susceptible to peer pressure at school, they tend to distance themselves from all that sets them and their friends apart. For this American-born first generation, a multi-racial religion like ISKCON can provide a greater sense of being American than they would be likely to feel attending an ethnically homogenous Hindu temple. This in turn may help them to negotiate their parents' basic spiritual beliefs in a way that does not seem so foreign.

Depending on how capable and willing the parents are to share their religious heritage, their children can be as unfamiliar with Hinduism as any other American youth. And in typically American fashion, they may interrogate their parents' beliefs with a voracity bewildering to their elders, who are often unable to respond convincingly. It is in this regard that ISKCON will continue to play a meaningful role, one which is readily recognized and even encouraged by many Indian elders. Western converts have little difficulty responding to young Indians whose philosophical perplexities are often quite similar to those of a new convert.

Most Indo-American youth will never move into an ISKCON ashram nor embrace the demanding disciplines and abstinence ISKCON expects of its initiates. But the positive rapport these Indo-American future adults establish with ISKCON will undoubtedly manifest when later they must choose for themselves not only whether to be a Hindu, but also which of the Hindu temples they wish to align with. As this next generation gradually succeeds their Indian-born parents, Hindu temples dependent entirely upon Indo-American congregations may have difficulty surviving. Already in India, there are instances of temple management succeeding to the hands of ISKCON despite Brahmin caste objections.

The alliance with the Indo-American community has been equally beneficial to ISKCON. Indeed, Western converts and Indo-Americans are tied inextricably to each other as spiritual siblings. Mother India nourishes the young convert like an adoptee, even as she expects to be supported by her begotten children in America. An indication of India's appeal to the convert can be understood when we consider the eager anticipation which precedes a visit to India. There is a sense of having arrived home after a journey of countless births. A convert enters India as a culturo-religious pilgrim, immersing himself in Hindu culture much as one submerges in a sacred river. For the North American devotee, the India experience substantiates what might otherwise have remained mere theorizing. It is an education which no amount of textual studies nor ashram living can equal.

Once having returned from the pilgrimage, the convert more easily recognizes the Indo-American as a brother or sister who reminds him of the sacred homeland. This sense of kinship is mutual, and it is not uncommon for the Indo-American to assume the role of an older sibling in relating with ISKCON devotees and their institution. Financial support is but one display of this relationship. Many ISKCON temples balance their budgets today more by way of contributions from the Indo-American community than from the sale of literature, the former mainstay of their financial support. And capital fund-raising projects in the millions of dollars have only been possible with the support of an affluent Indian membership.

A still more subtle result derived from the association with its Indian congregation has been a transferral of Hindu values. Sari styles and culinary expertise are but two of the more obvious manifestations. More substantially, the integrity of the Indian family unit has been admired, and through association, emulated by North American devotees. Most North American converts are now married (a sign of ISKCON's changing demographics) and occupy much of their time raising families. And apart from these dedicated Western converts, there is also a growing Western congregation of non-initiated lay persons who pattern their commitment to the institution on the example set by the Indo-American congregation. The change from ashram to household life and the growth of supportive congregations are two significant developments which should help ISKCON shed its cult image of the 1970s and 1980s.

Thus far I have spoken of the partnership of Western converts and the Indo-American Hindu community. Western converts can also make especially suitable Hindu partners in inter-religious dialogue. Who can be a more articulate Hindu spokesperson to the Judaeo-Christian world than one raised within it? Nor is such participation a purely selfless exercise, for we have a genuine need to understand as well as explain ourselves – to explain why we have left our Christian and Jewish homes and taken shelter of a strange God. We need to legitimate ourselves in the eyes of our parents and other relatives, our friends and acquaintances. To be whole, to be sane, we seek their acceptance. And this is as true for the new convert as a middle-aged monk like myself.

Age seasons one. Fervour and fanaticism are replaced by accommodation and reason. One re-examines what as a youth one rejected, surprised to find not only commonality but worthwhile differences. We recognize the distant 'other' as our long-lost companion. And it is in this sense that both inter-religious dialogue and its more academic studies can truly thrive.

Such studies are, as Francis Clooney has persuasively argued, 'a necessary luxury in the context of today's pluralism'.[7] For by crossing the boundaries into each other's belief system, we are in fact strengthening the walls that support our own faith with the mortar of borrowed wisdom. I believe he is correct in his assessment that few Hindus have been willing to study Christianity with as equal an urgency as some Christians have studied Hinduism. While I suspect that Western converts may be as lethargic in this regard as their Indian-born brethren, at least they will not find differing philosophical and cultural notions to be unassailable barriers separating the two civilizations, as some have suggested.[8] For the convert's life, after all, is a constant negotiation of these barriers, one in which he may feel equally at home in both worlds, while at other times peaceful in neither. But to accept these world views as finally discordant is to admit to hopeless schizophrenia. For the convert, bridging these two worlds is far more than a necessary luxury; it is necessary for survival. In this endeavour he will not allow economic constraints, which frustrate many an Indian scholar, nor any other obstacle to hinder his search. As I have tried to indicate earlier, he will be motivated unceasingly by the need to re-examine his own roots and find out if indeed his genes are Christian, Jewish, Hindu – or perhaps, a combination of all.

Many ISKCON communities are nearly miniatures of Indian village life in the midst of America. The dynamics of an ancient tradition struggling to understand itself in the context of modern society should intrigue anyone interested in the study of conversion, without demanding the ardour and expense of a trip to India. Those with the time and the inclination may make some astonishing discoveries, as I did in an ISKCON restaurant only the other day. Pizza, the waitress informed me, was a buttered *chapati* with curd and tomato *subji*. Apparently it has been added, along with peanut butter and jelly, to the canonical list of Vedic recipes. Without mushrooms, of course.

Notes

1. T. W. Smith, *A Report on the Socio-Economic Status of Ethnic Groups in the U.S.* (Chicago: University of Chicago, National Research Center, 1992).

2. J. Gordon Melton, 'The Attitude of Americans toward Hinduism from 1883 to 1983 with Special Reference to the International Society for Krishna Consciousness', in D. G. Bromley and L. D. Shinn (eds) *Krishna Consciousness in the West* (Lewisburg, PA: Bucknell University Press, 1992), pp. 79–101.

3. 'Invisible Americans: An Exploration of Indo-American Quality of Life' *Amerasia Journal* vol. 21, no. 3 (19), p. 27.

4. ISKCON: the International Society for Krishna Consciousness.

5. Bhagavad-gita 7.23: *antavat tu phalam tesam tad bhavaty alpamedhasam.*

6. For an indication of the Hindu community's objection to ISKCON's monotheistic position, and ISKCON's subsequent response, see Jayadvaita Swami, 'Is *Back to Godhead* an Offender?', *Back To Godhead*, The Magazine of the Hare Krishna Movement (January/February 1996), pp. 42–5.

7. Francis Clooney (1994) 'Hindu–Christian Studies as a Necessary Luxury in the Context of Today's Pluralism', *Hindu–Christian Studies Bulletin* 7 (19), pp. 39–44.

8. See Francis Clooney (ed.) (1995) 'Four Responses to Professor Dharmapal's *Bharatiya Chitta Manas and Kala*', *Hindu–Christian Studies Bulletin* 8 (19), pp. 2–19.

20. Cult conversions: controversy and clarification

Lorne L. Dawson

I have been teaching a course on 'cults' (see Richardson, 1993), or what sociologists of religion prefer to call new religious movements (NRMs hereafter), for many years, and I would say that interest in the topic is growing.[1] Certainly the enrolment in my own course has never been larger, even though we are now well past the peak of success enjoyed by such well known (or notorious) NRMs as the Unification Church, Scientology, Children of God, and Krishna Consciousness. Today much of the popular interest has shifted to a fascination with various expressions of neo-Paganism and the New Age movement, as well as some more secular psycho-therapeutic cults (e.g. Luhrmann, 1989; Heelas, 1996; Hanegraaff, 1996).

There is also a more general curiosity, though, about extreme religious commitments of all kinds. Much of this curiosity has been prompted by the approach of the next millennium and by the tragic deaths of the Branch Davidians at Waco, Texas in April 1993, the mass suicides of the members of the Solar Temple in October 1994 (and then again in December 1995, and March 1997) and of the Heaven's Gate group in March 1997, as well as the poison gas attack on the Tokyo subway by Aum Shinrikyo in May 1995 (see e.g. Tabor and Gallagher, 1995; Introvigne, 1995; Palmer, 1996; Reader, 1996). But whatever the reason for the growing interest in the subject, one question has been at the heart of most popular discussions of NRMs since the 1970s: Do the people who join these unconventional religions do so freely? Or are they the victims of some sort of psychological manipulation or even coercion? Put most bluntly, and in the terms popularized by the anti-cult movement in America

(Shupe and Bromley, 1980 and 1994), are converts to NRMs 'brainwashed' or subject to 'mind control'?

The public perception of NRMs continues to be strongly influenced by the fears raised about the possibility of coercive conversions (e.g. Enroth, 1977; Van Driel and Richardson, 1988; Pfeifer, 1992; Singer, 1979 and 1995). The resultant controversy has played an important role in numerous court cases involving 'cults' in the United States, Europe, and elsewhere (e.g. Richardson, 1991 and 1996; Anthony and Robbins, 1992 and 1995). But it has also stimulated a wide and diverse investigation into who joins NRMs and why by many sociologists, psychologists, and historians of religion (see Dawson, 1996 and 1998). We now have a much better grasp of the complicated process of religious conversion and the weight of evidence tips the scales decisively against the accusations of brainwashing levelled by the opponents of NRMs (i.e. disgruntled family members of converts, dissatisfied ex-members, members and leaders of competing religions, various government officials, and some psychologists and psychiatrists). Consequently, American courts have cease to entertain brainwashing claims. But the public remains relatively ignorant of the scholarly record and media reports of new religious activities still tend to instil an unwarranted measure of suspicion about cult conversions.[2]

In Europe NRMs are currently facing a rising tide of religious intolerance. Government-sponsored inquiries into new religious groups in France, Germany, Belgium, Switzerland, Russia, and elsewhere, have displayed a systematic bias in favour of the views of the anti-cult movement. Here talk of mind control has resurfaced and in many jurisdictions specific measures have been recommended for the legal suppression of hundreds of minority religions (Introvigne and Melton, 1997). The need persists, then, to promote a better understanding of who joins NRMs, how, and why.

To that end, this brief chapter surveys what we know about cult conversions, but by a rather unconventional means. What follows is the transcript of a typical media report about someone who joined a NRM, drawn from the height of the scare about cults in the United States. This is the transcript of a television programme, entitled *Cults: Choice or Coercion?*, first broadcast by CBS news in 1979.[3] The programme consists of an interview with Tom, a young and appealing ex-member of the Unification Church (i.e. the Moonies), interspersed with interviews with his parents, a so-called expert on mind control, the person who deprogrammed Tom, and some other footage dealing with members of the Unification Church. Much that is said by Tom and the others in this video is true, to a point. The interpretations given of the events, however, are speculative and incomplete, and, as we now know, at odds with the most reliable information available. Below the transcript I have provided a running commentary on many of the statements made in the programme, demonstrating how the programme fails to give an accurate insight into cult conversions.

In reading this chapter you may first wish to deal with the transcript of the programme in its entirety, and then consult my commentary. Alternatively, you may read the two in tandem. Some parts of the programme necessitate extensive comment, while others are passed over altogether. Thus to facilitate reading the analysis, the transcript has been divided into a series of ten numbered segments and these segments are matched with the numbered parts of the commentary. The overall format will not always lend itself to the most systematic or complete presentation of what we know about cult conversions. But the pertinent points do arise, and in a manner that better highlights their relevance to the real public discussion of cults.[4]

Cults: Choice or Coercion?

DIALOGUE (1)

TV HOST: The mass suicides of over 900 people in Jonestown, Guyana, brought the phenomenon of cults to the public eye in the most shocking manner. The hardest thing for most of us to understand is how any healthy person's mind could be influenced enough to make them do things that would be considered foreign to his nature. Call it brainwashing or mind control, it's hard to understand.

We went to California and met a young man who spent two and a half years in Reverend Moon's Unification Church. His personal story shows how someone is drawn into a cult and what happens to him when he gets out.

COMMENTARY (1)

The initial premise of most discussions of cult conversions is that they are different. Why? It is commonly assumed that these conversions are extreme in three ways: (i) the beliefs to which people are converting are thought to be very strange; (ii) the conversion is thought to be very sudden and unexpected; and (iii) some of the groups to which people have converted have committed extraordinary acts of violence – usually against their own members. As Eileen Barker (1984: 126–7) and other scholars of NRMs have observed, however, there are neither logical nor empirical reasons for accepting the anti-cult assertion that only someone who is brainwashed could believe some of the incredible doctrines of many NRMs. As the historical and anthropological record amply documents, there are few limits to the exotic character of the beliefs different peoples have held. The strangeness of the beliefs adopted does not, in and of itself, demonstrate or necessarily even imply the coercive nature of the process by which they were adopted. There are few if any universal criteria of reasonable belief, and all conclusions about the religious beliefs of others are a matter of perspective. As an old adage specifies, 'one man's meat is another man's poison' (cited by Barker, 1984: 158). The same holds true for the seeming suddenness of many cult conversions. 'Suddenness' is not *proof* of 'brainwashing'. There is considerable reason to believe, in any event, that the supposed 'suddenness' of these conversion is more apparent than real (see the last section of this commentary).

One must be leery too of the all too easy links made between all NRMs and the violent fate of a few. If one considers the claims made by the anti-cult movement about both the number of NRMs in existence (often stated to be 3,000 or more in the United States alone), and the number of people ever involved with such groups (often stated to be about ten million people in the United States), then the number of incidents of cult-related violence is not exceptional, especially set against the high levels of violent crime in America. In a similar vein, one need only think of the surprisingly numerous cases of child molestation that have recently scandalized the Catholic Church to appreciate that NRMs have no monopoly on deviant behaviour. Few people, however, would be inclined to condemn the Catholic Church as a whole for the errant ways of some of its members. Placed in proper cultural context, then, the crimes of most NRMs are rather ordinary, though nonetheless regrettable and truly worthy of condemnation. The tragedies of Jonestown, Waco, the Solar Temple, Heaven's Gate, and Aum Shinrikyo call out for special attention precisely because they are extraordinary, even within the context of other known incidents of cult-related violence.

The Moonies, the specific subject of this programme, have a history free of any violence. Their aggressive proselytizing, however, made them a primary target of the anti-cult movement and thus also of scholarly research (e.g. Barker, 1984; Parsons, 1986; Galanter, 1989). This research has largely exonerated the Unification Church, and other NRMs, of the charges of brainwashing brought against them.

DIALOGUE (2)

TOM: I rejected my family, my friends, they were all part of Satan's world. Moon says, in some of his speeches, the first point is that you give up your material possessions to God, through Moon. Then you give up your family, your friends, your emotional connections with the world. And then, finally you have to offer your mind to God. That is the ultimate offering, the sacrifice.

COMMENTARY (2)

Groups like the Moonies, Krishna Consciousness, or Children of God (now called The Family), evoked a strong negative response from many of the parents of their young converts because they demand a complete commitment to the cause. In historical reflection, this is not unusual. One need only think of the words of Jesus (Matthew 10:34–39): 'Do not think that I came to bring peace on the earth; I did not come to bring peace, but a sword. For I came to set a man against his father, and a daughter against her mother ... He who loves father or mother more than Me is not worthy of Me; and he who loves son or daughter more than Me is not worthy of Me. And he who does not take his cross and follow after Me is not worthy of Me. He who has found his life shall lose it, and he who has lost his life for My sake shall find it.' These and other lines of Scripture underlie the long tradition of monastic retreat from the world of Christendom, just as other ancient and sacred texts justify other forms of religious detachment throughout the world (e.g. the Buddhist *Sangha* or Hindu *sannyasin*). Only from the perspective of the presumed 'normalcy' of the contemporary American values of individualism, utilitarianism, materialism and secularism does this traditional religious vocation seem intrinsically strange and problematic.

DIALOGUE (3)

TV HOST: Today Tom Fuller is a sophomore at the University of California at Santa Cruz. In 1974, Tom was an idealistic 18-year-old on a break between high school and college. His father, a Congregational minister, had put him in touch with Christian volunteer programmes, and Tom was making his way across the country from group to group. In Missoula, Montana he accepted an invitation to dinner. Six days later he had given his life to the Unification Church, and he believed that the Messiah had come to earth, and that he was a Korean businessman by the name of Sun Myung Moon.

COMMENTARY (3)

Tom's experience and background are quite typical, we will see, of what research has revealed about those most likely to join NRMs – he was, as sociologists say, 'structurally available' to cult recruitment. However, the host's observations reflect several common misconceptions. First, in line with the literature of the anti-cult movement (e.g. Enroth, 1977; Hassan, 1988; Singer, 1995), it is implied, here and elsewhere in the programme, that cults target lonely, isolated individuals and conversions happen has a result of chance encounters with strangers in public places. Research has revealed otherwise, studies of conversion and case studies of specific groups have found that recruitment to NRMs happens primarily through pre-existing social networks and interpersonal bonds. Friends recruit friends, family members each other, and neighbours recruit neighbours (e.g. Harrison, 1974; Beckford, 1975; Lofland, 1977; Bainbridge, 1978; Snow *et al.*, 1980; Stark and Bainbridge, 1985; Rochford, 1985; Latkin *et al.*, 1987; Palmer, 1994; Wilson and Dobbelaere, 1994; Lucas, 1995). Groups like the Unification Church, Krishna Consciousness, and The Children of God have been criticized sharply for their aggressive and persistent forays into public places to disseminate literature and proselytize. Yet the evidence strongly indicates that these recruitment drives are rather dismal failures relative to the effort invested in them (e.g. with regard to the Moonies see the figures provided by Barker, 1984: 141–8, and Galanter, 1989: 140–1).

Second, it may often appear that cults target the lonely or vulnerable because cult involvement is strongly correlated with having fewer and weaker extra-cult ties (e.g. Lofland, 1977; Downton, 1979; Stark and Bainbridge, 1985; Balch, 1995). This accounts, in part, for the disproportionate representation of adolescents and young adults in NRMs. This segment of the population is simply free of countervailing social and economic commitments. They have the time and the opportunity to indulge their spiritual appetites and experiment with alternative lifestyles.

Third, an attempt is made in this passage to delegitimize Moon's religious claims by identifying him as a 'Korean businessman'. The statement is true enough, and it points to another source of controversy surrounding many NRMs (e.g. Scientology): they have blurred some of the traditional boundaries between the worlds of religion and business. Once again, however, one must watch for a measure of hypocrisy in the criticism. Many prominent and relatively respected American evangelical leaders head religious organizations that certainly could be called 'big business' – in style and monetary returns (e.g. Jerry Falwell, Pat Robertson, Jimmy Swaggart), while an examination of Moon's early life can leave little doubt about the genuineness of his belief in his religious mission. Entrepreneurship is not so foreign to religious endeavours, and in the contemporary hyper-capitalistic environment a greater fusion of these elements is assured (Moore, 1994).

DIALOGUE (4)

TOM: I totally disregarded anything that I knew in the past and finally came to a point where whatever Moon said was truth.

TV HOST: But how does an intelligent, articulate young man or woman get to the point that they would give up their mind, their capacity to think? We spoke with Dr Margaret Singer, a mind-control expert at the University of California at Berkeley. Dr Singer has done extensive research on people coming out of cults.

DR MARGARET SINGER: I think we need to take a slightly different look and see how active and sophisticated the recruiting by the cults are [sic]. The approaches usually are made in public places to people who look lonely by the cult recruiters. With some of the cults they don't realize that it is a cult; they think they are joining a communal living or altruistic group.

TV HOST: Wearing a hidden microphone, producer Joseph Lovit passed by a recruiting station of the Creative Community Project in San Francisco, to see if he would be approached.

STREET RECRUITER: Howdy.

TV PRODUCER: Hi.

. . .

TV HOST: Though they do not say so, the Creative Community Project is affiliated with Rev. Moon's Unification Church.

TV PRODUCER: Is this a religious group?

STREET RECRUITER: No, not really. Not any fixed religion. But most people come from some sort of spiritual background. We try to see what we have in common. There is a God. We believe in God. We're having an open house tonight, if you'd like to come . . .

TOM: There's a process, I mean it begins the first time you run into somebody on the street, that's one point. And then, three months later it is a deeper commitment, and by the time I was in for six, eight, ten months, I was totally in – I was a true believer.

COMMENTARY (4)

Many different and important points are raised in this longer passage. First and most obviously, the programme repeats the anti-cult charge that converts to NRMs actually lose 'their capacity to think', to realistically assess their situation. This supposed loss of critical reflection is presented as the most telling symptom of brainwashing (e.g. Enroth, 1977; Singer, 1979 and 1995). Yet no reliable evidence has ever been collected to support the charge, beyond pointing to the obstinacy with which converts hold to their 'distasteful' beliefs. Any regular interaction with the membership of these organizations quickly dispels the illusion that they are cognitive 'zombies'. But what is more, the record of psychological testing, of many kinds, consistently reveals that converts to NRMs score within the normal range on all scales of psychological functioning (e.g. Levine, 1984; Rochford et al., 1989; Richardson, 1995).

Second, in the debate about cults one must learn to be wary of the sources of information. Dr Singer has made her living providing advice about NRMs. When the efforts of other scholars denied her the opportunity to earn fees serving as an expert witness on cult brainwashing in court cases, she attempted to sue them for millions of dollars for loss of livelihood. She has long had a vested interest in keeping the cult controversy alive. Contrary to the introduction provided in this programme, moreover, she has never been a faculty member at the University of California or anywhere else.

Third, no participant observation studies of NRMs to date have revealed the kind of sophisticated recruitment techniques that Singer and others repeatedly claim cults use. The Moonies and other groups work hard at recruiting new members and in the process they use some high pressure social tactics – much like other kinds of salespeople and missionaries. One significant fact, however, would seem to cast considerable doubt on the efficacy and sophistication of their efforts: careful studies conclude that about 90 per cent of converts leave the groups they joined, voluntarily, within two years (e.g., Barker, 1984; Levine, 1984; Wright, 1987; Jacobs, 1989). Such a high rate of attrition does not suggest that mind control has been used, or if so, very effectively.

Fourth, at several points the programme, like the anti-cult movement in general, focuses on the use of deception by the Moonies. As the programme demonstrates, to a certain limited extent this is true. But the actual deception shown is only consequential if it is assumed that within a few days recruits can be brainwashed into joining the Unification Church and not just the Creative Community Project (in this instance). Moreover, what the programme does not realize or say, is that the Creative Community Project was part of a particular and rather atypical sub-group of the Unification Church known as the Oakland Family. This group was the most notorious component of the Church, it was unrepresentative of their work elsewhere, and it was eventually censured by Moon.

Fifth, this last point leads us to another common problem in media discussions of cults: a persistent tendency to lump all NRMs together. By repeated implication, accusations made against any one group are generalized to almost all other new religions, ignoring their marked differences in origins, doctrines, practices, objectives and organizational structures. 'Atrocity stories' are opportunistically drawn from an indiscriminate array of NRMs and used to 'prove' the accusations levelled with little regard for the varied nature and circumstances of the groups cited. No systematic means of comparison is even attempted, because it is incorrectly assumed in advance that all cults are essentially the same (e.g. Bromley *et al.*, 1983).

DIALOGUE (5)

TV HOST: Gary Scharf says that mind control was deliberately practised in the Unification Church. He should know. During his four years in the Church he indoctrinated new recruits for Rev. Moon.

GARY SCHARF (DEPROGRAMMER): Our goal at that point was to surround them with a very particular kind of atmosphere to inundate them with affection, with the ideas of the lecture, exploring all the different reaches of a person's emotions whether it be exuberance, or intense guilt, or longing for an ideal world, piling all those emotions together to totally capture a person's heart and experience.

COMMENTARY (5)

This part of the programme raises two concerns. First and most straightforwardly, in rereading the words of Gary Scharf, ask yourself whether his description of the process of brainwashing matches the image conjured in your own mind? Or does the passage more simply suggest the kind of intense missionizing effort many religious (and other) groups often make to win others to their vision of the truth? What is it that the anti-cultists actually have in mind in speaking of brainwashing or mind control? As classically delineated, with primary reference to the fate of some modern prisoners of war (e.g. Hunter, 1951; Sargent, 1957; Lifton, 1961), the processes of brainwashing roughly conform to a three-stage model of radical resocialization by which an old identity is stripped and new one is welded. In the first stage or phase, sometimes called the 'unfreezing', the victims of brainwashing are subjected to various incapacitating physical, psychological, and social conditions designed to induce a near complete cognitive, emotional and social breakdown. The two primary means used are various forms of either sensory deprivation or sensory overload.

296

Physically weakened and psychologically disoriented by such practices, the sense of reality and of self of those being brainwashed is fractured, supposedly, leaving them susceptible to suggestions for alternative ways of ordering their lives and re-establishing peace and sanity. In the second stage or phase of brainwashing, called the 'changing', this openness to suggestion is used to impose a new identity – a new set of thoughts, feelings and behaviours. Those being brainwashed are systematically and ever more intensely introduced to new daily routines, expectations, group activities, and rewards and punishments. The third and final stage or phase, the 'refreezing', seeks to consolidate and reinforce the changes induced by rapidly and thoroughly immersing the subjects of brainwashing in a new, stable, and supportive social environment, suffuse with appropriate ritualized activities. By the repeated and relentless control and manipulation of the external behaviour of the subjects of brainwashing (their words and deeds), it is assumed that these people can be conditioned to continue to censor and refashion themselves. The change effected should be permanent, short of another round of counter-brainwashing (like the 'deprogramming' attempted by anti-cultists). It is also assumed that the change in behaviour is indicative of a true change in the person's self-conception, even personality.

As indicated here and in the passage below, where Tom discusses what happened to him (section 8), the NRMs are said to employ a number of techniques to brainwash: (i) the recruiters are trained to look for personal weaknesses in the potential converts; (ii) these 'targets' are talked into signing up for a rapidly escalating series of lectures, workshops, and retreats, using deception if need be; (iii) once engaged in the activities the recruits are never left alone and all their doubts are deflected by intense social pressure to maintain a sense of group harmony and individual happiness; (iv) they are bombarded with affection and loving kindness; (v) they are kept very busy and systematically deprived of sufficient food and sleep; and (vi), once they are sufficiently tired and disoriented they are drawn into various confessional activities through which information is collected and used to play upon their natural feelings of guilt and anxiety about their past experiences and future uncertainties; then (vii) the recruits are taught and shown, through various spiritual exercises (ranging from singing to praying to guided imagery exercises and meditation), how they can relieve themselves of their guilt and fears by fully dedicating their lives to the newly revealed truth of the NRM.

Is this picture of cult recruitment accurate? Does it constitute 'brainwashing'? Reliable research has left most scholars of religion sceptical. But before I explain why, we must deal with another more preliminary issue raised by this part of the programme. Gary Scharf is a deprogrammer, and as the TV Host later reveals, he was deprogrammed himself just five months earlier. This state of affairs is typical and it points to a systematic sampling bias in the popular literature on cults and this television programme. The brainwashing scenario of NRMs relies heavily on the testimony of individuals who have undergone deprogramming or 'exit-counselling'. The latter is the non-coercive equivalent of the former. These people are under great pressure to account for their aberrant behaviour (joining a cult) and to direct blame away from themselves, their families and the community. This may be necessary to make peace with their families and regain entry into other community groups (e.g. returning to school or a job), or simply to resolve the cognitive dissonance they are experiencing from the contrast of their present and past behaviour. The brainwashing scenario, to which they are 'programmed,' provides a non-stigmatizing way to absolve everyone, most importantly themselves, of responsibility and actually securing the sympathy of others for themselves (Richardson and Derks, 1986; Bromley, 1988). Similarly, the books and articles of the anti-cultists tend to selectively employ small and non-random samples of stories drawn from sources that are either inadequately identified or not identified at all (see Barker, 1984: 128–31). Several academic studies, on the other hand, have revealed a marked and consistent discrepancy between the post-involvement attitudes of converts who leave these groups voluntarily and those who are deprogrammed. Only the latter show a strong statistical correlation with negative views of their cult experience (e.g. Solomon, 1981; Wright, 1984; Lewis, 1986; Lewis and Bromley, 1987; Galanter, 1989). Most individuals who leave a NRM voluntarily (which accounts for most who leave), continue to express some very positive feelings about their involvement.

TOM: I was gullible. I was looking for this. I wanted to believe it. I wanted the Messiah to be here. So, I kept overlooking the little incongruities, the little half truths.

COMMENTARY (6)

Tom, quite obviously, fits the profile of most witnesses against the cults: he has been deprogrammed. But from his own comments and those of his parents, in many respects he also seems to fit the best social-psychological profile we have of the people who join NRMs. In media reports two stereotypes are often repeated: converts are either naive and duped or social losers seeking refuge. Tom is cast in the former role here, yet his words tell us more. A great many of the people drawn to NRMs have been 'seekers'. They have been reading religious and philosophical literature, attending different lectures and church services, asking the so-called 'big questions' in life (e.g. What is the meaning of life? Is there a God? Is there life after death? How does my life matter?). Some have already established a 'conversion career'. They have belonged to several other conventional and unconventional religions before. Tom acknowledges that he became a Moonie because he strongly 'wanted to believe' in something. He was at least a nascent seeker.

Like most converts, Tom is also young (most are in their twenties), from middle- to upper-class backgrounds, and better educated than most people in the United States, Canada and Britain (see Dawson, 1996 or 1998). In fact for many 'cults' the levels of education are well beyond the national averages (e.g. Scientology, The Church Universal and Triumphant, Rajneesh / Osho movement, Vajradhatu / Shambhala). In the words of two of the leading sociologists of NRMs, Stark and Bainbridge (1985: 395), the successful cults of today seem to 'skim more of the cream of society than the dregs'.

This is not to say that converts are not attracted to the NRMs by some unfulfilled needs. Usually they are experiencing some form of what sociologists call 'relative deprivation' (Glock, 1964). They may not be poor or socially marginal in any obvious sense, but we have reason to believe that many of them share certain less apparent psychological and social needs. In their detailed studies of hundreds

299

of converts to the Unification Church and many other NRMs, Barker (1984) and Levine (1984) independently discovered that these 'joiners' tended to be idealistic people who came from fairly happy and very respectable homes. Their families tended to place a priority on the importance of public service and doing one's duty over acquiring material wealth. These households were also sheltered environments, however, in which the future converts were encouraged and rewarded for being over-achievers at school and in other activities, but seem to have had their emotional development retarded. They did not tend to experience the usual crises of adolescence until a later point in life. Therefore, many seem to have been psychologically ill-equipped to handle the disappointments, hurt and disillusionment they experienced when they first ventured out into the world on their own. As a psychiatrist, Levine further speculates that many have been experiencing greater than normal difficulties in separating themselves from their parents and establishing their own identities. In ways their parents may not have noticed, because they were 'good kids', these potential converts often have been struggling quietly with a crisis of self-esteem and self-understanding for years.

Enduring this kind of acutely felt tension, these young people yearn for a quick fix to their sense of isolation and confusion. They seek a sense of full belonging and purpose in life, independent of their families, but without engaging in the serious analysis of their situation required to find and shape their own identity. With so little real self-esteem in place, they seek to avoid, for a time, the responsibility of making choices. Then at a moment of crisis they encounter the missionaries of one or another NRM offering just such an alternative path to (or temporary detour from) maturity.

Whatever the nature of the psychological processes involved, it is interesting, as Barker notes, that the radical separation from the parents achieved by converting to a NRM is in some respects not a departure from them at all. Moonies, for instance, 'do not appear to be rejecting the values that were instilled into them during their childhood; they appear, on the contrary, to have imbibed these so successfully that they are prepared to respond to the opportunity (which society does not seem to be offering them) to live according to those very standards' (1984: 210–11). Arthur Parsons (1986) and Susan Palmer (1994: 92, 100) were led to like conclusions in their interactions with the Moonies. The pattern may well vary for other

NRMs, but Palmer found elements of it in each of the seven NRMs she studied and her findings are reminiscent of the views expressed by Tipton (1982) in his well-known comparative study of a fundamentalist Christian group, an American Zen centre, and the clients of the human potential movement *est*. This perspective certainly accords with the finding that most of the people who join NRMs leave voluntarily within about two years – presumably when their identity crises have been resolved adequately. Does Tom fit this more precise profile? We do not know enough to say, but in listening to his parents there are indications that he may.

DIALOGUE (7)

TV HOST: Tom's mission in the Church was fund-raising, selling flowers for up to 18 hours a day, seven days a week. Even though it sounds like a minor assignment, some months Tom brought in as much as $12,000.

TOM: I spent my days running around a parking lot. I'd have a bundle of flowers, I'd go up to someone and say, 'Hi, my name's Tom. I'm working with a Christian Youth Program. Can you help out by buying some flowers?' And, I would go from one person, to another, to another. It was more the smile, the connection, that did it. They didn't know. I mean, we lied to people.

TV HOST: Tom, we've heard the term 'heavenly deception'. Can you explain that to me? What is it, exactly?

TOM: Heavenly Deception is . . . well like . . . lying, okay. Take for instance the idea that if I told them I was raising money to help lay the financial foundation for the physical Kingdom of God on earth, you would think I was crazy. So, I say something to you that you can understand and relate to – you got kids, Christian Youth, America, and so on.

TV HOST: But how did you justify in your mind, the fact that you were standing there lying to people?

TOM: I didn't think about it. I couldn't think about it. It was a basic contradiction to my own upbringing, and the values that I had when I was growing up. But if I was going to be a good Moonie I wasn't going to question.

COMMENTARY (7)

Regrettably, there is good reason to believe Tom's account of how he spent his days. But once again we know that his situation was rather extreme because of the particular faction of the Unification Church he joined. Both the Moonies and the Hare Krishna movements became excessively preoccupied with fund-raising in the mid-to-late 1970s. The abuses of the situation cost them members and led to internal crises, calls for reform, and changes in their policies (see Rochford, 1985; Richardson, 1988). The daily life of most converts to these prominent NRMs is now quite different as these groups have abandoned their more aggressive forms of proselytizing and fund-raising.

DIALOGUE (8)

TOM'S FATHER: His critical mind was just not functioning. Then we began to say what is our responsibility as a parent? What is my responsibility to an 18-year-old? Should I intervene?

TV HOST: As liberal parents, Rev. and Mrs Fuller were anguished over the idea of intervening in their son's life.

TOM'S FATHER: I think that 18-year-olds should go out and want to be on their own. I believe in freedom of religion, that people should celebrate their religious faith without government interference, or outsiders. The question is holding that over against my son and what was happening to him.

TOM'S MOTHER: We had been thinking: we don't like this, but it's his choice. We can't intervene between him and a choice that he is making. And you know what? What we finally realized was that it wasn't a choice. That's the thing that is really, really hard to get and that took us two years to understand.

TV HOST: What do you mean that it wasn't a choice?

TOM'S MOTHER: That, he had made a choice to accept an invitation to dinner, and then we come to the end of his choosing.

TV HOST: We use the term 'brainwash,' what does that really mean? How do they do that? And do it so quickly?

TOM: It is a complicated process. You've probably heard that a lot of it is through food and sleep deprivation. I slept an average of five hours a night for 27 months. And I was working, like I said, 12, 15, 18, 20 hours a day. So, I was kind of a walking, running, talking zombie. Believe me. But that's okay. You can fund raise from that state, but other than that when I'm coming in I get a very limited amount of information, okay. It's only what Moon tells me. I'm not allowed to contact my family, to check things out with them, to talk to them or my friends. I don't, I'm not allowed to read any other books, any other magazines, any other newspapers.

DR MARGARET SINGER: If they do begin to question, they are afraid to leave because the contents of the cult have made them feel that they have totally separated from all their past family, all that was meaningful. They've got out of the mainstream of life. The cult has convinced them that all the problems in their life were worse than they can actually really remember them being. And, they feel that there is no other life except life within the group.

TV HOST: After two and a half years of soul searching, Tom's parents decided to take drastic steps to retrieve their son. Knowing that Tom was based in Kansas City on a fund-raising team, they applied for, and were granted, a legal conservatorship putting Tom in their custody like a child, or a mental incompetent, for a court-limited 45 days. (pause) How were you picked up? Who got you?

TOM: Okay. My sister had been working on the east coast for a year and a half and she was travelling back to Berkeley and she was going to stop in Kansas City and visit me. The night she was supposed to come in, I finished fund-raising at about 11 o'clock. They let me out of the van and I went down to the motel where she was staying, and I had my flowers, and I knocked on the door and she answered, and I gave her my flowers -- I was glad to see her. And, she took the flowers and gave me a big hug and she stepped back and two policemen jumped out of the bathroom and two more from the other room and the lawyer, and everybody. I got deprogrammers, Satan's agents in the flesh, had me.

TV HOST: Is that what you thought?

TOM: Oh yeh! Oh yeh! Because we were programmed against the deprogrammers, you know. And mad!! (squeals ahhh ...). I was mad, I was resentful, I was bitter, because I knew my parents were behind it. They weren't there, but I knew they were behind it.

TV HOST: Tom co-operated, and within 48 hours they had begun to turn him around. Gary Scharf, who had been deprogrammed just five months before, was one of Tom's deprogrammers.

DEPROGRAMMER (GARY SCHARF): It was difficult for Tom just to be still, there was an actual physical unrest in him. But underneath Tom was a person who really was trying to do what was right for his life. And there was a concern, a sensitivity, an integrity in Tom that I really felt coming through from him.

TOM: It wasn't a violent experience at all. They were very gentle because I think they understood, it's been awhile, exactly what it was from me, and it was basically talking. They were challenging me to look at my own experience, like look at what about heavenly deception, and what about all those doubts and questions you've just been repressing? They came up, finally! I was in an alternative situation where I wasn't constantly singing and chanting and programming my self, where finally they could come up.

COMMENTARY (8)

Having said all this, is it still appropriate, however, to call the actual process of conversion to NRMs brainwashing? The evidence will not support such a claim. In the first place, there is considerable doubt that anyone has ever been brainwashed. Two psychiatrists hired by the CIA to do a definitive study of the possibility concluded, for example, that when thought reform techniques do seem to have worked, it is simply the result of behavioural compliance brought on by threats of violence and the experience of physical abuse (Hinkle and Wolff, 1956, as discussed in Anthony and Robbins, 1994: 460–1). This is what happened to the American prisoners of war turned against the United States for propaganda purposes by the Communist Chinese during the Korean War. But no evidence has been found that any of the NRMs charged with brainwashing have ever physically constrained or harmed their recruits in the attempt to produce a conversion. Rather, physical force plays a role when converts are deprogrammed. In deprogramming people are kidnapped, held against their will, and systematically harassed and abused for days and weeks. It is deprogramming, that is, that comes closest to replicating the classic pattern of brainwashing, as attempted with prisoners of war. In this regard, it is interesting to note that Tom and the programme producers say little about the coercive aspect of his own deprogramming.

Second, we must simply pause to seriously consider if the things most commonly cited as evidence of brainwashing by the anti-cult movement hold up to scrutiny. Are the loving attention heaped on new recruits, their busy schedules of activity, combined with possible elements of food and sleep deprivation the elements of brainwashing? Observing and participating in such communities and interviewing members who left voluntarily, scholars have been unable to document any systematic pattern of abuse and exploitation (e.g. Lofland and Stark, 1965; Richardson et al., 1979; Barker, 1984; Levine, 1984; van Zandt, 1991; Lucas, 1995). Considerable social pressure is brought to bear on new recruits, and in some instances errors of judgement are made. But are the converts somehow deprived of their very capacity to think for themselves? This is not what most converts and ex-converts report, and to dismiss their denials of brainwashing as being in turn the products of brainwashing is to carry us into a circular and nonsensical line of argument that cannot be refuted. To warrant stigmatizing the cult conversion process as brainwashing or mind control the proponents of such a claim must find evidence that can be tested independently of the pre-judgements of the anti-cult movement. By the loose standards of discrimination applied in the anti-cult literature a wide array of similar such activities in other contexts, from fraternity initiations through army boot-camp to many forms of athletic training, could be accused of brainwashing as well. Clearly, in the end, the difference between these activities and those of the NRMs is that the beliefs and values of these other organizations are in harmony with the beliefs and values of the anti-cultists (see Pfeifer, 1992).

Singer (1995: 139) argues, for example, that NRMs use meditation to relax and diminish the critical faculties of their followers, rendering them passively suggestive to the supposedly bizarre views of the cult leaders. But what then are we to make of the long lineage of meditation instruction common to almost all of the great religious traditions of the world, and the growing use of similar techniques in psychotherapy and the treatment of cancer and other physical ailments? Speaking, it is apparent, with little personal or professional understanding of the nature of meditation, Singer provides no reliable means to discriminate between these various uses of meditation other than her distaste for some of the ideas that some NRMs are seeking to inculcate through meditation. But she cannot acknowledge this, for the nature of people's religious beliefs is not subject to legal determination. In most Western societies, ideological disagreement is no longer grounds for the denial of religious freedom.

Third, and most tellingly, we know that the success rates of cult recruiters are in fact extremely low, while the rates of voluntary defection of members, as mentioned already, are extremely high. In her comprehensive study of the Moonies in Britain, for example, Barker (1984: 144–8, 259) calculated that no more than 0.5 per cent of prospective converts who visit a Unification centre will be part of the movement two years later (see Wright, 1987: 2 as well). If the cults are engaging in brainwashing then, they are not doing it very well!

TOM'S MOTHER: Just because you discovered that you had been had, and that you want to leave the organization, all that veneer that's been laid on you, and the way of feeling, and thinking and being doesn't just drop off.

TOM'S FATHER: The last two years of his life just disappeared, not the normal kind of life experience of an 18 to 20 year-old. So what do you talk to somebody else about, you've not been the same place that they've been?

TOM'S MOTHER: He didn't know what had been going on in the world. He didn't know what was in the news, or what the music was.

TOM'S FATHER: All the clues, you know, we pick up from society, all the clues that orient us to this reality they've been shut away from so it took him a long time to start coming back into another earth, another planet. To get reoriented.

TOM: I think the hardest thing for me was wondering whether I was ever really going to be able to pull it back together. Being deprogrammed, my world was exploded in a lot of ways and I mean there were times where I would wake up in the morning and I would feel so depressed, like six months later, that I was never going to get a direction for myself, you know, get a purpose for my life, that I was just going to be floating. And that was very scary, I thought I was losing my head at certain times. There is a lot of doubt for many, many months – well, is Moon ... who is right?, you know, am I damning myself to hell for coming out of the organization?

. . .

TOM: I'm just finally really starting to deal with the fact that I was really ripped off by Moon. Finally allowing myself to be angry that he had exploited my good intentions the way that he did. And the way that he is exploiting the good intentions of everybody in that organization.

As Tom tells the TV Host, he experienced a lot of distress for months after his deprogramming. 'Being deprogrammed,' he says, 'my world was exploded in a lot of ways ... I thought I was losing my head at certain times.' Tom's parents, and the programme, interpret the psychological difficulties he experienced as a direct result of his cult involvement. The years spent in the Moonies are seen as lost years, years in which Tom was out of touch with 'reality'. Thus his stress stems from his inability to return to his old self and adapt to a changed world. On first hearing, this account seems most plausible. Things change, however, when one learns that psychological studies of current and ex-members of NRMs show that few believers or voluntary defectors display any psychological dysfunction, while deprogrammed individuals frequently do (see the summaries of studies provided in Rochford *et al.*, 1989; Saliba, 1993; Richardson, 1995). John Saliba (1993: 106) reports that 'more than 75 per cent of studies of [active members of NRMs] ... show that the psychological profiles of individuals tested fall well within "normal" bounds'. Likewise the psychiatrist Saul Levine (1984: 4) says that the hundreds of converts and ex-converts he interviewed 'showed no more sign of pathology ... than is found in any youthful population'. In fact the strong correlation found by sociologists between people with negative views of their cult involvements and the experience of deprogramming or exit counselling (e.g. Solomon, 1981; Wright, 1984; Lewis, 1986; Lewis and Bromley, 1987) supports the counter-charge that the only deleterious brainwashing, and hence psychological impairment, experienced by anyone comes with deprogramming. It is not difficult to understand why deprogrammed ex-members report far more psychological problems in adapting to life after their cult experiences than those who have left of their own volition. As Wright (1987) and Ebaugh (1988) have each established, the process by which anyone gives up any role in life, whether an occupation, a marriage, or a religious identity, tends to follow a fairly set pattern of stages by which the person psychologically and socially anticipates and prepares for the impending change (see Wright and Ebaugh, 1993: 124–8). That process is short-circuited by deprogramming, which leaves involuntary ex-members ill-prepared to assume a new identity. In place of gradually forging new grounds of self-worth and purpose in life, those who are deprogrammed are assigned, and often assume, the identity of a victim. But this passive identity causes them to feel vulnerable and in need of completing the process of role exiting. The resultant quest for some more secure identity may explain why so many of the deprogrammed have become deprogrammers themselves. Gary Scharf, Tom's deprogrammer, it will be recalled, had been deprogrammed only five months before.

In Tom's case, like most others, we need more reliable

information and testing to really understand what happened. Perhaps Tom's claim is correct, he is simply angry that he allowed Moon to exploit his good intentions. But in surveying the existing literature Saliba concludes (1993: 107): 'the brainwashing model begs the questions it purports to ask and has generated little productive research'. Certainly we have ample reason to be more careful in our judgements about cult conversions and their consequences.

DIALOGUE (10)

TV HOST: Who's vulnerable to this kind of thing? Who's vulnerable to a Moonie recruiter?

TOM: I think anybody who is willing to listen to somebody coming up to them on the street is vulnerable. I think anybody is vulnerable and it's not just dumb kids or kids that are lost, or kids that have just broken up with their girlfriend, it's a very seductive temptation to be taken care of, to have a family, to have a direction, to know that you're right with God, to be free. It's a very quick process, a transformation, totally turned around, brainwashed, if you will.

STREET RECRUITER: You should come by tonight. We've got a special tonight. A lot of people will be out. Try to come by.

TOM: I mean people say, you know, that the people who died in Jonestown were crazy, but I have a lot more sympathy for that situation, because I know that they were following their good intentions and they just kind of veered off to the left a little bit and there you have it. And, I think the way things are nowadays we don't really have any traditions or understandings of truth that we're really sure about, so it's very easy to be taken for a ride. And, it can happen to anybody.

COMMENTARY (10)

By this point it is clear probably that Tom is correct when he says that 'it's not just dumb kids or kids that are lost' that join NRMs. Equally clearly, perhaps, he is off-the-mark in saying that 'anybody who is willing to listen to somebody coming up to them on the street' may be drawn into a cult. While many different people will convert to many different NRMs for many different reasons, we know with greater precision who really is structurally available to conversion. Few people actually do join, however, despite their exposure to these groups, and even fewer become true converts. Thus our delimitation of the reasons for converting and the process of conversion is still too crude. Much more careful research is required.

The research already prompted into the nature of cult conversions by the charges of brainwashing has reversed, though, the long-standing tendency to understand conversion as something that happens to someone. Contrary to the assumptions of the anti-cult movement, most traditional (e.g. Christian), and previous social scientific conceptions of conversion, people are not so much converted to new religions as they convert themselves. Conversion is a much more active process than previously realized.

St Paul may have been paradigmatically smitten blind by a brilliant flash of light from which Jesus spoke to him, and then suddenly, unexpectedly, and permanently converted to Christianity (Acts 9:1–19). But the conversions of many members of contemporary NRMs are much more gradual affairs, born of a search for spiritual insight or help and an interactive process of exchange and negotiation of commitments between the convert and the religious organization. In-depth interviews with converts and participant observation studies of various cults have revealed much more rational calculation and conscious lifestyle experimentation than anticipated. Converts are much more aware of their situation than social scientists expected, assessing circumstances, weighing the advantages and disadvantages of affiliation. Often they even display latent reservations about their actions long after converting. It seems likely that most converts learn to act the part of a convert, adapting their behaviour to group expectations for some time before they then change in their attitudes and finally their beliefs and self-conceptions (see, e.g. Straus, 1979; Richardson, 1985; Neitz, 1987; Dawson, 1990; Machalek and Snow, 1993).

In the end Tom may be right, in part. In a time when more and more people are experiencing ever greater anomie in the face of a life rich in choices and possibilities, but short on clear guidelines for behaviour and a sense of greater purpose, the promise of a life with real meaning, shared with a small and supportive band of like-minded people, may be strong. But in the last analysis, people choose to convert, just like they may choose to deconvert, if and when the time is right for them. What we need is a better understanding of the criteria that inform their choices.

Notes

1. This chapter draws directly on material presented in much greater detail in Dawson (1998).
2. As I write this chapter, for example, the cover story of the March 1998 issue of *Homemakers*, a magazine distributed by mail to most homes in Canada, is 'Cults: The Next Wave – Everyone is Vulnerable'. This article repeats, without qualification, the half-truths and misconceptions about cults that have been in circulation for almost thirty years, with particular attention to the charge of brainwashing.
3. The programme is 24 minutes long and was part of a show called *April Magazine* (MTI Production Co.).
4. The transcript has been edited at a few points to remove some non-essential parts.

References

Anthony, Dick and Thomas Robbins (1992) 'Law, Social Science and the "Brainwashing" Exception to the First Amendment.' *Behavioral Sciences and the Law* 10 (1): 5–27.

Anthony, Dick and Thomas Robbins (1994) 'Brainwashing and Totalitarian Influence.' Pp. 457–71 in *Encyclopedia of Human Behavior*, vol. 1. San Diego, CA: Academic Press.

Anthony, Dick and Thomas Robbins (1995) 'Negligence, Coercion and the Protection of Religious Belief.' *Journal of Church and State* 37 (3): 509–36.

Bainbridge, William Sims (1978) *Satan's Power: Ethnography of a Deviant Psychotherapy Cult*. Berkeley, CA: University of California Press.

Balch, Robert W. (1995) 'Waiting for the Ships: Disillusionment and the Revitalization of Faith in Bo and Peep's UFO Cult.' Pp. 137–66 in J. R. Lewis (ed.), *The Gods Have Landed: New Religions from Other Worlds*. Albany, NY: State University of New York Press.

Barker, Eileen (1984) *The Making of a Moonie: Choice or Brainwashing?* Oxford: Basil Blackwell.

Beckford, James (1975) *The Trumpet of Prophecy: A Sociological Study of Jehovah's Witnesses*. New York: Oxford and Halsted Press.

Bromley, David G. (1988) 'Deprogramming as a Mode of Exit from New Religious Movements: The Case of the Unificationist Movement.' Pp. 185–204 in D. G. Bromley (ed.), *Falling From the Faith: Causes and Consequences of Religious Apostasy*. Newbury Park, CA: Sage.

Bromley, David G., Anson D. Shupe, Jr. and J. C. Ventimiglia (1983) 'The Role of Anecdotal Atrocities in the Social Construction of Evil,' Pp. 139–60 in D. G. Bromley and J. T. Richardson (eds), *The Brainwashing/*

Deprogramming Controversy: Sociological, Psychological, Legal and Historical Perspectives. Lewiston, NY: Edwin Mellen Press.

Dawson, Lorne L. (1990) 'Self-Affirmation, Freedom, and Rationality: Theoretically Elaborating "Active" Conversions.' *Journal for the Scientific Study of Religion* 29, pp. 141–63.

Dawson, Lorne L. (1996) 'Who Joins New Religious Movements and Why: Twenty Years of Research and What Have We Learned?' *Studies in Religion* 25 (2): 193–213.

Dawson, Lorne L. (1998) *Comprehending Cults: The Sociology of New Religious Movements*. Toronto and New York: Oxford University Press.

Ebaugh, Helen Rose Fuchs (1988) *Becoming an Ex: The Process of Role Exit*. Chicago: University of Chicago Press.

Enroth, Ronald (1977) *Youth, Brainwashing, and the Extremist Cults*. Grand Rapids, MI: Zondervan.

Galanter, Marc (1989) *Cults: Faith, Healing and Coercion*. New York: Oxford University Press.

Glock, Charles Y. (1964) 'The Role of Deprivation in the Origin and Evolution of Religious Groups.' Pp. 24–36 in R. Lee and M. Marty (eds), *Religion and Social Conflict*. New York: Oxford University Press.

Hanegraaff, Wouter J. (1996) *New Age Religion and Western Culture*. Leiden, The Netherlands: E. J. Brill.

Harrison, Michael (1974) 'Sources of Recruitment to Catholic Pentecostalism.' *Journal for the Scientific Study of Religion* 13 (1): 49–64.

Hassan, Steven (1988) *Combatting Cult Mind-Control*. Rochester, VT: Park Street Press.

Heelas, Paul (1996) *The New Age Movement: The Celebration of the Self and the Sacralization of Modernity*. Oxford: Blackwell.

Hinkle, L. E. and Wolff, H. E. (1956) 'Communist Interrogation and the Indoctrination of "Enemies of the States".' *American Medical Association Archives of Neurological Psychology* 76: 117–27.

Hunter, Edward (1951) *Brainwashing in Red China*. New York: Vanguard Press.

Introvigne, Massimo (1995) 'Ordeal by Fire: The Tragedy of the Solar Temple.' *Religion* 25 (2): 267–83.

Introvigne, Massimo and J. Gordon Melton (1997) 'The Attack Upon Religious Groups in Present-Day Europe: A Special Report.' Paper presented to the American Academy of Religion, San Francisco.

Jacobs, Janet Liebman (1989) *Divine Disenchantment: Deconverting from New Religions*. Bloomington, IN: Indiana University Press.

Latkin, Carl, R. Hagan, R. Littman and N. Sundberg (1987) 'Who Lives in Utopia? A Brief Report on the Rajneeshpuram Research Project.' *Sociological Analysis* 48 (1): 73–81.

Levine, Saul V. (1984) *Radical Departures: Desperate Detours to Growing Up*. New York: Harcourt Brace Jovanovich.

Lewis, James R. (1986) 'Reconstructing the Cult Experience: Post-Involvement Attitudes as a Function of Mode of Exit and Post-Involvement Socialization.' *Sociological Analysis* 47 (2): 151–9.

Lewis, James R. and David G. Bromley (1987) 'The Cult Withdrawal Syndrome: A Case of Misattribution of Cause?' *Journal for the Scientific Study of Religion* 26 (4): 508–22.

Lifton, Robert Jay (1961) *Thought Reform and the Psychology of Totalism*. New York: Norton.

Lofland, John F. (1977) *Doomsday Cult: A Study of Conversion, Proselytization and Maintenance of Faith*. Enlarged edition. New York: Irvington Pub.

Lofland, John and Rodney Stark (1965) 'Becoming a World-Saver: A Theory of Conversion to a Deviant Perspective.' *American Sociological Review* 30 (6): 863–74.

Lucas, Phillip C. (1995) *The Odyssey of a New Religion: The Holy Order of MANS from New Age to Orthodoxy*. Bloomington, IN: Indiana University Press.

Luhrmann, T. M. (1989) *Persuasions of the Witch's Craft: Ritual Magic in Contemporary England*. Cambridge, MA: Harvard University Press.

Machalek, Richard and David A. Snow (1993) 'Conversion to New Religious Movements.' Pp. 53–74 in D. G. Bromley and J. K. Hadden (eds), *Religion and the Social Order, Vol. 3, The Handbook on Cults and Sects in America (Part B)*. Greenwich, CT: JAI Press.

Moore, Laurence R. (1994) *Selling God: American Religion in the Marketplace of Culture*. New York: Oxford University Press.

Neitz, Mary Jo (1987) *Charisma and Community: A Study of Religious Commitment within the Charismatic Renewal*. New Brunswick, NJ: Transaction.

Palmer, Susan Jean (1994) *Moon Sisters, Krishna Mothers, Rajneesh Lovers: Women's Roles in New Religions*. Syracuse, NY: Syracuse University Press.

Palmer, Susan Jean (1996) 'Purity and Danger in the Solar Temple.' *Journal of Contemporary Religion* 11 (3): 303–18.

Parsons, Arthur S. (1986) 'Messianic Personalism: A Role Analysis of the Unification Church.' *Journal for the Scientific Study of Religion* 25 (2): 141–61.

Pfeifer, Jeffrey E. (1992) 'The Psychological Framing of Cults: Schematic Representations and Cult Evaluations.' *Journal of Applied Social Psychology* 22 (7): 531–44.

Reader, Ian (1996) *A Poisonous Cocktail? The Aum Shinrikyo Path to Violence*. Copenhagen: The Nordic Institute of Asian Studies.

Richardson, James T. (1985) 'The Active vs. Passive Convert: Paradigm Conflict in Conversion/Recruitment Research.' *Journal for the Scientific Study of Religion* 24 (2): 163–79.

Richardson, James T. (ed.) (1988) *Money and Power in New Religions.* Lewiston, NY: Edwin Mellen Press.

Richardson, James T. (1991) 'Cult/Brainwashing Cases and Freedom of Religion.' *Journal of Church and State* 33 (1): 55–74.

Richardson, James T. (1993) 'Definitions of Cult: From Sociological-Technical to Popular-Negative.' *Review of Religious Research* 34 (4): 348–56.

Richardson, James T. (1995) 'Clinical and Personality Assessment of Participants in New Religions.' *The International Journal for the Psychology of Religion* 5 (3): 145–70.

Richardson, James T. (1996) ' "Brainwashing" Claims and Minority Religions Outside the United States: Cultural Diffusion of a Questionable Concept in the Legal Arena.' *Brigham Young University Law Review* (4): 873–904.

Richardson, James T., Mary White Stewart and Robert B. Simmonds (1979) *Organized Miracles: A Study of a Contemporary, Youth, Communal, Fundamentalist Organisation.* New Brunswick, NJ: Transaction.

Richardson, James T. and Jan van der Lans, and Frans Derks (1986) 'Leaving and Labeling: Voluntary and Coerced Disaffiliation from Religious Social Movements.' Pp. 97–126 in L. Kriesberg (ed.), *Research in Social Movements, Conflicts and Change.* Greenwich, CT: JAI Press.

Rochford, E. Burke, Jr. (1985) *Hare Krishna in America.* New Brunswick, NJ: Rutgers University Press.

Rochford, E. Burke, Jr., Sherly Purvis and NeMar Eastman (1989) 'New Religions, Mental Health, and Social Control.' Pp. 57–82 in M. Lynn and D. Moberg (eds), *Research in the Social Scientific Study of Religion*, vol. 1. Greenwich, CT: JAI Press.

Saliba, John A. (1993) 'The New Religions and Mental Health.' Pp. 99–113 in D. G. Bromley and J. K. Hadden (eds), *Religion and the Social Order, Vol. 3, The Handbook on Cults and Sects in America (Part B).* Greenwich, CT: JAI Press.

Sargent, William (1957) *Battle for the Mind.* London: Heinemann.

Shupe, Anson D., Jr. and David G. Bromley (1980) *The New Vigilantes: Deprogrammers, Anti-Cultists and the New Religions.* Beverly Hills: Sage.

Shupe, Anson D., Jr. and David G. Bromley (1994) 'The Modern Anti-Cult Movement 1971–1991: A Twenty-Year Retrospective.' Pp. 3–31 in A. Shupe and D. G. Bromley (eds), *The Anti-Cult Movements in Cross-Cultural Perspective.* New York: Garland.

Singer, Margaret T. (1979) 'Coming Out of the Cults.' *Psychology Today* (January): 72–82.

Singer, Margaret T. (1995) *Cults in Our Midst: The Hidden Menace in Our Everyday Lives.* San Francisco, CA: Jossey-Bass.

Snow, David A. and Louis A. Zurcher, Jr. and Sheldon Ekland-Olson (1980) 'Social Networks and Social Movements: A Microstructural Approach to Differential Recruitment.' *American Sociological Review* 45 (5): 787–801.

Solomon, Trudy (1981) 'Integrating the "Moonie" Experience: A Survey of Ex-members of the Unification Church.' Pp. 275–95 in T. Robbins and D. Anthony (eds), *In Gods We Trust.* First edn. New Brunswick, NJ: Transaction Press.

Stark, Rodney and William Sims Bainbridge (1985) *The Future of Religion: Secularization, Revival and Cult Formation.* Berkeley, CA: University of California Press.

Straus, Roger (1979) 'Religious Conversion as a Personal and Collective Accomplishment.' *Sociological Analysis* 40 (2): 158–65.

Tabor, James and Eugene Gallagher (1995) *Why Waco?* Berkeley, CA: University of California Press.

Tipton, Steven M. (1982) *Getting Saved from the Sixties.* Berkeley, CA: University of California Press.

Van Driel, Barend and James T. Richardson (1988) 'Print Media Coverage of New Religious Movements: A Longitudinal Study.' *Journal of Communication* 38 (3): 37–61.

Van Zandt, David E. (1991) *Living in the Children of God.* Princeton, NJ: Princeton University Press.

Wilson, Bryan and Karel Dobbelaere (1994) *A Time to Chant: The Soka Gakkai Buddhists in Britain.* Oxford: Clarendon Press.

Wright, Stuart A. (1984) 'Post-Involvement Attitudes of Voluntary Defectors from Controversial New Religious Movements.' *Journal for the Scientific Study of Religion* 23 (2): 172–82.

Wright, Stuart A. (1987) *Leaving Cults: The Dynamics of Defection.* Washington, DC: Society for the Scientific Study of Religion Monograph Series, Number 7.

Wright, Stuart and Helen Rose Ebaugh (1993) 'Leaving New Religions.' Pp. 117–38 in D. G. Bromley and J. K. Hadden (eds), *Religion and the Social Order, Vol. 3, The Handbook on Cults and Sects in America (Part B).* Greenwich, CT: JAI Press.

21. Rediscovering Islam: a Muslim journey of faith

Sophie Gilliat-Ray

Introduction

> Transformation or conversion is a difficult phenomenon to account for.
> Sometimes it is a sharp, clear break between the past and a new future,
> but often it is not. Paul Tillich described grace in his famous sermon on
> this subject in this way: 'You are accepted. After such an experience we
> may not be better than before, and we may not believe more than before.
> But everything is transformed.'[1]

In common parlance, the term 'conversion' is often regarded as a
move away from one set of beliefs towards another; the acceptance of
a new lifestyle; the membership of a new faith community; a dramatic
change in religious identity, and so on. However, the quotation which
introduces this chapter serves as a fitting reminder that the
phenomenon of religious 'conversion' is so broad, so diverse, so
complex, that sometimes our understanding of it has to be enlarged
so that we might comprehend nor lose sight of the vast scope of
experiences that the term in fact describes. Ali Kose, in his study of
British converts to Islam, points out that indeed, 'the term "religious
conversion" comprises diverse experiences: increased devotion within
the same religious structure, a shift from no religious commitment to
a devout religious life, or a change from one religion to another'.[2] It is
especially the first of Kose's descriptions – 'increased devotion within
the same religious structure' – that this chapter will explore.

Extensive and detailed research has already been done on the
subject of conversion, or rather the 'subjects' of conversion. Studies
abound on the sociological and psychological profile of converts to
different faiths, the motivational factors behind conversion, and so
on.[3] However, little empirical research has been done on intra-

religious conversion in particular and the tenacity of some religious identities, and there is scope for more study in this area.[4]

A good dictionary definition of 'conversion' utilizes a range of familiar terms and phrases to define the word, such as 'to turn from one thing, condition, opinion, party or religion to another'.[5] But *Chambers English Dictionary* also uses the words 'change', and 'alter' to define conversion, and both these words allude to the somewhat more subtle connotations that the term 'conversion' may have, and which are more suitable for a discussion of 'intra-faith conversion'. By this term 'intra-faith conversion', I am referring to the process whereby an individual makes a dramatically renewed commitment to their existing faith tradition, and their religious identity and conviction become altered, changed, stimulated, strengthened, energized, revived and invigorated. The changes that can take place as a response to personal searching, mission, local, national or worldwide events, can be tantamount to a 'conversion'. And yet, in the words of Paul Tillich, individuals who undergo such an experience may not 'believe more than before', and yet 'everything is transformed'.

To situate and contextualize this phenomenon of intra-faith conversion, I will be looking in particular at the current experiences of some young Muslims in Britain. My interest in them especially stems from my observation of the apparently conversion-like experience that growing numbers of them seem to be undergoing, often during their late teenage years. The resurgence of Islam on the world stage is mirrored, in microcosm, by the experiences of individual young Muslims in Britain who, for a diversity of reasons, may begin to take a renewed interest in the faith of their birth. They are the 'twice born', having been born and raised into a faith from birth, but then undergoing a 'rebirth' within it later in life.

Some particular characteristics of intra-faith conversion

Before contexualizing this discussion by looking at some of the intra-faith conversion experiences of young Muslims in Britain, some answers are needed to the question, 'What are the characteristics of intra-faith conversion in particular which set it apart from inter-religious conversion in general?'. To attempt a response to this question, the following section will consider how intra-faith conversion *differs* from more conventional conversion experiences.

MOTIVATIONAL AND PROCESSUAL DIFFERENCES

One common characteristic that often motivates conversion to a new religion is a growing dissatisfaction with previous beliefs leading to the ultimate rejection of certain doctrines. This is unlikely to feature as a motivational factor for the intra-faith convert. Rather, they are likely to move from a position of indifference about the doctrines of their faith, towards a much deeper attachment and comprehension. Secondly, many conversion experiences are preceded by a cognitive quest prior to the acceptance of a new religion. Converts are often perplexed by existential questions, social and moral issues, as well as religious doubts. While intra-religious conversion *may* be preceded by similar searching questions in these areas, it appears to figure less strongly as an antecedent to a conversion experience, as this chapter will later demonstrate in relation to young Muslims. For example, it would be unlikely that a young Muslim would describe their journey towards a renewed and committed attachment to Islam in the way that a native British convert to Islam did so: 'I was looking for a religion and an explanation, a way of life, a philosophy that was explaining and giving meaning to life and answering questions I felt very fundamental about myself, about existence, about creation . . .'.[6] Thirdly, many converts to a new faith are prompted to begin a cognitive search as a result of personal traumas. It is often in the wake of some kind of emotional distress, whether it be a divorce, an illness, or a bereavement, that they begin the process of finding spiritual answers to the questions that these events often initiate. Again, this kind of motivational factor is likely to figure *less* prominently as a precedent to an intra-faith conversion experience (though not always so), particularly in relation to young Muslims in Britain.

The process of actually converting to a new faith involves a variety of different forms of ritual, and other chapters in this collection will have discussed them in further detail. New Buddhists may 'Go for Refuge' or take the 'Precepts' as a way of demonstrating and marking their change in religious identity. Christian converts might 'accept Jesus as their personal Saviour' during a religious rally, or as a result of personal contact with missionaries. The process of converting to Islam involves testifying, in the presence of two witnesses, that one accepts 'There is no God but Allah, and Muhammad is His Messenger'. This process of 'taking the *Shahadah*' and bearing witness to the central tenets of Islam is unlikely to feature in the Muslim journey of faith, and intra-religious converts in other traditions are also unlikely to undergo a formal conversion process. Somehow such a ritual is often not regarded as a necessary part of their journey.

DIFFERENCES OF IMPLICATION

The consequences of conversion are likely to be very different for those who accept a new faith compared to those who make a renewed commitment to their existing tradition. New converts often become involved with a new community, perhaps adopting a new name, possibly wearing different clothing, learning a whole new language of social codes, and often dealing with pressure, perplexity, resentment or misunderstanding from their families. The intra-religious convert, while undergoing no less of a radical process of inner transformation, will be unlikely to have to deal with major social implications. But this does not mean that they escape difficulties (there have been numerous reports in the British Muslim press over the last few years regarding the experiences of Muslim women whose employment is terminated once they have started wearing *hijab*).[7] There may well be pressures and expectations upon intra-faith converts, but often these come primarily from the in-group of committed fellow believers they have joined. It is likely that they will be expected to adopt stricter observance of religious practices more immediately, in contrast to the convert who is often given a period of 'grace' to learn unfamiliar rituals and new normative patterns for social behaviour.

Why are young Muslims 'converting' to Islam?

So far the discussion has centred around broad generalizations which attempt to illustrate some of the ways in which intra-faith conversion contrasts with other types of conversion. This has served to lay some foundations for a more analytical examination of the particular reasons that appear to underlie the current upsurge in adherence and observance of Islam by many young Muslims in Britain. To explore some of the factors which might explain this process of intra-faith conversion, I suggest that there are three main headings under which some answers may be found. Firstly, the socio-structural position of young Muslims in Britain; secondly, general features of modern Western social life; and thirdly, some characteristics of Islam itself. The substantial part of the remainder of this chapter will be concerned with each of these three issues in turn, but particularly the first. The limitations of space, however, does mean that the discussion can only skim the surface of each, therefore failing to do justice to the complexity of the issues.

Before turning to these three headings, we need to briefly describe the kinds of experiences that some young Muslims are undergoing and which might be classified as intra-religious conversion events. We need to hear some of the voices of Muslim youth before we try to explain their experiences:

As a child I hated Muslims and Muslim countries. I thought they were backward, fanatic. When I started studying the intellectual tradition of Islam, I began to change ...' (Rashida).[8]

Although children here are sent to the mosque from a very early age, many young Muslims go through a phase where they begin to question everything to be certain that their beliefs have a sound basis (Saqib).[9]

I think more and more girls will turn to Islam to find a way out of their problems, the problems of their parents and the society.[10]

Scholarly observers of the Muslim community in Britain have also noted that there is a radical rediscovery of Islam taking place among young Muslims. 'There are indications that a growing number of youth ... are engaged in the reapplication of Islamic sources. It is here that some of the most radical new formulation of Islamic ideals may be found.'[11]

In a study conducted by Kim Knott and Sajda Khokher on young Muslim women in Bradford, one of their interviewees said that 'she felt strongly drawn to a more committed position ... saying that had she not been born a Muslim she would have converted to Islam'.[12]

There is also evidence that other sizeable Muslim communities in Britain are spawning newly committed young Muslims. In London's East End, where pressure to observe Islamic dress codes used to result from parental influence, now 'demands for a stricter Islamic dress code come mainly from peers'.[13,14]

A new Muslim identity is being forged among the young female members of Britain's Islamic community, whether imposed or enthusiastically embraced. In the East End, teenagers with Turkish, Bengali and Middle Eastern backgrounds form a generation of Muslims whose religious approach differs from the traditional practices of their parents. They find their parents too immersed in cultural traditions and detached from the global Islamic community. The parents are often ignorant of Islamic doctrine, whereas these young Muslims analyse the Koran, attend discussions on religious topics and dream of the ideal Islamic state ... For most girls the *hijab* is a symbol of this new awareness. A group of seven girls at college recently decided to adopt the stricter dress code, some in the face of parental opposition. 'My mother was appalled'. It turns out that they have hardly a free moment between fund-raising, meetings of the Islamic society and educating other girls.[15]

From some of these descriptions and quotations it is possible to identify some of the critical antecedents and manifestations of an intra-religious conversion-like experience: nominal belief in the tenets of Islam turning into a critical quest for 'Truth'; the decision to 'do something about it' by making changes to outward identity as well as inner identity as a visible marker of transformation (such as changes in dress); a concern to 'educate' others; the cognitive search for meaning in the face of societal problems, and so on. To say that some of these young Muslims are simply becoming 'more observant' undermines the impact of their new-found commitment and the intensity of their search. But a note of caution should be added here. The revival of interest in Islam by many young Muslims is certainly not typical of *all* of them. Paul Vallely and Andrew Brown, writing about young Muslims in Britain in *The Independent* note that 'for every child who returns home with a belief in a revitalised form of Islam, another drifts into the moral relativism of contemporary Western values'.[16] But having made this qualification, let us move on to examine some reasons why some young Muslims are turning to their faith with renewed vigour by examining three factors that can be associated with the socio-structural position of young Muslims.

The socio-structural position of young Muslims in Britain

The current resurgence of Islam among young British Muslims could have been predicted soon after the arrival of their elderly relatives in the 1950s and 1960s. This section will examine why there are three particular historical socio-structural circumstances which have made the renewed commitment of many young Muslims to Islam almost inevitable: (a) the change from a communally defined to an individually defined sense of identity; (b) the structural situation of young Muslims as a minority group who, whether individually or communally are aware of racism and anti-Muslim prejudice; and, (c) the fact that they constitute membership of a third generation, twice removed from the migration experiences of their elder relatives.

GENERATIONAL CHANGES IN IDENTITY

For many Muslim youth in British society, their origins lie in the different countries that constitute the Indian subcontinent. Their parent and grandparents migrated particularly from Pakistan, India, and Bangladesh, to Britain between the 1950s and 1970s. By now there are well-established Muslim communities in those towns and cities which could offer employment to the first generation migrants, such as Bradford, London, Birmingham, Glasgow, the Lancashire milltowns, and Manchester. The history of some of these communities is well documented, so I shall not repeat the findings of earlier work here,[17] save to remind the reader that most migrants were from poor rural areas, few had any formal education, and many were illiterate. Their primary motive for migration was the prospect of wealth and prosperity through employment in unskilled and semi-skilled occupations in the wake of the post-Second World War expansion of manufacturing industry.

The world-view and identity of this first group of migrants had a number of characteristics that appear to contrast sharply when compared to the current young generation. For them, identity was based upon belonging to a community, or more especially the *biraderi*; a complex network of kinship ties. Many of this generation remained, and for those who are still alive they continue to remain, strongly attached to the absolute value of their previous identity gained from their village lives in Pakistan, India, and so on.

This has meant the importation into Britain of communally defined concepts of social honour and reputation, as well as the behaviour patterns to support such notions. In her study of Mirpuris in Bradford and Mirpur (a district in Azad Kashmir), Verity Saifullah-Khan writes:

> The concept of an individual self apart from a family, kin and village is beyond comprehension. Personality is less important that status, and individualism as we know it is neither highly cherished nor desirable. A man or woman in Pakistani society must be conceptualised as existing in a complex network of rights and duties which extend from the central core or his immediate family to a wide set of kin relationships. He, or she, is not an individual agent acting on his own behalf but exists only in relation to family and kin.[18]

Identity, to the extent that it is a meaningful concept to this first generation, was unquestioned, taken-for-granted, and ascribed to them as a consequence of belonging to a communal network of family ties, especially among female members. So too their religious identity as Muslims was in general ascribed, assumed, unquestioned, and deeply embedded and justified by cultural traditions.

Such a communally and traditionally defined world-view and identity contrasts with the outlook and self-perceptions of the young generation of British Muslims, many of whom are twice-removed from the migration experience. They are looking to the future as a way of organizing the present, contrary to their grandparents who used their experiences of the past to structure life in the present. It is a matter of contrast between the first generation identity based upon 'who we were', compared to the identity of the third generation orientated around 'who we want to be'. For increasing numbers of this young generation the answer to the question, 'Who do we want to be?' is derived from an Islamic heritage. But for many the question is far more personal. It is more a matter of ,'Who do I want to be?' Simply the change of one word in this question betrays the fact that young Muslims in Britain now have a much stronger sense of personal, individual identity compared to their migrant relatives. And one thing is for sure, conversion of any type in modern Western society appears to rely upon a strong sense of 'self', and an individualized sense of personality. The cognitive quest that often precedes conversion is a uniquely interior, self-orientated personal journey. The intra-faith conversions typical of young Muslims to

Islam would not be possible without the more individually, orientated identity that many have adopted since the migration of their elderly relatives.[19, 20]

What might be termed the politicisation of Muslims, a worldwide phenomena in Islam but especially prevalent in diaspora populations in North America and Europe, has led to a heightened sense of identity being felt through the affirmation of distinctive Islamic practices. Another way of expressing this is as 'the Islamisation of the self' and the use of Islamic symbols to provide identity on a personal level.[21]

MEMBERSHIP OF A MINORITY GROUP

The particular experience of being members of a minority faith group also appears to underpin the quest for, and the commitment to, a renewed Islamic identity among Muslim youth in Britain, not to mention the racial and anti-Muslim prejudice that can accompany this minority position. In the face of these pressures, whether experienced personally or communally, Rohit Barot notes that 'for a group which is defined as being both different and inferior and denied opportunities to assume identity and status relevant to the mainstream of the metropolitan society, self-conception and self-esteem may increasingly focus on religious belief and practices'.[22] The title of a paper by Dr Zaki Badawi, Director of the Muslim College in London says it all: 'Ingrained racism brings Muslim youth back to Islam'.[23] The experience of being part of a minority group can sharpen the contours of identity, especially when combined with hostility and prejudice from the wider society. Young Muslims are part of Western society which at one and the same time seems to 'embrace them as part of itself and to exclude them on account of their "otherness" '.[24] All this makes many of them ask the question, 'How am I relevantly different?', and for some it is a sense of identity as Muslims, perhaps at times only a latent identity, that marks them out. As a consequence a new and stronger sense of religious identity begins to come to the fore, and in some the processes of identity renewal, through intra-faith conversion, can be identified: the disruption to existing social relationships, new confrontations with the self, and 'the buttressing of established forms of inclusiveness or the emergence of new expressions of exclusiveness and separateness'.[25] A Birmingham-based psychiatrist regards the popularity of radical groups like Hizb ut Tahrir as appealing to young Muslims for the sense of identity that they can bring through its exclusiveness: 'the radical groups function as clubs, providing support, friendship. They give them an identity which British society hasn't'[26] on account of their 'otherness' as members of a minority Muslim community in a non-Muslim society.

'WHAT THE SON WISHES TO FORGET ...'

Though somewhat dated now, the classic text *Protestant Catholic Jew* by Will Herberg notes the pervasiveness of religious self-identification in America, and the particular impact of what he calls the 'dialectic of "third generation interest" '.[27] He suggests that there is something particular about the experience of being a member of a third generation, twice removed from the experience of mass migration, that explains the 'return to religion' among this generation in particular. So significant was this generation for Herberg that he dedicates his book thus: 'to the Third Generation upon whose "return" so much of the future of religion in America depends'. But what light does the 'dialectic of third generation interest' throw upon the situation of young Muslims in Britain, many of whom are themselves members of a third generation? Herberg offers some clues:

> The third generation, coming into its own with the cessation of mass immigration, tried to recover its 'heritage' so as to vie itself some sort of 'name' or context of self-identification and social location in the larger society. 'What the son wishes to forget' – so runs 'Hansen's Law' – 'the grandson wishes to remember'. But what he can remember is obviously not his grandfather's foreign language, or even his grandfather's foreign culture; it is rather his grandfather's *religion* ... This religion he now remembers in a form suitably 'Americanized' and yet in a curious way also 'retraditionalized'.[28]

Herberg identifies here some of the dynamics involved in the third generation British Muslim 'return' to Islam: the primacy of religious associations and affiliations as a way of finding identity, and the return to the original sources of the faith (retraditionalization).[29] But he also goes on to note that this 'return' is also part and parcel of other wider social processes at work such as 'the collapse of all secular securities in the historical crisis of our time, the quest for a recovery of meaning in life, (and) the new search for inwardness and personal authenticity amid the collectivistic heteronomies of the present-day world'.[30] The third generation 'return to religion' therefore cannot be isolated from the processes at work in modern society at large.

The modern search for meaning

The apparent problem of the 'meaninglessness' that characterizes modern society has been well documented by several generations of social theorists. Far more could be said about this in relation to young Muslims than space permits here. But for young Muslims this 'meaninglessness' and confusion might be expressed through questions of identity: 'Who am I? Pakistani, British, Muslim? What makes me different?'.[31] However, the concern with questions of identity and meaning appears to be a particularly late twentieth-century interest, and certainly not peculiar to young British Muslims. They are, however, inevitably encompassed by this wider concern with questions of identity, arising mainly from the consequences of modernity. The perplexity of young Muslims with questions of identity represents in microcosm a process of human self-understanding that appears to be going on at a much broader level.

> It is terms such as contradiction, fluidity, multiplicity which come most readily to mind when conceptualising the contemporary experience of modernity ... Contemporary culture represents a rupture with the past, throwing previous assumptions to the wind, undermining accepted ideas ... Each one of us, as individual 'subjects of modernity' struggles to come to terms with and resolve the tension. Usually we try to do this by constructing a stable self which can make sense of and integrate the various forces impinging upon us ...[32]

For some young Muslims, their project of constructing a 'stable self' is resting upon their religious identity. The sense of community that Islam provides is offering a context in which to begin the building process. For them, the Islamic way of life provides a framework to fulfil their particular search for meaning:

> Islam is presented as an ideological movement confronted with the ideology of the West and of capitalist secular society. Whereas the latter is said by Muslims to have lost its moral signposts, they claim that Islam

proposes a sense of purpose with moral precepts ... To the overriding selfish individualism of the West is contrasted Muslim collective responsibility.[33]

Young Muslims are looking towards the stability that comes from religious identification as a basis for their self-perception. The tenets of Islam are regarded as more enduring when compared to the transience, and increasingly, the irrelevance of nationalistic ties[34] as sources of identity, especially when combined with the constantly shifting trends of modern life itself.

But though modern society offers young Muslims the freedom to explore, for the more committed and militant members they run into a problem, as yet unresolved. They have noticed that

the society which harbours hermeneutists, as it harbours so much else, is pervaded by pluralism, doubt, half-heartedness and an inability to take its own erstwhile faith literally and practise it to the full. They are not quite clear whether they despise it for its tolerance, or rebuke it for not being tolerant enough, notably of their own intransigence: they are liable to be pervaded by both these sentiments at once.[35]

This paradox is particularly being played out in the debate about Muslims in British schools, and the calls for separate Islamic schools.[36]

Some inherent characteristics of Islam

There appears to be something particular to Islam as a faith that is drawing young Muslims towards a stronger attachment to their religion. In view of all that has been said above about the problems of meaninglessness, the plurality of values, and the fragmented nature of modern Western society, Islam is offering to its youth a counterbalancing and complete package of 'alternative' values and meanings, combined with a sense of community and belonging. Many Muslims describe Islam as 'a way of life' encompassing as it does nearly every aspect of human life; from worship and spiritual life to economic and political life; from the way one washes to the way one treats others. Furthermore, the central tenets of Islam are non-negotiable 'Truths', and few Muslims would entertain doubts about the conviction that 'There is no God but Allah and Muhammad is His Messenger'. In other words, Islam is offering a sense of cognitive and spiritual security as a result of its 'completeness' as a way of life and due to the fact that it has drawn boundaries around what may be questioned and developed, and what remains timeless and ultimate. This is proving to be enduringly attractive for young Muslims as they negotiate questions of identity in British society. As Jessica Jacobson found in her study of young Pakistani Muslims in Britain, even the less observant Muslims remained convinced of the truth of Islam. One respondent commented:

> Everything I've been told about the religion has been true. There's not been something that I've thought about as being wrong, because when somebody tells you something right, you know it's right. You might not want it to be right, and you'd *hate* it if it was right, but still it's right.[37]

She interprets statements such as these by viewing the conservatism of Islam, often criticized as a failure to take up the challenge of progressive reform, as paradoxically one of its strengths. 'For in this society, where almost everything is open to question, it may seem all the more appealing or even essential to turn for meaning in life to a religion whose foundations have not pandered or succumbed to liberal attack.'[38]

One of the ways in which the revival of interest in Islam might be attributed to something particular to the faith itself, as opposed simply to socio-structural and / or personal factors, can be seen from the fact that young Hindus and Sikhs in Britain, who share the same kind of social and historical background as their Muslim counterparts, do not apparently seem to be turning with similar enthusiasm nor to the same extent, to the religious traditions of their heritage. Though the numbers of Hindus and Sikhs in Britain are much smaller (even when combined together) compared to the numbers of Muslims, we do not see the younger members of the Hindu and Sikh communities making radical recommitments to their faiths in the way that has typified some young Muslims.[39]

Another reason for the intra-faith conversion of young Muslims, particular to the nature of Islam itself (though not on philosophical grounds), is the fact that for various reasons it has been the subject of worldwide attention. Numerous events have seen Muslims coming to the public defence of Islam. The Rushdie affair meant that the non-negotiable truths of Islam had to be defended and otherwise 'passive' Muslims came out of their communities to defend their faith; the Gulf War meant that the historic and sacred spaces of Islam had to be protected; the atrocities faced by the minority Muslim community in Bosnia reminded the Islamic community in Britain that it was their 'brothers' and 'sisters' in another European minority situation facing persecution and bloodshed. All these events have sharpened the identity of Muslims worldwide, but especially within minority contexts.

> The impact of external events – from Iran and the Salman Rushdie affair, Saddam and the Gulf War, to the persecution of Muslims in Bosnia – has prompted an emotional identification with the idea of what it means to be a Muslim. Many of those so aroused have begun a more serious exploration of the faith and have begun to practise. The result is an Islamic revival. The rising Islamophobia ... has provoked an emotional response in non-practising Muslims, and from this reinforced sense of Islam as a cultural if not a religious identity many have begun to explore their faith. Many of those who are reviving their faith are those born in this country. The seriousness of many young people is a reaction against what they see as the nominalism of their parents' religious practice.[40]

Conclusion

As I suggested earlier in this chapter, in many ways the process of intra-faith conversion among young Muslims in Britain is to some extent a reflection in microcosm of the resurgence of Islam on a worldwide scale. In localized communities, perhaps in the East End of London, or in certain parts of Bradford or Birmingham, this might be regarded as a communal intra-faith renewal, thus lessening the particularly individual significance of the process. Given that the central practices of Islam have profound social as well as personal dimensions, this process of revival among young British Muslims could be seen as a reflection of Islam's community-orientated aspects and its space–time location in modern Western society. But this would be to undermine the personal implications of Islam, and the fact that the response to the message of Islam has to be made by individuals. Though whole communities respond to the *muezzin*'s call to prayer, and while congregational worship has important communal implications, the response and involvement in both require the will and initiative of the individual.

By way of conclusion to his study of native British converts to

Islam, Ali Kose suggests that religious conversion does not arise due to one single influence, but the 'mutual interaction of various forces that make a person sensitive to conversion'.[41] In the case of British Muslims, their 'sensitivity' towards Islam and the process of renewing their religious identity may rely not only upon the most typical antecedents of conversion (the cognitive quest; emotional traumas; loss of earlier beliefs), but also upon circumstances that are extremely particular to their social situation as third generation members of a minority community in Western society, combined with some characteristics unique to Islam.

Young Muslims in Britain are inheritors of two generations of experience of living in 'submission to Allah' (Islam) in this country. As a legacy of the migration of their parents and grandparents, they are placed in a social setting which enables new understandings of how Islam can contribute to the sacralization of identity. They draw upon a precarious balance between what is old and what is new; reaction and innovation. But in many ways the whole of Islam rests upon balance (*wasat*), particularly when this touches upon the relationship between this world and the next.

Notes

1. W. Lesher, 'Meanings of Globalization', in *The Globalization of Theological Education*, ed. R. Evans, A. Evans and D Roozen (New York: Orbis, 1993), p. 37.

2. Ali Kose, 'Native British Converts to Islam: Who Are They? Why Do They Convert?', *The American Journal of Islamic Social Sciences*, vol. 12, no. 3 (1995).

3. See, for example, Edwin Starbuck, *The Psychology of Religion* (New York: Charles Scribner's Sons, 1900) or more recently V. Bailey Gillespie, *Religious Conversion and Personal Identity: How and Why People Change* (Birmingham: Religious Education Press, 1979). For studies of converts to Islam see Kose 'Native British Converts to Islam', or Larry Poston, *Islamic Dawah in the West: Muslim Missionary Activity and the Dynamics of Conversion to Islam* (New York: Oxford University Press, 1992).

4. One of the few scholars to have done work that approaches this subject in relation to young Pakistani Muslims in Britain is Jessica Jacobson. For example, her paper 'The Persistence of Islamic Identity among Young British Pakistanis' presented at the BSA Sociology of

Religion Study Group Conference, Lincoln, 1995. However, I would question her use of the word 'persistence' to describe the enduring nature of the religious identity of young British Pakistani Muslims. 'Persistence' seems too soft a word to describe what I would call more a process of *rediscovering of Islam* which is often a significant life event (like conversion itself) for young Muslims.

5. *Chambers English Dictionary* (Edinburgh and Cambridge: Chambers and Cambridge University Press, 1988).

6. Kose, 'Native British Converts to Islam'.

7. For one of the most recent incidents of 'Hijabophobia' see *Q News* 8–14 November 1996.

8. Interview with Rashida Butt, *The Independent*, 5 July 1993.

9. Interview with Saqib Qureshi, *Eastern Eye*, 14 December 1993.

10. From an interview conducted by R Sharif, 'Young Muslim Women of Pakistani Origin', MA thesis, University of Birmingham, 1985, p. 117.

11. Jørgen Nielsen, 'Muslims in Britain: Searching for an Identity', *New Community,*, vol. 1, no. 3 Spring 1987.

12. Kim Knott and Sajda Khokher, 'Religious and Ethnic Identity among Young Muslim Women in Bradford', *New Community*, vol. 19, no. 4, 1993.

13. Peer pressure appears to be an important dynamic behind the resurgence of Islamic identity among young Muslims. Reporting from conference for young Muslims in Britain (see note 19), Miriam Jilani noted:

> when you are constantly reminded by your peers that you are different the chances are you go in one of two directions. Some feel they have to eradicate their "difference" ... if they ignore it so will everyone else. Only a few realize that it isn't as simple as that. Others feel they have to explore that "difference" and once they discover its true nature, they embrace it to suffocation. Only some find a balance between the two.

14. Asla Aydintasbas, 'Why they can't turn their backs on the veil', *The Independent*, 28 April 1994.

15. Ibid.

16. *The Independent*, 6 December 1995.

17. See for example, S. Barton, *The Bengali Muslims of Bradford* (Leeds: University of Leeds, 1986).

18. Verity Saifullah-Khan, 'Pakistani Villagers in a British City – the World of the Mirpuri Villager in Bradford and in his Village of Origin', PhD thesis, Community Religions Project, University of Leeds, Monograph Series, 1974, pp. 367, 416.

19. There is a dispute among some scholars as to the effect that migration

has upon religious commitment. Hans Mol asserts that 'in the countries of immigration, migrant churches have always been the most effective bastions of ethnic preservation' and they are at the centre of social activities, with religious commitment intensified due to the migration experience (*Identity and the Sacred*, Oxford: Blackwell, 1975, p. 174). However, Stephen Barton found that after migration to Bradford, Bengali Muslims 'suffered an almost total lapse of religious observance ... the migrant lived and worked in Britain on behalf of his family, who, it may be surmised, prayed on his behalf' (*The Bengali Muslims of Bradford*, p. 177).

20. There are other indicators to show that young Muslims are more independently minded and individualistic than their parents, especially in terms of lifestyle choices. For example, many now aspire to living in a nuclear family rather than the more typical joint family system of their more elderly relatives. In a study by Muhammad Anwar, he found that 'fifty-eight per cent of young Muslims agreed with the statement: "When I have a home of my own, I would prefer to have only my husband/wife and children living with me". The main reasons were ... privacy, independence, and "having a home of one's own"' (*Young Muslims in Britain: Attitudes, Educational Needs and Policy Implications*, Leicester: The Islamic Foundation, 1994, p. 25).

21. A. Rippin, *Muslims: Their Religious Beliefs and Practices, vol. 2 – The Contemporary Period* (London: Routledge, 1993), p. 117.

22. Rohit Barot (ed.), *Religion and Ethnicity: Minorities and Social Change in the Metropolis* (Kampen, Netherlands: Kok Pharos, 1993), p. 8.

23. Published in *New Horizon*, London, April–May 1988, p. 25.

24. Jessica Jacobson, 'The Persistence of Islamic Identity'.

25. E. Epstein, *Ethos and Identity* (London: Tavistock, 1978), pp. 99–102.

26. Kathy Evans, 'Radical time-bomb under British Islam', *The Guardian*, 7 February 1994.

27. Will Herberg, *Protestant Catholic Jew* (New York: Anchor Books, 1960), pp. 256–7.

28. Ibid., p. 257.

29. There is good evidence to suggest that young Muslims, in the process of 'retraditionalization', are turning directly to the sources of Islam – Qur'an, Sunnah, and Shari'ah. See note 10.

30. Ibid.

31. The weekly Muslim newspaper *Q News* held a forum in 1993 as part of its 'Body Mind and Soul Project'. One of its first gatherings had the theme of 'Beyond Beards, Scarves and Halal Meat: Is there a British Muslim Identity in the 21st Century?'. See the reports in vol. 2, (nos. 3–4). This was in part a reflection of research carried out by the

newspaper about issues concerning its readership. For young Muslims, the topic of 'identity' figured prominently as an issue of concern.

32. Stephen Frosh, *Identity Crisis: Modernity, Psychoanalysis and the Self* (London: Macmillan, 1991), pp. 6–7.

33. Daniele Joly, 'Making a Place for Islam in British Society: Muslims in Birmingham', in Tomas Gerholm and Yngve Georg Lithman, *The New Islamic Presence in Western Europe* (London: Mansell, 1988), p. 40.

34. Many young Muslims are resisting nationalistic labels as a way of identifying themselves. For some, their sense of connection with the homeland of their parents and grandparents may mean very little, especially if they have not made visits to the home village or town. Similarly, the idea of being 'British' is resisted by others, due to their sense of 'difference' whether in terms of religion, dress or skin colour. In a *Q News* survey, 'when asked to describe themselves as one of the following: Asian, Pakistani, Arab, European, or Muslim, an overwhelming majority (males 90 per cent and females 78 per cent) wanted it to be known that they were Muslims. Only 4 per cent of both sexes ticked "Asian"' (*Q News*, 8–15 April 1994).

35. Ernest Gellner, *Postmodernism, Reason and Religion* (London: Routledge, 1992), p. 74.

36. See Paul Vallely, 'How much intolerance can we tolerate?', *The Independent*, 4 March 1996.

37. Jacobson, 'The Persistence of Islamic Identity'.

38. Ibid.

39. *The UK Christian Handbook* (1996–7) gives the combined total number of Hindus and Sikhs in Britain as 900,00, whereas the Muslim community alone is estimated to have 1,200,000 members.

40. See note 15.

41. Kose, 'Native British Converts to Islam'.

Index

This book is due for return on or before the last date shown below.

Printed in Great Britain
by Amazon.co.uk, Ltd.,
Marston Gate.